As Europe proceeds towards economic and monetary union, fiscal convergence and the prospect of a common money are at the centre of discussion. This volume from the Centre for Economic Policy Research brings together theoretical, applied and historical research on the management of public debt and its implications for financial stability.

Gale fills a gap in the literature, using a consistent framework to investigate the welfare economics of public debt, while Calvo and Guidotti analyse the trade-off between indexation and maturity when it comes to minimizing debt service.

Confidence crises have become relevant again today in view of the high debt ratios in countries such as Belgium, Italy and Ireland. Alesina, Prati and Tabellini develop a formal model of the propagation of a debt run and use it to interpret Italian debt panics. Giavazzi and Pagano concentrate on how inappropriate debt management can precipitate a run on the currency while Makinen and Woodward review a broad sweep of historical experience.

Three historical studies examine what happens when debts get too large. Eichengreen develops a simple model to examine why capital levies so rarely succeed. De Cecco studies a successful Italian consolidation, while Brown reviews all of US public debt history.

Miller, Skidelsky and Weller offer a formal analysis of confidence effects in a modern version of the Mundell–Fleming model. Finally, Aghion and Bolton develop a neat political model of debt, which may become a common tool of analysis.

Public debt management: theory and history

The Italian Macroeconomic Policy Group

The Italian Macroeconomic Policy Group first met in 1986. It consists of a small group of Italian economists who wish to promote discussion of economic policy issues that are relevant not only to Italy, but also of more general interest. The Group periodically commissions papers from economists based in Italy and elsewhere. Subsequently these papers are discussed by an international panel at meetings convened by the Group.

Current members of the Group are:

Giorgio Basevi
Marcello de Cecco
Mario Draghi
Francesco Giavazzi
Alberto Giovannini
Mario Monti
Paolo Onofri
Antonio Pedone
Luigi Spaventa

Centre for Economic Policy Research

The Centre for Economic Policy Research is a network of 130 Research Fellows, based primarily in European universities. The Centre coordinates its Fellows' research activities, providing central administrative services and communicating research to the public and private sectors. CEPR is an entrepreneur, developing research initiatives with the producers, consumers and sponsors of research. Established in 1983, CEPR is already a European economics research organization, with uniquely wide-ranging scope and activities.

CEPR is a registered educational charity. Grants from the Leverhulme Trust, the Esmée Fairbairn Charitable Trust, the Baring Foundation, the Bank of England and Citibank provide institutional finance. The ESRC supports the Centre's dissemination programme and, with the Nuffield Foundation, its programme of research workshops, while the Alfred P. Sloan and Ford Foundations support the Centre's programme of research in International Macroeconomics. None of these organizations gives prior review to the Centre's publications nor do they necessarily endorse the views expressed therein.

The Centre is pluralist and non-partisan, bringing economic research to bear on the analysis of medium- and long-run policy questions. The research that it disseminates may include views on policy, but the Board of Governors of the Centre does not give prior review to such publications and the Centre itself takes no institutional policy positions. The opinions expressed in this volume are those of the authors and not those of the Centre for Economic Policy Research.

30 November 1989

Public debt management: theory and history

Edited by

RUDIGER DORNBUSCH

and

MARIO DRAGHI

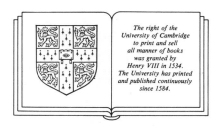

The right of the
University of Cambridge
to print and sell
all manner of books
was granted by
Henry VIII in 1534.
The University has printed
and published continuously
since 1584.

CAMBRIDGE UNIVERSITY PRESS

Cambridge

New York   Port Chester   Melbourne   Sydney

Published by the Press Syndicate of the University of Cambridge
The Pitt Building, Trumpington Street, Cambridge CB2 1RP
40 West 20th Street, New York, NY 10011, USA
10 Stamford Road, Oakleigh, Melbourne 3166, Australia

First published 1990

Printed in Great Britain at the University Press, Cambridge

British Library cataloguing in publication data

Public debt management: theory and history.
1. Governments. External debts. Financing
I. Dornbusch, Rudiger   II. Draghi, Mario
336.343

Library of Congress cataloguing in publication data

Public debt management: theory and history/edited by
Rudiger Dornbusch and Mario Draghi.
    p.   cm.
Based on a conference on 'Capital Markets and Debt Management'
held at Castelgandolfo in June 1989
Includes index.
ISBN 0 521 39266 7
1. Debts, Public – Italy – History – Congresses.
2. Debts, Public – Europe – History – Congresses.
3. Debts, Public – United States – History – Congresses.
4. Deficit financing – History – Congresses.
I. Dornbusch, Rudiger   II. Draghi, Mario.
HJ8675.P83 1990
336.3'6'09 – dc20   90-38550 CIP

ISBN 0 521 39266 7   hardback

CE

Contents

Contents   xi

Figures

xiv   **List of figures**

Tables

Preface

This volume presents the third in an annual series of collaborations between the Italian Macroeconomic Policy Group and the Centre for Economic Policy Research. It contains the papers and proceedings from a conference on 'Capital Markets and Debt Management' held at Castelgandolfo in June 1989. Earlier volumes in this series are *High Public Debt: The Italian Experience* (edited by Francesco Giavazzi and Luigi Spaventa) and *A European Central Bank? Perspectives on Monetary Unification after Ten Years of the EMS* (edited by Marcello de Cecco and Alberto Giovannini), both published by Cambridge University Press.

The research and conference programme has over the years created a close and stimulating interaction between scholars in macroeconomics in Italy and their counterparts in other European countries and in the United States. CEPR has been an invaluable resource in fostering this interaction.

We are grateful to Euromobiliare SpA, Centro Europa Ricerche, Prometeia and Alitalia, who provided financial support for the conference, and to the Ente Nazionale Idrocarburi, who hosted the meeting at Villa Montecucco in Castelgandolfo. We are especially grateful to Paul Compton at CEPR, for extremely fast and efficient handling of all the arrangements necessary to publish this volume, and to John Black for his efforts as production editor.

Rudiger Dornbusch
Mario Draghi

Conference participants

Philippe Aghion *MIT*
Alberto Alesina *Harvard University and CEPR*
David Begg *Birkbeck College, London, and CEPR*
Giuseppe Bertola *Princeton University*
Olivier J. Blanchard *MIT*
Patrick Bolton *l'Ecole Polytechnique*
Barry Bosworth *The Brookings Institution*
William H. Branson *Princeton University and CEPR*
Cary Brown *MIT*
Guillermo Calvo *IMF*
Remy Cohen *Euromobiliare SpA*
Jean-Pierre Danthine *Université de Lausanne and CEPR*
Marcello de Cecco *European University Institute, Firenze*
Enrica Detragiache *Johns Hopkins University, Baltimore*
Rudiger Dornbusch *MIT and CEPR*
Mario Draghi *The World Bank*
Allan Drazen *Princeton University*
Barry J. Eichengreen *University of California at Berkeley and CEPR*
John Flemming *Bank of England*
Douglas Gale *MIT*
Giampaolo Galli *Banca d'Italia*
Francesco Giavazzi *Università di Bologna and CEPR*
Alberto Giovannini *Columbia University and CEPR*
Vittorio Grilli *Yale University*
Pablo Guidotti *IMF*
Cesare Imbriani *Ministero del Tesoro, Roma*
Gail Makinen *US Library of Congress*
Marcus Miller *University of Warwick and CEPR*
Mario Monti *Università Bocconi, Milano*
Maurice Obstfeld *Harvard University*

xviii

Paolo Onofri *Università di Bologna*
Fiorella Padoa-Schioppa *LUISS, Roma*
Marco Pagano *Università di Napoli and CEPR*
Richard Portes *CEPR and Birkbeck College, London*
Alessandro Prati *Banca d'Italia*
Pietro Reichlin *European University Institute, Firenze*
Andrea Ripa di Meana *Ministero del Tesoro, Roma*
Riccardo Rovelli *Università Bocconi, Milano*
Robert Skidelsky *University of Warwick*
Luigi Spaventa *Università di Roma 'La Sapienza' and CEPR*
Lars Svensson *Institute for International Economic Studies, Stockholm, and CEPR*
Guido Tabellini *University of California at Los Angeles and CEPR*
Wendy Thompson *CEPR*
Ignazio Visco *Banca d'Italia*
Paul Weller *Cornell University and CEPR*

1 Introduction

RUDIGER DORNBUSCH and
MARIO DRAGHI

In the 1980s the US public debt has grown rapidly and raised questions about the sustainability of deficits. The same issue has been raised in Europe where debt management is a topic of considerable concern today. While in Germany fiscal retrenchment was the result of a fiscally conservative philosophy, in other countries the debt issue has moved to the forefront because debts were reaching perilous levels. Belgium, Ireland and Italy all have ratios of debt to GDP of 100% or more and Greece is rapidly getting there. Debt service absorbs a significant share of government revenue in these countries, and shocks to real interest rates or to economic growth threaten to launch debt-income ratios onto an explosive path.

This introductory chapter spells out some of the issues and then offers a preview of the papers in this collection.

1 A brief tour of debts and deficits

Table 1.1 shows the evolution of debts in the 1980s. Every country, with the exception of Luxemburg and the UK, had higher debt ratios at the end of the decade than at the beginning. The reason for the generalized increase in indebtedness are three:

– The sharp increase in real interest rates, in many cases a shift from negative to positive rates. When in the early 1980s the US shifted to a sharply anti-inflationary monetary stance and other countries joined, in part to avoid even further dollar appreciation and imported inflation, world real interest rates turned sharply positive. The extent of the shift in the United States is well summarized by the decadal averages of real interest rates: -0.1% in the 1950s, 1.9% in the 1960s, -0.1% in the 1970s and then an extraordinary 4.7% in the 1980s. Higher positive real interest rates meant, other things equal, a larger burden of interest payments to be financed by larger non-interest surpluses or by more debt.

1

	1981			1988		
	Debt	Deficit Total	Primary	Debt	Deficit Total	Primary
Europe-10	40.6	3.8	1.4	58.7	2.9	−1.8
Belgium	75.7	12.6	4.8	126.5	5.9	−4.5
Denmark	39.3	6.9	1.6	62.5	−1.0	−8.5
Germany	32.7	3.7	1.4	44.7	0.8	−2.0
Greece	28.8	11.0	7.9	73.6	12.8	3.2
Spain	18.2	3.9	3.1	47.7	3.2	−0.3
France	24.6	1.9	−0.1	36.5	1.7	−1.1
Ireland	76.8	13.4	6.8	118.6	5.1	−4.3
Italy	58.5	11.3	5.2	94.1	9.9	1.0
Luxemburg	13.6	3.6	2.7	10.0	−5.6	−6.7
Netherlands	45.9	5.5	1.0	78.5	4.5	−1.5
Portugal	37.1	9.2	4.1	72.2	6.1	−2.4
UK	52.3	2.6	2.4	48.6	−1.2	−4.7
USA	37.1	1.0	0.7	51.5	1.7	0.3
Japan	57.1	3.9	2.5	68.3	−0.2	−2.8

Table 1.1. Debt and deficits, 1981–88
(% of GDP, General government)
Note: Gross debt/GDP ratios. The primary budget deficit excludes interest payments. A minus (−) sign denotes a surplus.
Source: European Community for EC countries and OECD for other countries.

– Growth in the 1980s, while not unsatisfactory, was low by comparison with previous decades. The combination of high real interest rates and only moderate growth implied more rapid growth in debt-income ratios.
– Non-interest budget surpluses could in principle stop the growth of debt. But it took a while before countries managed to turn around their balances. In the meantime growth of the debt-income ratio was the rule.
By the late 1980s virtually all countries had initiated severe adjustment programs in their budgets. Debt service had grown for all of them, but a major improvement of non-interest balances was in place to slow down or even reverse the growth of debt ratios. Germany and the US, for example, had stable debt ratios by 1989, and in the UK a major debt reduction program was being carried out, partly with resources obtained from the sale of public assets. But in some countries debts and budgets were so far out of line that even serious adjustment, where it did take place, could not swing the balance. As a result there are now four problem debtor countries in Europe. Table 1.2 shows their situation.[1]

	Belgium	Ireland	Italy	Greece
Debt/GNP	127.9	117.5	97.8	76.5
Deficit:				
Total	5.9	5.1	9.9	12.8
Primary	−4.5	−4.3	1.0	3.2
Real interest	7.1	5.7	3.8	−0.7

Table 1.2. The European problem debtors, 1989
(% of GDP)
Source: European Community.

The experience of the 1980s raises three broad sets of issues:
— What is the microeconomic rationale for governments to run up public debt rather than balance budgets all the time?
— Are there significant macroeconomic implications running from the size of the debt, or from decisions to entertain debt finance, to economic activity and interest rates?
— How did countries historically deal with large debts? Were they typically retired, repudiated or ignored?
   When debts are large, are there theoretical reasons to favour a particular maturity structure or indexation regime? Should a government favour short rather than long debt, debt denominated in foreign exchange or indexed to the price level to debt that is denominated in home currency? And are there 'equilibrium' debt structures? This latter topic is new in the literature; the recent interest is clearly a reflection of the need to 'manage' debts when they become as large as they have in the problem debtor countries. We now comment briefly on each of these topics.

2   Debt neutrality and the microeconomics of debt

Government bonds represent an asset to their holders, but they are simultaneously a liability to the tax-payers who must ultimately redeem them. According to the Ricardian Equivalence view, assets and liabilities cancel each other across time and generations so that changes in the level of government debt should not affect the households' net worth and aggregate spending.
   The main counterargument to this view holds that assets and liabilities do not cancel across generations. Therefore debt represents net wealth for its holders who do not take into full account the corresponding liabilities of future generations, and debt-financed government deficits do increase

total spending. Most of the macroeconomic literature in this area focussed on the issues of whether these government-induced intergenerational transfers do actually take place and, if so, whether they affect private spending.

Dornbusch and Poterba (1990) review some of the main arguments in favour of either position. Most US government debt is repaid while the original beneficiaries of the deficits which originated the debt are still alive, which seems to indicate that intergenerational transfers are not large. Also substantial private transfers in the form of bequests would likely cancel out any effect that the government-induced transfers might have on spending. On the other side of the controversy are the arguments which point to the household's liquidity constraints, to possible underestimates of future tax liabilities, or, more simply, to the possibility of a steady growth rate larger than the real rate of interest, so that tax revenues would grow faster than interest payments on government debt. It is the first of these counterarguments from which a still tenuous stream of literature has started to develop. If individuals cannot borrow privately so as to offset shocks in their incomes, the introduction of deficit-financed government benefits allows them to do so from their offspring, and therefore expands their budget constraint.

In recent time this area has attracted the interest of both the macro and the microeconomist. The first asks how quantitatively important are the households which are potentially subject to a liquidity constraint, and to which income-class they belong. On a different side of the professional spectrum, the second is engaged in recasting this problem within the Arrow-Debreu framework, of which several models are presented by Douglas Gale in this book. He offers what in our view is likely the first systematic paper on public debt viewed from the general equilibrium standpoint of the financial economics of uncertainty. One feature of his various results deserves particular attention: in his models the government is 'important' to the extent that it completes from a financial viewpoint markets which are assumed to be incomplete. They are so because agents are prevented from making short sales – which is the equivalent of the liquidity constraint in macroeconomics – or because, under uncertainty, only spot markets are assumed to exist. This second case outlines a novel role for the government which has an impact on the economy as a financial innovator issuing new securities that allow investors to make trades previously impossible. From this viewpoint, it is not the size of debt that matters, but the set of financial instruments created in order to finance it. Even a small quantity of a new instrument induces a substantial welfare improvement if investors may take large open positions in such an instrument.

Many questions like: 'Why are the markets incomplete? Is it reasonable to assume that the government has a comparative advantage over the private sector in the creation of new securities? What is the explanation for the use of public debt in order to accomplish intergenerational transfers which the government can achieve through lump-sum taxation?' remain, as Gale himself reminds us, largely unanswered.

There are also two entirely different tracks of analysis to which several papers presented in the conference were addressed. One was stimulated by the Blanchard (1985) treatment of households which made the discussion of deficit finance highly operational. In this setting, where consumers are viewed as finitely lived, debt is non-neutral and important questions can be asked about the impact of debt finance, present or future, on current economic activity. The long-term interest rate, formed in a rational, forward-looking fashion plays a key role in this system.

In this environment a present tax cut, financed by an increase in future taxes will be expansionary in respect to aggregate demand. The fact that individuals are mortal makes them participate more fully in the current benefits than in the future taxes. The term structure, in a Keynesian fixed-price, constant money supply setting, would become negatively sloped as demand expands today but is expected to decline in the future. The model helps explain why empirically there is no strong evidence of a stable link between debt or deficits and interest rates, at least for the case of the US.[2] An exact timing of benefits and taxes is required to generate predictions, and none of the empirical work has come close to this.

The alternative treatment, in the tradition of the new classical economics, sets out an agenda for monetary and fiscal policy. The most uncompromising statement of this position is Lucas (1986). Here it is argued that there are only two interesting issues about debt: first, how to avoid the time consistency problem of the temptation of debt repudiation and second, the imperative of tax smoothing. The repudiation issue arises because once a debt exists it is tempting to write it off rather than incur the social cost of distortionary taxation required for its service. But if it is expected that governments will do just this, as must be expected in this framework, then there will be no lending. The tax smoothing point addresses the concern that unless tax rates are flat over time, they introduce incentives for socially unproductive intertemporal substitution of consumption or labour effort.

Guillermo Calvo and Pablo Guidotti bring together the issues of market completeness, price indexation of public debt and its optimal maturity structure. The first is shown to be the crucial dividing line between alternative views of public debt, and they, like Gale in a different context, find that when markets are complete 'the maturity structure of public debt is totally irrelevant'. On the other hand, if there is some form of liquidity constraint, and if indexation represents a credible commitment by the government, they find several cases where the effect of optimal indexation of debt to the price level is strengthened by the choice of long-term maturities. In particular, they show how governments through maturity management can alter the time profile of the tax-base.

3   Debt structure

When debts are large and precarious creditors shy away. To continue borrowing governments must make concessions: the debt has to have short maturities and it must be indexed or denominated in foreign exchange. And if the perception of risk is even more acute there may simply be no credit other than what is self-liquidating and fully collater-alized such as trade credit for Latin America today. The literature by Sargent and Wallace (1981) on unpleasant monetarist arithmetic, and the earlier writing on inflationary liquidation of debt by Keynes (1923) and Clark (1945), are the setting for this strand of enquiry: the public is concerned that inflation or depreciation, or repudiation will catch up with them if they are trapped in long-term debt denominated in a soft currency.

The process by which government moves from a situation where the *structure* of debt is not an issue to a situation where maturities are short and payments indexed is exceptionally interesting. It starts, harmlessly, with a premium on long-term bonds reflecting uncertainties about tax-ation or inflation, or about the exchange rate over a significant horizon. In response to the rising term premium governments, eager to minimize their debt service (perhaps 'their' means debt service during their term of office) respond by shifting to shorter maturities. The average maturity of the debt thus shortens and if the lack of confidence intensifies that process accelerates. There is no limit to the shortening; in fact a situation may be reached where debt is all of one-day maturity so that the entire public debt is rolled over every single day.

As a way of illustration, the process of maturities shortening can be suggested by a very simple, static formulation. Imagine a government has a linear quadratic loss function with two arguments: the interest cost of the debt, I, and the liquidity L.

$$V = \alpha I^2 + \beta L^2 \tag{1}$$

where L is an index that runs from zero to 1 with the value of unity denoting instantly maturing debt. Suppose further that there is a linear relation between debt interest and maturity imposed by the capital market.

$$I = i(1 - \sigma L) \quad 1 > \sigma > 0 \tag{2}$$

with i the rate applying to the longest maturities. The government will select an optimal maturity, L^* given by:

$$L^* = \frac{1}{\lambda + \sigma} \quad \text{where} \quad \lambda = \beta/(\alpha \sigma i^2) \tag{3}$$

Too much liquidity is a problem and so is the payment of term premia that would make for a less liquid debt. Now note from (3) that when interest rates rise the government will opt for more liquid debt. It can also be shown that the same thing happens when capital markets charge a higher term premium. There is ample evidence only starting to be studied on this endogenous maturity process.

Of course, the shortening of maturities brings with it the risk of a funding crisis. High enough interest rates, in principle might avert a crisis because they compensate the lender for the risk from here to tomorrow. But high interest rates create their own problem because they make debts grow so fast that insolvency is involved, if not now then tomorrow. In such a situation the market may simply dry up and a government shifts to inflationary finance because debt cannot be sold.

With an eye to the oncoming European Monetary Union, Francesco Giavazzi and Marco Pagano address the optimal maturity issue within the context of an open economy with fixed exchange rates and free capital movements. If a speculative attack against this country's currency takes place, exchange-rate support will require higher interest rates. But suppose also that a large chunk of government debt comes due at the same time and that the government, unwilling to further raise interest rates, refinances it through new money creation. Then investors may develop a crisis of confidence in the ability of the Central Bank to maintain the fixed exchange rate and they would require an even higher nominal interest rate which in turn would increase the refinancing needs of the Treasury and the probability of a devaluation. Such situations can best be avoided when the amount of debt outstanding is not high and when its maturities are not concentrated at few dates but are evenly distributed through time.

'It is the identity of the debtor, and not the nature of the instrument, that is feared by the market.' Alberto Alesina, Alessandro Prati and Guido Tabellini point to the risk of a confidence crisis or of a default as an important determinant of the risk premium paid on Italian government debt during the 1980s. Their finding is based on extensive evidence, of which the most intriguing piece is the one showing the existence of a positive and substantial interest-rate differential between Treasury Bills and Certificates of Deposit with the same maturity issued by Italian commercial banks. Furthermore, using a model based on the analogy between runs on commercial banks and runs on government debt, they reach policy conclusions which are not dissimilar from those of Gia- vazzi and Pagano: 'A confidence crisis is least likely to exist if only long-term debt is issued, and if the same amount of debt matures in each period'.

The preference for liquidity on the part of creditors can easily involve an illusion. Every creditor prefers short to long debt because they believe they can opt out, at short notice, by allowing their claims to run off. Long debts would suffer capital losses, short debts run off and are thus paid at par. But it is clear that if there is a debt problem then it is impossible for all debts to be paid on demand. The classical bank run situation emerges and the fact that the capital market understands the situation certainly does not make it better. On the contrary, all actors become more trigger happy, the debts shortens more and more and self-generating runs become a live possibility.

The indexation issue follows much the same logic. It is well known that when inflation is unstable the long-term capital market dries up. Govern- ments can respond to the premium required to borrow for anything but very short maturities by indexation. But indexation means that now *real* government liabilities are fixed; the policy may reduce the cost of borrow- ing if no adverse circumstances occur. But if they do then more of the burden of adjustment has to fall on taxation, making returns to physical and human capital less certain, or the possibility of partial or total default more real. Indexation, like shortening maturities, is a spontaneous response of a government that is either confident or myopic; in either case it may turn out to be a serious risk. In Mexico, for example, dollar deposits in the banking system went into default and Brazil's indexed debt by early 1990 had become so incredible that the average maturity had shrunk to less than a day. Maturity management or indexation are not substitutes for serious fiscal policy.

4   Debt histories

Alesina (1988) raised the question of how large debts end. There is no simple answer. Some are inflated away, some are repudiated and some are worked down by budget surpluses and growth. In the 1920s, in the aftermath of the Great War, European debts ran high and debt service forced the serious choice between inflation, taxation and repudiation. Germany and Austria fell into hyperinflation, solving their debt problems without doubt, but opening new problems that changed the course of

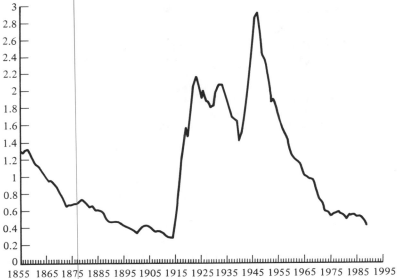

Figure 1.1   The UK debt–income ratio, 1855–1989

history. France, too, eliminated much of her debt by inflation. Not so, however, the UK whose experience is shown in Figure 1.1.

The UK case is striking for a number of reasons. First, debts reached extraordinary levels of nearly 300 percent of GNP in the late 1940s. Second, there was never any default, except by inflation. (An immediate point is that by comparison with the UK case, debt ratios of 100 percent are by no means extreme.) And inflation certainly was not the rule until the period after the Second World War. In fact, in the 1920s the debt ratio declined in the face of steady and even declining prices!

Perhaps most strikingly, today British debt is declining absolutely, partly as the result of receipts from privatization. And as debt is being retired the budget automatically improves, creating room for improvements in the tax structure. The debt reduction program is so dramatic that some observers even speculate what to do after all the debt is gone, – tax cuts or more government spending programs? The British case certainly contradicts the assertion that government, always and anywhere, will spend every penny of resources it can lay its hands on.

Traditional public finance held the view that debts were allowed to rise during wars, but that they had to be worked off soon afterwards. Certainly there was a presumption for debt reduction which today is altogether absent. At full employment budget deficits stood in the way of growth.[3] It bears rereading James Tobin's (1960) essay 'Growth Through Taxation' where he writes:

> Increased taxation is the price of growth. We must tax ourselves not only to finance the necessary increase in public expenditure but also finance, indirectly, the expansion of private investment. A federal budget surplus is a method by which we as a nation can expand the volume of saving available for private investment. The means are at hand; to use them we will need to muster more wisdom, maturity, leadership and sense of national purpose than we displayed in the 1950s.

The model today is one of 'debt-drift' – meaning that deficit finance is altogether appropriate provided the debt ratio is not rising, except during recession. This contrasts sharply with the philosophy prevalent right up to the end of the 1960s when balanced budgets continued to be the rule.

The striking shift made worldwide deficit financing as acceptable and the change must have occurred in the 1960s when the notion of full-employment budgets legitimized deficit finance. In the 1970s there was never a good time to bring deficits under control, and by the 1980s growing debts and deficits started drawing alarm.[4]

It is not clear how far the pendulum of fiscal restraint will swing. If Europe experiences a boom in the 1990s, if real interest rates remain high because of a shortage of saving relative to investment rates driven by a high productivity of capital, it is quite plausible to see a call for budget surpluses. In the United States deficits persist, but the debate about the undesirability of deficits at full employment is certainly alive. Of course, one must note that in the US the budget deficits, and the resulting threat of financial instability, are seen by some as the only check against ever rising government spending. And up to a point it has proven an effective threat in that spending programs have been trimmed substantially. But there are diminishing returns to this game. The deficit translates into increasing debt service and ultimately a situation develops where total government spending stabilizes, but rising interest payments requires more and more non-interest spending cuts.

Several papers addressed these issues from an historical perspective, and one is tempted to outline a few of their main messages:

– Little comfort comes from history for those who consider a capital levy as an adequate way to resolve debt problems in Western Europe. Only under exceptional circumstances, requiring extraordinary measures, would bond-holders accept a capital levy as a legitimate policy instrument to reduce debt service: only in such a case would the government's market access not be damaged. Barry Eichengreen reviews this century's historical experience and cannot find one example of successful peacetime capital levy which was not frustrated by the powerful resistance of the interested groups. He singles out the Japanese experience in this area as unique because it was carried out during a military occupation, when domestic distributional conflicts were suppressed, and reputational consequences on future governments were not in question.

– There is no historical evidence of spontaneous 'debt runs'. Gail Makinen and Thomas Woodward's provocative analysis sharply contrasts with the view by which funding crisis would be caused by lack of confidence among creditors, usually induced by unsound fiscal policies. The three funding crises they discuss took place in countries where government budgets were either in surplus or almost balanced. They conclude that wrong debt management policies whereby governments insisted in paying to bondholders an interest rate below the equilibrium level were the main factor of crisis.

– Excellent placement techniques, careful financial diplomacy, and perfect timing with the conditions prevailing on the international capital markets were the preconditions for a series of successful debt conversions undertaken by the Italian government during 1903–06. Marcello de Cecco reviews this experience and compares it with others less fortunate which were to be implemented by the fascist government in later years.

– Small, poorly managed and often defaulted by the States was the US public debt during the 19th century. Cary Brown reviews its history and highlights how it was considered more of a residual variable, in a country where the main focus was on trade policies, and where high tariff revenue and limited government intervention kept budget deficits low.

5   Debt and politics

A new and fruitful discussion is developing in the political economy literature.[5] Debt links one government to another, it affords the possibility of reaping benefits today at the cost of another administration or it creates an opportunity to limit the scope for action of one's successor.

The typical setting involves a current government that must choose a public finance strategy in view of an uncertain future government. Burdening future governments with a large debt makes certain that they cannot spend, and, if the debt is short-dated and denominated in hard currency, the problems for the successors are even worse.

The political economy strand of public finance, so much in fashion today, exploits in a game-theoretic framework this issue to ask what debt strategies are likely to emerge depending on political polarization and election probabilities. One rather striking implication is that conservative governments run large deficits (resulting from low taxation) so as to limit their successor governments with burdens that make it impossible to spend!

Also considered by Calvo and Guidotti, this subject constitutes the main topic of Philippe Aghion and Patrick Bolton's contribution. How can public debt be used as a political instrument to ensure reelection of the incumbent government? If there is no risk of default, public debt has no strategic role, although, as in Calvo and Guidotti, it may be used to constrain the policies of future administrations. However, if there is risk of default, if the government can credibly promise not to default and such a promise is not credible when made by the opposition, then the government in power has an incentive to excessive accumulation of public debt. In so doing, it will increase the number of bond-holders who are going to be potentially hurt by a default and who will therefore vote for the government in power.

The psychological aspects of private agents' response to government policies are discussed by Marcus Miller, Robert Skidelsky and Paul Weller. They construct a model where conventional fiscal policies, like increases in deficit spending, produce surprising results, like decreases in aggregate demand, because the private agents' consensus objects to their policy-makers' intentions and successfully offsets them. The authors analyse this 'psychological crowding-out' in a setting where agents are concerned about the level of public debt and are convinced that, if this were to exceed a certain threshold, they would have to pay more taxes. These are assumed to fall on the coupon of their bond holdings. The authors show that anticipation of such tax measures has relevant current effects on output only if the economy has a reduced capacity to service debt.

The political economy literature is easily dismissed as oversimplified if not simplistic. But that would be throwing away an important source of insight into political processes. Debt is not only the result of macro-economic decisions, high real interest rates and low growth. It clearly involves important intertemporal political jockeying as the US case makes so clear.

NOTES

1 In a recent study Stournaras (1989) places the Greek debt in 1989 at 100 percent of GDP and calculates a primary deficit of 9 percent of GDP. The data in this study by the Bank of Greece are possibly more authoritative than others and thus suggest that Greece is a problem debtor on any definition.
2 See the survey by Iden and Sturrock (1989).
3 One of the best formal developments of this theme is Auerbach and Kotlikoff (1987).
4 See Stein (1976) for a history of fiscal policy and philosophy in the United States.
5 In addition to the work reported in this volume see especially Persson and Tabellini (1989).

REFERENCES

Alesina, A. (1988). 'The End of Large Public Debts', in Francesco Giavazzi and Luigi Spaventa *High Public Debt: The Italian Experience*. Cambridge: Cambridge University Press.

Auerbach, A. & L. Kotlikoff (1987). *Dynamic Fiscal Policy*, Cambridge: Cambridge University Press.

Blanchard, O.J. (1985). 'Debt, Deficits and Finite Horizons', *Journal of Political Economy* **93**, 223–47.

Clark, C. (1945). 'Public Finance and Changes in the Value of Money', *Economic Journal*, December.

Dornbusch, R. & J. Poterba (1990). 'Debt and Deficits', forthcoming in volume to be published by the American Enterprise Institute.

Iden, G. & J. Sturrock (1989). 'Deficits and Interest Rates. Theoretical Issues and Empirical Evidence', mimeo, Congressional Budget Office, January.

Keynes, J.M. (1923). *A Tract on Monetary Reform*, London: Macmillan.

Lucas, R.E. (1986). 'Principles of Fiscal and Monetary Policy', *Journal of Monetary Economics* **17**, 117–34.

Persson, T. & G. Tabellini (1989). *Macroeconomic Policy, Credibility and Politics*, mimeo, University of California, Los Angeles.

Sargent, T. and N. Wallace (1981). 'Some Unpleasant Monetary Arithmetic', Federal Reserve Bank of St. Louis, *Quarterly Review*, Fall.

Stein, H. (1976). *The Fiscal evolution in America*, Chicago: University of Chicago Press.

Stournaras, Y. (1989). 'Public sector debts and deficits in Greece: The Experience of the 1980s', mimeo, Bank of Greece.

Tobin, J. (1960). 'Growth through Taxation', *The New Republic*, July 25, reprinted in his *National Economic Policy*, New Haven: Yale University Press.

2 The efficient design of public debt

DOUGLAS GALE

1 Introduction

With a few notable exceptions, such as Fischer (1983), Peled (1985) and Bohn (1988a, b, c), the literature on public debt has concentrated on positive issues, such as the neutrality of the debt (Barro, 1974; Tobin, 1971). In this paper I want to concentrate instead on welfare issues, in particular, the impact of debt policy on the efficiency of risk sharing.

As a prelude to the central part of the paper, Section 2 reviews the familiar issue of the neutrality of the debt. The classical Ricardian equivalence theorem assumes that markets are complete. Nonetheless, even if markets are incomplete, there is an analogue of the classical neutrality theorem. A theorem of this sort is proved in Section 2 for a generic economy with incomplete markets. It shows that changes in the size and composition of the debt are neutral as long as the set of debt instruments issued by the government is unchanged. This result is similar to the Modigliani-Miller theorem of Wallace-Chamley-Polemarchakis (see Wallace, 1981, and Chamley and Polemarchakis, 1984). On the other hand, if markets are incomplete, it is clearly possible for the government to have an impact on the economy by introducing new securities that expand risk-sharing opportunities.

There is a tension between these two results. It seems that a tiny amount of a new security has a large impact while a large change in the amount of an existing security has no impact at all. The explanation for this asymmetry lies in the assumption that agents can take unlimited short positions. Introducing a small amount of a new security is like opening a new market. It can have a big impact on the economy simply because it allows a large open interest in the security. The discontinuity disappears as soon as short sales are constrained. It is well known, of course, that neutrality also disappears if short sales are constrained. Thus, at the theoretical level, we have to accept a discontinuity in the impact of public

14

debt policy in order to have neutrality. This ought to give us pause for thought.

The core of the paper begins in Section 3, which studies the impact of particular financial innovations. For this purpose, I use a simple overlapping generations (OLG) model with identical generations that last two periods. There is a risky, constant returns to scale investment technology. The young can save for their retirement by investing in this risky technology, but that will mean that all the risk at any date is borne by only one of the two generations alive at that date. It is not hard to show that intergenerational risk-sharing can be improved by introducing 'safe' securities that give the old a claim on the next young generation. (This kind of result has been obtained by Weiss, Fischer and Pagano.) By introducing a safe, short-dated security it is possible to allow each generation to transfer some risk from the second to the first period of its life. Under certain circumstances, this shift may be Pareto-improving *ex post*.

An even better allocation of risk can be achieved, however, if long-dated securities are used. If productivity shocks are positively serially correlated, bond prices will be low when returns to capital are high. This is because high returns to capital lead to expectations of future high returns which make bonds less attractive. Thus, the yield on long-dated securities will be negatively correlated with the return on capital, which makes long-dated securities an even better hedge against productivity shocks.

It is well known that in infinite-horizon economies with overlapping generations, competitive equilibrium may be inefficient, even if markets are complete. The failure of the First Theorem of Welfare Economics is partly responsible for the possibility of improving welfare through debt policy. It is known, however, that under some conditions the competitive equilibrium is efficient. In particular, if there exist durable assets producing positive returns at a zero interest rate, the competitive equilibrium is efficient when there are complete markets and no uncertainty. (This result, discovered by many for the steady-state case has been proved in general by Scheinkman. His result, which remains unpublished, appears to be under-appreciated in the literature.) The question, then, is whether these conditions are sufficient to ensure efficient risk-sharing in the presence of uncertainty. If the answer is yes, then the possibility of improving risk-sharing through debt policy also disappears.

In Section 4 I consider the efficiency of equilibrium when there are durable assets. It is shown that under certain conditions the equilibrium allocations cannot be Pareto-dominated by any stationary allocation. In particular, this means that debt policy cannot improve welfare in a stationary equilibrium. At first glance, this appears to undermine the analysis of the preceding section. However, the result is not quite as strong as it appears at first. Apart from the restriction to comparisons with stationary allocations, the result depends on the assumption that the returns to the durable asset are greater than the rate of growth with probability one. It also depends on the use of the *ex post* welfare criterion, which distinguishes individuals by the state in which they are born. There is still the possibility of obtaining a welfare improvement using the weaker *ex ante* criterion. (The *ex ante* criterion is used by Fisher, 1983; also, in another context, by Gale, 1988.)

At the end of Section 4 there is a discussion of the problem of characterizing an efficient, contingent debt policy. The problem can be broken into two parts. The first is the problem of choosing an efficient tax-transfer scheme. The second is the problem of implementing it via an appropriate public debt policy. In very simple models (e.g., Fischer, 1983; Pagano, 1988), there may be no essential difference between the tax-transfer scheme and the debt policy. One can simply reinterpret the one as the other. In general, this will not be the case. If the government can make efficient transfers directly, there is no reason to use security markets. If there is some reason to use security markets to implement efficient intergenerational risk-sharing, then the problem of choosing an efficient debt policy is inherently more difficult than simply choosing an efficient tax-transfer scheme. Relatively simple transfers may require complicated debt policies. It can be shown that within the general class of models studied in the second half of the paper, an optimal debt policy will typically be unable to implement the allocation achieved by the optimal tax-transfer policy. To understand the force of this result it is helpful to restate it. In the optimal tax-transfer problem it is assumed that the government implements the entire allocation by fiat. In the very simple OLG models studied in the paper, a debt policy is equivalent to making lump-sum, intergenerational transfers. So the optimal tax-transfer problem corresponds to finding the first-best allocation and the optimal debt policy problem corresponds to finding prices at which the first-best allocation can be supported as an allocation with lump-sum, intergenerational transfers. The additional constraint under the debt policy is that asset markets must be in equilibrium. In particular, agents must be willing to hold the durable asset at the prevailing prices. What the theorem says is that the first-best allocation achieved by a tax-transfer policy (including transfers of the asset) cannot be supported as an equilibrium with lump-sum transfers.

Once we have incomplete markets, it is not hard to obtain non-neutral effects from the debt and even to find scope for welfare-improving changes in the size or the structure of the debt. But an important question is begged as long as the market structure is taken as exogenous. Why should we assume that there is a role for the government as a financial innovator? If markets are missing they are presumably missing for a reason. The government may be able to replace these missing markets, but it does not necessarily have a cost advantage over the private sector. Is it clear that, if these costs were taken into account, it would be socially desirable to introduce the new securities?

A related question is why, assuming there is a role for the government to improve risk-sharing opportunities, it should choose to do so by introducing new securities (or altering the mix of existing securities) rather than making lump-sum transfers, for example. These issues are discussed in Section 5.

Inevitably, some important issues have been left out. Perhaps the most important omission is the exclusion of any discussion of monetary issues. This is particularly unfortunate because a significant part of the risk of holding nominal government securities comes from uncertainty about the price level. Nonetheless, in what follows attention is restricted to real models. Although this approach is undoubtedly restrictive, I think one learns enough from it to justify the approximation. From an antidote to the present approach, the reader is directed to the excellent work on nominal debt by Henning Bohn. (See also the work on the role of money in intergenerational risk-sharing by Weiss, 1979 and by Bhattacharya, 1982.) A second omission is the exclusion of time-consistency issues (see Lucas and Stokey, 1983). A third is the exclusion of the problems raised by distortionary taxation (see Barro, 1979; Lucas and Stokey, 1987). For all these, the excuse is simply the impossibility of including everything, in a coherent way, in a finite space.

2   Neutrality, incomplete markets and financial innovation

From the point of view of financial economics, the classical theorems on the neutrality of the debt are special cases of general results on linear spaces generated by sets of assets. They are part of a family that includes the familiar results on Arrow securities, the Modigliani-Miller theorem, the Black-Scholes option pricing theory and so forth. This perspective suggests that the classical neutrality theorems are very general. It also suggests some limitations. One of these is the need to allow unlimited short sales. An asset is redundant in these theories if it can be expressed as a linear combination of other assets. This notion of 'spanning' assumes that it is possible to *sell* as well as to *buy* any amount of an asset at the prevailing price. For obvious reasons, however, there is an asymmetry between short and long positions. It is unrealistic to assume unlimited short sales and as we shall see, even if unlimited short sales are allowed there are purely theoretical problems that arise as a result of this unrealistic assumption. As we shall see in Section 5, constraining short sales is not an insignificant change in the theory.

The essential ideas that lie behind debt neutrality are often obscured by the details of specific results. Re-expressing these arguments abstractly, with a minimum of unnecessary detail, makes clear the essential unity of all these results. In particular, it makes clear that the same arguments work whether markets are complete or incomplete. However, when markets are incomplete, there is a tension between the neutrality theorem, which holds when the set of securities is not changed, and the non-neutrality that results if new securities are introduced. In this section I first state a neutrality theorem and then discuss the importance of short sales in this context.

2.1 A model of incomplete markets

Let X and Z be finite-dimensional Euclidean spaces. Call X the *commodity space* and Z the *security space*. An element of X represents a commodity bundle and an element of Z represents a trade in securities. The returns to trading securities are represented by a linear function $A: Z \to X$. A trade $z \in Z$ results in a vector of returns Az. Security prices are also represented by elements of Z. Let $\otimes$ be a bilinear function from $Z \times Z$ to Z. For any $(q, z) \in Z \times Z$, the value of (q, z) under $\otimes$ is denoted by $q \otimes z$. If q denotes the prices of securities and z denotes the security trade, then $q \otimes z$ is the value of the trade.

There is a finite number of agents indexed by $i = 1, 2, \ldots, n$. Each agent is defined by a consumption set $X_i \subset X$ and a utility function u_i on that set. The elements of X_i represent net consumption after the initial endowment has been subtracted.

There is also a government that consumes goods, levies taxes and trades in securities. The government's net consumption is denoted by $g \in X$, and its taxes are denoted by $H \in X$. Both are assumed to be exogenous. Let h_i denote the tax obligations of agent $i = 1, 2, \ldots, n$ where $H = \Sigma h_i$, and let $h = (h_1, \ldots, h_m)$.

Each agent $i = 1, 2, \ldots, m$ is assumed to choose a consumption bundle $x_i \in X_i$ and a security trade $z_i \in Z$ subject to the budget constraints $x_i + h_i + q \otimes z_i \leq Az_i$. Similarly, the government chooses a security trade $z_0 \in Z$ that satisfies the budget constraints $g - H + q \otimes z_0 \leq Az_0$.

Fix the government's expenditures $g \in X$ and taxes $h \in X$. An *equilibrium* relative to (g, h) is defined to be a price vector $q \in Z$ and an allocation $(z_0, (x_1, z_1), \ldots, (x_m, z_m))$ satisfying the following conditions:

(i) (x_i, z_i) is maximal with respect to u_i in the set

$\{(\xi, \zeta) \in X_i \times Z \mid x_i + h_i + q \otimes z_i \leq Az_i\}$ for $i = 1, 2, \ldots, m;$

(ii) $z_0 \in Z$ satisfies $g - H + q \otimes z_0 \leq Az_0;$

(iii) $\Sigma_{i=1}^m x_i + g = 0$ and $\Sigma_{i=0}^m z_i = 0.$

2.2 The neutrality theorem

Let $\langle q, z_0. (x_1, z_1), \ldots, (x_m, z_m) \rangle$ be a fixed but artibrary equilibrium, relative to some policy (g, h). Suppose that the government decides to change its financial policy while keeping its expenditures g fixed. The new policy must satisfy the government's budget constraint. Let (g, h') denote the new policy. Then there exists a security trade $z_0' \in Z$ satisfying $g - H' + q \otimes z_0' = Az_0'$, where $H' \equiv \Sigma_i h_i'$. The policy change will be neutral if there is no redistribution of the tax burden among the individual agents. The change of policy will have no distribution effects if, for each $i = 1, 2, \ldots, m$, there is a security trade that agent i can make that will convert his new tax into the old one. More precisely, for each $i = 1, 2, \ldots, m$, there exists $\zeta \in Z$ so that $h_i' - h_i + q \otimes \zeta = A\zeta$. Then for each $i = 1, 2, \ldots, m$ there exists a security trade z_i' such that $x_i + h_i' + q \otimes z_i' = Az_i'$. Since the agents' budget sets have not changed, $(q, (z_0', (x_1, z_1'), \ldots, (x_m, z_m')))$ is an equilibrium relative to the new policy (g, h'). The allocation of goods is unchanged in the new equilibrium so the policy change is *neutral*.

Theorem 1: A change in financial policy which leaves government expenditure unaltered and has no distributive effects is neutral.

This is all there is to the neutrality of the debt. I have deliberately used a rather roundabout argument in order to make explicit the role of securities. A more compact argument is possible if securities are eliminated.

Let $X(q)$ denote the set of commodity bundles that can be generated by security trades when the security prices are given by q. That is, $X(q) = (\xi \in X \mid \xi \leq Az - q \otimes z, \exists z \in Z\}$. Then the budget constraints for the agents and the government can be written compactly as $x_i + h_i \in X(q)$ and $g - H \in X(q)$, respectively.

In this notation, an equilibrium is defined by an n-tuple of consumption bundles $(x_1, \ldots, x_m) \in X_1 \times \ldots \times X_m$ and a price vector $q \in Z$, satisfying the following conditions:

(i) x_i maximizes $u_i(x_i)$ subject to $x + h_i \in X(q) \cap X_i$, for $i = 1, 2, \ldots, m;$

(ii) $g - H \in X(q);$

(iii) $\Sigma_{i=1}^m x_i + g = 0.$

Note that if these conditions are satisfied, there exists a security trade z_i for each $i = 1, 2, \ldots, m$ such that $x_i + h_i + q \otimes z_i \leq Az_i.$

If we define $z_0 = \Sigma_{i=1}^{m} z_i$, then condition (iii) implies that
$g = H + q \otimes z_0 \leq Az_0$. Thus, the definition of equilibrium is consistent
with equilibrium in the securities markets.

Now consider a change in the government's financial policy. Government consumption is kept constant but its security trade and taxes may
change. The budget constraint must be satisfied so $g - H' \in X(q)$, if h'
denotes the new taxes. The new taxes are divided up among agents so
that their individual shares of the tax burden are not changed. This is
interpreted as the requirement that $x_i + h_i' \in X(q)$, for $i = 1, 2, \ldots, m$.
Then, clearly, nothing has changed. If (x, q) is an equilibrium relative to
the old pattern of taxes, it is an equilibrium relative to the new pattern.

2.3   Financial innovation and short sales

The preceding argument does not depend in any way on the completeness or incompleteness of markets. However, it does depend on the
fact that Z is fixed. If the government can change Z by introducing a
new security, for example, then clearly it can have a real impact on the
economy.

This fact, which is fairly obvious, is nonetheless somewhat puzzling on
the surface. On the one hand, we have a neutrality theorem that says the
quantity of government securities outstanding does not have any real
effect as long as the set of traded securities does not change. On the
other hand, the introduction of a small amount of a new security may
have a large effect, by changing the dimension of the set of consumption
bundles that can be reached by trading securities. There is a *discontinuity*
in the effect of debt policy when financial innovation occurs.

The reason for this discontinuity is the implicit assumption that there
are no constraints on short sales of securities. Agents are allowed to buy
and sell as much of any security as they like. As soon as the government
introduces a small amount of a new security, the volume of trade on the
new market may explode. It is the volume of trade in the new security
that matters, not the amount of the security that is issued by the government. On the other hand, if short sales were not allowed, the volume of
trade would be restricted to the amount of the security issued by the
government and there would be no discontinuity. However, as everyone
knows, restricting short sales would destroy the neutrality of the debt. In
order to undo the effects of the change in the government's debt policy,
the private sector has to be able to short sell government securities.

Thus, one must either accept the existence of a discontinuity in the
impact of government securities or abandon the neutrality theorem for
incomplete markets.

3   Public debt in an infinite-horizon model

From the preceding discussion it is clear that the introduction of new securities can have an impact on the risk-sharing opportunities in the economy. But this theoretical possibility is not very interesting unless we can say something precise about the securities being introduced and the welfare effects of their introduction. A simple overlapping generations (OLG) framework provides the structure that is needed for this exercise.

Implicit in the OLG structure is the assumption that markets are incomplete. More precisely, there is *incomplete participation*. Each generation can only participate in the markets that are open during its lifetime. In the present context, this makes it impossible for an investor to write risk-sharing contracts with generations yet unborn. There is a role for long-lived institutions, of which the government is one, to act as intermediaries.

The idea that intergenerational risk-sharing could be facilitated by government-issued assets appears in Weiss (1979). (I am indebted to Sudipto Bhattacharya for this reference.) Weiss characterized the optimal monetary policy in an OLG economy with a risky investment technology. He showed that, under certain conditions, an activist monetary policy that stabilized the value of money was welfare-increasing. The effect of this policy was to redistribute risk between the generations. The role of money in facilitating intergenerational risk sharing was studied further in Bhattacharya (1983). A particularly transparent example of intergenerational risk sharing with indexed debt was presented by Fischer (1983). He studied the efficiency properties of a pure exchange, OLG economy with two-period-lived agents. Fischer assumed that the aggregate endowment of the economy was constant but that the distribution between old and young was random. He showed that various arrangements, some of which could be interpreted as (indexed) debt, would lead to an *ex ante* increase in welfare. Peled (1985) studied a related set of issues in the context of a pure exchange, OLG economy with money. He showed that a stationary monetary equilibrium was *ex post*, stationary-efficient. That is, it was efficient when agents were distinguished by the state in which they are born and when the equilibrium allocation was compared only with other stationary allocations. He also argued that the introduction of indexed debt was destabilizing.

An *empirical* analysis of dynamic inefficiency is contained in Abel *et al.* (1989).

In this section we shall see that introducing public debt can lead to *ex post* increases in welfare. This result is stronger than Fischer's and appears to contradict Peled's. However, as we shall see in the next section, the introduction of durable assets, such as shares in firms or fiat money, changes the story somewhat.

3.1   A model of an OLG economy

There is an infinite sequence of dates indexed by $t \in T = \{1, 2, \ldots, \infty\}$. At each date $t \in T$, a random variable $\tilde{s}_t$ is observed. The stochastic process $\{\tilde{s}_t\}$ is assumed to be a finite Markov chain with a stationary transition probability matrix. Let $S = \{s_1, \ldots, s_n\}$ denote the values of the random variables $\{\tilde{s}_t\}$ and let $a_{ij} > 0$ denote the probability of a transition from state s_i to state s_j, for $i, j = 1, 2, \ldots, n$. At each date there is a single good that can be either consumed or invested. One unit of the good invested at date t produces $\tilde{R}_t$ units of the good at date $t + 1$. The return to the investment technology is assumed to be a function of the current state, that is, $\tilde{R}_t = R(\tilde{s}_{t+1})$.

Each generation consists of a single representative investor who lives for two periods. The generations have identical preferences that can be represented by a von Neumann–Morgenstern utility function $u(c_1, c_2)$, where c_τ denotes net consumption in the τth period of life.

In what follows, only stationary equilibria are considered. In a stationary equilibrium the stock of government securities is constant over time. Then the government's budget constraint requires that expenditure must be paid for out of current taxes, except possibly at the first date. In that case, we can assume without loss of generality that government expenditure is zero after the first period.

The government is assumed to issue (non-contingent) real bills of different maturities. Greater improvements in welfare could be achieved if the government were to issue more exotic securities. But endowing the government with the ability to create very complex securities may exaggerate the scope for improvements in risk-sharing. If the market has not produced certain kinds of securities, it may be because the costs outweigh the benefits. In that case, it is inefficient for the government to issue them, unless it has a cost advantage. By restricting attention to simple (non-contingent) securities we at least avoid the mistake of ascribing unrealistic powers to the public sector. Contingent securities will be considered in Section 4. The question of the government's role as a financial innovator is considered in more detail in Section 5.

A k-period bill issued at date t is a promise to deliver one unit of the consumption good at date $t + k$. Suppose that bills of maturities $k = 1, 2, \ldots, K$ have been issued. Then a price system is a function $v \colon S \to \mathbf{R}_+^K$. For any $s \in S$, $v(s)$ is the vector of security spot prices in terms of the consumption good if state s is observed.

Let B_k denote the stock of k-period bills outstanding at each date and let $B = (B_1, \ldots, B_K)$. A k-period bill issued at date t becomes a $(k - 1)$-period bill at date $t + 1$. Thus, to maintain a constant stock of securities, the government has to issue $B_k - B_{k+1}$ new k-period bills each period. Alternatively, one can think of the government as retiring all bills after one period and issuing a new stock of B_k k-period bills. In either case the budget constraint is

$$B \cdot \hat{v}(s) - B \cdot v(s) = H(s) \tag{1}$$

where $H(s)$ denotes total tax revenue collected in state $s \in S$ and

$$\hat{v}(s) = (1, v_1(s), \ldots, v_{K-1}(s)) \tag{2}$$

is the resale value of the bills after one period in state $s \in S$. To avoid intergenerational transfers as a result of asymmetric tax treatment, it is assumed that all taxes are imposed on the young generation. The government's tax policy is represented by the function $h: S \to \mathbf{R}_+$, where $h(s)$ represents the tax levied on a young investor born in state $s \in S$.

In the first period of his life, a typical individual chooses an investment in the risky technology and a portfolio of securities to hold. His consumption at each date in each state is then determined by his budget constraint. Let $y: S \to \mathbf{R}_+$ denote an investor's investment choice and $b: S \to \mathbf{R}_+^K$ denote his portfolio choice. Then the investor's consumption is given by

$$c_1(s) = -v(s) \cdot b(s) - y(s) - h(s) \tag{3}$$

$$c_2(s, s') = R(s')y(s) + \hat{v}(s') \cdot b(s) \tag{4}$$

for any $(s, s') \in S \times S$. The investor chooses the functions c_1, c_2, y and b to maximize his expected utility conditional on the state in the first period.

An *equilibrium* for the OLG economy is an array $\langle y, b, h, B, v \rangle$ satisfying the following conditions:

(i) (b, y) maximizes $E[u(c_1(s), c_2(s, s')) | s]$ where c_1 and c_2 are defined by the budget constraints.

$$c_1(s) = -v(s) \cdot b(s) - y(s) - h(s), \quad \forall s \in S;$$
$$c_2(s, s') = R(s')y(s) + \hat{v}(s') \cdot b(s), \quad \forall (s, s') \in S \times S.$$

(ii) $B \cdot \hat{v}(s) - B \cdot v(s) = h(s)$, for any $s \in S$.

(iii) $b(s) = B$, for any $s \in S$.

The following assumptions are maintained throughout the remainder of this section.

(A.1) $u(c_1, c_2) = U(c_1) + V(c_2)$ for any $(c_1, c_2) \in \mathbf{R}^2$, where U and V are C^2, strictly increasing and strictly concave functions from $\mathbf{R}$ to $\mathbf{R}$;

(A.2) $U'(0) < V'(0) \Sigma_{j=1}^{n} a_{ij} R(s_j)$,   for $i = 1, \ldots, n$.

Theorem 2: Under the maintained assumptions, there exists an equilibrium of the OLG economy for any $B \geq 0$.

Note that consumption is unbounded below.

3.2   Intergenerational risk-sharing with short-dated securities

In order to understand the role of public debt in promoting more efficient risk-sharing, it is useful to think of it as a kind of social security scheme. Imagine an economy in which there were no government securities. Since investors in different generations cannot issue securities to each other, equilibrium is autarkic. The only way for investors to transfer wealth between dates is to invest in the risky technology. Since R_t is random, their first-period consumption will be certain but their second-period consumption will be risky. What each investor wants is to shift some of this risk from the second period of his life to the first. The only way this can be achieved is for the old to shift some of the risk to the young generation at each date. One way to do this is by introducing a social security scheme.

Define a function y^* from S to $\mathbf{R}_+$ by putting

$$y^*(s_i) = \arg\max \Sigma_{j=1}^{n} a_{ij}[U(-y) + V(R(s_j)y)], \quad \text{for} \quad i = 1, \ldots, n$$
(5)

(A.1) implies that $y^*(s) > 0$ for all $s \in S$. y^* is the optimal investment policy in the absence of government securities and social security. The question is whether the introduction of social security would increase welfare. The social security scheme requires each investor to pay a contribution σ when young and promises to pay him a benefit σ when old. An increase in σ will change the optimal y, but from the envelope theorem, the effect on utility is negligible. Thus, the effect on expected utility of a small change in σ is given by

$$\{-U'(-y^*(s_i)) + \Sigma_{j=1}^{n} a_{ij} V'(R(s_j)y^*(s_i))\}d\sigma + o(d\sigma)$$
(6)

If the term in braces is positive for each $s \in S$, then an increase in σ will increase welfare for every $s \in S$. In other words, welfare increases even if we distinguish investors by the state in which they are born.

Proposition: If $U'(-y^*(s_i)) < \Sigma_{j=1}^{n} a_{ij} V'(R(s_j)y^*(s_i))$ for $i, \ldots, n$, a social security scheme in which $\sigma = 0$ is dominated by one in which $\sigma > 0$.

Social security is like an asset with a zero rate of return. Although capital has a higher expected return, an investor may be willing to invest in the safe asset as a hedge. In fact, the inequality of the Proposition will always be satisfied if $\tilde{R}_t$ is random and the investor is sufficiently risk-averse. Under the same conditions, there will be a demand for public debt. Public debt operates like a social security scheme by offering the investor a safe asset which is in fact a claim on the next generation. To see this, let $\langle b, y, h, B, v \rangle$ be a stationary equilibrium in which only 1-period bills are issued. That is, $B_k = 0$ for $k = 2, \ldots, K$. In the first period of his life, an investor pays a tax of $h(s) = (1 - v_1(s)) B_1$ and buys bills worth $v_1(s) B_1$. His first-period consumption will be $c_1(s) = -y(s) - B_1$ and his second-period consumption will be $c_2(s, s') = R(s') y(s) + B_1$. Thus, putting $\sigma = B_1$ we see that his consumption will be exactly the same in an equilibrium with 1-period debt as it would be in an equilibrium with a social security scheme and no government securities. Conversely, if y is an optimal investment policy corresponding to a social security scheme σ, there is an equilibrium with government securities that implements the same consumption allocation. This equilibrium can be defined by putting $B_1 = \sigma$, $h(s) = (1 - v_1(s)) B_1$, $\forall s \in S$, and choosing v to satisfy the first-order condition

$$U'(-y(s_i) - B_1) v_1(s_i) = \Sigma_{j=1}^n a_{ij} V'(y(s_i) R(s_j) + B_1) \qquad (7)$$

Theorem 3: Corresponding to any equilibrium with a social security scheme and no government securities, there exists an equilibrium with 1-period bills that has the same consumption and investment. Conversely, corresponding to any equilibrium with 1-period bills there is an equilibrium with a social security scheme and no government securities that has the same consumption and investment.

In a precise sense, public debt is equivalent to a social security scheme. Since (short-dated) public debt is riskless, it provides a hedge against the risky investment technology. Each generation is providing insurance to the preceding generation and, since there is an infinite horizon, they can all be better off. Thus, there is a role for public debt to improve risk-sharing in the economy even if there is no continuing need to finance government expenditure.

It is useful to compare this role for public debt to the one discovered by Diamond (1965). In Diamond's model there is no uncertainty and markets are complete. However, equilibrium may be inefficient because of overaccumulation of capital. In that case, an increase in public debt would crowd out part of the capital stock and so lead to a Pareto improvement. In the present case, in addition to an infinite horizon and an OLG structure, we have risk and incomplete markets. The expected rate of return on capital can be greater than zero, so there is no overaccumulation, yet there is still the possibility of an increase in welfare. The inefficiency arises not from overaccumulation but simply from unexploited opportunities for risk-sharing.

3.3   *Intergenerational risk-sharing with long-dated securities*

The preceding analysis shows that the existence of public debt can improve risk-sharing in a simple, OLG economy. If short-term debt can improve welfare, is there a role for longer-dated securities? Under certain circumstances, as we shall see, lengthening the maturity structure of the debt can improve welfare even further.

Short-dated securities (1-period bills) offer a safe return. Longer-dated securities are inherently more 'risky' because changes in the interest rate lead to random capital gains and losses. However, riskiness of this sort can be an advantage. Suppose that the observation of a high (low) value of R_t causes investors to expect high (low) future values of R_t and hence lowers (raises) the price of long-dated securities. If the price of bonds is high when the return to capital is low, then risky, long-dated securities will be an even better hedge against the risky investment technology than the safe, short-dated securities.

To make this argument precise, a general-equilibrium analysis is needed. Fix an equilibrium $\langle y, b, h, B, v \rangle$ and consider the effect of a small change in B. If $u^*(s_i)$ denotes the equilibrium expected utility of an investor born in state s_i, then the impact of the change in B is easily calculated to be

$$\frac{du^*(s_i)}{dB} = U'(c_1(s_i))\left\{ - B\frac{dv(s_i)}{dB} - \frac{dh(s_i)}{dB} \right\}$$

$$+ \sum_{j=1}^{n} a_{ij} V'(c_2(s_i, s_j)) B \frac{d\hat{v}(s_j)}{dB} \qquad (8)$$

where $\hat{v}(s) \equiv (1, v_1(s), \ldots, v_{K-1}(s))$.

One fact is immediately apparent from this formula. If there are no government securities in the initial equilibrium, then the welfare effect of introducing short-dated securities is determined entirely by the tax effect. Putting $B = 0$, the formula tells us that

$$\frac{du^*(s_i)}{dB} = - U'(c_1(s_i)) \frac{dh(s_i)}{dB} \qquad (9)$$

This result can be explained as follows. The change in the equilibrium expected utility of an investor can be divided into three parts. First, there is the effect of the change in the investor's portfolio (y, b). Second, there is the wealth effect of the change in the prices v. Third, there is the effect of the change in taxes. The first of these effects vanishes by the Envelope Theorem. If $B = 0$, the second effect also vanishes. We are left with the tax effect. What the formula says is that welfare is increased if and only if taxes *fall* as a result of the introduction of short-dated securities.

At first glance, this may seem strange. Since taxes are used to pay the interest on the debt, an increase in debt would seem to require an increase in taxes. However, under the conditions of the Proposition, the interest rate must be negative. Recall that an intergenerational transfer is like a safe asset with a zero rate of return. If there is a demand for this asset, the expected marginal utility of future consumption is greater than the marginal utility of present consumption. This is what the Proposition assumes. Then in order for markets to clear when the supply of 1-period bills is zero, the price of these bills must be greater than unity, i.e., the interest rate is negative. Then the government can make a profit by issuing these bills: at each date the cost of redeeming last period's issue will be less than the revenue from the sale of this period's issue. To satisfy its budget constraint, the government will make transfers to investors. These transfers measure the increase in welfare.

The same argument can be used to analyze the welfare effects of introducing longer-dated securities. Suppose that $B = 0$ and a small quantity of k-period bills are introduced. If these bills are redeemed at maturity then, in a stationary equilibrium there must be bills of all maturities from 1 to k. More precisely, if the government issues $\epsilon > 0$ k-period bills each period, the equilibrium stock must be

$$B_i = \begin{cases} \epsilon & \text{if} \quad i = 1, \ldots, k \\ 0 & \text{otherwise.} \end{cases} \tag{10}$$

The change in taxes will be approximately $(1 - v_k(s))\epsilon$ in state $s \in S$, so from the earlier formula

$$\frac{du^*(s_i)}{dB} = -U'(c_1(s_i))(1 - v_k(s_i)) \tag{11}$$

As an illustration of what can happen when there is a positive stock of debt already in existence, suppose there is a positive quantity of 1-period bills outstanding and none of higher maturities. That is, $B_1 > 0$ and $B_k = 0$ for $k = 2, \ldots, K$. Now consider the effect of introducing a small amount of two-period debt. Note that what is held constant is the *flow* of newly issued 1-period bills. The *stock* of 1-period bills increases to accommodate the issue of 2-period bills. Thus, if the government issues ϵ units of 2-period bills at each date, the stock of 1-period bills will be $B_1 + \epsilon$.

Let $\langle y, b, h, B, v \rangle$ be a fixed but arbitrary equilibrium. Substituting these assumptions into the formula, we see that the change in equilibrium expected utility is

$$\frac{du^*(s_i)}{dB_2} = -U'(c_1(s_i))\left\{ -B_1\frac{dv_1(s_i)}{dB_2} - \frac{dh(s_i)}{dB_2} \right\} \tag{12}$$

Imagine that the government's budget is divided into two parts, one devoted to servicing the existing one-period debt and one devoted to servicing the new two-period debt. Let h_k denote the tax payment from the young that is required to service the k-period debt. For any $s \in S$, $h_1(s) = (1 - v_1(s))B_1$. Holding the issue of 1-period bills constant, the change in h_1 is just offset by the change in the value of 1-period bills issued each period. In other words, the wealth effect and the tax effect cancel out for 1-period bills. Thus, the change in expected utility is determined by the change in h_2:

$$\frac{du^*(s_i)}{dB} = - U'(c_1(s_i)) \frac{dh_2(s_i)}{dB_2} \tag{13}$$

The introduction of long-dated securities is welfare improving if and only if an increase in B_2, evaluated at the point $B_2 = 0$, reduces h_2. To determine the effect on taxes, simply differentiate the government's budget constraint:

$$\frac{dh_{12}}{dB_2} = \frac{d(1 - v_2)B_2}{dB_2} = (1 - v_2) \tag{14}$$

when $B_2 = 0$. So the introduction of long-dated securities will be welfare improving if and only if $1 < v_2$. A similar argument holds for k-period bills.

These results are summarized in the following theorem.

Theorem 4: Let $\langle y, b, h, B, v \rangle$ be an equilibrium of the OLG economy. Issuing a small amount of k-period bills will increase the expected utility of every type of investor if $v_k(s) > 1$ for every $s \in S$ and either (i) $B = 0$ or (ii) $B_i = 0$ for $i = 2, \ldots, K$ and $k \geq 2$.

These results may suggest that a lengthening of the maturity of the debt is always beneficial. This is not the case. As a counterexample, consider the case of a perpetuity offering a constant coupon of one unit per period. To keep things simple, suppose that the security in existence is a one-period bill. Introduce a small amount of the perpetuity. The change in the price of 1-period bills is offset by the change in the taxes needed to redeem them. The change in the price of the perpetuity has no effect because the stock of perpetuities is zero. The introduction of the perpetuities affects welfare only through its effect on the taxes required to service them. In a stationary equilibrium, perpetuities are issued only once, at the first date. At each subsequent date, their existence must give rise to a positive demand for revenue. So taxes must rise, regardless of the price at which the perpetuities are sold initially.

4   The efficient design of public debt

Section 3 explored the role of public debt in facilitating intergenerational risk sharing. By issuing debt, the government acts as an intermediary between generations that cannot trade directly with each other. It appears that here the government can do something the market cannot do, but that is only because we have assumed that there are no other long-lived institutions besides the government. In fact, other institutions capable of creating long-lived securities do exist. For example, firms issue equity. It is not clear that public debt will have the same role to play when there exist alternative, long-lived securities.

There is an analogy here with the inefficiency of equilibrium in OLG economies with no uncertainty. It is well known that the equilibrium of an OLG economy can be inefficient even if markets are complete. This is true both for pure exchange models and for models with production subject to constant returns to scale. However, this inefficiency disappears if one introduces a scarce durable factor such as land or a firm that can earn positive profits at a zero interest rate.

4.1   The efficiency of equilibrium with long-lived assets

Consider a pure exchange economy with an OLG structure. Each generation consists of a single, representative agent who lives for two periods. Agents are identical and have preferences represented by a utility function $U(c_1) + V(c_2)$ satisfying the usual properties. There is no production and the only security traded at each date is a 1-period bill. The only possible equilibrium allocation is the no-trade allocation. If $U'(0) < V'(0)$, the market-clearing interest rate must be less than zero and the equilibrium is inefficient. In fact, everyone can be made better off if each generation except the first transfers a small amount $\epsilon > 0$ of the good to the preceding generation.

Now suppose there is a durable asset that produces a constant output of R units per period. The asset is initially owned by the first generation, but after receiving the output of the asset the first generation will sell it to the second and so on. In equilibrium, there will be no borrowing or lending. The only trade between generations will be the exchange of goods for the asset. Let q be the price of the asset in a stationary equilibrium. The first-order condition for an agent's optimum is

$$U'(- q)q = V'(R + q)(R + q) \tag{15}$$

Since $R > 0$, we must have $U'(- q) > V'(R + q)$. The interest rate is positive so efficiency follows by the Cass criterion (Cass, 1972).

One way to understand the result is the following. The value of the asset is the present value of the stream of outputs it produces. If the interest rate gets too small, the value of the asset will become very large. But that means that each generation will have low first-period consumption and high second-period consumption, so the interest rate must be high in order to clear the market for bills. Thus, the interest rate cannot get 'too low'.

Stationarity is not needed to establish efficiency. Scheinkman (1980) has proved the result for the general case. The result was also discovered by Wallace. Weiss (1979) proves a similar result for the case of a monetary economy in steady-state equilibrium. The Scheinkman theorem is a powerful result. It says that if there are any long-lived assets, equilibrium will be efficient. However small the yield of the durable asset, the interest rate will adjust so that the value of the asset is adequate to support an efficient level of saving. Since there can never be an inadequate supply of long-lived securities, public debt cannot improve the allocation of resources (compare Diamond, 1965).

Something similar happens when there is uncertainty. To illustrate the importance of durable assets, we can adapt the OLG framework from Section 3 as follows. As before, there is assumed to be an infinite sequence of dates. At each date, a single representative investor, who lives for two periods, is born. There is a single good and investors have a zero endowment of the good in each period of their lives. Their identical preferences are represented by the von Neumann-Morgenstern utility function $U(c_1) + V(c_2)$ satisfying (A.1) and (A.2). Uncertainty is represented by the finite Markov chain $\{s_t\}$ with stationary transition probabilities $\{a_{ij}\}$. So far the model is indentical with the one described in Section 3. But here, instead of assuming the existence of a constant returns to scale investment technology, I assume there is a single unit of a perfectly durable and non-reproducible asset. The asset produces a random output $\tilde{R}_t = R(\tilde{s}_t)$ at each date $t = 1, 2, \ldots, \infty$. Let q_t denote the price of the asset at date t. In a stationary equilibrium the asset price will be a function of the current state: $q_t = q(\tilde{s}_t)$.

Let $y: S \rightarrow \mathbf{R}_+$ denote the investor's demand for the asset in each state. Then consumption is given by

$$c_1(s) = -q(s)y(s), \quad \forall s \in S \tag{16}$$

$$c_2(s, s') = (R(s') + q(s'))y(s), \quad \forall (s, s') \in S \times S \tag{17}$$

The investor chooses the functions c_1, c_2, and y to maximize his expected utility conditional on the state in the first period.

An *equilibrium* for this OLG economy is an array $\langle y, q \rangle$ satisfying the following conditions:

(i) y maximizes $E[u(c_1(s), c_2(s, s')|s]$ where c_1 and c_2 are defined by the budget constraints

$$c_1(s) = -q(s)y(s), \quad \forall s \in S \tag{16}$$

$$c_2(s, s') = (R(s') + q(s'))y(s), \quad \forall (s, s') \in S \times S \tag{17}$$

(ii) $y(s) = 1$, $\forall s \in S$.

Since markets are incomplete, equilibrium will not be Pareto-efficient. In this sense, Scheinkman's result does not hold. However, it does not follow that a simple, non-contingent debt policy of the kind studied in Section 3 can make every one better off. In fact, even if the government pursues a contingent debt policy, it cannot make every type of investor better off in a stationary equilibrium. To see this, consider the more general problem in which the government makes state contingent transfers between generations. Define a *stationary transfer scheme* to be a function $Q: S \to \mathbf{R}$ with the interpretation that $Q(s)$ is the amount of the good transferred from the young generation to the old in state $s \in S$ at any date. The government is restricted to use a stationary transfer scheme. Assume without loss of generality that the old consume the return to the asset at each date. Then the consumption of the young and old generations are $c_1(s) = -Q(s)$ and $c_2(s) = R(s) + Q(s)$, respectively, in state $s \in S$.

To analyze the problem further it is convenient to have a slightly different notation. Let Q_i denote the transfer from the young generation to the old generation in state s_i at each date and let $Q = (Q_1, \ldots, Q_n)$. Also, let $R_i = R(s_i)$, and $q_i = q(s_i)$ for $i = 1, 2, \ldots, n$. Then the expected utility of an investor both in state s_i can be denoted by $u_i^*(Q)$, where

$$u_i^*(Q) = U(-Q_i) + \Sigma_{j=1}^n a_{ij} V(R_j + Q_j) \tag{18}$$

for $i = 1, \ldots, n$. In a stationary equilibrium the equilibrium price function q is the transfer scheme, i.e., the net transfer from young to old in state $s \in S$ is $q(s)$. The question is whether it is possible to make everyone better off by choosing some other value of Q. A necessary condition for this to be true is that $u_i^*(Q) \geq u_i^*(q)$, for $i = 1, \ldots, n$, and $Q \neq q^0$. (This condition is not sufficient because it ignores the welfare of the first generation).

Let q^0 be an equilibrium price vector. From the definition of equilibrium q^0 must satisfy the condition

$$U'(-q_i^0)q_i^0 = \Sigma_{j=1}^n a_{ij} V'(R_j + q_j^0)(R_j + q_j^0) \text{ for } i = 1, \ldots, n. \tag{19}$$

The equilibrium conditions can be written in matrix form as

$$B_q^0 = CR \tag{20}$$

where $B = [b_{ij}]$ is an $n \times n$ matrix with elements

$$b_{ij} = \begin{cases} a_{ii} V'(R_i + q_i^0) - U'(-q_i^0) & \text{if } i = j \\ a_{ij} V'(R_i + q_j^0) & \text{if } i \neq j \end{cases} \tag{21}$$

for $i, j = 1, \ldots, n$, and $C = [c_{ij}]$ is an $n \times n$ matrix with elements

$$c_{ij} = a_{ij} V'(R_j + q_j^0) \tag{22}$$

for $i, j = 1, \ldots, n$. Suppose there exists a Q such that $u_i^*(Q) \geq u_i^*(q^0)$ for $i = 1, \ldots, n$ and $Q \neq q^0$. By the strict concavity of the utility function.

$$- U'(- q_i^0) \delta Q_i + \Sigma_{j=1}^n u_i^* a_{ij} V'(R_j + q_j^0) \delta Q_j > 0 \tag{23}$$

for $i = 1, \ldots, n$, where $\delta Q = Q - q^0$. These inequalities can be written in matrix form as

$$B \delta Q \gg 0 \tag{24}$$

Suppose that $R_i > 0$ for $i = 1, \ldots, n$. Then q^0 must be strictly positive. Since $b_{ij} > 0$ for $i \neq j$, the equilibrium conditions imply that B has negative diagonal and positive off-diagonal elements. In fact, the equilibrium conditions imply that B has a dominant diagonal. This in turn implies that δQ must be strictly negative. Then the first generation must be made worse off in each state. There cannot be a Pareto improvement.

To see that $\delta Q \ll 0$, write $\delta Q = \xi_i q_i^0$ for $i = 1, \ldots, n$ and assumes the numbers ξ_i are indexed so that $\xi_i \leq \xi_{i+1}$, for $i = 1, \ldots, n - 1$. Then the inequality

$$- U'(- q_n^0) \xi_n q_n^0 + \Sigma_{j=1}^n a_{nj} V'(R_j + q_j^0) \xi_j q_j^0 > 0 \tag{25}$$

implies that

$$- U'(- q_n^0) \xi_n q_n^0 + \Sigma_{j=1}^n a_{nj} V'(R_j + q_j^0) \xi_n q_j^0 > 0 \tag{26}$$

From the equilibrium condition, however,

$$- U'(- q_n^0) q_n^0 + \Sigma_{j=1}^n a_{nj} V'(R_j + q_j^0) q_j^0 < 0 \tag{27}$$

This can only be true if $\xi_n < 0$, in which case $\xi_i < 0$ for all $i = 1, \ldots, n$. This proves that $\delta Q \ll 0$ so there can be no Pareto improvement.

Note that if δQ_i were non-negative for some $i = 1, \ldots, n$ it would be possible to implement a (weak) Pareto improvement. One would simply begin the transfer scheme at the first date if $s = s_i$ and not otherwise.

Theorem: If $R_i > 0$, for every $i = 1, \ldots, n$, then it is impossible to make every type of investor better off using a stationary transfer scheme.

The theorem implies that it is impossible to use the kind of debt policy studied in Section 3 to bring about an increase in welfare. To see this, one only has to examine the investor's budget constraints. Let B denote the stock of bills outstanding at each date. Then in equilibrium the consumption of a young investor in state $s \in S$ will be

$$c_1(s) = - q(s) - B \cdot v(s) - h(s) \tag{28}$$

$$= - q(s) - B \cdot v(s) + (B \cdot v(s) - B \cdot \hat{v}(s)) = - q(s) - B \cdot \hat{v}(s)$$

Similarly, the consumption of an old investor in state $s \in S$ will be

$$c_2(s) = R(s) + q(s) + B \cdot \hat{v}(s) \qquad (29)$$

Putting $Q(s) = q(s) + B \cdot \hat{v}(s)$ for each $s \in S$, it is clear that any consumption allocation that can be supported as a stationary equilibrium with a constant stock of debt B can also be implemented by a stationary transfer scheme Q. The theorem implies that introducing debt cannot make every type of investor better off in a stationary equilibrium.

The sense in which equilibrium is shown to be efficient is a very weak one. Apart from the restrictions of stationarity, we have distinguished investors by the state in which they are born. It is not obvious that this is the right notion of Pareto efficiency to use. For example, Fischer (1983) uses the notion of *ex ante* efficiency (which Peled, 1985, calls unconditional efficiency). The *ex ante* notion regards the investor born at date t as being the same individual, regardless of the state in which he is born. An increase in his expected utility, *ex ante* the realization of the state in which he is born, counts as an increase in welfare for him, even if he is worse off in some states. The theorem leaves open the possibility that debt policy can improve welfare according to this criterion.

A result analogous to Theorem 4 is proved in Peled (1985). (See also Peled, 1984.) In Peled's model, it is the existence of valued fiat money that ensures the efficiency of equilibrium. Both results suggest that the absence of durable assets may be a restrictive feature of the analysis in Section 3, as also of Fischer (1983). However, the efficiency result is also special. It relies on the assumption that $R(s) > 0$ for all $s \in S$. If negative returns are possible, then an appropriate debt policy may lead to a welfare improvement. The following example makes this clear.

Example: Consider the special case of the model in which there are two states, $S = \{H, L\}$. The returns to the asset are R_H and R_L, respectively. Suppose that the states $\{s_t\}$ are i.i.d. and the high and low states have equal probability. In that case, the price of the asset is constant in a stationary equilibrium and the equilibrium conditions can be written as follows:

$$2U'(-q)q = V'(R_H + q)(R_H + q) + V'(R_L + q)(R_L + q) \qquad (30)$$

For a sufficiently small but positive expected rate of return, the equilibrium must be inefficient. To see this consider the limiting case where $R_H + R_L = 0$. The equilibrium condition reduces to

$$[2U'(-q) - V'(R + q) - V'(-R + q)]q$$
$$= [-V'(R + q) - V'(-R + q)]R < 0 \qquad (31)$$

where $R = R_H = -R_L$. Then it is possible to make every generation better off simply by making a non-contingent transfer of $\epsilon > 0$ units of the good from the young to the old at each date. By making the expected return sufficiently close to zero, the same result is obtained.

The source of the inefficiency is the same as the one exploited in Section 3. It seems clear that it can be used in the presence of durable assets to derive results similar to those found in Section 3.

The assumption that the return to the asset be negative with positive probability may seem quite strong. In a growing economy, the corresponding condition is that the returns be less than the rate of population growth with positive probability. This assumption seems much more acceptable.

Where does this leave us? The range of application of the results in Section 3 is clearly limited by the existence of durable assets yielding positive returns. But that still leaves considerable scope for welfare-improving debt policies. If the asset returns are negative with positive probability, or if it is considered appropriate to use the *ex ante* welfare criterion, then debt policy may lead to a Pareto-improvement.

4.2   *Characterization of efficient, contingent debt policies*

Up to this point, only non-contingent debt instruments have been considered. If no restriction is placed on the government's ability to create new securities, the analysis becomes trivial. The government should simply replace all missing markets and implement the first best. This is not a plausible solution. Markets are missing for a reason, often because of transaction costs or lack of information. The government is subject to similar restraints and it is not sensible to assume it can costlessly issue any security it likes.

On the other hand, there may be circumstances in which the government has an advantage in providing insurance against some contingencies. One of these may be the provision of insurance against the business cycles. Since macroeconomic shocks tend to affect most asset returns in a similar way, it may be difficult for investors to hedge against the cycle by holding a diverse portfolio. The government, on the other hand, can provide insurance by arranging intergenerational risk-sharing. The idea is to exploit the law of large numbers by spreading the risk of the cycle over many generations. In this context, contingent debt can be regarded as an extension of traditional countercyclical policy. It may be interesting, then, to consider briefly the problem of choosing an efficient, contingent debt policy.

To fix ideas, suppose the government issues a single, contingent bond. The bond matures after one period and pays a return that depends on the state at the redemption date. The bond is defined by a payoff function

$P\colon S \to \mathbf{R}$, where $P(s)$ is the payoff to one unit of the bond in state $s \in S$. Without loss of generality it can be assumed that the government issues one unit of the bond at each date. The young investor at each date chooses a quantity of the bond and the durable asset to hold. As before, let $b(s)$ and $y(s)$ denote the holdings of the bond and asset, respectively, in state $s \in S$ and let $v(s)$ and $q(s)$ denote the prices of the bond and asset, respectively, in state $s \in S$. Then an *equilibrium* for the economy is defined to be an array $\langle y, b, h, P, q, v \rangle$ satisfying the following conditions:

(i) (y, b) maximizes $E[u(c_1(s), c_2(s, s'))|s]$ where c_1 and c_2 are defined by the budget constraints

$$c_1(s) = -q(s)y(s) - v(s)b(s) - h(s), \quad \forall s \in S;$$

$$c_2(s, s') = (R(s') + q(s'))y(s) + P(s')b(s), \quad \forall (s, s') \in S \times S;$$

(ii) $(y(s), b(s)) = (1, 1), \quad \forall s \in S$.

Notice that the kind of debt policy studied earlier is, in a certain sense, a special case of the stationary, contingent debt policy defined here. The portfolio B of non-contingent bills is equivalent to a single, contingent bond. Simply put $P(s) = B \cdot \hat{v}(s)$ for every $s \in S$ and put the price of one unit of the bond equal to $B \cdot v(s)$ in state $s \in S$. Then it is clear that a stationary equilibrium with a stock of bills B can be replicated as a stationary equilibrium with a single contingent bond with payoff function P.

Note also that Theorem 4 implies that it is impossible to improve welfare by introducing contingent debt. If $\langle y, b, h, P, q, v \rangle$ is an equilibrium with contingent debt, it is clear that the same consumption allocation can be attained by making the lump-sum transfers $Q = q + P$. Even though it is impossible to increase the expected utility of every type of investor, one might still want to pursue a contingent debt policy if, for example, one were willing to make distributional tradeoffs. In that case, one would need to characterize the efficient, contingent debt policy.

We are used to thinking that an efficient allocation can be decentralized, that is, supported as an equilibrium with lump-sum transfers. We have seen that a contingent debt policy makes lump-sum transfers between generations. This suggests the following approach to characterizing an efficient, contingent debt policy. First, characterize an efficient allocation. Then show it can be supported as an equilibrium with a contingent debt policy. In fact, this approach does not work, because the first-best cannot be decentralized in this way. Nonetheless, it is interesting to see what goes wrong, because it shows that the problem of choosing an efficient debt policy is more complicated than merely choosing efficient lump-sum transfers.

Start by considering the efficient transfer policy. The problem is to choose a stationary transfer scheme $Q = (Q_1, \ldots, Q_n)$ that is maximal in the sense that it is impossible to make every type of investor better off by choosing some alternative transfer scheme. (The effect on the initial generation is ignored in what follows). Since the utility functions are concave in Q, any choice of Q that is efficient in this sense must maximize a weighted sum of expected utilities. Let Q^* denote an efficient transfer scheme. A necessary and sufficient condition for efficiency is that, for some vector $\lambda = (\lambda_1, \ldots, \lambda_n) > 0$, Q^* is a maximum of $\Sigma_{i=1}^n \lambda_i u_i^*(Q)$, where

$$u_i^*(Q) \equiv U(-Q_i) + \Sigma_{j=1}^n a_{ij} V(R_j + Q_j) \tag{32}$$

for $i = 1, \ldots, n$. Note that this maximization problem can be thought of as the limiting case, as the discount factor $\delta \to 0$, of maximizing a weighted sum of all investors' expected utilities, where investors are distinguished only by birth state. The objective function in that case is

$$\Sigma_{t=1}^\infty \delta^{t-1} \Sigma_{i=1}^n \lambda_i u_i^*(Q) + \Sigma_{i=1}^n \lambda_i V(Q_i) \tag{33}$$

In any case, Q^* must satisfy the first-order conditions

$$\Sigma_{i=1}^n \lambda_i a_{ij} V'(R_j + Q_j) = \lambda_j U'(-Q_j) \tag{34}$$

for $j = 1, \ldots, n$. These conditions completely characterize the efficient transfer scheme Q^*.

The efficient transfer scheme always provides insurance against macroeconomic shocks. Other things being equal, an increase in $R(s)$ will be associated with a decrease in $Q(s)$. However, it is only in very special circumstances that the efficient policy provides the old with complete insurance against macroeconomic shocks. Suppose, for example, that the policy maximizes the expected utility of a representative investor. In that case, the weights λ are the invariant probability distribution of the stochastic process $\{\tilde{s}_t\}$ and hence satisfy the invariance condition

$$\Sigma_{i=1}^n \lambda_i a_{ij} = \lambda_j \tag{35}$$

for $j = 1, \ldots, n$. From the first-order condition it is clear that $U'(-Q_i) = V'(R_i + Q_i)$ for all $i = 1, \ldots, n$.

The problem of choosing an optimal transfer policy has been studied by Fischer (1983), by Pagano (1988) and, in a monetary context, by Bhattacharya (1982). Fischer (1983) discusses at length the problem of implementing efficient risk-sharing arrangements by means of debt policy. Because of the special structure of his model (pure exchange, no aggregate uncertainty) efficient solutions can be implemented by fairly simple institutional arrangements. Pagano (1988) studies the optimal transfer problem in a model that is very similar to Fischer's. He interprets the resulting transfer scheme as an optimal debt policy. Now, if the government can make transfers directly, there is no need to bother with security markets. On the other hand, if there is some reason to use security markets to implement efficient intergenerational risk-sharing, then the problem of choosing an efficient debt policy is inherently more difficult than simply choosing an efficient Q. These difficulties are studied by Bhattacharya, who stresses the informational asymmetries that may prevent the implementation of the first-best transfer scheme. Informational asymmetries are ignored here, but they must be important in explaining why the government would want to use financial markets rather than make lump-sum transfers directly. Even with complete information, however, implementing the optimal Q by an appropriate choice of contingent debt policy may not be possible, as we see below.

Once Q^* is determined, the next step is to see whether the same allocation can be supported as an equilibrium with contingent debt for some debt policy. Suppose that it can. Let $\langle y, b, h, P, q, v \rangle$ denote an equilibrium such that $Q^*(s) = q(s) + v(s)$ for $s \in S$. Letting $P(s_i) = P_i$, $q(s_i) = q_i$ and $v(s_i) = v_i$, for $i = 1, \ldots, n$, the conditions for equilibrium can be written

$$U'(- Q_i^*)q_i = \Sigma_{j=1}^{n} a_{ij} V'(R_j + Q_j^*)(R_j + q_j) \tag{36}$$

and

$$U'(- Q_i^*)v_i = \Sigma_{j=1}^{n} a_{ij} V'(R_j + Q_j^*) P_j \tag{37}$$

for $i = 1, \ldots, n$. The first set of equations must be used to define the equilibrium value of $q = (q_1, \ldots, q_n)$. P can be defined by the identify $Q^* = q + P$. Then the second set of equations can be used to define the equilibrium value of $v = (v_1, \ldots, v_n)$. Thus, the possibility of supporting the efficient allocation as an equilibrium is equivalent to the possibility of solving the equilibrium conditions for q.

Recall the first-order conditions for the solution of the efficient transfer problem:

$$\Sigma_{i=1}^{n} \lambda_i a_{ij} V'(R_j + Q_j) = \lambda_j U'(- Q_j) \quad (j = 1, \ldots, n) \tag{38}$$

and substitute them into the equilibrium conditions above:

$$U'(- Q_i^*)q_i = \Sigma_{j=1}^{n} a_{ij} U'(- Q_j^*)\lambda_j(R_j + q_j)/\Sigma_{k=1}^{n} a_{kj}\lambda_k \tag{39}$$

Rewrite these equations in matrix form as

$$Bq = - CR \tag{40}$$

where $B = [b_{ij}]$ is an $n \times n$ matrix with elements

$$b_{ij} = \begin{cases} (a_{ii}\lambda_i/\Sigma_k a_{ki}\lambda_k - 1)\, U'(-Q_i^*) & \text{for} \quad i = j \\ a_{ij}\lambda_j/\Sigma_k a_{kj}\lambda_k\, U'(-Q_j^*) & \text{for} \quad i \neq j \end{cases} \tag{41}$$

for $i, j = 1, 2, \ldots, n$ and $C = [c_{ij}]$ is an $n \times n$ matrix with elements

$$c_{ij} = a_{ij}\lambda_j/\Sigma_k a_{kj}\lambda_k\, U'(-Q_j^*) \tag{42}$$

for $i, j = 1, \ldots, n$. To solve this equation generally requires B to be a non-singular matrix. Divide the j-th column of B by $U'(-Q_j^*)/\Sigma_k a_{kj}\lambda_k$, for $j = 1, \ldots, n$. Multiply the i-th row by λ_i, for $i = 1, \ldots, n$. These operations do not change the rank of the matrix. The columns of the resulting matrix sum to zero, proving that B is singular. Unless by accident $- CR$ lies in a linear subspace of dimension less than n, there will exist no q satisfying the equilibrium conditions. The efficient transfer scheme cannot be supported as an equilibrium with contingent debt.

It appears that the singularity is peculiar to the efficient allocation, so a small perturbation will remove it. Thus, it ought to be possible to implement an allocation that is very close to the efficient allocation. Yet even here there seems to be difficulties. It is worth pursuing this possibility because it reveals a little more of what goes wrong in the attempt to implement the efficient allocation. Consider the case mentioned earlier where the efficient allocation maximizes the expected utility of the representative investor. In that case, $U'(-Q_i^*) - V'(Q_i^* + R_i)$ for every $i = 1, 2, \ldots, n$. Suppose that Q is a transfer scheme very close to Q^* and let $u_i = U'(-Q_i)$, $v_i = V'(Q_i + R_i)$ and $\epsilon_i \equiv u_i - v_i$ for every $i = 1, 2, \ldots, n$. Substituting these definitions into the equilibrium conditions for asset prices, we get

$$(v_i + \epsilon_i)q_i = \Sigma_{j=1}^n a_{ij}v_j(R_j + q_j) \tag{43}$$

for $i = 1, 2, \ldots, n$. Multiplying by a_i and summing over i gives us

$$\Sigma_{i=1}^n a_i(v_i + \epsilon_i)q_i = \Sigma_{i=1}^n a_i v_i(R_i + q_i) \tag{44}$$

or

$$\Sigma_{i=1}^n a_i \epsilon_i q_i = \Sigma_{i=1}^n a_i v_i R_i \tag{45}$$

Now suppose that $Q \to Q^*$. From the equation above it is clear that as long as $\Sigma_{i=1}^n a_i v_i R_i$ is bounded away from zero, $q_i \to \infty$ for at least one i and hence by the equilibrium conditions it must be so for all i. In order for this behaviour of prices to be consistent with Q approaching Q^*, it must be the case that $P_i \to - \infty$ for each i. Theoretically, this is possible but it seems somewhat implausible. In practice, the volatility of prices and the problems associated with negative face-value bonds would seem to rule out this kind of scheme.

The result is in any case somewhat surprising since by issuing the contingent debt instrument (and adopting an appropriate tax policy to balance its budget), the government is effectively making lump-sum transfers between generations. This is clear from the expression for the equilibrium expected utility of a typical investor. Nonetheless, the fact that investors are subject to additional risk in the form of capital gains and losses on the durable asset puts the attainment of the first-best allocation beyond the government's reach. In effect, the market frustrates the government's attempt to achieve the best possible risk-sharing arrangement.

There is a family resemblance between this result and an example found in Bhattacharya (1982). In Bhattacharya's setup, there is no durable capital good, only an investment technology. Generations live for two periods, have an endowment of one unit in the first period and none in the second, and have additively separable preferences. The government uses taxes and transfers to maximize a weighted sum of utilities, in which the utility of future generations is slightly discounted. Call this the first-best allocation. Formally, the maximization problem is like that of an infinitely-lived individual with appropriately specified period utility functions. Bhattacharya asks whether this allocation can be implemented by injecting money in the form of transfers to the young. He shows that when agents have logarithmic utility functions, the answer is 'no'. In the context of Bhattacharya's example, some difficulties are clear even without uncertainty. Suppose that the return on invstment is a constant $R > 1$ and that the rate at which future generations' utility is discounted is small. Since the first-best problem is formally the same as a single, infinitely-lived individual's maximization problem, we know that the amount of capital invested must grow without bound. Then eventually there must be transfers from old to young. But this cannot be accomplished in a monetary equilibrium, where by definition goods are transferred only from young to old. Introducing uncertainty will not eliminate this problem.

Whether monetary policy fails in general to implement the first best and what the reasons for that failure might be, is not clear. In any case, the result is evidently rather different from the one derived above. In the model studied in this section, the debt policy is equivalent to a lump-sum transfer scheme. The result derived above can be interpreted as showing that a transfer scheme alone can do better than a transfer scheme operating in conjunction with a market for a durable capital good. Bhattacharya, on the other hand, compares the allocation implemented by a transfer scheme with the allocation implemented by a monetary policy, both operating in conjunction with an independent investment technology.

The question remains of what can be done by means of debt policy to improve risk-sharing. What follows is a sketch of the efficient debt problem. Suppose that in some open neighbourhood of the efficient debt instrument P^* we can solve the equilibrium value of q as a C^1 function of P, say $q = \zeta(P)$. Then P^* must be a local solution to the constrained maximization problem

$$\text{Max} \, \Sigma_{i=1}^n \lambda_i \left\{ U(-q_i - P_i) + \Sigma_{j=1}^n a_{ij} V(R_j + q_j + P_j) \right\}$$

s.t. $q = \zeta(P)$.

The first-order conditions are

$$- \lambda_i U'(-q_i - P_i) + \Sigma_{j=1}^n \lambda_j a_{ji} V'(R_j + q_j + P_j) + \mu_i = 0 \tag{46}$$

and

$$- \lambda_i U'(-q_i - P_i) + \Sigma_{j=1}^n \lambda_j a_{ji} V'(R_j + q_j + P_j) + \Sigma_{j=1}^n \mu_j \zeta_{ji}(P) = 0 \tag{47}$$

where μ_i is the Lagrange multiplier attached to the i-th equilibrium condition and $\zeta_{ij}(P) \equiv \partial \zeta_i(P)/\partial P_j$, for $i, j = 1, \ldots, n$. Comparing these two equations, we see they imply that

$$\mu_i = \Sigma_{j=1}^n \mu_j \zeta_{ji}(P) \tag{48}$$

for $i = 1, \ldots, n$. In matrix notation,

$$\mu(I - D\zeta) = 0 \tag{49}$$

where $D\zeta = [\zeta_{ij}]$. Comparing the first-order conditions with those for the efficient transfer problem, we see that they differ only in the terms involving the multipliers μ. If μ were zero, the solutions would be identical. In a precise sense, μ measures the wedge between the efficient transfer outcome and the outcome of the efficient debt policy.

Pagano (1988) has suggested that the government should issue securities that are negatively correlated with the market portfolio. This proposal has a family resemblance to the contingent bonds described above. Pagano's argument is that since the negatively correlated securities can be sold at a higher price than safe securities, the government would make a profit that would allow it to retire the debt. The argument is essentially partial equilibrium in nature. As we have seen, the problem of achieving a genuine welfare improvement may be more complicated than the partial equilibrium argument suggests. In the first place, one has to pay attention to the government's budget constraint and its implications for different generations' tax liabilities. Second, one has to pay attention to the general-equilibrium effects of the debt policy on prices. When these effects are taken into account it is not clear that issuing a security which is negatively correlated with the market portfolio will be sufficient to ensure an increase in welfare. At the very least, the securities will have to be carefully designed and the informational requirements may be beyond the capacity of the government.

5   Privately issued debt

We have so far assumed that the private sector is only capable of developing a rather rudimentary capital market. As a result, the government has been the only source of long-dated securities. In this framework it has been relatively easy to show how public debt policy can have far-reaching consequences for the risk-sharing possibilities in the economy. Financial innovation by the public sector can make markets more complete and under certain circumstances lead to Pareto improvements.

The point of these exercises is not to suggest that financial innovation is the prerogative of the public sector. That is clearly not the case. On the other hand, it may be that there are gaps in the market that public debt instruments can fill. What makes the preceding exercises rather artificial is that we have not provided any reasons why the private capital market should be incomplete in the first place. By assuming that the private capital market is restricted to a single instrument, we have artificially provided a large role for the government as a financial innovator. If, instead, we had started by assuming the existence of a highly sophisticated financial market, providing perfect substitutes for most of the securities issued by government, the conclusion could have been quite different. To justify the analysis of the preceding sections, one should at least provide an explanation of why the private capital market might be incomplete in the first place. There are two types of arguments that might be used to justify a role for the public sector as a financial innovator. One is that the government has some kind of comparative advantage in providing certain kinds of securities to the market. In that case, even if the private sector can provide these securities, it may be efficient to let the public sector do the job. The second kind of argument is concerned with the incentives for innovation in the private sector. Even if the private sector has the capacity to issue certain securities, it may choose not to do so. In that case, there may be a case for government provision. The first kind of argument will not be pursued here. Instead, we concentrate on the private incentives for financial innovation.

In a series of papers (Allen and Gale 1988, 1989a and 1989b), Franklin Allen and I have investigated some of the issues concerning efficient financial innovation. Under certain conditions it appears that, in a competitive equilibrium, financial innovation is constrained efficient. What this means is that a planner, who was subject to the same technology, could not make everyone better off. However, the circumstances in which the equilibrium market structure will be efficient are restrictive. For example, it must be assumed that no short sales are allowed or that short sales are so costly that they are effectively bounded. If unlimited short sales are allowed, there are strong reasons for believing that the perfect competition assumption will not be satisfied. In Allen and Gale (1989a) it is shown that when unlimited short sales are allowed, the number who innovate in equilibrium may be small, even if the number of potential innovators is large. In order to give adequate incentives to innovate, it is necessary that the innovators have some monopoly power. But this implies that in equilibrium the number of securities is too small.

Part of the explanation of this inefficiency is that innovators create positive externalities. In a competitive equilibrium they may not be able to internalize these externalities and so they cannot extract all the rents from their innovation. One might think that a monopolist would have a better chance to introduce an efficient market structure. Allen and Gale (1989b) examine a situation where the innovator has a monopoly that allows him to extract all the rents from the innovation. Nonetheless, it turns out that in this situation as well, the equilibrium market structure may still be inefficient. The social value of the innovation is measured by the maximum amount the investors are willing to pay for the innovation before it occurs. The problem is that, since the innovation may have general-equilibrium effects, the surplus to be extracted after the innovation may be different from the surplus that existed *ex ante*. As a result, there may be too much or too little innovation.

There are some differences between the models described in Allen and Gale (1988, 1989a and 1989b) and the ones employed here. The former are restricted to two time-periods and trade only occurs in the first of these periods. Also, financial innovation consists of issuing securities with different patterns of returns across states of nature at the second date. In the present class of models, only non-contingent debt instruments are traded, but investors can adopt dynamic trading strategies which increase the possibilities of spanning states of nature. Because of these structural differences one must be careful about drawing analogies between the two classes of models. Nonetheless, it appears that similar arguments do apply in the present context.

A complete analysis of (private sector) financial innovation is out of place here. Instead, an extended example is analyzed to illustrate the sort of things that can happen. The point of this example is to show that even if the private sector can produce a socially desirable security, there may not be an incentive for any individual or institution to produce it. The example is constructed to demonstrate this point in the simplest possible way, but the same phenomenon will occur in more realistic contexts.

There are assumed to be three agents, two investors indexed $i = 1, 2$ and an entrepreneur indexed $i = 3$. The entrepreneur represents a large firm, say, General Motors, which has the capacity to issue securities with characteristics similar to public debt. There are three dates indexed $t = 1, 2, 3$. The entrepreneur's endowment can be interpreted as the firm's revenues. The entrepreneur has an endowment of goods at dates 2 and 3, but he only values consumption at the first date. Since the entrepreneur only values consumption at the first date, he will want to sell his future endowment in exchange for consumption at the first date. More precisely, he will sell securities which are claims against the future endowment.

Each agent $i = 1, 2, 3$ has a von Neumann–Morgenstern utility function $W_i(c_1, c_2, c_3)$, where c_t denotes consumption at date $t = 1, 2, 3$. By assuming that $W_i(c_1, c_2, c_3) = -\infty$ if $c_t < 0$ for some $t = 1, 2, 3$, we can restrict attention to the case where $(c_1, c_2, c_3) \in \mathbf{R}^3_+$. The three utility functions are assumed to satisfy:

$$.W_1(c_1, c_2, c_3) = c_3 \tag{50}$$

$$W_2(c_1, c_2, c_3) = c_1 + u(c_3), \quad \text{where} \quad u'(1) = 1 \tag{51}$$

$$W_3(c_1, c_2, c_3) = c_1 \tag{52}$$

for any $(c_1, c_2, c_3) \in \mathbf{R}^3_+$. The function $u(\cdot)$ is assumed to satisfy all the usual neoclassical properties. The agents' endowments are given by:

$$e_1 = (1, 0, 0) \tag{53}$$

$$e_2 = (2, 0, 0) \tag{54}$$

$$e_3 = (0, 1, 1) \tag{55}$$

A single producer maximizes profits subject to the usual constant returns to scale investment technology. At date 1 the return to investment is assumed to be $R_1 = 0$. At date 2 the return to investment is random, taking the values $r_H = 1.5$ and $r_L = 0.5$ with equal probability. The producer earns zero profits in equilibrium.

There is assumed to be a market for one-period bills at each date. Investors can save (buy bills) but they cannot borrow (issue bills). Investors can also purchase securities issued by the entrepreneur but they cannot take short positions. The producer issues one-period bills in order to finance production.

The investors take prices as given and trade the available securities at each date in order to maximize expected utility. (Each of the investors represents a continuum of identical agents.) The entrepreneur, on the other hand, is a genuinely 'big' agent.

To keep things simple, the entrepreneur is only given two options. The first is to sell equity only. One unit of equity entitles the holder to the endowment stream e_3. The other option is to split the endowment stream into two pieces, $(0, 1, 0)$ and $(0, 0, 1)$, and sell them separately. This option corresponds to issuing a one-period bill with face value of one unit and one unit of levered equity.

Suppose the entrepreneur chooses to issue two securities at the first date. Both securities sell for a price of one unit. Investor 1 buys all of the one-period bills and investor 2 buys all of the two-period bills. At date 2, investor 2 receives one unit of consumption. Since he does not value consumption at date 2 he will reinvest the entire amount and consume the proceeds at date 3. The supply of one-period bills at date 2 comes from the producer, so the price of one-period bills at date 2 is determined by the investment technology, i.e., the price is $1/R_2$. Investor 2 holds his security for the full two periods and consumes the dividend at date 2.

To see that this is an equilibrium, note first of all that the expected rate of return on both assets at date 1 is zero if they are held to maturity. Since investor 1 is risk-neutral his action is optimal at date 1. Investor 2 is also behaving optimally at date 1 since the marginal utility of consumption is one at dates 1 and 3. At date 2, it is optimal for investor 1 to reinvest everything and for investor 2 to hold on to his one-period bills. At date 3 they can only consume. The value of the firm in this equilibrium is $V = 2$.

Now suppose that there is only one security (equity). Both investors must now hold the same security at date 1. Furthermore, there is no opportunity to trade at date 2. As before, the dividends received at date 2 must be reinvested. The supply of one-period bills at date 2 must come from the producer so the price of one-period bills will be determined by the investment technology. Once the rate of return on investment is observed at date 2, the uncertainty has disappeared so there is no possibility of hedging. Each agent can only reinvest his dividend and hold on to the bills purchased at date 1. Without loss of generality, we can treat a unit of equity as a claim to $(1 + R_2)$ units of consumption at date 3, since we know the interim dividends will be reinvested at the rate R_2. If V is the price of equity at date 1 and E is the quantity held by investor 2, the first order condition that must be satisfied for an interior optimum is:

$$V = \{u'(2.5E)2.5 + u'(1.5E)1.5)\}/2 \tag{56}$$

Since investor 1 will use all of his first-period endowment to buy equity, the market-clearing condition is:

$$1 = V(1 - E) \tag{57}$$

It is easy to see that these two equations have a unique solution (V^*, E^*) with $0 < V^*$ and $0 < E^* < 1$. Furthermore, $V^* > 2$ if we assume that:

$$\{u'(1.25)2.5 + u'(0.75)1.5)\}/2 > 2 \tag{58}$$

which is consistent with $u'(1) = 1$. Thus, the value of the firm is higher when there is only one security.

The equilibrium with two securities is obviously Pareto-efficient because all the risk at date 3 is borne by the risk-neutral investor. In the equilibrium with one security, the risk-averse investor bears some risk at date 3. As a result that equilibrium is Pareto-inefficient. Thus, the entrepreneur has the ability to choose an effectively complete market structure that leads to an efficient equilibrium. But it is in his interest to chose an incomplete market structure that leads to an inefficient equilibrium. This is not to say that the two-security equilibrium Pareto-dominates the one-security equilibrium, since the entrepreneur is better off in the latter. However, a transfer at the first date could make everyone better off in the two-security equilibrium than he was in the one-security equilibrium. In this sense, the one-security equilibrium is not constrained efficient.

This brief discussion is obviously inadequate to settle any issues about the role of the government as a financial innovator. That important question must be left to future research. Another question that has not even been mentioned, is why the government would want to use debt policy to affect risk-sharing opportunities, rather than using lump-sum transfers. Bhattacharya (1982), in an intriguing and suggestive paper, has suggested that incomplete information may be the explanation. Asset markets may solve some of the incentive problems better than the available alternative institutions. This is an idea that should certainly be followed up. However, even if one finds the use of debt policy as a tool for achieving optimal risk-sharing fanciful, there is little doubt that the public debt does have an impact on risk-sharing opportunities. Understanding this mechanism would seem to be important for the formulation of sound policy.

NOTE

An earlier version of this paper was presented at a seminar at the Wharton School. I am grateful to the participants for their comments. The discussants at the

Castelgandolfo conference, Olivier Blanchard and Sudipto Bhattacharya also made helfpul comments.

REFERENCES

Abel, A., G. Mankiw, L. Summers and R. Zeckhauser (1989). 'Assessing Dynamic Efficiency', *Review of Economic Studies* **56**, 1–20.
Allen, F. and D. Gale (1988). 'Optimal Security Design', *Review of Financial Studies* **1**.
 (1989a). 'Arbitrage, Short Sales and Financial Innovation', Rodney L. White, Center for Financial Research, University of Pennsylvania, Working Paper.
 (1989b). 'Incomplete Markets and the Incentives to Set Up an Options Exchange', *Geneva Papers on Risk and Insurance*, forthcoming.
Barro, R. (1974). 'Are Bonds Net Wealth?', *Journal of Political Economy* **82**, 1095–118.
 (1979). 'On the Determination of Public Debt', *Journal of Political Economy* **87**, 940–71.
Bhattacharya, S. (1982). 'Aspects of Monetary and Banking Theory and Moral Hazard', *Journal of Finance* **37**, 371–84.
Bohn, H. (1988a). 'A Positive Theory of Foreign Currency Debt', Rodney L. White, Center for Financial Research, University of Pennsylvania, Working Paper 19-88.
 (1988b). 'Tax Smoothing with Financial Instruments', Rodney L. White, Center for Financial Research, University of Pennsylvania, Working Paper 27-88.
 (1988c). 'Time Consistency of Monetary Policy in the Open Economy', Rodney L. White, Center for Financial Research, University of Pennsylvania, Working Paper 33-88.
Cass, D. (1972). 'On Capital Overaccumulation in the Aggregative, Neoclassical Model of Economic Growth: A Complete Characterization', *Journal of Economic Theory* **4**, 200–23.
Chamley, G. and H. Polemarchakis (1984). 'Asset Markets, General Equilibrium and the Neutrality of Money', *The Review of Economic Studies* **51**, 129–38.
Diamond, P. (1965). 'National Debt in a Neoclassical Growth Model', *American Economic Review* **55**, 1125–50.
Fischer, S. (1983). 'Welfare Aspects of Government Issue of Indexed Bonds', in R. Dornbusch and M. Simonsen (eds.), *Inflation, Debt and Indexation*, Cambridge MA., MIT Press, 223–46.
Gale, D. (1988). 'Underinvestment and the Demand for Liquid Assets', University of Pittsburgh, mimeo.
Lucas, R. and N. Stokey (1983). 'Optimal Fiscal and Monetary Policy in an Economy without Capital', *Journal of Monetary Economics* **12**, 55–93.
 (1987). 'Money and Interest in a Cash-in-Advance Economy,' *Econometrica* **55**, 491–514.
Pagano, M. (1988). 'The Management of Public Debt and Financial Markets', in F. Giavazzi and L. Spaventa (eds.), *High Public Debt: the Italian Experience*. Cambridge: Cambridge University Press, 135–66.
Peled, D. (1982). 'Informational Diversity over Time and the Optimality of Monetary Equilibria', *Journal of Economic Theory* **28**, 255–74.
 (1984). 'Stationary Pareto Optimality of Stochastic Equilibria with Overlapping Generations', *Journal of Economic Theory* **34**, 396–403.

(1985). 'Stochastic Inflation and Government Provision of Indexed Bonds', *Journal of Monetary Economics* **15**, 291–308.

Scheinkman, J. (1980). 'Notes on Asset Trading in an Overlapping Generations Model', University of Chicago, mimeo.

Tobin, J. (1971). 'An Essay on the Principles of Debt Management', in *Essays in Economics, Vol. 1*, Chicago: Markham.

Wallace, N. (1981). 'A Modigliani-Miller Theorem for Open Market Operations', *American Economic Review* **71**, 267–74.

Weiss, L. (1979). 'The Effects of Money Supply on Economic Welfare in the Steady State', *Econometrica* **48**, 565–76.

Discussion

OLIVIER JEAN BLANCHARD

The paper by Douglas Gale is an important contribution to the analysis of the role of public debt in affecting intertemporal allocations. To my taste, the most interesting part is without question that which deals with the role of debt in overlapping generation models. I shall concentrate my comments on that part.

We are used to thinking of the role of government debt in the context of models with certainty. In such models, the crucial issue is that of capital accumulation. Individual utility maximization may still lead to overaccumulation of capital, in which case issuing debt and reducing capital accumulation is Pareto-improving. The source of the welfare failure is that those currently alive do not hold claims to all future resources, and the crucial criterion is, assuming growth to be zero, whether the net rate of return on capital is negative (this is a loose characterization, the exact one being given by the Cass criterion). If it is negative, issuing some debt is Pareto-improving. Otherwise, it is not.

Under uncertainty, a different aspect of overlapping generation models comes into play, namely the incompleteness of markets. Finite lives imply that intergenerational insurance is limited, opening a second and conceptually distinct role for debt policy and government intergenerational transfers. Despite a number of papers on the subject, we know much less about the positive and normative effects of debt in that context. This is where Gale makes substantial advances. In addition to introducing a clear conceptual framework and incorporating existing contributions, he reaches a number of important results. Among them:

(1) The economy may have a positive expected rate of return on capital, but still allow for Pareto-improving transfers. This result is not all that surprising when one realizes that there may be scope for intergenerational insurance, whatever the average rate of return. What is more surprising is the form that some of these transfers may take:

(2) Even if the economy has a positive expected rate of return on capital, the introduction of non-contingent debt, that is debt paying a fixed coupon, may well provide insurance and be Pareto-improving. The issuance of longer-maturity debt may be Pareto-improving, even when the issuance of short-term debt would not be. The reasons for those results are made clear by showing the equivalence of non-contingent debt policies to contingent tax-transfer schemes. The issuance of longer-maturity debt is equivalent to tax-transfer schemes which are more sensitive to contingencies, and thus provide more insurance.

(3) While simple non-contingent debt may be welfare-improving, even fully contingent debt policy cannot however in general replicate optimal tax-transfer schemes. This result shows the limitations of earlier results to the contrary.

The second set of results speaks very much to what has emerged as one of the main themes of the conference, that of the *maturity of the debt*. Should the government issue short or long-term debt, and does it matter? The paper, focusing on the insurance aspect, gives a clear set of answers. I have found it useful, in preparing my comments, to play with simple examples, and I shall now present them. They do not add to Gale's basic results, but may help the intuition.

1   When is issuing one-period bonds bonds Pareto-improving?

Absent bonds and taxes, the utility of a consumer in the Gale economy is given by $U(e - y) + E[V(yR)|\cdot]$, where e is the non-random endowment, y is savings, and R is the random gross rate of return on storage. Throughout, I ignore time indices for variables and conditioning sets; the context makes them clear.

With a fixed quantity, b, of one-period bonds, sold at price v_1 and redeemed at 1, the budget constraint of the government is given by $v_1 b + h = b$, so that the utility of the consumer is then given by $U(e - y - v_1 b - h) + E[V(yR + b)|\cdot]$.

Replacing the government budget constraint in the utility function gives: $U(e - y - b) + E[V(yR + b)|\cdot]$. This shows the first result emphasized by Gale, namely the equivalence of the debt policy to a tax-transfer scheme, in this case one in which a non-contingent b is transferred from the young to the old each period.

It follows that the condition for a small transfer to be Pareto-improving is that the following holds for any conditioning set:

$$- U'(e - y) + E[V'(yR)|\cdot] > 0$$

The price v_1 is itself determined, from the first-order conditions of the consumer, by:

$$- v_1 U'(e - y) + E[V'(yR)|\cdot] = 0$$

A comparison of these two equations shows that the issuance of debt is Pareto-improving if and only if $v_1 > 1$, if the net rate of return on one-period bonds is negative, the second result emphasized by Gale.

Suppose now that $U(\cdot)$ and $V(\cdot)$ are both logarithmic, with no discounting. Suppose also that the R is i.i.d., log normal, with $E[\ln(R)] = \mu - (1/2)\sigma^2$, and $V[\ln(R)] = \sigma^2$. These assumptions imply that $E[R] = \exp(\mu)$. The condition for the introduction of one-period bonds to be Pareto-improving is:

$$v_1 = \exp(-\mu + \sigma^2) > 1, \quad \text{or equivalently}$$

$$\mu - \sigma^2 < 0$$

Thus, for σ large enugh, it is quite possible for the average net rate of return on capital to be positive, i.e. for $\mu > 0$, while at the same time the introduction of one-period bonds is Pareto-improving, $\mu - \sigma^2 < 0$.

2   When is issuing two-period bonds Pareto-improving?

Suppose that, each period, the government issues instead two-period bonds, in quantity b, at price v_2, buying them back after one period at price v_1, the price of then one-period bonds. This way, the only bonds in existence in the economy are two-period bonds. The budget constraint of the government is thus $v_2 b + h = v_1 b$, and the utility function is given by $U(e - y - v_2 b - h) + E[V(yR + v_1 b)|\cdot]$.

Replacing the government budget constraint in the utility function gives $U(e - y - v_1 b) + E[V(yR + v_1 b)|\cdot]$. (Note that the first v_1 corresponds to the price of one-period bonds this period while the second one, in the expectation operator, corresponds to the price of one-period bonds next period). Thus, a constant stock of two-period debt is equivalent to a contingent tax-transfer scheme.

Intuition suggests that, if E is serially correlated, a low realization of R will be associated with expectations of low R, thus of high bond prices, of high v_1. This suggests that two-period bonds will do well when returns from storage are low, thus providing some insurance against technological uncertainty. This in turn suggests that their introduction is more likely to be Pareto-improving than that of one-period bonds, a result emphasized by Gale. Intuition is confirmed as follows:

The condition for utility to improve is that:

$$ - v_1 U'(e - y) + E[v_1 V'(yR)|\cdot] > 0 \quad \text{in any state of nature.} $$

The condition can again be related to the price of one- and two-period bonds. v_1 is given by the same expression as above. And, from the first-order conditions, v_2 is given by:

$$ - v_2 U'(e - y) + E[v_1 V'(yR)|\cdot] = 0 $$

This implies that the introduction of two-period bonds will be Pareo-improving if, in any state of nature, $v_2 > v_1$. Note that this condition does not require $v_1 > 1$.

Turning to simple functional forms and distribution assumptions, suppose again that $U(\cdot)$ and $V(\cdot)$ are logarithmic, and there is no discounting. The condition for the introduction of two-period bonds to be Pareto-improving becomes:

$$ - v_1 + E[v_1/R|\cdot] > 0 \quad \text{where} \quad v_1 = E[R|\cdot] $$

Again, the first v_1 is the price of one-period bonds this period, while v_1 in the expectation operator is the price of one-period bonds next period, a random variable as of today.

Under the previous assumption that R is i.i.d., it is clear that the price of one-period bonds, v_1, is non-random, so that two-period bonds do not provide more of a hedge than one-period bonds did earlier. It is easy to check that in this case the conditions for Pareto-improvement are exactly the same for one-period and two-period bonds. Thus, going to the extreme, I assume instead that $\ln(R)$ follows a random walk, with a drift of $(-1/2)\sigma^2$, and a normally distributed innovation with mean zero, and variance σ^2. This assumption implies that $E[R|\cdot] = R_{-1}$.

It is clear that this assumption implies that non-contingent bonds cannot be Pareto-improving. This is for two different reasons. Any assumed degree of serial correlation, together with the assumption that the support of the innovation, and thus of $\ln R$, is unbounded, implies that there is some positive probability of states with large enough conditional expected value of R that any condition for bonds to be Pareto-improving will not be satisfied. The second reason is that the random walk assumption itself eventually implies unbounded support for R even if the innovation itself had finite support. I nevertheless use the assumption because it shows clearly the difference between the conditions for Pareto improvement by one-period and two-period bonds. One can think of the assumption as a limiting case to a case of bounded support and high serial correlation, and interpret the results below in this light.

Under the random walk assumption, the condition for the introduction of one-period bonds to be Pareto-improving becomes:

$$\mu - \sigma^2 < 0, \quad \text{where} \quad \mu \equiv \ln(R_{-1})$$

The condition for the introduction of two-period bonds to be Pareto-improving is instead:

$$\mu - 2\sigma^2 < 0, \quad \text{where} \quad \mu \equiv \ln(R_{-1})$$

This makes clear how the insurance that two-period bonds provide against serially correlated technological shocks makes their introduction potentially Pareto-improving, even if the introduction of one-period bonds is not itself Pareto-improving.

The answers given by Gale generate in turn a number of questions. Among them:

Is there an optimal maturity of the debt and what does this depend on? In the example above, it appears that longer maturity (although not infinite, as Gale shows) is always better, but this is likely an artefact of the random walk assumption.

How different would the analysis be if the shocks were shocks to income distribution, as examined by Fischer (cited by Gale)?

Also, in contrast to the simple model, actual generations live for many periods so that there is substantial overlap between them; is there a sense in which the problem of the lack of insurance markets in the simple model decreases with the extent of overlap, with a corresponding decrease in the role of debt policy?

I wish I had some of the answers. I do not, but I feel that Gale has helped us start thinking about them.

3 Indexation and maturity of government bonds: an exploratory model

GUILLERMO A. CALVO and PABLO E. GUIDOTTI

1 Introduction

Very few economists would nowadays deny that the stock of money and the price level are closely related variables. In fact, cross-country empirical analyses (see, e.g., Vogel, 1974; Lucas, 1980; Lothian, 1985; Calvo, 1987) and even a cursory look at the data eloquently shows that a nonbeliever in this basic 'monetarist' proposition would have a hard time making his case (except, perhaps, for recent periods when the very definition of the relevant stock-of-money concept is somewhat controversial). However, if money growth is the main cause of inflation, and the relationship is well understood, why is it then that inflation has not been completely eradicated? A possible answer is that at times countries rely on the inflation tax as a source of fiscal revenue. In fact, Phelps (1973) has given rise to a literature which suggests that a sensible reliance on the inflation tax could even be socially optimal (see, e.g., Végh, 1989; Guidotti and Végh, 1988; and the references therein). Interestingly, however, there are many instances in which the inflation tax appears to be larger than any sensible social welfare function would dictate. The phenomenon becomes self-evident in hyperinflation episodes.[1] An answer to this puzzle was given in Calvo (1978) where it is shown that money creation becomes an attractive fiscal revenue source when its present use has little effect on expectations about future monetary/fiscal policy (a characteristic of non-reputational rational-expectations equilibria). Thus, for *each* successive government it is optimal to engineer 'high' inflation. But since individuals are assumed to be rational, they take this inflationary bias into account, leading to an almost total inability to collect revenue through the inflation tax.[2]

It is still too early to judge whether the rational-discretion approach is the key to explain the above-mentioned puzzle. Our present empirical knowledge, however, strongly suggests that precommitment-only models

52

are unable to explain even the most basic stylized facts (see, e.g., Poterba and Rotemberg, 1988; Obstfeld, 1988), and that the rational-discretion approach could provide some of the missing links.[3] Thus, whatever is the final verdict, a sensible study of monetary policy issues appears to necessitate the use of rational-discretion methods. And this is the approach that this paper will take.

We will focus on a somewhat relegated character of the inflation drama, namely, government bonds. Its potential relationship with the inflationary process has been recently rediscovered – Keynes (1971) knew it well enough himself – due partly to the experience of some heavily indebted LDCs as well as that of some industrialized ones like Belgium and Italy. However, the theoretical work using post-Keynesian (New Classical?) tools has only started (see, for instance, Lucas and Stokey, 1983; Persson and Svensson, 1984; Persson, Persson and Svensson, 1987; Bohn, 1988; Calvo, 1988a; Obstfeld, 1988). Some of the results that emerge from this literature are quite striking. Take, for instance, the work of Lucas and Stokey (1983), and Persson, Persson and Svensson (1987). Their central message is that a careful management of the maturity structure can be so effective that it could actually succeed in replicating the full-precommitment optimum in a rational-discretion world. This remarkable result is bought at the cost of making some unrealistic assumptions,[4] but it strongly suggests that in a rational-discretion world, the structure of debt maturity could become a highly relevant policy instrument.[5]

The present paper relaxes the assumption of complete markets – to make the model more realistic – and introduces actual-inflation costs (i.e., anticipated and unanticipated inflation are both costly). The latter has been shown to be almost a necessary assumption in the context of the above-mentioned first-best-through-discretion literature (see Calvo and Obstfeld, 1989, and Persson, Persson, and Svensson, 1989).[6] The model is, otherwise, very simple.

The central issue addressed in the paper is the impact and optimality of different price indexation coefficients and debt maturity structures. We first examine the indexation issue in terms of a two-period model where government in period 0 decides the proportion of total debt – a predetermined variable – that will be indexed to the price level. The only source of uncertainty is (exogenous) government expenditure. We study the cases in which the nominal interest rate can be indexed to the state of nature, and some of those in which it cannot. The optimal solution with a state-contingent interest rate is referred to as the first best, and is our benchmark for our consumer-surplus type welfare calculations.

Most of the discussion in the paper deals with the realistic case in which the interest rate on government debt is not indexed to the state of nature (i.e., government expenditure).[7] However, we allow debt to be indexed to the price level. The latter is a useful device whenever there are rational-discretion type elements, because price indexation lessens the incentives to use inflation to liquidate the real value of the outstanding debt – and thus lowers the deadweight-loss of conventional taxes associated with debt service. Like in the Gray-type papers (see, Gray, 1976; Aizenman and Frenkel, 1985), however, full price indexation is shown not to be necessarily optimal, because the government would be completely prevented from applying the inflation tax on bonds to smooth out conventional taxes. There exists, therefore, a nontrivial optimization problem, and it is carefully discussed in Section 2 employing, as an intermediate step, the case in which the government in period 0 can precommit the actions of its successor (i.e., government 1).

In Section 3 we look at a three-period model in which government 0 can determine, in addition, the maturity structure of the outstanding debt, i.e., the amount of indexation characteristics of the debt obligations that government 0 passes along to governments 1 and 2. Interesting insights can already be shown in the context where government 1 can fully precommit the actions of government 2, but government 0 has to rely on 'incentives' in order to influence next governments' (i.e., governments 1 and 2) policies. We find that optimal maturity depends very strongly on whether government 0 is able to index optimally. If the latter holds then it is optimal to issue only long-term maturity bonds. Otherwise, if no price indexation is possible, for example, there is a clear tendency for optimal debt maturity to have a strong short-term bias.

Section 4 shows several ways in which the above model's assumptions can be relaxed and, for the sake of realism, it examines the situation in which all debt is nominal (i.e., no price indexation is possible) and no government can precommit the actions of any of its successors. Interestingly, here we observe a reversion towards long-term debt.

In sum, then, with some precommitment and optimal indexation, long-term debt is optimal. With no indexation optimal debt maturity shortens considerably. But, with no precommitment the optimal term structure becomes longer once again. The intuition behind these different cases is carefully discussed, and numerical examples are shown to assess possible welfare implications.

Section 5 closes the main text of the paper with some conclusions and suggestions for further work. An Appendix collects the relatively more technical material.

2   A two-period model

Consider a two-period economy. Government in period 0 has a debt b (> 0 unless otherwise explicitly stated) which passes on to government in period 1. To simplify, we assume throughout that this decision has already been taken. We will first study the case in which the government in period 0 can completely control the actions of the government in period 1 (full precommitment).

In period 1 the relevant government budget constraint is:

$$x = g + (1 - \theta)b(1 + i^*) + \theta b(1 + i)/(1 + \pi) - k\pi/(1 + \pi) \qquad (1)$$

where i^* is the one-period international rate of interest, g is (exogenous) government spending, x are conventional taxes, i and π are the one-period nominal interest rate and rate of inflation (i.e., $\pi = P_1/P_0 - 1$, where P_t is the price level in period $t = 0, 1$) and, finally, $(1 - \theta)$ is the share of b which is indexed to the price level and $k\pi/(1 + \pi)$ is the inflation tax on cash balances.[8] Implicit in the above formulation is the assumption of perfect capital mobility. This is reflected in the second term of the RHS of equation (1), where the interest rate on indexed debt is equated to the international one.[9] Variables x, g, and b are measured in terms of (homogenous) output.

From the perspective of period 1, variables θ, b, i^* and i are predetermined. On the other hand, variables π, the rate of inflation, and x, taxes, are in principle under the control of government in period 1, subject to budget constraint (1). However, in the case of full precommitment we assume that also those last two variables are chosen by the government in period 0.

We will allow for stochastic shocks on g. In period 0, therefore, the value of g is, in principle, unknown. However, we assume that the government in period 0 (or government 0, for short) knows its probability distribution. Social welfare, as seen by government 0, is a negative function of taxes and inflation or deflation. More concretely, we assume the loss function, l, takes the following form:

$$l = E[(Ax^2 + \pi^2)]/2 \qquad (2)$$

where A is a positive parameter and E is the expectations operator based on information available in period 0 which, by assumption, is the full structure of the model except for the realization of g.

Suppose first that the nominal interest rate, i, could be made contingent on the state of nature, g. The formal problem faced by government in period 0 is, thus, to minimize (2) by choosing θ and schedules $i(g)$ and $\pi(g)$, subject to budget constraint (1), and

$$E\{[1 + i(g)]/[1 + \pi(g)]\} = 1 + i^* \tag{3}$$

The last condition is equivalent to saying that investors are risk-neutral in terms of output.

A quick look at this problem immediately reveals that the optimal solution exhibits constant x and π. In particular, if the base of the (conventional) inflation tax, k, is zero, then optimal inflation is zero (i.e., equal to Friedman's optimal inflation in the present context), and $i(g)$ is chosen so as to keep x constant subject to (1), which in the present context boils down to

$$x = g + (1 - \theta)b(1 + i^*) + \theta b[1 + i(g)] \tag{1'}$$

Notice that $i(g)$ is effective as a tool to keep x constant only if debt indexation to the price level is less than perfect, i.e., if $\theta \neq 0$. The constant optimal value of x is, of course, unique because, by (3) and (1'),

$$x = \bar{g} + b(1 + i^*) \tag{4}$$

where $\bar{g}$ is expected government expenditure. This shows, incidentally, that the degree of price indexation is irrelevant as long as it is not perfect.[10]

State-contingent contracts are not easy to write or to enforce, particularly when moral hazard considerations are present. In the above optimal solution, for example, the rate of interest must fall as g rises. Hence, if the government had any control on g, it might be to its advantage to increase g and pretend that it was due to unavoidable circumstances. This shows why it is relevant to examine the case in which the nominal interest rate is independent of the state of nature.

Letting i denote the fixed nominal interest rate on the non-indexed portion of the domestic debt, equation (3) becomes:

$$E\{(1 + i)/[(1 + \pi(g)]\} = 1 + i^* \tag{3'}$$

and the government loses an important tax-smoothing device, since now it is only the rate of inflation that could be employed for that purpose. In using it, however, the government gives up inflation smoothing, which is costly.

Let us assume that the share θ satisfies $0 \leq \theta \leq 1$. Then it can be readily seen that an optimal solution to the above minimization problem (subject now to a fixed i and (3')) calls for setting $\theta = 1$, i.e., no debt indexation. This remarkable result is due to the following facts: (1) fluctuations of π are costly; and (2) the base of the inflation tax – particularly the third term of the RHS of (1) – increases with θ. Therefore, with the same inflation cost, the larger is θ, the larger will be the capability to smooth out taxes with inflation (more on this below).

Setting $\theta = 1$, the minimization problem faced by government 0 becomes:

$$\text{Min } l \text{ with respect to } \pi(\cdot) \text{ and } i \qquad (5a)$$

subject to

$$x(g) = g + b(1 + i)/[(1 + \pi(g)] - k\pi(g)/[1 + \pi(g)] \qquad (5b)$$

and to (3'). One can easily check that at an optimum solution inflation, π, is an increasing function of government expenditure, g. This is true even when k, i.e., the base of the conventional inflation tax, is equal to zero. This is a point worth emphasizing, because when $k = 0$ the *expected* revenue from inflation is zero. To prove this, note that the latter is given by

$$Eb(1 + i)/(1 + \pi(g)) = b(1 + i^*) \qquad (6)$$

where the equality follows directly from (3'). Hence, changes in the rate of inflation have, on average, no effect on revenue. Despite this, however, π varies with g because it is a way to smooth out x (although, by previous considerations, $\bar{x}$ is invariant with respect to the π schedule).

The above discussion assumed that θ lies between zero and one. However, there is in principle no natural bound for θ. If $\theta > 1$, for example, the amount of indexed debt, $1 - \theta$, would be a negative number, meaning simply that the government is a net *creditor*, in indexed bonds. Interestingly, as noted above, the larger is θ, the larger will be the base of the inflation tax. We already noticed that a bigger θ enlarges the base but not the expected revenue from inflation. However, a larger base implies that the same smoothing of x could now be obtained by smaller changes in π. Thus, a larger θ always lowers minimum loss (this is the same argument behind the proof that $\theta = 1$ is optimal when $0 \le \theta \le 1$). In the limit as θ becomes infinitely large (or small, for that matter), the variance of π necessary to smooth out x goes to zero, and *perfect* smoothing of x and π is possible. As a matter of fact, one can show that in the limit the optimal value of the loss function equals that obtained if the nominal rate of interest, i, could be made contingent on the state of nature, g.

A more inflexible nominal rate of interest, i, is equivalent to decreasing the number of available contracts. Therefore, it is to be expected that when i is independent of the state of nature the remaining instruments will tend to be used more intensively in order to compensate for such a loss. In the example the only loss of making i inflexible is its power to smooth out x. There is no *expected* revenue loss because equation (3) holds. That is why an unbounded enlargement of θ is enough to recover the smaller degrees of freedom of an inflexible i. It should be noted, however, that this device of increasing the base of the inflation tax to smooth out x gives rise to the temptation to use 'unanticipated' inflation or deflation in order to increase government revenues. This is ruled out by assumption in the present case, but will play a key role in the ensuing discussion.

To show the above results in a simpler manner and to increase our understanding of more complicated scenarios, we will linearize the budget constraint (1). Using the first-order terms of the Taylor series corresponding to the RHS of equation (1), and expanding at the point $i = \pi = i^* = 0$, we get[11]

$$x = g + (1 + \theta)b + \theta b(1 + i - \pi) - k\pi \tag{7}$$

We can now solve problem (5) substituting (7) for (5b). Given θ, we prove in the Appendix that optimal π and x satisfy:[12]

$$\pi(g) = \frac{A(\theta b + k)}{1 + A(\theta b + k)^2}(g - \bar{g}) + \frac{Ak}{1 + Ak^2}(\bar{g} + b) \tag{8}$$

$$x(g) = \frac{1}{1 + A(\theta b + k)^2}(g - \bar{g}) + \frac{1}{1 + Ak^2}(\bar{g} + b) \tag{9}$$

The above equations confirm the intuitions discussed in the previous paragraphs. Thus, by (8), inflation is positively (negatively) correlated with the level of government expenditure if the base of the inflation tax (i.e., $\theta b + k$) is positive (negative) and likewise, by (9), taxes increase with g. Furthermore, as θ becomes infinitely large (in absolute value), functions $\pi(g)$ and $x(g)$ tend to become completely independent of g, i.e., perfect smoothing of π and x can be arbitrarily approximated by setting θ sufficiently large (in absolute value).

A payoff of linearizing the budget constraint is that the second term of equation (8) can be interpreted as the certainty-equivalent optimal full-precommitment inflation tax on cash balances when g equals its expected value, $\bar{g}$. For, under perfect certainty and full precommitment, the budget constraint (1) becomes (recalling that $i^* = 0$):

$$x = g + b - k\pi \tag{10}$$

Thus, minimizing l, given by equation (2), with respect to π subject to equation (1) calls for setting π equal to the second term of the RHS of equation (8). Consequently, optimal inflation associated with government expenditure g – as given by equation (8) – is the sum of certainty-equivalent optimal inflation and a linear term in the level of government expenditure.

Employing equations (8) and (9) in expression (2) yields that, given θ, at its minimum the loss function satisfies:

$$l(\sigma, p) = \left[\frac{\sigma^2}{1 + A(\theta b + k)^2} + \frac{1}{1 + Ak^2} (\bar{g} + b)^2 \right] \frac{A}{2} \tag{11}$$

where σ^2 is the variance of government expenditure, g, and p stands for 'precommitment'. Clearly, at optimum (given θ), social loss is an increasing function of the variance and expected value of government expenditure. Moreover, the relationship with respect to θ is ambiguous but, confirming our earlier discussion, the loss l can be set arbitrarily close to its minimum (or, rather its infimum) with respect to θ by setting θ sufficiently large. Finally, one can easily show that at the limit (i.e., as θ converges to plus or minus infinity), the value of the loss function converges to its optimum without uncertainty – as asserted for the nonlinear case.

We now turn to examine the case of no precommitment with respect to π. We assume that government in period 1 (or government 1, for short) has the same utility function as that of government 0, but knows the value of g. On the other hand, government 1 takes the nominal interest rate and the degree of indexation as given. Therefore, government 1 faces a problem without uncertainty; the only variables under its control are the rate of inflation π and taxes x. The solution to this problem is of relevance for government 0 given that its choices of i and θ will affect π and x.[13]

Formally, the problem faced by government 1 is to minimize

$$l_1 = [Ax^2 + \pi^2]/2 \tag{12}$$

with respect to π and x, subject to equation (7). The first-order condition with respect to π (taking into account constraint (7)) is

$$Ax(\theta b + k) = \pi \tag{13}$$

where $\theta b + k$ is the total base of the inflation tax in period 1 (i.e., cash balances k plus non-indexed debt θb), and Ax is, by (12), the marginal cost of conventional taxes, x. Similarly, π is the marginal cost of inflation. Thus, equation (13) simply tells us that at optimum government 1 will choose the rate of inflation so that a marginal increase in π will reduce the cost of taxation by as much as it increases the cost of inflation. By (7) and (13), we get

$$\pi = \frac{A(\theta b + k)}{1 + A(\theta b + k)^2} [g + b(1 + \theta i)] \tag{14}$$

and

$$x = \pi/[A(\theta b + k)] \tag{15}$$

As in the full precommitment case here also π and x are increasing (decreasing) functions of the level of government expenditure, g, when the base of the inflation tax is positive (negative).

We now return to period 0 in order to examine the problem faced by government 0. To simplify the analysis, we assume that equilibrium condition (3′) can be approximated by:

$$E(i - \pi) = i^* \tag{16}$$

This, by equations (14)–(16), we get the following equilibrium relationships:

$$\pi(g) = \frac{A(\theta b + k)}{1 + A(\theta b + k)^2} (g - \bar{g}) + \frac{A(\theta b + k)}{1 + Ak(\theta b + k)} (\bar{g} + b) \tag{17}$$

$$x(g) = \frac{1}{1 + A(\theta b + k)^2} (g - \bar{g}) + \frac{1}{1 + Ak(\theta b + k)} (\bar{g} + b) \tag{18}$$

Interestingly, the first terms of the RHS of equations (17) and (18) are the same as in equations (8) and (9), corresponding to full precommitment. The second terms are equal only if $\theta = 0$, full indexation. In general, however, it can be shown that the second term of the RHS of the inflation equation (17) is the optimal rate of inflation under certainty *without precommitment* and when g equals the expected value of government expenditure, $\bar{g}$. As in previous cases, there exists a positive (negative) association between the rate of inflation and government expenditure if the base of the inflation tax is positive (negative), and between the latter and taxes. It is worth noting that, unlike the full precommitment case, perfect-certainty inflation – given by the second term on the RHS of equation (17) – under incomplete indexation (i.e., $\theta \neq 0$) would be different from zero, even when there is no demand for real monetary balances (i.e., $k = 0$). This is so because when $k = 0$ government 1 can still collect revenue from inflation on account of the share of total debt which is not indexed to the price level – although, as shown below, on average government 1 will not be induced to employ this source of revenue. To see this, notice that, by (18), when $k = 0$ we have:

$$Ex = \bar{g} + b \tag{19}$$

which implies, recalling that the international rate of interest was assumed to be zero, that on average conventional taxes, not the inflation tax, will bear the brunt of financing government expenditure and debt amortization.

By (2), (17), and (18), the expected loss of government 0 is given by:

$$l(\sigma) = \left[\frac{\sigma^2}{1 + A(\theta b + k)^2} + \frac{1 + A(\theta b + k)^2}{[1 + Ak(\theta b + k)]^2}(\bar{g} + b)^2 \right] \frac{A}{2} \qquad (20)$$

Comparing (20) with (11), we notice that

$$l(\sigma) - l(0) = l(\sigma, p) - l(0, p) \equiv \mu(\sigma) \qquad (21)$$

which means that the cost differential between total and partial precommitment is entirely due to the differential that would occur under perfect certainty (i.e., $\sigma = 0$). Clearly, the minimum of $l(0)$ is attained at $\theta = 0$, and, furthermore, $l(0, p) = l(0)$ at $\theta = 0$, i.e., with full indexation. Therefore, recalling (21), the extra social loss associated with the smaller degree of precommitment (i.e., $l(\sigma) - l(\theta, p)$) is captured by the increased value of $l(0)$ when $\theta \neq 0$, and it is, thus, no longer true in general that l is minimized by setting θ unboundedly large in absolute value.

Obviously, by equation (21),

$$l(\sigma) = \mu(\sigma) + l(0) \qquad (22)$$

To develop the intuition behind the optimal choice of θ, consider first the effect of θ on $l(0)$ – i.e., the loss if $\theta = 0$. Without uncertainty, social loss is minimized with full indexation, which ensures that inflation is set to its optimal full-precommitment value. When $\theta \neq 0$, the presence of nominal debt (credit) affects the temptation of government 1 to inflate (deflate). Since, with no uncertainty, inflation collects revenue on cash balances only, the presence of non-indexed debt (combined with partial precommitment) serves no useful purpose and, hence, results in a larger $l(0)$. It is interesting to note that if the demand for real cash balances is zero, i.e., $k = 0$, then $l(0)$ goes to infinity as θ grows without bound (in absolute value), but converges to a finite value if $k > 0$. The reason for this is that when $k = 0$ then, obviously, inflation does not collect any revenue. Thus, for instance, if θ goes to plus infinity the temptation of government 1 to inflate away the swelling nominal debt is not offset by any other indirect cost. Hence, recalling that inflation costs are quadratic, optimal inflation from the perspective of period 1 goes to plus infinity, which explains the unbounded growth of $l(0)$. On the other hand, if $k > 0$, larger inflation implies larger revenues. As π grows without bound, those revenues will eventually be so large that they will have to be disposed of through negative taxes, i.e., through subsidies, which, by (2), are socially costly. In the limit as π goes to infinity the associated subsidies would also go to infinity, which, recalling the loss function (2), would provoke an unbounded growth in social costs. However, since government 1 internalizes the relationship between unbounded π and infinite social costs, this puts some additional restraint on its temptation to inflate away nominal debt as θ goes to infinity. This helps to explain why the social loss as perceived by government 0, $l(0)$, does not go to infinity as θ grows without bound (in absolute value).[14]

By (21), the uncertainty-related part of social loss, μ, is the same as in the full-precommitment case, which shows basically the same arguments that were discussed in connection with that case apply here. It is worth recalling that this term vanishes as θ becomes infinitely large in absolute value. In view of the above discussion about $l(0)$, it clearly follows that optimal θ could now turn out to be finite. For example, we show in the Appendix that if $k = 0$, then in the realistic case in which $\sigma < \bar{g} + b$ the optimal solution calls for perfect indexation, i.e., $\theta = 0$. This is a dramatic illustration of the importance of precommitment. In this example, lack of precommitment implies complete renunciation of the use of the inflation tax for (conventional) tax-smoothing purposes.

We show in the Appendix that when $k > 0$ then optimal $\theta > 0$.[15] The comparative statics of this case are relatively straightforward. Thus, we show in the Appendix that optimal debt indexation to the price level, i.e., $1 - \theta$, decreases with the variance of g, σ^2, and increases with the expected value of g, $\bar{g}$, and the level of debt, b. Notice, incidentally, that the negative association between the variance of real shocks and indexation is in line with the findings of Gray (1976) and related literature (e.g., Aizenman and Frenkel, 1985). In contrast with that literature, however, in the present model the real shock is intertwined with monetary decisions, so that the reduced form contains elements that could also be identified with monetary shocks.[16]

The intuition behind the above-mentioned comparative statics results is as follows. An increase in σ affects only $\mu(\sigma)$ in equation (22) and, *ceteris paribus*, increases the variability of government revenues. The latter enhances the attractiveness of widening the base of the inflation tax through less debt indexation (in order to smooth out the increased variability). A higher expected g, on the other hand, only affects the term $l(0)$ in equation (22) and, *ceteris paribus*, brings about higher expected taxes and inflation. The latter raises the marginal costs of nominal debt and partial precommitment – which explains why it is optimal to increase the indexation parameter $1 - \theta$. Finally, by equation (20), a higher debt level increases expected inflation, taxes, and the (total) base of the inflation tax, i.e., $\theta b + k$. The first two effects lead to higher indexation for the same reasons discussed in connection with a larger expected government expenditure. The implications of a bigger inflation tax base, on the other hand, are harder to explain, but, obviously, under these conditions the marginal cost of reducing θ – which lowers the inflation tax base – ought to be smaller, reinforcing the previous effects.

3   A three-period model

We turn now to examine an extension of the above example to a three-period world in order to be able to examine the optimal maturity of government debt. As before, government 0 passes on to future governments b units of debt (in real terms). However, it now has to decide the quantities that will be allocated to each future government, i.e., governments 1 and 2. We denote those quantities by b_{01} and b_{02}, respectively, and, of course, constraint them to satisfy:

$$b = b_{01} + b_{02} \tag{23}$$

For the sake of brevity, we assume that the interest rate on the non-indexed portion of these debt instruments is not state-contingent, and we denote them by i_{01} and i_{02}, respectively.

Let us begin by examining the case of full precommitment, that is to say, the case in which government 0 can predetermine all the policies of governments 1 and 2. To simplify, we further assume that the international interest rate, i^*, is constant over time, and that both i^* and the demand for real cash balances, k, are equal to zero.[17] Hence, linearizing (like in equation (7)) the budget constraint faced by government 0, we get:

$$x_1 + x_2 = g + b + \theta b_{01}(i_{01} - \pi_1) + \theta b_{02}(i_{02} - \pi_1 - \pi_2) \tag{24}$$

where g is the sum of government expenditure in periods 1 and 2, and the subscripts on x and π indicated their timing.

Objective function (2) is now written as follows:

$$l = E[Ax_1^2 + \pi_1^2 + Ax_2^2 + \pi_2^2]/2 \tag{25}$$

We assume that the state of nature is fully specified by g, and that the latter is known in period 1. We will allow government 0, however, to design its inflation policy as a function of the state of nature (this is similar to the second exercise developed in Section 2).

The first optimization problem that will be examined is the minimization of l in equation (25) with respect to π and x for each period and state of nature, and with respect to i_{0j} for $j = 1, 2$, given θ and b_{0j} for $j = 1, 2$, and subject to budget constraint (24) and the no-arbitrage conditions:

$$E(i_{01} - \pi_1) = 0 \tag{26a}$$

$$E(i_{02} - \pi_1 - \pi_2) = 0 \tag{26b}$$

Conditions (26) are linearizations like in equation (16), and take into account the assumption of a zero international interest rate, i.e., $i^* = 0$.

We show in the Appendix that at optimum:

$$x_1 = x_2 = x(g) = \frac{g - \bar{g}}{2 + A(\theta b)^2 + A(\theta b_{02})^2} + \frac{\bar{g} + b}{2} \tag{27}$$

$$\pi_1(g) = A\theta b(x - Ex) \tag{28}$$

$$\pi_2(g) = A\theta b_{02}(x - Ex) \tag{29}$$

Equation (27) states that it is optimal to smooth out taxes completely over time, a standard result under full precommitment when the real rate of interest is equal to the rate of discount, as in the present case. Furthermore, by equations (27)–(29), there exists a positive association between government spending and taxes, and a relationship between government spending and inflation whose sign depends, as in the previous section, on the signs of the respective inflation tax bases (i.e., recalling equation (24), θb for period-1 inflation and θb_{02} for period-2 inflation).[18]

By equations (25), (27)–(29), expected loss of government 0 satisfies:

$$l(\sigma, p) = \{\sigma^2/[2 + A(\theta b)^2 + A(\theta b_{02})^2] + (\bar{g} + b)^2/2\}A/2 \tag{30}$$

where the definition for precommitment loss $l(\sigma, p)$ in equation (30) substitutes for that in equation (11). As in the precommitment case of Section 2, the optimal indexation policy would be to set θ unboundedly large in absolute value, and the reasons are the same. The new character in this play, however, is the level of debt issued in period 0 and that matures in period 2, i.e., b_{02}; or, recalling (23), the maturity structure of the debt issued by government 0. First we note that if there is no uncertainty, i.e., $\sigma = 0$, then the maturity structure has no effect. This 'irrelevancy' result is quite familiar in the presence of complete markets and full precommitment. With uncertainty, however, markets become incomplete because we do not allow governments to make state-contingent interest contracts. Therefore, it is to be expected that debt maturity begins to matter, and that is precisely what is implied by equation (30). Remarkably, the role of b_{02} is very similar to that of θ. In fact, the optimal policy consists of setting non-indexed b_{02} unboundedly large (in absolute value) which, in view of (23), implies that it is optimal to swap an infinite amount of non-indexed short against non-indexed long-term maturity debt, or vice versa. The principles behind this result are essentially the same that we discussed in connection with optimal indexation under precommitment. Examination of budget constraint (24) shows that, for example, an increase in b_{02} at the expense of b_{01} increases the inflation tax base in period 2, which permits to obtain the same path of x with smaller fluctuations in π_2 or, alternatively, to reduce the fluctuations of x with the same path of π_2. Given the discussion in Section 2, it should by now be obvious that an unboundedly large b_{02} can attain perfect smoothing of x with (in the limit) no inflation cost, thus mimicking the complete-markets solution.

An interesting theme that emerges from the above arguments, and that appears to be relatively novel in the public policy literature, is that when markets are incomplete, a tax that collects nothing on average could be socially desirable, and, perhaps more surprising, that 'artificially' increasing the base of the tax through, for instance, offsetting subsidies could help achieve the complete-markets optimal fiscal policy solution. In our problem, the artificiality of the optimal inflation tax base is glaringly apparent when $b = 0$. Initially there is no debt of any kind and so, in principle, there is no inflation tax base either (recall that $k = 0$); however, government 0 will find it optimal to increase non-indexed long-term debt (i.e., increase the period-2 inflation tax base), say, by making short-term loans to the private sector – and the more, the better!

As in the two-period example, however, the above type of optimal solution raises serious questions about policy credibility. A key element of the solution is the blowing up of some component of the inflation tax base. The objective is, of course, to be able to smooth out taxes with a minimum of inflation cost; however, government 1 may be tempted to inflate more (less) than it was optimal from the perspective of government 0 if the inflation tax base is positive (negative). It is, therefore, important to study solutions that take into account the temptation of governments 1 and/or 2 to depart from the original plan. Our next exercise moves in that direction by relaxing the assumption that the policies of government 1 can be precommitted by government 0, but still assuming that government 1 can fully precommit the policies of government 2.

The optimal problem of government 1 under the above precommitment assumptions is essentially equivalent to the one we discussed in Section 2 when government 0 can precommit the policies of government 1. The details, however, are somewhat different because government 1 can choose both (π_1, x_1) and (π_2, x_2) taking as predetermined the interest rates and indexation coefficient on the government-0 debt. When government 0 takes into account the optimal response of government 1 then, as shown in the Appendix, we have that $x_1 = x_2 = x$ for all g, and

$$x(g) = \frac{g - \bar{g}}{2 + A(\theta b)^2 + A(\theta b_{02})^2} + \frac{\bar{g} + b}{2} \tag{31}$$

$$\pi_1(g) = A\theta bx \tag{32}$$

$$\pi_2(g) = A\theta b_{02}x \tag{33}$$

Comparing (27) with (31) we note that the optimal tax formula is the same as with full precommitment.[19] Moreover, comparing (32)–(33) with

(28)–(29), we note that with full precommitment, expected inflation is zero in both periods, while in the present case expected inflation depends on expected taxes and the inflation tax base for each of the two periods. The intuition for this should be clear from the above discussion, since the temptation to inflate or deflate is obviously related to the corresponding inflation-tax base.

Consequently, expected loss at time 0, taking equations (25) and (31)–(33) into account is:

$$
l(\sigma) = \left[\frac{\sigma^2}{2 + A(\theta b)^2 + A(\theta b_{02})^2} + \frac{2 + A(\theta b)^2 + A(\theta b_{02})^2}{4}(\bar{g} + b)^2 \right] \frac{A}{2}
$$

(34)

where the definition for $l(\sigma)$ replaces that of equation (20).

Clearly, if there is no uncertainty, then it is optimal to fully index debt to the price level, i.e., set $\theta = 0$, like in the two-period example. Failing that, a second best is to set $b_{02} = 0$, meaning that all debt should exhibit short-term maturity, i.e., $b = b_{01}$.[20] This is an illustration of the possible optimality of short-term maturity debt when governments are tempted to generate 'excessive' inflation – a theme that will recur in the more general cases examined in the ensuring simulations.[21]

When there is uncertainty (i.e., $\sigma > 0$), then optimal θ could be larger than zero and, thus, maturity begins to matter. Notice, by (32), that if $b_{02} = b$ then inflation will be constant over time, which is a valuable feature for our planners. Surprisingly, the optimal solution actually requires setting $\pi_1 = \pi_2$, even when $k > 0$ (see the Appendix). The intuition for this result is that long-term debt is part of the inflation-tax base for π_1 and π_2, while the real value of short-term debt can only be affected by π_1. Thus, when all debt is long-term, government 1 will make equal use of both instruments, which is an efficient way to collect the inflation tax. This may still not be optimal, however, because the base could be too large or too small. But the size of the inflation tax can be directly controlled by the indexation parameter, $1 - \theta$. This is the reason why a first-best type property (like $\pi_1 = \pi_2$) holds in a second-best world.

The picture changes drastically if governments are constrained to have a degree of debt indexation different from the optimal. As the ensuing simulations wil illustrate, when no indexation is possible (i.e., $\theta = 1$), then optimal debt maturity shortens by a considerable amount. This can also be explained in an intuitive manner. When no indexation is possible and the unconstrained optimal solution calls for some debt indexation, then the inflation tax bases are large relative to their unconstrained optima.

Under the present conditions, the monetary authority cannot lower the inflation tax base for period 1. However, by shortening the debt maturity structure, it can still lower the inflation-tax base for period 2 – which is, quite naturally, what the second-best solution requires.

Table 3.1 shows some simulations to develop some feeling about the possible empirical relevance of these issues. In our experiments we assume that the average (conventional) tax revenue is 40 percent of GNP,[22] and that the standard deviation of shocks to government expenditure (i.e., σ) is 3 percent of GNP. Finally, we chose $A = 0.5$ in order to make the inflation rates associated with the case of (1) no debt indexation; (2) 100 percent debt-to-GNP ratio; and (3) $k = 15$ percent of GNP quantitatively similar to the anual inflation rates for Italy in the 1980s. Columns denoted by l show the extra cost in relation to the first-best, and it is given in terms of the extra government expenditure that would have to be incurred under first-best conditions, as a percentage of GNP, to generate the same rise in social cost. The inflation columns correspond to expected inflation, and are expressed as percentages per period. The numbers for the b and b_{02} columns are percentages of GNP and b, respectively. Numbers in parenthesis correspond to $k = 8$ per cent of GNP, while the others are generated under the asumption that $k = 15$ percent of GNP.

The salient features of Table 3.1 are that there is a substantial cost associated with government 0 losing its ability to precommit the rates of inflation for periods 1 and 2; the cost is about 1.1 percent of GNP and does not vary with the initial debt level.[23][24] Furthermore, optimal indexation is larger than 95 percent in all cases, despite having chosen a relatively high standard deviation for g (3 percent of GNP).

Social loss increases if no debt indexation is possible, and even more so if, in addition, all debt is long-term maturity. The importance of this effect grows significantly with the debt level, and relatively big losses are found when the debt is 50 percent of GNP or larger. As asserted before, Table 3.1 shows that optimal debt maturity shortens significantly if no indexation is possible. In the examples, optimal short-term debt is never less than 95 percent of initial debt. Finally, when indexation is not possible, inflation rates are not equalized and could be substantially different, depending on the initial debt.

4   Interpretation and extensions

The previous analysis has given us yet another example of the importance of precommitment for macroeconomic policy. We showed that with full precommitment, debt indexation and maturity structure are close substitutes, because a large nominal debt (in absolute value) – achieved either

b	$b_{02} = b$				$\theta = 100$ percent				$\theta = 100\%$ $b_{02} = b$	
	$E\pi_{fp}$	l	θ	$E\pi$	l	b_{02}	$E\pi_1$	$E\pi_2$	l	$E\pi$
25	3	1.1	3.6	3.1	1.37	5	7.8	3.2	1.6	7.8
	(1.6)	(1.1)	(1.9)	(1.7)	(1.38)	(2.5)	(6.5)	(1.7)	(1.65)	(6.5)
50	3	1.1	1.8	3.1	2.1	4	12.6	3.3	3.1	12.4
	(1.6)	(1.1)	(0.96)	(1.7)	(2.2)	(2)	(11.4)	(1.8)	(3.2)	(11.3)
100	3	1.1	0.9	3.1	5.1	4.8	21.9	3.8	8.3	21.2
	(1.6)	(1.1)	(0.48)	(1.7)	(5.3)	(2.5)	(21.1)	(2.0)	(8.9)	(20.7)

Table 3.1. Simulations under full and partial precommitment (in percent)
Note: π_{fp} is expected inflation under full precommitment.

by swapping short against long-term maturity bonds, or by indexation, e.g., by swapping nominal by real debt – is useful to smooth out fluctuations in conventional taxes. However, with partial precommitment, a careful choice of indexation and maturity are both necessary for an optimum. Interestingly, the optimal policy is quite sensitive to the instruments that can be controlled. Thus, if one can freely choose indexation and maturity, then it is optimal to concentrate all debt on long-term maturity bonds; but, on the other hand, if it is not possible to index, then our simulations suggest that optimal maturity will shorten by a considerable amount.

The last model that was examined in Section 3 assumes that government 0 cannot precommit the actions of future governments. Government 1, instead, is assumed to be able to precommit the policies of government 2. This 'partial precommitment' assumption can be easily relaxed if government 1 is free to choose the indexation level on its own debt. By assumption, uncertainty is fully resolved in period 1, and, hence, government 1 operates under perfect certainty. Thus, it is easy to see that if the nominal debt inherited by government 2 equals b_{02}, and its total debt (including the fully indexed part) is equal to the optimal level corresponding to the case in which government 1 can precommit the actions of government 2 (the partial-precommitment case), then government 2 will actually replicate the policy that government 1 would like it to follow. In other words, the model's implications apply equally to the case in which no government can tie the hands of any future administration.[25]

If optimal indexation is not possible, then the inability to precommit has a substantial effect on the nature of optimal policy. Consider, for example, the case in which debt indexation to the price level is not possible (i.e., $\theta = 1$). By previous discussion, if government 1 can precommit the actions of government 2, then most of the debt (in fact, 100 percent of the debt if $k = 0$) should optimally be placed in the form of short-term bonds. However, when no precommitment is possible, the latter type of policy tends to generate 'too much' tax revenue in period 1. This is so, because, in contrast to the partial-precommitment case, when government 1 considers transferring part of its inherited debt to government 2, it realizes that it simultaneously increases government-2 debt-liquidation incentives. Thus, if following the prescriptions of the partial-precommitment model of Section 3, government 0 puts most of its debt in the form of short-term maturity instruments, government 1 will tend to repay a share of total debt which is higher than that of the partial-precommitment optimum (i.e., the optimal solution when government 1 can precommit the policies of government 2). Consequently, government 0 will find it optimal to issue more long-run debt than in the partial-precommitment case.

The analytics behind the above intuitions are presented in the Appendix. Table 3.2 shows some simulations corresponding to the case in which government 1 cannot precommit the actions of government 2, there is no debt indexation (i.e., $\theta = 1$), and perfect certainty prevails.[26] For the sake of comparison, all other parameters are the same as in Table 3.1.

Confirming the above discussion, Table 3.2 shows that under no precommitment the maturity structure tends to become more uniform – in fact, numbers range from 40 to 60 percent – and long-term debt increases with the size of the initial debt. Finally, maturity is important (in terms of social cost) in the case of partial precommitment (i.e., when government 1 can precommit the policies of government 2), but its relevance diminishes considerably when there is no precommitment.

These results suggest that there may be some wisdom behind the observed trend towards short-term debt that accompanied the recent accumulation of domestic government debt. Although we do not provide a rationale for the existing high proportion of nominal debt (except for the somewhat unrealistic case in which the monetary authorities can precommit the future rates of inflation), our simulations suggest that with low levels of debt indexation it may be optimal *and important* to shorten the maturity structure if some precommitment is feasible. On the other hand, this policy would not be optimal if governments could not precommit future inflation. In that case, however, maturity-structure mistakes do not appear to be very costly. Hence, as a rule of thumb, we reach the tentative conclusion that *when government debt is not indexed to the price level short maturities look like a reasonably fair bet: they could make a*

Table 3.2. Simulations under partial and no precommitment (in percent)

b	Partial precommitment				No precommitment				Partial precommitment $b_{02} = b$		No precommitment $b_{02} = b$		
	l	b_{02}	π_1	π_2	l	b_{02}	π_1	π_2	l	π	l	π_1	π_2
25	0.3	1.5	7.8	3.0	0.4	43.6	7.8	5.3	0.6	7.8	0.4	7.8	5.6
	(0.3)	(0.6)	(6.5)	(1.6)	(0.4)	(39.2)	(6.5)	(4.0)	(0.6)	(6.5)	(0.4)	(6.5)	(4.3)
50	1.15	2.4	12.6	3.1	1.41	50.6	12.5	7.6	2.2	12.4	1.5	12.4	8.3
	(1.2)	(1.2)	(11.4)	(1.7)	(1.5)	(47.2)	(11.4)	(6.4)	(2.3)	(11.4)	(1.6)	(11.4)	(7.1)
100	4.3	4.1	21.9	3.6	5.1	60.4	21.3	12.5	7.7	21.2	5.4	20.7	14.1
	(4.5)	(2.1)	(21.1)	(2.0)	(5.5)	(57.3)	(20.7)	(11.4)	(8.3)	(20.7)	(5.6)	(20.4)	(13.1)
												$b_{02} = 0$	
100											5.8	23.5	10.3
											(6.1)	(22.8)	(9.5)

sizable contribution to social welfare and, at worst, their costs appear to be low.

5 Final remarks

(1) In a world of complete markets where policy makers can make credible announcements, price indexation can easily be substituted by other policies, and the maturity structure of government debt is totally irrelevant. Departures from that Alice-in-Wonderland case, however, could turn these instruments into extremely useful tools for policy making. Our analysis suggests that if indexation is credible – in the sense that it is not expected to be nullified by interest taxation or sheer debt repudiation – then there exists a variety of realistic cases in which it is optimal to index a high proportion of the debt to the price level. Moreover, the effect of optimal indexation is further enhanced by choosing long debt maturities. Our simulations show that the contribution of long maturities to welfare could be quite important when the debt-to-GNP ratio exceeds 50 percent. But, on the other hand, if indexation was not possible and there was a relatively low degree of credibility of policy announcements then, interestingly, it was hard for us to find realistic examples in which the marginal cost of selecting a 'wrong' maturity structure exceeded 0.3 percent of GNP.

(2) Our discussion revealed that the relevant base for the inflation tax includes *all* nominal government liabilities, not just the noninterest-bearing part. The reason is rather obvious: the price level affects the real value of the whole set of nominal assets. Some economists, however, would prefer to subtract the interest-bearing part because *in equilibrium* the interest rate on those assets may tend to include the expected rate of inflation, point for point, and, consequently, in *equilibrium* no inflation revenue will be collected on that account. Although we do not disagree, in principle, with this methodology for calculating the actual proceeds from the inflation tax, our analysis shows that it could be very misleading to abstract from the interest-bearing part of government nominal liabilities *if one is trying to come up with a 'positive' theory of inflation*: they are as much a temptation to inflate as high-powered money. In fact, we showed examples where inflation is positive even though at equilibrium it collects no revenue whatsoever – i.e., there is no demand for high-powered money – and it is first-best optimal to generate zero inflation. This inflationary potential of government bonds is precisely one of the fundamental reasons why debt maturity may matter. By changing the maturity structure of nominal government debt, the policy maker changes the time profile of the inflation base, and is thus able to affect the incentive-compatible inflation path.

(3) The paper made enough assumptions to ensure *uniqueness* of equilibrium solutions. However, uniqueness is not a very robust property of
these types of models. In fact, multiplicity of equilibria is relatively easy to
generate when there exists a positive stock of non-indexed bonds (see
Calvo, 1988a, b). The intuition is that the nominal interest rate reflects
inflationary expectations. Thus, if the public expects 'high' inflation then,
ex post, the government will be tempted to validate those expectations;
for, otherwise, the *real* interest rate will be 'high', calling for 'high'
distorting conventional taxes. But, on the other hand, if inflationary
expectations are 'low' then, for similar but opposite reasons, the government could be led to generate 'low' inflation. Consequently, the monetary
authority may end up being the passive reflector of average opinion.

A way to try to avoid the non-uniqueness problem is to index the entire
stock of bonds to the price level, but this could be costly in an uncertain
environment. Hence, maturities are once again likely to be of some help.
We conjecture that, when non-uniqueness is a problem, the optimal
maturity structure will tend to be shorter than otherwise. This appears to
be a promising area for future research.[27]

(4) We need to develop a better intuition about inflation costs, in
particular, and debt-repudiation costs, in general. They are central to the
analysis and essential for policy implications. In our model, for example,
if there is no uncertainty then the optimal solution is to index the
government debt fully to the price level. This is the best one can do
because full indexation removes the incentive to 'inflate away' the real
value of government bonds – a completely wasteful activity in equilibrium. However, in more realistic economies, inflation is not the only
policy that can be employed to lower the real value of government debt.
Wealth or interest taxes, for example, could yield the same effects.
Consequently, in a more general framework complete neutralization of
the inflation tax on bonds may give rise to other forms of debt repudiation, which may turn out to be more costly. Until the microeconomics of
these costs is better understood, therefore, we should be very cautious
about the relevance of our policy conclusions.[28]

Appendix: technical notes

1   Two-period model, full precommitment

Government 0 chooses functions $\pi(g)$, $x(g)$, and a constant i to minimize l,
given by equation (2), subject to budget constraint (7), and equilibrium
condition (16), for given θ. The first-order conditions of this minimization
problem imply that:

$$- Ax(\theta b + k) + \lambda + \pi = 0 \tag{A.1}$$

$$A \theta b Ex - \lambda = 0 \tag{A.2}$$

where λ is the Lagrange multiplier associated with equilibrium condition (16). The fact that costs are quadratic and the constraints are linear ensures that l attains a unique (global) minimum. Using equations (7), (16), and (A.2), equation (A.1) can be written as:

$$\begin{aligned} - A(\theta b + k)[g + b(1 + i^*) + \theta b(E\pi - \pi) - k\pi] \\ + \pi + A\theta b[\bar{g} + b(1 + i^*) - kE\pi] = 0 \end{aligned} \tag{A.3}$$

We conjecture that the optimal $\pi(g)$ is a linear function:

$$\pi(g) \equiv B + Cg \tag{A.4}$$

where B and C are unknown positive constants. To verify the conjecture we find unique values of coefficients B and C for which equation (A.3), combined with (A.4), holds as an identity. This yields the following values of B and C:

$$B = \frac{Akb(1 + i^*)}{1 + Ak^2} - \frac{A\theta b[1 - kA(\theta b + k)]}{(1 + Ak^2)[1 + A(\theta b + k)^2]}\bar{g} \tag{A.5a}$$

$$C = A(\theta b + k)/[1 + A(\theta b + k)^2] \tag{A.5b}$$

Using (A.5a) and (A.5b), and assuming that $i^* = 0$, optimal $\pi(g)$ is given by equation (8). Similarly, using (A.1), (A.2) and (7), it follows that also optimal $x(g)$ is given by equation (9). Moreover, taking into account the fact that $EX^2 = E[X - EX]^2$ for $X = x, \pi$, and equations (8) and (9), it is easy to check that expected loss at time 0 is given by equation (11).

The optimal value of the non-indexation parameter θ is that which minimizes l in equation (11). As discussed in the text, l can be set arbitrarily close to its infimum with respect to θ by setting θ sufficiently large in absolute value.

2   Two-period model, no precommitment

Government 0 chooses optimal θ to minimize l in equation (20). As discussed in the text, equation (20) is obtained by taking into account the optimal response of government 1. Consider first the case in which $k = 0$. The minimization problem faced by government 0 is equivalent to choosing z to minimize the value of the following function $h(z)$:

$$h(z) = \alpha/z + \beta z \tag{A.6}$$

where α and β are positive constants and $z \in [1, \infty)$. Let us study the same problem with the exception that $z \in (0, \infty)$. From equation (A.6) we have

$$h'(z) = -\alpha/z^2 + \beta \tag{A.7}$$

$$H''(z) = 2\alpha/z^3 > 0 \tag{A.8}$$

for $z > 0$. Hence, $h(\cdot)$ is strictly convex and its global minimum is attained where

$$h'(z) = 0 \quad \text{i.e., at } z = (\alpha/\beta)^{1/2} \tag{A.9}$$

Hence, at a minimum,

$$h(z) = 2(\alpha/\beta)^{1/2} \tag{A.10}$$

If z is constrained such that $z \geq 1$ then, due to the convexity of h and equation (A.9), we have

$$\operatorname*{argmin}_{z \geq 1} h(z) = 1 \quad \text{iff} \quad (\alpha/\beta)^{1/2} \leq 1 \tag{A.11}$$

In terms of loss function (20), $\alpha \equiv \sigma^2$, $\beta \equiv (\bar{g} + b)^2$, and $z \equiv 1 + A(\theta b + k) = 1 + A\theta b$ since $k = 0$. Therefore, equation (A.11) implies that, in the case in which $k = 0$, optimal $\theta = 0$ if and only if $\sigma \leq \bar{g} + b$, as asserted in the text.

Consider the case in which $k > 0$. Minimizing the value of loss function (20) with respect to θ is equivalent to choosing z to minimize the value of $f(z)$, defined by:

$$f(z) = -\frac{\alpha}{\beta} + \beta \frac{z}{[1 + k(z-1)^{1/2}A]^2} \tag{A.12}$$

where $z \geq 1$ (note that $f(z) \equiv h(z)$ when $k = 0$.)

It can be checked that

$$f(1) < f(\infty) \quad \text{iff} \quad \alpha + \beta(1 - 1/k^2 A) < 0 \tag{A.13}$$

$$f'(z) = -\alpha/z^2 + \beta(w - kA)/w(1 + kw)^2 \tag{A.14}$$

where $w \equiv [A(z-1)]^{1/2}$. Hence,

$$\lim_{z \to 1} f'(z) = -\infty \tag{A.15}$$

Thus, if equation (A.13) holds, a minimum exists and optimal $z > 1$.

When a minimum occurs at $z < \infty$ we have $f'(z) = 0$ which, by equation (A.14), requires

$$w > kA \tag{A.16}$$

Since, in terms of loss function (20), $z \equiv 1 + A(\theta b + k)$ and $w = A(\theta b + k)$, equation (A.16) implies that optimal θ satisfies

$$\theta b > 0 \qquad\qquad (A.17)$$

Thus, if $b > 0$ then optimal $\theta > 0$.

The comparative statistics with respect to σ and $\bar{g}$ are easily computed from the first order condition $f'(z) = 0$. Using the definitions of α and β, condition (A.16), and the fact that at a minimum $f''(z) > 0$, it can be checked that optimal θ increases with σ and decreases with $\bar{g}$ and b.

3   Three-period model, full precommitment

Government 0 chooses functions $\pi_1(g)$, $\pi_2(g)$, $x_2(g)$, $x_2(g)$, and constants i_{01} and i_{02} to minimize l in equation (25), subject to the budget constraint

$$z_1 + x_2 = g + b + \theta b_{01}(i_{01} - \pi_1)$$
$$+ \theta b_{02}(i_{02} - \pi_1 - \pi_2) - k(\pi_1 + \pi_2) \qquad (A.18)$$

and equilibrium conditions (26a) and (26b), for given θ. The first-order conditions for this minimization problem include:

$$Ax_1 - \mu = 0 \qquad\qquad (A.19)$$

$$Ax_2 - \mu = 0 \qquad\qquad (A.20)$$

$$\pi_1 - \mu(\theta b + k) - \lambda_1 - \lambda_2 = 0 \qquad\qquad (A.21)$$

$$\pi_2 - \mu(\theta b_{02} + k) - \lambda_2 = 0 \qquad\qquad (A.22)$$

$$E \mu \theta(b - b_{02}) + \lambda_1 = 0 \qquad\qquad (A.23)$$

$$E \mu \theta b_{02} + \lambda_2 = 0 \qquad\qquad (A.24)$$

where $\mu(g)$ is the multiplier associated with constraint (A.18) and λ_1 and λ_2 are the multipliers associated with equilibrium conditions (26a) and (26b). Existence of a global minimum is ensured by the fact that costs are quadratic and the constraints are linear. The above first order conditions imply

$$x_1 = x_2 = x \qquad\qquad (A.25)$$

$$\pi_1 = A \theta b(x - Ex) + Akx \qquad\qquad (A.26)$$

$$\pi_2 = A \theta b_{02}(x - Ex) + Akx \qquad\qquad (A.27)$$

From equations (A.18) and (A.25)–(A.27) we obtain:

$$Ex = (\bar{g} + b)/2(1 + Ak^2) \qquad\qquad (A.28)$$

$$E\pi_1 = E\pi_2 = Ak(Ex) \tag{A.29}$$

Using (A.18) and (A.25)–(A.29) one can verify that optimal $x(g)$, $\pi_1(g)$, and $\pi_2(g)$ are linear functions that satisfy

$$x(g) = \frac{g - \bar{g}}{2 + A(\theta b + k)^2 + A(\theta b_{02} + k)^2} + Ex \tag{A.30}$$

$$\pi_1(g) = \frac{A(\theta b + k)(g - \bar{g})}{2 + A(\theta b + k)^2 + A(\theta b_{02} + k)^2} + E\pi_1 \tag{A.31}$$

$$\pi_2(g) = \frac{A(\theta b_{02} + k)(g - \bar{g})}{2 + A(\theta b + k)^2 + A(\theta b_{02} + k)^2} + E\pi_2 \tag{A.32}$$

Using equations (A.30)–(A.32), one can check that expected loss at time 0 satisfies:

$$l(\sigma, p) = \left[\frac{\sigma^2}{2 + A(\theta b + k)^2 + A(\theta b_{02} + k)^2} + \frac{(\bar{g} + b)^2}{2(1 + Ak^2)} \right] \frac{A}{2} \tag{A.33}$$

Hence, as discussed in the text, social loss can be set arbitrarily close to its infimum with respect to θ and b_{02} by making θ or b_{02} arbitrarily large in absolute value.

4   Three-period model, partial precommitment

After the realization of g, government 1 chooses x_1, π_1, x_2, and π_2 to minimize l in equation (25) subject to budget constraint (A.18), taking as predetermined θ, b_{01}, b_{02}, i_{01}, and i_{02}. After taking into account equilibrium conditions (26a) and (26b), the formulas describing the reaction function of government 1, faced by government 0, when $k > 0$ are:

$$x(g) = \frac{g - \bar{g}}{2 + A(\theta b + k)^2 + A(\theta b_{02} + k)^2}$$
$$+ \frac{\bar{g} + b}{2 + Ak[\theta(b + b_{02}) + 2k]} \tag{A.34}$$

$$\pi_1(g) = A(\theta b + k)x \tag{A.35}$$

$$\pi_2(g) = A(\theta b_{02} + k)x \tag{A.36}$$

where the fact that, at optimum, $x_1 = x_2 = x$ has been used. From equations (25) and (A.34)–(A.36), expected loss at time 0 satisfies:

$$l(\sigma) = \left[\frac{\sigma^2}{2 + A(\theta b + k)^2 + A(\theta b_{02} + k)^2} \right.$$
$$\left. + \frac{2 + A(\theta b + k)^2 + A(\theta b_{02} + k)^2}{\{2 + Ak[\theta(b + b_{02}) + 2k]\}^2} (\bar{g} + b)^2 \right] \frac{A}{2} \tag{A.37}$$

Government 0 chooses θ and b_{02} to minimize l in equation (A.37). This problem is equivalent to minimizing $F(y, n)$, defined below, with respect to y and n:

$$F(y, n) = \frac{\alpha}{2 + A(n^2 + y^2)} + \frac{2 + A(n^2 + y^2)}{[2 + Ak(n + y)]^2} \beta \qquad (A.38)$$

where $n, y \in (-\infty, \infty)$ except where $2 + A(n + y) = 0$. If (y^*, n^*) minimizes $F(y, n)$ then (y^*, n^*) must also solve the following problem:

$$\text{Min } F(y, n) \qquad (A.39a)$$
$$\underset{n, y}{}$$

subject to

$$n + y = n^* + y^* \qquad (A.39b)$$

Under equation (A.39b) we have

$$z' \equiv 2 + A(n^2 + y^2) = 2 + A[n^2 + (n^* + y^* - n)^2]$$

which attains its minimum where

$$n = (n^* + y^*)/2, \quad \text{i.e., at } z' = 1 + (A/2)(n^* + y^*)^2 \qquad (A.40)$$

Consequently, we can express problem (A.39) as follows:

$$\text{Min } \alpha/z' + \beta' z' \qquad (A.41a)$$
$$\underset{z'}{}$$

subject to

$$z' \geq 1 + (A/2)(n^* + y^*)^2 \qquad (A.41b)$$

where

$$\beta' \equiv \beta/[2 + Ak(n^* + y^*)]^2 \qquad (A.42)$$

By equation (A.10), if problem (A.41) has an interior solution, we have that the minimum value of the function in (A.41a) is

$$2(\alpha/\beta)^{1/2}/[2 + Ak(n^* + y^*)] \qquad (A.43)$$

Hence, solutions to the original problem do not lead to interior solutions of problem (A.41), because otherwise the value of F could be lowered by changing $(n^* + y^*)$. Thus, by (A.41), at the optimum

$$z' = 1 + (A/2)(n^* + y^*)^2 \qquad (A.44)$$

which, by definition of z' and equation (A.40), requires setting

$$n = y \qquad (A.45)$$

Interestingly,

$$F(n, n) = \tfrac{1}{2}\left[\frac{\alpha}{1 + An^2} + \frac{1 + An^2}{(1 + Akn)^2}\,\beta\right] \tag{A.46}$$

Minimizing the value of $F(n, n)$ with respect to n is equivalent to minimizing the value of $f(z)$ in equation (A.12) with respect to z. In terms of loss function (A.37), $y = \theta b + k$ and $n = \theta b_{02} + k$. Thus, the above discussion implies, by equation (A.45), that if $\theta \neq 0$ then $b = b_{02}$, otherwise if $\theta = 0$ then the maturity structure does not matter. Moreover, since the choice of n to minimize the value of $F(n, n)$ in equation (A.46) is equivalent to choosing optimal θ in the two-period model, then optimal θ in the three-period model is the same as in the two-period model. By equation (A.17), when $k > 0$ and $b > 0$, optimal $\theta > 0$. Finally, by equation (A.35) and (A.36), $\pi_1 = \pi_2$ at the optimum.

5   Three-period model, no precommitment, $\sigma = 0$, $\theta = 1$

Government 2 chooses x_2 and π_2 to minimize l_2 given by

$$l_2 = (Ax_2^2 + \pi_2^2)/2 \tag{A.47}$$

subject to the budget constraint

$$\begin{aligned} x_2 = g/2 + b_{02} + b_{12} + b_{02}(i_{02} - \pi_1 - \pi_2) \\ + b_{12}(i_{12} - \pi_2) - k\pi_2 \end{aligned} \tag{A.48}$$

where b_{12}, and i_{12} denote (nominal) debt issued in period 1 with maturity in period 2, and the interest rate applying to b_{12}, respectively. It can be verified that at optimum

$$\pi_2 = A(b_{02} + b_{12} + k)x_2 \tag{A.49}$$

With perfect certainty, equilibrium requires (recalling that $i^* = 0$)

$$i_{12} = \pi_2 \tag{A.50}$$

Government 1 chooses x_1, π_1, and b_{12}, taking into account the optimal response of government 2, which chooses x_2 and π_2 as described above. The minimization problem of government 1 is equivalent to choosing x_1, x_2, π_1, π_2, and b_{12} to minimize social loss

$$l = (Ax_1^2 + \pi_1^2 + Ax_2^2 + \pi_2^2)/2 \tag{A.51}$$

subject to equations (A.48), (A.49), (A.50), and the period-1 budget constraint

$$x_1 = g/2 + b_{01} + b_{01}(i_{01} - \pi_1) - k\pi_1 - b_{12} \tag{A.52}$$

The solution to this minimization problem, along with equilibrium conditions

$$i_{01} = \pi_1 \qquad (A.53)$$

$$i_{02} = \pi_1 + \pi_2 \qquad (A.54)$$

characterizes the reaction function of government 1 faced by government 0.

Equation (A.49), along with the following set of equations, characterizes the reaction function of government 1:

$$x_1 + x_2 = g + b - k(\pi_1 + \pi_2) \qquad (A.55)$$

$$\frac{x_1 - x_2}{\pi_2 - Ax_2(b_{02} + k)} = \frac{2x_2 - g + k(1 + \pi_2)}{1 + A(b_{02} + k)[x_2 - g + k(1 + \pi_2)]} \qquad (A.56)$$

$$\pi_1 = Ax_1(b + k) - \frac{Ab_{02}x_2(x_1 - x_2)}{2x_2 - g + k(1 + \pi_2)} \qquad (A.57)$$

Government 0 chooses b_{02} to minimize l in equation (A.51) taking into account the optimal responses of governments 1 and 2. Formally, this is equivalent to choosing x_1, x_2, π_1, π_2, and b_{02} to minimize l in equation (A.51) subject to incentive compatibility constraints (A.49) and (A.55)–(A.57). Simulations presented in Table 3.2 are computed by solving numerically the minimization problem of government 0.

NOTES

The authors wish to acknowledge useful comments from William Branson, Allen Drazen, Malcolm Knight, Juan Pablo Nicolini, Maurice Obstfeld, Gerardo della Paolera, Torsten Persson, Thomas Reichmann, Carlos Végh and seminar participants at Castelgandolfo, the World Bank, the Federal Reserve (Washington, D.C.), and the University of Houston.

1 Friedman (1971) was one of the first papers to focus squarely on this issue.
2 Barro and Gordon (1983a, b) have expanded this line of research in several important directions. Persson and Tabellini (1989) provide a comprehensive discussion on the importance of binding incentive constraints for government policy.
3 Obstfeld (1988) shows, for example, that a rational-discretion type model can explain the failure of the inflation-rate series to behave like a martingale, which is an implication of standard precommitment-only models with quadratic and time-separable utility functions (see Mankiw, 1987).
4 For example, existence of complete markets is assumed. It should also be noted that the problem may exhibit multiple equilibria, so decentralization of the good may be at risk (see Calvo, 1988a).
5 This contrasts sharply with the well-trained economists' bias that 'debt maturity is irrelevant, all that matters is present value.'

6   These costs play an important role in the Barro and Gordon (1983a, b) papers. They are assumed away in Persson, Persson and Svensson (1987) but, as shown by Calvo and Obstfeld (1989), their absence prevents attaining the full-precommitment solutions under rational discretion, except in very special cases.

7   This is, incidentally, how incomplete markets will come into the picture.

8   We assume the demand for real monetary balances $k (\geq 0)$ is completely inelastic with respect to its opportunity cost. Relaxation of this assumption is possible but results are not significantly affected.

9   We assume the existence of only one homogenous good, and the strict validity of PPP. Furthermore, we assume that international prices are constant, implying that i^* is also the *real* international rate of interest.

10   In fact, full indexation, i.e., $\theta = 0$, could also achieve the same optimum if we allowed for the interest rate on indexed debt to be a function of the state of nature g.

11   Henceforth we will assume, without loss of generality, that the international interest rate $i^* = 0$.

12   The following results are based on a linearization of equation (3'), as given by equation (16) below.

13   For the sake of brevity, we will concentrate our discussion on the case in which the nominal interest rate i is not state-contingent.

14   A similar argument can be made for the case in which θ goes to minus infinity, because the temptation to generate an infinitely large *de*flation can be shown to be pared down by the undoubtedly large costs of the associated taxes.

15   With perfect certainty, optimal $\theta = 0$ because we have assumed that the demand for money is interest inelastic. It can be shown, however, that if the demand for money is interest elastic, then optimal $\theta < 0$. An optimal $\theta < 0$ is consistent with Persson, Persson and Svensson's (1987) notion that governments should leave net nominal claims on the private sector to their successors.

16   It would be interesting to extend this example in order to account for shocks on k. However, the exercise is not trivial because the problem appears to be inherently nonlinear.

17   The appendix contains the formulas for $k > 0$. In the text, however, the reader will be alerted whenever substantive results change if $k > 0$.

18   Expected inflation in both periods is zero. This follows from the assumption that the conventional base of the inflation tax, k, is assumed to be zero, but it is also a consequence of our linearizations.

19   As shown in the appendix, this does not hold with $k > 0$.

20   As shown in the appendix, if $k > 0$ then optimal $b_{02} > 0$.

21   Spaventa (1987), for example, suggests that the temptation to inflate away the debt could be behind the decision by some governments, like Italy, to load up the short-term end of the maturity spectrum.

22   This is equivalent to setting $\bar{g} + b = 0.8$. Revenues constancy is assumed in order to isolate the total equilibrium revenue requirements from changes in the level of debt, b, which is the focal point of our analysis.

23   As can be seen in the appendix, if $\bar{g} + b$ is held constant then only the product θb matters at optimum (recall, also, that $b_{02} = b$ at optimum). Thus, in Table 3.1, changes in b generate changes in θ that leave θb unchanged. This explains the invariance of cost with respect to b.

24   By way of comparison, notice that the above-mentioned loss would be zero if there were no uncertainty (i.e., $\sigma = 0$). Hence, these costs are intimately related to the randomness of g.

25 This equivalency, however, would break down if uncertainty is not fully resolved in period 1.
26 Uncertainty does not seem to be essential for the following discussion. It should be noted, however, that even under our previous linearizations, the optimum problem of government 1 becomes highly nonlinear, which substantially complicates the analysis of the stochastic case.
27 Some progress on this front has been made by Giavazzi and Pagano (1988).
28 Rogers (1986) is a forerunner in this line of research. Distributional incentives are also discussed by Persson and Tabellini (1989).

REFERENCES

Aizenman, J., and J.A. Frenkel (1985). 'Optimal Wage Indexation, Foreign Exchange Intervention, and Monetary Policy', *The American Economic Review* **75**, 402–23.
Barro, Robert J., and David B. Gordon (1983a). 'A Positive Theory of Monetary Policy in a Natural Rate Model', *Journal of Political Economy* **91**, 589–610.
    (1983b). 'Rules, Discretion and Reputation in a Model of Monetary Policy', *Journal of Monetary Economics* **12**, 101–21.
Bohn, Henning (1988). 'Why Do We Have Nominal Government Debt?', *Journal of Monetary Economics* **21**, 127–40.
Calvo, Guillermo A. (1978). 'Optimal Seigniorage from Money Creation: An Analysis in Terms of the Optimum Balance of Payments Problem', *Journal of Monetary Economics* **4**, 503–17.
    (1987). 'Inflation and Financial Reform', unpublished (University of Pennsylvania).
    (1988a). 'Servicing the Public Debt: The Role of Expectations,' *The American Economic Review* **78**, 647–61.
    (1988b). 'Controlling Inflation: The Problem of Non-Indexed Debt' Washington: International Monetary Fund, Working Paper No. WP/88/29.
Calvo, Guillermo A. and Maurice Obstfeld (1989). 'Time Consistency of Fiscal and Monetary Policy: A Comment', Institute for International Economic Studies, Seminar Paper No. 427 (Stockholm, Sweden), forthcoming in *Econometrica*.
Friedman, Milton (1971). 'Government Revenue from Inflation', *Journal of Politica Economy* **79**, 846–56.
Giavazzi, Francesco, and Marco Pagano (1988). 'Confidence Crises and Public Debt Management', unpublished (Università di Bologna, CEPR, NBER, and Universita' de Napoli).
Gray, Jo Anna (1976). 'Wage Indexation: A Macroeconomic Approach', *Journal of Monetary Economics* **2**, 221–35.
Guidotti, Pablo E., and Carlos A. Végh (1988). 'The Optimal Inflation Tax when Money Reduces Transaction Costs: A Reconsideration' (Washington: International Monetary Fund), unpublished.
Keynes, John M. (1971). *A Tract on Monetary Reform*, Macmillan–St. Martin's Press for the Royal Economic Society, London.
Lothian, James R. (1985). 'Equilibrium Relationships Between Money and Other Economic Variables', *American Economic Review* **75**, 828–35.
Lucas, Robert E., Jr. (1980). 'Two Illustrations of the Optimum Quantity of Money', *American Economic Review* **70**, 1005–14.

Lucas, Robert E., Jr., and Nancy L. Stokey (1983). 'Optimal Fiscal and Monetary Policy in an Economy Without Capital', *Journal of Monetary Economics* **12**, 55–94.

Mankiw, J. Gregory (1987). 'The Optimal Collection of Seigniorage: Theory and Evidence', *Journal of Monetary Economics* **20**, 327–41.

Obstfeld, Maurice (1988). 'Dynamic Seigniorage Theory: An Exploration' unpublished (University of Pennsyvalia and NBER).

Persson, Mats, Torsten Persson, and Lars E.O. Svensson (1987). 'Time Consistency of Fiscal and Monetary Policy', *Econometrica* **55**, 1419–32.

   (1989). 'Time Consistency of Fiscal and Monetary Policy: a Reply', Seminar Paper No. 427, Institute for International Economic Studies (Stockholm, Sweden).

Persson, Torsten and Lars E.O. Svensson (1984). 'Time-Consistent Fiscal Policy and Government Cash Flow', *Journal of Monetary Economics* **14**, 365–74.

Persson, Torsten, and Guido Tabellini (1989). *Macroeconomic Policy, Credibility and Politics*, unpublished monograph.

Phelps, Edmund S. (1973). 'Inflation in the Theory of Public Finance', *Swedish Journal of Economics* **75**, 67–82.

Poterba, James M., and Julio J. Rotemberg (1988). 'Inflation and Taxation with Optimizing Governments' (mimeo).

Rogers, Carol Ann (1986). 'The Effect of Distributive Goals on the Time Inconsistency of Optimal Taxes', *Journal of Monetary Economics* **17**, 251–69.

Spaventa, Luigi (June 1987). 'The Growth of Public Debt: Sustainability, Fiscal Rules, and Monetary Rules' (Washington: International Monetary Fund), *Staff Papers* **34**, 374–9.

Végh, Carlos (1989). 'The Optimal Inflation Tax in the Presence of Currency Substitution', *Journal of Monetary Economics* **24**, forthcoming.

Vogel, R.C. (1974). 'The Dynamics of Inflation in Latin America, 1950–1969', *American Economic Review* **64**, 102–14.

Discussion

WILLIAM H. BRANSON

This complex and interesting paper explores the relationships among the ability of a government to 'precommit' and the optimal degree of debt indexation and maturity structure. The paper is essentially a series of examples using a government budget constraint and a loss function, with no specified model of how the economy works, so it is not clear how general the results are. But the results are intuitively clear. Precommitment and indexation are good, but not perfect, substitutes; indexation seems to me to be a form of precommitment. With precommitment, long debt is optimal, because it allows maximum flexibility in using the inflation tax to smooth the path of the tax burden once uncertainty about shocks is resolved. Without precommitment, the optimal maturity structure becomes shorter, to reduce the temptation on the government to use the inflation tax unexpectedly.

The paper is sufficiently complex that I had to spend quite a bit of time working through the models to see the results. Part of the difficulty comes from the authors' tendency to discuss results before deriving them. But part also is in the complexity of the problems being studied. So before I come to some critical questions at the end of this comment, I will provide a brief reader's guide to the paper, going over the model, the structure of the paper, and the results.

But first, a brief comment on terminology. What is the gain from using the term 'precommitment' instead of simply 'commitment'? My Webster's gives as the second definition of the latter: 'an agreement or pledge to do something in the future'. This seems sufficient to cover the prospective actions considered in this paper, and indeed in the literature on the topic. It is not at all clear what is added by the prefix 'pre' in this case; is it meant to weaken or strengthen the idea of commitment? I think the term should be dropped in favor of ordinary commitment.

The model in the paper is briefly summarized at the beginning of Section 2. The government in each of two or three periods faces a budget constraint of the form of equation (1), and attempts to minimize a loss function given in (2). Explicit taxes and inflation impose losses, and they are necessary to finance a stochastic path of worthless government spending, which provides the necessary uncertainty for the analysis. Strict PPP is assumed, with the world price level set at unity, so the realized inflation rate is the rate of exchange depreciation. Open interest parity is also assumed, with the world interest rate i^* set at zero, so the expected inflation rate is equal to the nominal interest rate i. The government's choice variables are explicit taxes, inflation, the degree of debt indexation, and, in the three-period model, the maturity of the debt. There is no model of the economy to determine the inflation rate or the realized interest rate.

The paper studies first the two-period, and then the three-period case. In each, the perfect-markets solution with the interest rate contingent on the realization for government spending is first obtained as a benchmark. Then solutions are obtained for cases with a fixed interest rate and different degrees of commitment. The government in time 0 (G0) may or may not be able to commit later governments (G1 and G2), or G0 cannot commit, but G1 can commit G2. Government spending is stochastic from the point of view of G0, and the uncertainty is resolved in time 1. In this structure, we look for the optimal, or at least good, degree of debt indexation and maturity structure.

The first result, in the two-period case with state-contingent i, is given in equation (4). With i^* set at 0, explicit taxes are set to finance expected spending plus debt repayment, and the interest rate varies inversely with the deviation of realized spending from expected. The next set of solutions are for fixed i on non-indexed debt, and committed inflation and tax schedules as functions of realizations on spending. These are equations (8) and (9). The second term of (9) is explicit taxes when g is at its expected value. If k is set at zero, this becomes (4). The second term of (8) is just Ak times the second term of (9). With commitment, the degree of indexation is set at zero to maximize the base for the inflation tax in order to minimize fluctuations in the inflation rate. In fact, the committed government would like to be a creditor in indexed bonds! In the discussion that follows, I will consider only cases in which the government has non-negative debt in all periods, since the case of the government as creditor for credibility purposes seems quite unrealistic.

The commitment to a predetermined inflation schedule in (8) raises a credibility question, so the paper turns next to the case of no commitment in the two-period model. The solutions are equations (17) and (18). Again, the second term of (18) is explicit taxes when g is at its expected value, and if k is zero, it becomes (4). With no commitment, the optimal degree of debt indexation becomes positive. With full indexation in both cases, so theta is set at zero, equations (17) and (18) with no commitment are the same as (8) and (9) with commitment. Thus indexation is a substitute for commitment; in fact, it seems to me to be a form of commitment. But it is not not a perfect substitute; the loss function (20) with full indexation is greater than (11) with no indexation.

Discussion of the three-period model begins with a case in which the zero-period government G0 can commit both subsequent governments. The model is simplified by assuming zero holdings of real balances. The solutions are given in equations (27)–(29). As in the two-period case, the optimal degree of indexation is zero with full commitment. In addition, the optimal maturity structure of the debt is 100% long debt, that is, b_{02} in (29) is the same as b in (28). This permits a uniform rate of inflation taxation in periods 1 and 2. This case again raises a credibility issue, so we move to a partial commitment case.

Here G0 cannot commit G1, but after the uncertainty about government spending is resolved in period 1, G1 can commit G2. The solutions are shown in equations (31)–(33), and the G0 loss function is shown in equation (34). In the absence of uncertainty, G0 would like to fully index debt to remove the temptation of G1 or G2 to inflate. This is again a form of commitment. The second best would be to make the debt structure 100% short debt, with b_{02} in the second term of (34) set at zero. With uncertainty, G0 will see that it may be optimal for G1 and G2 to use the inflation tax, setting the two inflation rates in (32) and (33) equal with 100% long debt, and then controlling the size of the inflation tax base by indexing a proportion of the debt. Thus the optimal policy with partial commitment will have long debt and partial indexation.

These results are reflected in the simulation results of Table 3.1. In the first set of simulations all debt is long, the fraction non-indexed is less than 4 percent (the theta and b_{02} columns are in percent), and the loss is a minimal 1.1 percent of GNP. In the second set, no indexation is allowed, the fraction of short debt rises to 95 percent, and the losses rise to a range of 1.4 to 5.1 percent of GNP as inherited debt rises. Thus imposition of the condition of no indexation induces a shift toward short debt, which is a good, but not perfect, substitute for indexation. Finally, imposing no indexation and 100 percent long debt raises the losses to a range of 1.6 to 8.3 percent of GNP. These results make sense, and improve our understanding of the relations among commitment, indexation, and debt maturity.

My satisfaction with the results is undermined a bit by some doubts about the structure of the assumptions behind them. First, government spending is stochastic about its mean, and even its mean is in the loss function, because it has to be financed. I would have mean government spending as a positive good, set by traditional public finance considerations, and perhaps necessary deviations from it as losses. Second, while the authors say at the beginning of Section 4 that 'the optimal policy is quite sensitive to the instruments that can be controlled', they assume that the government can control inflation and the interest rate, but not its own spending, and provide no model of inflation. I would reverse these assumptions. Third, the government can commit indexation, but not other policies; why? The paper lacks a discussion of commitment technology. These aspects of the paper limit it to a series of interesting examples with no underlying model of the economy. Thus we cannot have a clear idea of the generality of the results, even though they are interesting and plausible. The authors still have an intriguing research agenda.

Discussion

ALLAN DRAZEN

1   Introduction

On first reading this paper looks quite daunting. Calvo and Guidotti present a highly stylized and streamlined model, so that a casual reader may get sidetracked into quarrelling with their specialized set-up, or with the assumptions that make it work. This would be a mistake, because the model is highly stylized for a very good reason: Calvo and Guidotti want to present a lot of results in a relatively short space. In this they are quite successful, one may say even too successful. Results 'pour out' of the model, and one is led to ask which assumptions are behind a given result. This question seems especially relevant as simple changes in structure often induce sharp changes in the degree of optimal indexation or the optimal maturity structure of the debt.

I therefore think it is quite useful to organize the results in a way which may help clarify what is driving them. I will argue that in these models there are two general effects of indexation and debt maturity structure which may arise in the various models in the paper, and optimal policy choices may be understood in terms of how these effects can be traded off given the number of instruments available to hit multiple goals. A change in structure which significantly alters the results does so because the change often eliminates a key tradeoff. A further goal of these comments is to ask to what extent the Calvo and Guidotti model provides a positive theory of inflation, indexation, and debt maturity. Here too, viewing things in terms of tradeoffs may be enlightening.

Calvo and Guidotti begin with a world where markets are not perfect and one can not write the necessary state-contingent contracts to get precommitment, as in the work of Lucas and Stokey or Persson, Persson, and Svennson. In the absence of precommitment there exists a tradeoff in designing policy. On the one hand, by reducing the flexibility of a future policymaker, it is possible to get closer to the precommitment solution. Call this the *anti-temptation* motive in policy design. But, by reducing the flexibility of a future policymaker, one limits his ability to respond to future shocks, that is, his ability to smooth a variable tax path. Call this the *smoothing* motive in policy design. The question in deciding on a debt maturity or an indexation structure is how to trade off these two motives. Various cases can be thought of as pure smoothing, pure anti-temptation, or a tradeoff of the two. The striking result in the paper that seemingly small changes in model specification lead to sharp changes in optimal indexation debt maturity structure arises because a change in specification will often eliminate some of the possible tradeoffs.

2   Indexation

Consider first the issue of optimal indexation in Calvo and Guidotti's two-period model, so that no issues of debt maturity arise. The period-one government must levy taxes to pay for current expenditures (which are stochastic) and pay off principal and interest on debt inherited from the period-zero government. I assume throughout that money demand k is identically zero, so that inflation affects the fiscal position of government 1 via the nominal value of the debt it must redeem. This simplifies the exposition, but doesn't change the main conclusions.

When government 0 can precommit government 1 in its choice of inflation, there is no anti-temptation motive for government 0 in deciding on how debt is to be divided between nominal and real. There is only the unavoidable loss from the distortionary taxes needed to pay off government expenditure and debt plus the loss from variance in taxes and inflation due to government expenditures being random. With only the smoothing motive operative the optimal solution is to go to a corner, that is, set the indexation parameter θ as high as possible (high θ means a low level of indexation). To see why, consider inflation as a function of realized government expenditure, (equation (8) in Calvo and Guidotti, where mathematical symbols are the same as their paper except as noted), namely

$$\tau^P(g) = \frac{A\theta b}{1 + A\theta^2 b^2} (g - \bar{g}) \tag{1}$$

where the P superscript denotes the precommitment case. g should be interpreted as government expenditure net of any available non-distortionary taxes. Substituting this and the analogous schedule $x(g)$ for regular (distortionary) taxes into equation (2) in Calvo and Guidotti, expected loss under precommitment may be written

$$l^P = \frac{A}{2}\left[(\bar{g} + b)^2 + \frac{\sigma^2}{1 + A\theta^2 b^2}\right] \tag{2}$$

This formulation highlights the two sources of loss in this basic case, from payoff of expected fiscal requirements plus the loss from variance in government expenditure. Optimal θ is chosen to minimize expected social loss. Clearly the higher is θ in absolute value, the lower is the variance of taxes and the lower is the loss.

The result is intuitive when one realizes that a high value of θ, meaning a large amount of nominal debt widens the tax base for the inflation tax. This allows the same variance in revenue collected for smaller variance in tax rates. The general lesson of course is to widen the tax base as much as possible if variability of tax rates is costly. Allowing θ to go to infinity would introduce lump-sum taxation via the back door.

Suppose now that no precommitment is possible. Interest rate parity means that the known temptation of period-1 government to engage in surprise inflation will be reflected in higher *ex-ante* nominal interest rates. In deciding on the optimal degree of indexation, and hence the optimal tax schedules, the period-zero government must tradeoff the smoothing benefit of higher θ against the anti-temptation benefit of lower θ. In this case the optimal inflation schedule (Calvo and Guidotti's (17)) may be written

$$\pi^D(g) = \pi^P(g) + A\theta b(\bar{g} + b) \tag{3}$$

where the D superscript denotes the solution under discretion. Expected loss of government 0 becomes

$$l^D = \frac{A}{2}\left[(\bar{g} + b)^2 + \frac{\sigma^2}{1 + A\theta^2 b^2} + A\theta^2 b^2(\bar{g} + b)^2\right] \tag{4}$$

showing the two earlier sources of loss, plus a new term yielding the loss due to non-indexed debt giving government 1 the temptation to inflate. Note that while the loss from reduced ability to smooth depends on the variance of g, the temptation for the period one government to deviate, and thus the expected loss from the inability to precommit, depends on the level of g. This observation will be useful below in assessing these results as a basis for a positive theory of government policy.

We see clearly the tradeoff in choosing θ is a tradeoff between the smoothing and the anti-temptation motives. If σ is zero, we go to the other corner of setting $\theta = 0$ (full indexation), since there is only the pure anti-temptation motive. If σ^2 is positive, the tradeoff in choosing optimal indexation depends on the level versus the variance of g. If $\sigma^2 \leq (\bar{g} + b)^2$, then optimal θ is 0. The anti-temptation motive implies a strong anti-inflation policy.

One should be somewhat hesitant to put too much weight on specific results such as this, as well as on some of the specific simulation results. These results are very much dependent not simply on parameter values chosen for a given form of the objective function (for example A), but on the form of the objective function itself. This problem is common, but the criticism may be especially relevant here. What drives the model theoretically is that *actual* inflation has a welfare cost. Here and later on we find that for 'realistic' parameter values, the anti-temptation motive leading to an anti-inflationary policy dominates in choice of indexation. Hence what may be the most problematic assumption is the crucial one in the optimal indexation results. One is then led to ask what are the welfare costs of actual inflation. It would be unrealistic to expect Calvo and Guidotti to flesh out the model sufficiently to specify these costs. But one would like to know how robust are the results on indexation to changes in the loss function. To take but one example, in reality a non-indexed nominal income tax means that π and x interact. How might that affect the results?

3   Debt maturity structure

The second basic issue that Calvo and Guidotti consider is that of optimal debt maturity. Here they use a three-period model, the current period again being zero, the future periods being 1 and 2. Though total debt b is given, government 0 can decide on the amount coming due in period 1, namely b_{01}, and the amount coming due in period 2, b_{02}. Similarly, government 0 has two inflation decisions, over both inflation between periods 0 and 1, namely π_1, and inflation between periods 1 and 2, π_2. Since inflation is obviously cumulative, note that the maturity structure of nominal debt does not affect choice of π_1.

With more periods there are more possible effects to be traded off: the smoothing (for both regular distortionary taxes and inflation) and anti-temptation effects can be thought of as operating both between time 0 and 'the future', meaning periods 1 and 2 taken together, as well as between periods 1 and 2. Different assumptions about the structure of the model reduce the dimensionality of the problem by eliminating some of the possible tradeoffs, and thus may radically alter the nature of optimal policy. In all cases, Calvo and Guidotti assume that g is realized in period one, so that the incentive for regular taxes x to vary between periods one and two for smoothing purposes is eliminated.

Once again, the first case to consider is one where only one of the two main motives operates. In the case of full precommitment, where government 0 can precommit the actions of both governments 1 and 2, there is no anti-temptation motive in choice of indexation and debt maturity structures. Given the assumption about the realization of g in period one, two smoothing motives remain: choice of an average value of x over both future periods for tax smoothing; and choice of π_1 and π_2 for inflation smoothing. Once again we can derive optimal tax schedules. For example inflation in period 2 under full precommitment is

$$\pi_2^P(g) = (A\theta b_{02}/H)(g - \bar{g}) \tag{5}$$

where $H = 2 + A(\theta b)^2 + A(\theta b_{02})^2$. Using this and the analogous schedules for π_1 and x, expected loss becomes

$$l^P = \frac{A}{2}\left[(\bar{g} + b)^2/2 + \sigma^2/H\right] \tag{6}$$

We see there is only the payoff effect (the first term of (6)) and the smoothing effect (the second term). As in section two, indexation and debt maturity cannot affect the loss from the necessary payoff of debt plus average government expenditure. Minimizing (6) with respect to these variables means that either $\theta = \infty$ or $b_{02} = \infty$, or both. Substituting this back into (5) (and the analogous expression for π_1) one finds that with only one motive operative, inflation in both periods is optimally zero. As in the indexation case, it is optimal to go to a corner and increase the inflation tax base as much as possible with no fear of temptation for future governments.

The main case that Calvo and Guidotti consider is an intermediate case of 'partial' precommitment. Government 1 can commit government 2, but government 0 cannot precommit its successors. This means there are the effects from the previous paragraph plus temptation effects on future governments relative to government 0's inflation choices. Denoting this case by D, we have the schedule for π_2 of the form

$$\pi_2^D(g) = \pi_2^P(g) + (A\theta b_{02}/H)\left(\frac{\bar{g} + b}{2}\right) \tag{7}$$

The expected loss function becomes

$$l^P = \frac{A}{2}\left[(\bar{g} + b)^2/2 + \sigma^2/H + \frac{A\theta^2(b_{02}^2 + b^2)}{4}\right] \tag{8}$$

In (8) we see the problem of trading off the smoothing motive (the second term) and the anti-temptation motive (the third term).

In the case where $\sigma^2 = 0$, the optimal structure is full indexation ($\theta = 0$). This solves the temptation problem faced by both governments 1 and 2. The next best solution, if θ is not a choice variable, is to set $b_{02} = 0$. With government 0 unable to index debt fully, having all debt come due in period one means that at least the temptation of government 2 to inflate can be removed. There is an important general lesson here. Short maturity of nominal debt has the effect of indexing. When temptation to inflate is a problem but indexation is not possible, the appropriate debt maturity structure can partially compensate.

Now consider the case where there is partial precommitment and σ^2 is positive, so that both smoothing and anti-temptation motives are present.

Calvo and Guidotti find that if θ is not a choice variable, it is optimal to have very short maturity debt (b_{02} small), as in the pure temptation case, while if θ can be optimally chosen, optimal maturity policy is to go to the other extreme of the longest possible maturities ($b_{02} = b$), as in the pure smoothing case! How can we explain this 'flip-flop' of optimal policy?

With several tradeoffs possible, government 0 knows some inflation is optimal by future governments. It must decide on both the average level of inflation in the future, as well as the relative levels of π_1 and π_2. If θ can be chosen optimally, use $b_{02} = b$ to hit the target of inflation smoothing, that is $\pi_1 = \pi_2$, since the *relative* future inflation rates are affected only by the debt maturity choice, and debt maturity cannot be used to affect average future inflation. This leaves only tradeoffs between the present and the future (periods 1 and 2 taken together). θ should then be used to hit the optimal tradeoff between temptation and tax smoothing between present and future. In short, the structure of the model implies that one instrument and one 'target' are perfectly matched, so that the existence of tradeoffs still implies a corner solution for this instrument.

When θ is not a choice variable, debt maturity cannot be dedicated simply to inflation smoothing and b_{02} must be chosen with all tradeoffs in mind. The parameter values that Calvo and Guidotti consider for the case of θ constrained to be unity (no indexation) imply that the tradeoff favours the anti-temptation motive, with short maturities proxying for indexation.

Finally, Calvo and Guidotti consider the case of no precommitment whatsoever, but where the degree of indexation is fixed and where $\sigma^2 = 0$. The fixed level of indexation knocks out an instrument, and the assumption on σ^2 knocks out any smoothing motives. Only two anti-temptation motives remain to be traded off: the temptation of future governments relative to government 0's optimum; and the temptation of government 2 relative to government 1's optimum. We saw above that partial precommitment means only the first effect is present, and there is nothing to be traded off. Even with indexation not a choice variable, we would have a corner solution. With both anti-temptation motives present but only one instrument, we have an interior solution for b_{02}, meaning a lengthening of maturities relative to the partial precommitment case.

4   Towards a positive theory of government policy

Does the model help explain observed patterns of indexation, inflation, and debt maturity structure? It seems to me that the anti-temptation effect has some predictive power; the smoothing effect is less compelling as a positive theory. This latter criticism is not specific to this paper: I am quite doubtful that monetary or inflation policy can be explained in terms of tax smoothing.

To be more specific, the anti-temptation motive as a positive theory would run as follows. Countries with high financing needs relative to their ability to raise non-distortionary taxes are perceived as likely to succumb to the temptation to use surprise inflation, so that we should observe use of indexation and short maturities of nominal debt to enable them to move closer to a precommitment solution. Israel comes to mind as a good example of this prediction; other examples could be given.

The problem with the smoothing motive as a positive theory is suggested by the following question: can either the lack of indexation or long maturities of the debt be explained by high variance of expenditures? Here one would be doubtful. It is true that once a country has widespread indexation or significant use of foreign currency-denominated financial instruments, policymakers become especially aware of the lack of flexibility this implies and try to move away from such arrangements. Israel, for example, has put limitations on the types of foreign currency-denominated assets that individuals may hold because of the feeling that widespread holding of such assets limited the effectiveness of policy. But the move away from indexation (or analogous asset market arrangements) is not viewed in Israel or elsewhere in terms of tax smoothing. Nor does one really think that the US has *chosen* less indexation to give it more flexibility.

In terms of understanding the results of the paper, it is useful to think about tradeoffs between problems of future tax smoothing and problems of future temptation to deviate from previously announced policies. But in terms of a positive theory of economic policy, the implied tradeoff may be somewhat misleading. As indicated above, high average government expenditures lead to a strong anti-temptation motive in designing policies, high variance of government expenditures to a strong smoothing motive. Hence a positive theory would ask: in a given economy which of the two effects, one related to high mean g, the other to high variance of g, is more important?

To see why this tradeoff may be misleading, consider two economies, the first with *no* non-distortionary tax base; the second with the ability to collect non-distortionary taxes up to an amount τ. For the same pre-distortionary-tax distribution of expenditures, the second economy clearly has lower $\bar{g}$, net-of-nondistortionary-tax average expenditures (and probably lower b inherited from the past as well). Therefore it faces less of a temptation problem. However, given its ability to collect non-distortionary taxes up to an amount τ, the second economy will also have a lower variance of net-of-nondistortionary-tax expenditures.[1] Hence there is less of a smoothing problem as well. Thus for the first economy both temptation and smoothing are problems. For the second neither is. That is, an economy with a poorly-developed and distortionary tax system will find both motives strong, and the notion of looking at different economies as lying at different points on a given tradeoff frontier is not very useful.

The basic problem may be put as follows. A really successful positive theory of indexation and debt maturity structure would link these to more basic characteristics of an economy than the level or variance of government expenditures. The Calvo and Guidotti model is quite successful in investigating how indexation or short debt maturities can substitute for precommitment when government expenditures are random, and the stylized nature of the model is crucial in that success. Its stylized nature makes the model less adequate however as a positive theory of indexation and debt maturity.

NOTE

1 The ability to use non-distortionary taxes *up to* amount τ means that economy two's distribution of g is a truncated version of economy one's distribution, implying a lower variance.

4 Public confidence and debt management: a model and a case study of Italy

ALBERTO ALESINA, ALESSANDRO PRATI and GUIDO TABELLINI

1 Introduction

With a public debt projected to remain close to 100% of GNP for several years in the future, the Italian authorities face two goals: first, to keep the cost of debt service as low as possible; second, to guarantee monetary and financial stability while carrying out the financial liberalization required by the EC accords. This paper investigates the role of public debt management in the achievement of these two goals.

Section 2 of the paper briefly summarizes the debt management policies followed in Italy during the 1980s. Even though in the first half of the decade these policies were quite successful, they may have planted the seeds of the difficulties of the Summer of 1987, which marked a turning point. Unlike in the pre-87 period, the government has been unable to issue long-term debt at low cost. A difficult dilemma has arisen: should the government pay a premium in order to prevent a shortening of the maturity of its debt; and what kind of debt instruments should be issued?

The answers to these questions depend on the nature of the risk premium currently paid on long-term debt. Section 3 asks whether the return on the Italian public debt currently incorporates a premium against the risk of a confidence crisis, or more generally of a government default. This is a difficult question, and any attempt to answer it must be regarded as tentative and not conclusive. However, we do find some evidence that such a premium may exist and may have been rising in recent years.

Section 4 analyses a simple model that begins to address some of the questions relating to debt management and confidence crises. The central result is that the maturity structure of public debt may influence the likelihood of a confidence crisis on the debt: the shorter and more concentrated are the maturities, the more likely is a confidence crisis. This suggests that it may be worth it initially to pay a relatively high interest rate to lengthen the maturity structure: doing so can reduce the risk

94

Years to
maturity

Figure 4.1 Average maturity of Italian government debt, Jan. 1970–June 1989.
Source: Bank of Italy

premium on the whole stock of debt outstanding, since it makes a
confidence crisis less likely.

Finally, Section 5 concludes the paper with a discussion of some normative implications of our model about debt management policies.

2 Debt management in Italy during the 1980s

As shown in Figure 4.1, Italy approached the 1980s with a short and
rapidly declining maturity of public debt. In 1981, about 60% of the debt
had a maturity of less than a year; the average maturity of the whole debt
outstanding was less than one and a half years. Virtually all of it was
nominal domestic debt. Investors had suffered capital losses during the
late 1970s, due to rising inflation and high nominal interest rates. Afraid
of repeating the same mistakes, they were reluctant to hold long-term
fixed-interest nominal debt (see Pagano, 1988).

In order to lengthen the maturity of public debt, the authorities could
choose between three instruments: foreign currency debt, debt indexed to
the price level, or debt indexed to some short-term nominal interest rate.
The fourth option, fixed nominal interest debt, would have demanded an
excessively high premium against the inflation risk. The authorities opted
heavily for the third alternative. As indicated in Table 4.1, between 1982

	Total (% of GDP)	BOT	CCT	BTP (% of total Issues)	Foreign currency	Others
			Gross			
1980	35.97	90.78	9.21	0.01	0.00	0.00
1981	46.70	91.39	4.25	2.54	0.00	1.83
1982	59.71	83.95	14.51	0.94	0.44	0.16
1983	56.46	74.89	20.99	3.66	0.18	0.28
1984	47.34	66.51	27.82	5.18	0.49	0.00
1985	47.62	66.64	25.28	4.50	0.88	2.71
1986	44.96	66.39	19.79	13.30	0.52	0.00
1987	41.45	78.25	13.73	4.68	0.72	2.62
1988	42.27	77.01	5.14	14.19	3.23	0.43
			Net			
1980	6.24	104.64	11.04	−6.96	0.00	−8.72
1981	8.90	79.80	6.65	9.23	0.00	4.32
1982	10.32	56.80	47.70	−2.84	2.49	−4.15
1983	12.79	13.80	83.10	4.66	0.79	−2.35
1984	10.04	12.83	78.29	11.64	2.33	−5.09
1985	13.20	12.42	74.05	3.74	3.17	6.61
1986	10.87	9.98	55.10	36.05	2.14	−3.27
1987	8.57	30.17	42.28	16.07	3.48	8.00
1988	9.50	35.36	−7.65	58.31	15.21	−1.23

Table 4.1. Gross and net issues of Italian public debt, 1980–88

Note: Foreign currency = BTE + CTE.
Source: Bank of Italy.

and 1987 they increased considerably the net issues of CCT (Treasury Credit Certificates), medium-term notes whose coupons are indexed to the returns on 6-months or 1-year Treasury Bills (TBs). As shown in Figure 4.1, they succeeded in lengthening the average maturity of government debt from a minimum of 14 months in 1982 to a maximum of almost 4 years in the summer of 1987.

The authorities preferred financial indexation to price level indexation on the grounds that the latter would have reduced the Treasury's incentives to fiscal adjustment and it would have affected the credibility of their anti-inflationary policy (an essential part of which was a reduction of wage indexation). These concerns are clearly indicated in the 1981 'concluding remarks' of the Governor of the Bank of Italy (see Banca d'Italia 1981). These issues are also discussed in Spaventa (1988).

Other less compelling reasons have been suggested to explain this choice in favour of CCTs. It has been argued that financial indexation is preferred by the investor to price-level indexation or to foreign currency debt, and hence demands a lower premium, because it protects against inflation risk as well as against changes in the short-term real interest rate. However, this cannot be an argument for issuing *only* financially indexed long-term debt. An additional explanation is the fear that issuing real or foreign currency debt makes it impossible to reduce the burden of the debt by means of inflation or devaluation in case of an emergency. However, the government still retains other escape clauses, such as wealth taxation, forced consolidation, or outright repudiation. We discuss this issue in Section 5.

The almost exclusive reliance on financial indexation had two negative effects. First, it magnified the repercussions of monetary policy on the government budget. Any change in the short-term interest rate automatically affected the interest payments on a large fraction of the government debt. Thus, one of the purposes of lengthening the maturity was defeated.

Second, the choice of the indexation parameter (the rate on Treasury Bills) gave rise to a time-inconsistency problem. The value of this parameter is under the control of the authorities. Thus they have a temptation to keep it high at first, when the debt is issued, and to reduce it once the private sector is locked into an irreversible investment decision, thereby inflicting a capital loss on the debt holders. After 1985, perhaps the authorities were succumbing to this temptation. As indicated in Figure 4.2, after 1985 the rate of return on the 1-year TBs (to which much of the debt was indexed) remained systematically below that on the shorter-term TBs, right up to the crisis of 1987. At the same time, as shown in Figure 4.3, the return on the 1-year TBs was also generally below that on medium-term government bonds. The positive differential between 3-month (or 6-month) and 1-year TBs is particularly striking in the first half of 1987, just prior to the crisis. Presumably, at that time the market was expecting higher nominal rates in the future; and yet the authorities were not allowing the 1-year rate to budge.

As pointed out by Bencini and Tabellini (1987) and Ministero del Tesoro (1989), the perception of this time-inconsistency was probably one of the causes of the crisis in the Summer of 1987, even though other factors have played an important role.[1] In the few months after July 1987, the secondary market price of CCTs plummeted by more than 3 percentage points. Since then, the market for this debt instrument has not recovered, and the authorities have been unable to replace all of the CCTs as they became

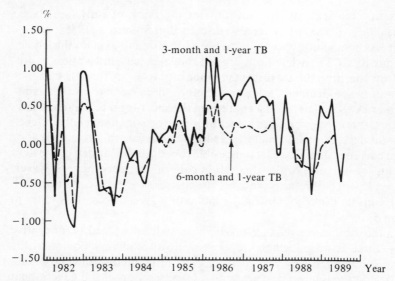

Figure 4.2   Interest differentials on Italian Treasury Bills (TB), 1982–89.
Source: Bank of Italy.

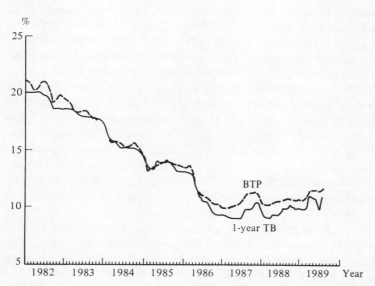

Figure 4.3   Rate of return on Italian medium-term government bonds and 1-year Treasury Bills, 1982–89.
Source: Bank of Italy.

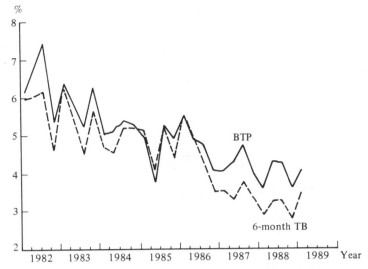

Figure 4.4 *Ex ante* **real returns on Italian medium-term government bonds (BTP) and 6-month Treasury Bills, 1982–89.**
Source: Bank of Italy and *Forum-Mondo Economico* (see text).

due. Since the summer of 1987, the sales of CCTs to the public have never been fully subscribed. At times the market bought even less than 50% of the amount offered.

This crisis marked a turning point. The previous strategy of financing the deficit by issuing CCTs had to be discontinued. Perhaps a new debt management strategy has not yet emerged. As indicated in Table 4.1, in 1988 the government had to resume the old policy of issuing large amounts of short-term Treasury Bills, implying a fall of the average maturity of the debt. The government also issued large amounts of medium-term fixed nominal-interest debt of a high interest rate. Figure 4.4 compares the *ex ante* real rates of return net of taxes on fixed-interest government bonds (BTP) and on 6-months Treasury Bills. Both rates display a common declining trend that reflects a decrease in real interest rates throughout the world. But since the Summer of 1987, the BTP have paid almost 1 percentage point in real terms more than Treasury Bills. A similar pattern emerges if one compares the real yield on the CCT and on the 6-months Treasury Bills.[2] Clearly, the market is unwilling to hold medium-long-term debt without compensation.[3]

The criticial question is: what is the nature of this risk premium? If the premium represents the expectation of forthcoming inflation and our measures of the *ex ante* real rates are wrong, then the course of action for

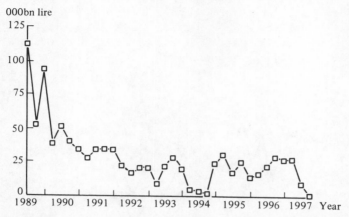

Figure 4.5   Maturing Italian government debt in 1989–97, as of April 1989.
000 mn lire: quarterly data at par value.
Source: Bank of Italy.

the government is clear. Foreign currency and real (i.e., indexed) debt should be issued in much larger amounts. This policy has been advocated by a committee of Italian economists, established by the Treasury ministry in 1988 – see Ministero del Tesoro (1989). There is however a second possibility. The high real interest rates currently paid on the Italian long-term debt may represent also a premium against a more general and vague risk of a financial crisis. In this second case, changing the nature of the debt instrument would not reduce the risk premium.

By financial crisis we do not mean that the government deliberately and unexpectedly chooses to default on its debt. This possibility seems very remote. In the current Italian situation it would probably have very high political costs, by disrupting the system of financial intermediation and causing arbitrary wealth redistribution. What we have in mind instead is the possibility of a crisis initiated by a reluctance of investors to roll over the public debt. In such an event, default or consolidation may be the only way out. But the realization that, in the event of a confidence crisis, the government would be forced to a default, may be enough to trigger a crisis. A run on government debt could be self-fulfilling, just like a bank run (see also Bencini and Tabellini, 1988). Figure 4.5 suggests that even disregarding the primary deficits, in the next few years the government is called on to roll over a large fraction of its outstanding debt. The authorities may be able to withstand a temporary crisis, as they did in 1982, when a large part of the maturing debt was bought by the Bank of Italy, who then resold it to the financial markets in the form of repurchase agreements. But would the system be able to survive a more prolonged confidence crisis? And even if the answer is positive, would the public believe that the system can survive? We now turn to some evidence suggesting that private investors may already fear negative answers to these questions.

3 Rates of return on the Italian public debt

This section asks what is the nature of the risk premium on the Italian public debt. We attempt to discriminate between two alternative sources of risk. (a) Inflation risk, due to the fact that most of the outstanding debt is nominal; (b) risk of a financial crisis leading up to public debt consolidation or default. To do so, we compare the returns on public debt to those on equivalent private financial instruments. We always find that the public debt pays a higher interest rate. This suggests that it is the identity of the debtor, and not the nature of the instrument, that is feared by the market.

3.1 Interest rate differentials on short-term debt

The only financial instruments similar to Treasury Bills (TBs) are the Certificates of Deposit (CDs) of corresponding maturity issued by banks. The differentials between the interest rates net of taxes paid on three- and twelve-month TBs and the interest rates on CDs of corresponding maturity are shown in Figures 4.6 and 4.7.[4]

These figures are striking. The TBs pay interest rates which are between two and four points above the interest rates paid on CDs. The differentials relative to 12-month TBs indicate again an increasing trend starting in 1987. It is also worth noting the peaks of March and April 1989, which reflect the issue difficulties of those months accompanied by a one-point increase of the official discount rate. A very similar pattern is followed by the differential between 6-month TBs and 6-month CDs.

This differential between TBs and CDs is high by international standards, as shown in Table 4.2. The high-debt countries are those in which the Treasury Bills pay a higher rate, while in the low-debt countries the relationship is reversed. We should note however that the size of the Italian differential could also be attributed to the illiquidity of the secondary market for TBs and to the possible existence of informal repurchase agreements for CDs between banks and depositors, which would make the CDs more liquid than the TBs. Since the Italian market for the CDs developed only recently, it is impossible to compute a differential before mid-1984. In that period the closest substitute for TBs was saving deposits. Figure 4.8 shows the interest differential between TBs and savings deposits for the

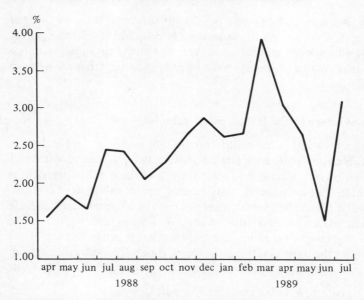

Figure 4.6 Interest differential between Italian 3-month Treasury Bills and 3-month certificates of deposit (CD), April 1988–July 1989.
Source: Bank of Italy.

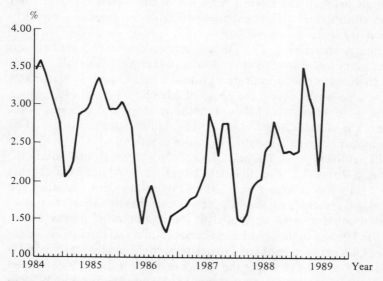

Figure 4.7 Interest differential between Italian 12-month Treasury Bills and 12-month certificates of deposit (CD), 1984–89.
Source: Bank of Italy.

	Debt/GDP (%)	TB3–CD3 Differential
Belgium	126	2.2
Italy	95	1.0 (2.7)[a]
Netherlands	80	0.9
Canada	69	−0.1
Japan	68	−2.1
United States	52	−1.1
Great Britain	45	−0.4
Germany	45	−0.1

Table 4.2. Short-term interest differential and debt–GNP ratios in selected countries, 1988

[a]All differentials are gross of taxes (the net of taxes Italian differential is reported in parenthesis and it is the 1988 average of the differential in Figure 4.6). For Belgium, Canada, Germany and the Netherlands, the interest rate on 3-month CDs corresponds to the interest rate on 3-month time deposits.
Source: Bank of International Settlements Databank.

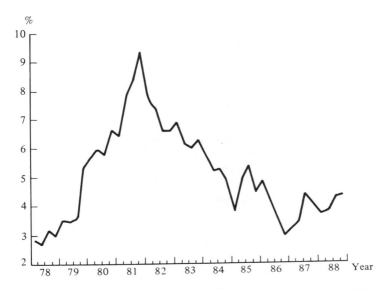

Figure 4.8   Interest differential between Italian 1-year Treasury Bills and savings deposits, 1978–88.
Source: Bank of Italy.

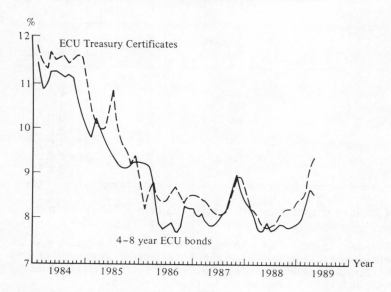

Figure 4.9   Secondary market yields of ECU bonds, 1984–89.
Source: Bank of Italy.

3.2   Interest differentials on medium/long-term debt

period 1978–88.[5] The differential is negatively correlated with the average maturity of government debt. This negative correlation is consistent with the predictions of our theoretical model of debt runs.[6]

The possibility of a risk premium on the Italian government debt can also be investigated by comparing the yield on ECU-denominated government bonds (CTE) with the average yield of ECU bonds of corresponding maturity (4–8 years). Figure 4.9 indicates that the yield net of taxes on the Italian bonds was higher on average than the yield on ECU bonds. The differential diminished and almost disappeared in 1987; since 1988, however, we can note again a premium on CTE. This evidence is again consistent with the view that the risk premium varies inversely with the average maturity of the debt. Note that the yield on CTE is net of taxes while that on ECU bonds is gross of taxes, so that the after-tax differential should be even more favourable to CTE.

Figure 4.10 shows the interest rates at issue on 2–3 year BTPs and 18–24 month certificates of deposit issued by special credit institutions. The differential is always favourable to the BTPs with peaks in 1987 and in the first months of 1989. The differential is even more remarkable if one considers that 1988 was a boom year for certificates of deposit of the

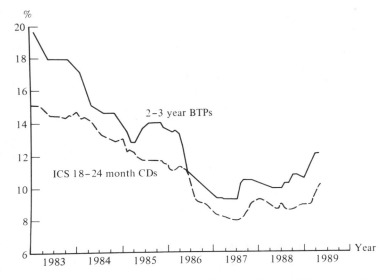

Figure 4.10 Interest rates at issue on Italian 2–3 year BTP and 18–24 month CD issued by special credit institutions, 1983–89.
Source: Bank of Italy.

special credit institutions: in spite of the differential, this kind of CDs increased by 41% relative to 1987.

Summarizing, this evidence suggests that private investors may fear a confidence crisis on the Italian public debt. We now turn to a theoretical model that analyses how such a crisis might take place.

4 A model of debt runs

The basic result of this section is that a crisis of confidence in the public debt can be self-fulfilling, like a bank run; but it is less likely to occur if the public debt has a long and balanced maturity structure.

4.1 Introduction and review of the literature

The idea that there may be an analogy between a bank run and a run on government debt has a long tradition, but the most recent treatments are in Parcu (1986) and Calvo (1988). The latter studies a two-period model of a small open economy: if the government repudiates its debt, it bears a cost proportion to the amount repudiated. Calvo shows that two equilibria exist: a 'good' equilibrium in which the government honours its debt, and a 'bad' equilibrium, in which investors expect the government to partially repudiate and demand a higher interest rate, and the government fulfills these expectations. Calvo's 'bad' equilibrium is similar to the banking panic studied by Diamond and Dybvig (1983); it reflects a coordination problem among investors making *simultaneous* portfolio decisions. If an investor expects all the other investors to demand a risk premium, he realizes that the government will be forced to partially repudiate in the future; thus, his optimal response is also to demand a risk premium.

The confidence crisis that we study in this paper, instead, reflects a coordination problem among individuals making investment decisions *at different dates*. We study an infinite-horizon model in which the optimal government policy is to roll over its debt for ever. There are two equilibria. In one this optimal policy is expected by investors and carried out by the government. In the other current investors refuse to buy any public debt, in the anticipation that future investors will do likewise, and the government is forced to repudiate. A second difference between Calvo's model and ours is in the specification of the cost of default. These differences imply that in our model, unlike in Calvo's, the larger is the stock of debt maturing in a given period, the greater is the range of parameter values for which a crisis can occur. This feature of our model provides a role for debt management.

Giavazzi and Pagano (this volume) derive results related to ours. However, in their paper, unlike in ours, the policy that gives rise to the debt run is not derived from the government optimization problem but is postulated exogenously. In addition, they focus on repudiation by means of exchange-rate devaluation; whereas we consider outright repudiation. Prati (1989) models a confidence crisis along lines similar to this paper, but focuses on nominal debt and disregards debt management.

4.2   The model

A small open economy is inhabited by an infinitely-lived representative consumer, maximizing:

$$U = \sum_{t=0}^{\infty} \beta^t u(c_t) \quad 1 > \beta > 0 \tag{1}$$

where c_t denotes consumption and $u(\cdot)$ is a well-behaved concave utility function. In each period he receives one unit of non-storable output and pays a distorting tax τ_t to the government. This tax is distorting: in addition to paying the tax, the consumer loses an amount $f(\tau_t)$ every time the tax is collected, where $f(0) = 0$, $f'(\cdot) >$, $f''(\cdot) > 0$. Thus, the consumer's disposable income in each period is

$$F(\tau_t) \equiv 1 - \tau_t - f(\tau_t) \tag{2}$$

This specification and, in particular, the convexity of $f(\cdot)$ captures in a very simple way the well-known idea that 'tax smoothing' is desirable. Alternatively, one could introduce a labour supply decision with a distortionary income tax. Such a model, however, introduces subtle time-consistency problems which we want to abstract from (see Lucas and Stokey, 1983, and Persson and Tabellini, 1990, on this point).

Consumers have access to perfect international capital markets in which they can borrow or lend at a risk-free gross real interest rate equal to their discount factor, $1/\beta$. External tax-free assets held by the consumers at the beginning of period t are denoted e_t. The government only issues one-period discount debt and there is no domestic government debt held abroad. With no loss of generality, there is no government spending. In each period the government decides how much tax revenue to raise and whether or not to honour its outstanding debt obligations; thus, policy commitments are ruled out. Debt repudiation is costly: the first time some debt is repudiated, the economy bears a cost proportional to output (which is normalized to 1); that is, output is reduced by a fraction $\alpha > 0$ in the period in which repudiation occurs for the first time. This cost represents the economic disruptions that may be brought about by a default on government debt, such as bankruptcies in financial markets, uncertainty, and disruption in the allocation of resources. With no change in the results, we could assume that this cost affects government utility rather than its budget constraint.

Based on these assumptions, we can write the private sector and the government intertemporal budget constraints respectively as:

$$q_t b_{t+1} + \beta e_{t+1} + c_t \leq F(\tau_t) + e_t + b_t(1 - \theta_t) - D(\theta_t) \tag{3}$$

$$b_t(1 - \theta_t) \leq \tau_t + q_t b_{t+1} \tag{4}$$

where b_t denotes the stock of domestic government debt at the beginning of period t, q_t is the market price at which new debt is issued, θ_t is the fraction of debt repudiated at time t, and $D(\theta_t)$ denotes the cost of repudiation. Our assumption about the costs of default is summarized by

$$D(\theta_t) = 0 \quad \text{if} \quad \theta_t = 0 \quad \text{or} \quad \theta_{t-i} = 1, \quad i > 0 \tag{5}$$

$$D(\theta_t) = \alpha \quad \text{otherwise}$$

Within each period, the timing of events is as follows. First, the government announces a price q_t at which it stands ready to sell the debt, and the maximum amount for sale. Then, on the basis of that price, the private sector chooses how much debt to buy. Finally, the government chooses the combination of τ_t and θ_t that satisfies the government budget constraint, given the amount of debt outstanding, b_t, and the debt just sold, b_{t+1}.

Alternatively, the timing of events could be as follows. First, the government announces the maximum amount of debt for sale. Then, the private sector chooses the price at which it is ready to buy the debt offered (β or zero, corresponding to $\theta^e_{t+1} = 0$ or $\theta^e_{t+1} = 1$, where e superscript denotes private expectations). Finally the government chooses the combination of τ_t and θ_t that satisfies the government budget constraint. The two timings correspond to different auction techniques. The technique used to auction TBs in Italy until March 1989 is very similar to the first timing of events, since the government announced a minimum price and an amount offered before the public made its bids. Since March 1989, the technique used to auction TBs corresponds to the second timing of events, since the government announces *only* the amount offered. Both timing assumptions guarantee the separation between the time at which the debt is offered and the time at which the public makes its bids, that is crucial for our results. Section 4.5 discusses alternative timing assumptions.

All private agents have the same (perfect) information as the government. Thus, a no-arbitrage condition between the returns on domestic and foreign assets implies

$$q_t = \beta(1 - \theta^e_{t+1}) \tag{6}$$

At time 0 a positive stock of debt outstanding b_0 is held by the consumer. For a discussion of this point see Section 4.5. Finally, the government maximizes the utility of the consumer.

An equilibrium is defined as a situation in which, in each period and for all sequences of previous aggregate histories: (i) The price q_t is optimal for the government, given the private sector reaction to the announced price. (ii) The private sector portfolio decision is optimal, given the price q_t announced by the government and the expected future equilibrium outcomes. (iii) The choice of taxes τ_t and θ_t is optimal for the government, given the private current investment decision and the effect of the current policy on the expected future equilibrium outcomes.[7]

4.3   Multiple equilibria with one-period debt

Any equilibrium must have the following properties: (a) Either $\theta_t = 0$ or $\theta_t = 1$. This is due to the lump-sum nature of the costs of defaulting.[8] Equation (6) then implies that the price at which investors are willing to buy government debt is either $q_t = \beta$ (if no default is expected) or $q_t = 0$ (otherwise). (b) If the government defaults, it always does it in period 0. Delaying the default does not reduce its cost, but it brings about more tax distortions while the debt is serviced.

We now characterize the 'good' equilibrium: by Property (b) we only need to consider period 0. If at time 0 the government defaults, then the consumer's consolidated budget constraint from time 0 onward is:

$$e_0 + \frac{1}{1 - \beta} - \alpha \geq \sum_{t=0}^{\infty} \beta^t c_t \tag{7}$$

Standard results of consumption theory imply that the optimal consumption path is constant, and by (7) it is:

$$c_t = (1 - \beta)e_0 + 1 - \alpha(1 - \beta) \equiv c^d \quad t = 0, 1, \ldots \tag{8}$$

Suppose instead that $\theta_t = \theta_{t+1}^e = 0$ for every t. The optimal policy is to raise taxes to pay interest on the debt and roll over the principal:

$$\tau_t = (1 - \beta)b_0 \equiv \tau^* \quad t = 0, 1, \ldots \tag{9}$$

Equation (9) captures the basic result of 'optimal tax smoothing'. The consumer now maximizes (1) subject to (2), where $D(\theta_t) = 0$, and chooses:

$$c_t = (1 - \beta)e_0 + 1 - f[(1 - \beta)b_0] \equiv c^* \quad t = 0, 1, \ldots \tag{10}$$

That is, in every period consumption is equal to disposable income plus the interest payments on the initial foreign assets.

In period 0, the government will choose *not* to repudiate if and only if:

$$c^* \geq c^d \tag{11}$$

(without loss of generality we assume that an indifferent government chooses *not* to repudiate). Using (8) and (10), condition (11) implies that repudiation occurs if and only if it costs less than the present value of the tax distortions needed to service the debt:

$$\alpha \geq \frac{1}{1 - \beta} f[(1 - \beta)b_0] \equiv \underline{\alpha} \tag{12}$$

A confidence crisis is triggered by the investor's beliefs that in the next period the government will *not* be able to roll over the debt and will be forced to default. Thus, if a crisis occurs in period t, $\theta_{t+1}^e = 1$; investors require immediate full repayment of the principal and invest in foreign assets. For the moment we take these expectations as exogenous; we show below under what conditions they are rational and self-fulfilling. Faced by a confidence crisis, the government has two choices:[9] (1) to raise taxes and repay the debt; (2) to default immediately. If the government chooses to default, from then onward consumption is c^d as defined in (8). If the government chooses to raise taxes, income falls by the amount of the tax distortions, $f(b_0)$. Clearly, raising taxes in response to a confidence crisis is superior to defaulting if and only if

$$\alpha \geq f(b_0) \equiv \bar{\alpha} \tag{13}$$

Lemma 1: $\bar{\alpha} > \underline{\alpha}$

Proof. $\bar{\alpha} > \underline{\alpha}$ is equivalent to $(1 + \beta)f(b_0) > f((1 - \beta)b_0)$. This inequality follows immediately from the strict convexity of $f(\cdot)$ and from $f(0) = 0$.

Q.E.D.

Proposition 1: *(i) If $\alpha < \underline{\alpha}$ there is a unique equilibrium in which default occurs in the first period: $\theta_0 = 1$, (θ_t^e, θ_t are indeterminate for $t > 0$). (ii) If $\alpha \geq \bar{\alpha}$ there is a unique equilibrium in which default never occurs, and $\theta_{t+1}^e = \theta_t = 0$ $\forall t$. (iii) $\underline{\alpha} \geq \alpha < \bar{\alpha}$ there are two Pareto-ranked equilibria. In the good equilibrium, default never occurs, i.e., $\theta_{t+1}^e = \theta_t = 0$ $\forall t$. In the bad equilibrium default occurs in the first period, i.e., $\theta_0 = \theta_1^e = 1$.*

Proof. (i) Follows immediately from (12). (ii) From (13) $\theta_t = \theta_{t+1}^e = 0$ is an equilibrium. To prove uniqueness, consider the event of a crisis: from (13), if $b_{t+1} = 0$, then $\theta_t = 0$ and taxes are raised to repay the debt. By (5) it then follows that $\theta_{t+1} = 0$. Hence $\theta_{t+1}^e = 1$ cannot be an equilibrium, since it violates rational expectations. (iii) By (12), $\theta_t = 0$ if $q_t = \beta$ and all the debt is rolled over. Hence, $\theta_t = 0$ is the government best response to $\theta_{t+1}^e = 0$. And $\theta_{t+1}^e = 0$ is the private sector best response to $\theta_{t+2}^e = 0$. But by (13), $\theta_t = 1$ if $\theta_{t+1}^e = 1$ and no debt is sold. Hence $\theta_t = 1$ is the government best response to $\theta_{t+1}^e = 1$. By repeating the same argument for period $t + 1$, $\theta_{t+1} = 1$ is the government best response to $\theta_{t+2}^e = 1$, irrespective of the value of θ_t – see also (5). As a consequence $\theta_{t+1}^e = 1$ is the private sector best response to $\theta_{t+2}^e = 1$. Q.E.D.

The crucial point is that if $\underline{\alpha} \leq \alpha < \bar{\alpha}$ there are two equilibria, with and without default, depending upon the occurrence of a confidence crisis.[10]

The proof relies on the lump-sum nature of these repudiation costs, which rules out partial default. Suppose that the repudiation costs were linear in the amount defaulted, and consisted of both a fixed and a variable component. The good equilibrium with no default would still be described as in Proposition 1. However, a confidence crisis could now take other forms in addition to those described in that Proposition. In particular, confidence crisis similar to those of Calvo (1988) would also be possible, in which a partial default occurs because investors fear a fall in the demand for public debt in the current period.

4.4   Multiple equilibria with multi-period debt

Let us assume that there exist 'short-term' debt (i.e., of one period) and 'long-term' debt (i.e., two periods). The consumer maximizes the same objective function as above, subject to the following new budget constraint, where $_ib_j$ ($i < j$) indicates debt issued in period i which matures in period j and $_iq_j$ is its market price:

$$c_t + \beta e_{t+1} + {}_tq_{t+1}\,{}_tb_{t+1} + {}_tq_{t+2}\,{}_tq_{t+2} \leq F(\tau_t)$$
$$+ e_t - D(\theta_t) + {}_{t-1}b_t(1 - \theta_t) + {}_{t-2}b_t(1 - \theta_t) \tag{14}$$

In (14) we assume that the default parameter (θ_t) is the same for both types of debt maturing at time t. The budget constraint of the government is:

$$_{t-1}b_t(1 - \theta_t) + _{t-2}b_t(1 - \theta_t) \le \tau_t + _tb_{t+1} \, _tq_{t+1} + _tb_{t+2} \, _tq_{t+2} \quad (15)$$

The no arbitrage conditions require:

$$_tq_{t+1} = \beta(1 - \theta^e_{t+1}) \quad _tq_{t+2} = \beta^2(1 - \theta^e_{t+2}) \quad (16)$$

Let us consider first under what conditions the government does not default in the absence of a crisis. The discounted present value of the debt outstanding at the beginning of period 0 is:

$$b \equiv \, _{-1}b_0 + \, _{-2}b_0 + \beta_{-1}b_1 \quad (17)$$

Hence the optimal tax rate is:

$$\tau_t = (1 - \beta)b \equiv \tau^*, \quad t = 0, 1, \ldots \quad (18)$$

Repeating the same argument illustrated in the previous subsection, we can conclude that the government will not repudiate in the absence of a crisis if the previous condition $\alpha \ge \underline{\alpha}$ holds, where $\underline{\alpha}$ is defined as in (12), except that now b replaces b_0.[11]

Consider now a confidence crisis in period t. Suppose first that the private sector followed an open-loop strategy, in the sense that the private expectations θ^e_{t+i}, $i > 0$, do not depend on the aggregate history of the game in previous periods. If $\theta^e_{t+i} = 1$, $i > 0$, then in period t the government can either default, in which case consumption from then onward is c^d as in (8), or it can repay the debt. In the latter case, since by hypothesis private expectations are given and equal to 1, taxes have to be as follows:

$$\tau_t = \, _{t-1}b_t + \, _{t-2}b_t \quad (19)$$

$$\tau_{t+1} = \, _{t-1}b_{t+1} \quad (20)$$

$$\tau_s = 0, \quad s > t + 1 \quad (21)$$

If the government chooses to repay, consumption from t onwards (C^R) is:

$$c^R_s = 1 + e_t(1 - \beta) - (1 - \beta)[f(_{t-1}b_t + _{t-2}\text{b}_t) \\ + \beta f(_{t-1}b_{t+1})] \quad s \ge t \quad (22)$$

From (8) and (22) it follows that in the event of a crisis the government chooses to repay if and only if:

$$\alpha \ge [f(_{t-1}b_t + _{t-2}b_t) + \beta f(_{t-1}b_{t+1})] \equiv \quad \bar{\alpha}_t \quad (23)$$

As in the previous subsection, it can be shown that, since no debt is repaid between periods 0 and t, $\bar{\alpha}_t > \underline{\alpha}$ for all t. Hence, if $\bar{\alpha}_t > \alpha \ge \underline{\alpha}$, there exists an (open-loop) equilibrium in which a confidence crisis occurs in period t or earlier.[12]

Clearly, by (23), $\bar{\alpha}_t$ depends on the maturity structure of public debt.

Proposition 2: *If the private sector plays an open-loop strategy, the equilibrium with a confidence crisis is least likely to exist if only long-term debt is issued, and if the same amount of debt matures in each period.*

Proof: By definition, $\underline{\alpha}$ depends only on the present value of the total debt outstanding, and not on its maturity composition. Consider the sequence $\{\bar{\alpha}_t\}$, $t = 0, 1, \ldots$, and define $\bar{\alpha}^*$ as the maximal element of that sequence. We want to find the maturity structure that minimizes $\bar{\alpha}^*$, for a given net present value of the total debt outstanding. A constant net present value of debt implies:

$$_{t-1}b_t + {}_{t-2}b_t + \beta\,{}_{t-1}b_{t+1} \equiv b, \quad t = 0, 1, \ldots \tag{24}$$

Consider the problem of minimizing $\bar{\alpha}_t$ as defined in (23), by choice of $_{t-2}b_t$, $_{t-1}b_t$ and $_{t-1}b_{t+1}$, subject to (24). The first order conditions of this problem imply:

$$_{t-1}b_t + {}_{t-2}b_t = {}_{t-1}b_{t+1} \tag{25}$$

The maximal element $\bar{\alpha}^*$ is minimized when all the elements of the sequence $\{\bar{\alpha}_t\}$ are minimized, which happens when (25) holds for all t. Combining (24) and (25) we then obtain that $_{t-1}b_t = 0$ and $_{t-2}b_t = {}_{t-1}b_{t+1}$ for all t. Only two-period debt must be issued, in equal amounts in each period.   Q.E.D.

This result is due to the convexity of the tax collection costs. When a large amount of debt falls due in a given period, the cost of repaying it in the event of a confidence crisis is high. Hence, a crisis is more likely to result in default. By holding a long and balanced maturity structure, the government reduces the cost of responding to a crisis by raising taxes, since the tax burden is distributed over several periods.

Proposition 2 can easily be generalized to a debt of more than two periods. In the limit, if all debt is consols, a confidence crisis is ruled out and $\bar{\alpha} = \underline{\alpha}$. In this limiting case, there is no need to roll over the principal, and taxes are raised just to pay interest on the debt.

Next, consider the case in which the private sector plays a feedback strategy. Thus, θ_{t+1}^e is now allowed to depend on the aggregate history up to period $t + i - 1$. In particular, in a sequentially rational Nash equilibrium, θ_{t+1}^e is a function of the stock of debt outstanding in the previous period, b_{t+i-1}. Suppose that $\theta_{t+1}^e = 1$. If the government chooses not to repudiate the debt, in period t it has to raise taxes in the amount:

$$\tau_t = {}_{t-1}b_t + {}_{t-2}b_t \tag{20'}$$

But now, the total stock of debt outstanding next period is $_{t-1}b_{t+1}$. Servicing this debt or even repaying it all at once entails smaller tax distortions. Hence, the continuation of the confidence crisis beyond period t is now less likely. If $_{t-1}b_{t+1}$ is sufficiently small (so that $\underline{\alpha} > (_{t-1}b_{t+1})$), the continuation of the crisis past period t is ruled out altogether. Thus, when the private sector plays a feedback strategy, long-term public debt has an additional advantage besides that discussed with reference to Proposition 2. Namely, it enables the government to regain the confidence of investors by partially repaying some of the debt outstanding. This point is developed by Lars Svensson, in his comments on this paper.

4.5   Extensions and discussion

4.5.1 Government spending, or where does the initial debt come from?
An alternative interpretation of our results is as follows. Suppose that there is no initial debt, but the government needs to issue debt to finance a temporarily high level of spending in period 0. The optimal policy is to issue debt in period 0 and roll it over for ever, so as to smooth tax distortions over time. If α is sufficiently high (higher than $\bar{\alpha}$) debt can be issued regardless of 'confidence'; if $\alpha < \underline{\alpha}$ debt cannot be issued and no tax smoothing can be achieved. In the intermediate case, $\underline{\alpha} \leq \alpha < \bar{\alpha}$, debt can be issued only as long as confidence crises do not occur. Thus, the possibility of confidence crises restricts the range of parameter values for which optimal tax smoothing can be achieved by issuing debt.

4.5.2 Debt auctions
The timing of events postulated in the previous pages corresponds to a particular method for selling government debt. Namely, the government fixes a base price and lets the market determine the amount bought. The nature of the equilibrium, and in particular the possibility of a confidence crisis, depends critically on the features of this auction. Suppose for instance that government debt is sold through the following more sophisticated auction method: the government fixes a base price for short-term debt; if any short-term debt remains unsold, then the government sells the remaining debt as consols, at whatever interest rate the market will require to absorb it. As remarked above, if all debt was consols, a confidence crisis would never occur in this simple model. Hence, in the event of a confidence crisis, the government would always be able to sell consols with no risk premium. Knowing that the government can rely on this option rules out the bad equilibrium with the confidence crisis, for *any maturity* of the debt outstanding: the maturity of the outstanding debt is completely irrelevant! What matters is only that the government retains the *possibility* of selling long-term debt.

However, in a more realistic environment, where long- and short-term instruments are not perfect substitutes from the point of view of investors, this alternative auction method may not rule out completely the bad equilibria. But this example suggests that a careful selection of auction methods may contribute to ensure financial stability in a high-debt economy. A more careful study of this issue is an important task for future research.

4.5.3 Risk premium

Our model is deterministic, thus it is impossible to address the issue of the risk premium in a precise way. More generally, in a model with some uncertainty a risk premium on government debt might be requested by the investors. Giavazzi and Pagano (this volume) have analysed this issue. We conjecture that the nature of their results would carry over to our optimizing framework.

Suppose that a confidence crisis occurs in every period with probability Q_t, exogenously given. That is, in every period t, $\theta^e_{t+1} > 0$ with probability Q_t and $\theta^e_{t+1} = 0$ with probability $1 - Q_t$.[13] Assume that the true value of α is unknown to the consumer, who only assigns a probability distribution to α, $\phi(\alpha)$. If $\theta^e_{t+1} = 0$ no default occurs with certainty, but if $\theta^e_{t+1} = 1$ the probability of a default is equal to $\text{Prob}(\alpha < \bar{\alpha}) \equiv \phi(\bar{\alpha})$ where $\bar{\alpha}$ has the same interpretation as above. Thus, in every period t, the probability of default is $\phi(\bar{\alpha})Q_t$. If a confidence crisis occurs and $\alpha \geq \bar{\alpha}$ the government repays the debt; if $\alpha < \bar{\alpha}$ the government defaults. In either case there is no debt left after the crisis. Until a confidence crisis occurs, the government has to pay a risk premium on its liability to compensate for the default risk. As shown above, $\bar{\alpha}$ is lower the 'more balanced' and the longer is the maturity structure of the debt. Thus, the risk premium can be reduced by lengthening and balancing the maturity structure of government debt.

4.5.4 Consolidation

A third option, in addition to repudiating or raising taxes, is available to the government in the event of a confidence crisis: to consolidate the debt. 'Consolidation' is defined as a compulsory transformation of short-term debt due for maturity into long-term debt. If the secondary market for public debt is perfectly efficient, a consolidation would cause only a minor capital loss by the current holders of the debt. Thus, if private investors could be sure that the government would respond to a crisis by consolidating the debt rather than by repudiating it, they would not 'fear' the crisis. But this in turn would seem to make the occurrence of a crisis less likely. Indeed, it can be shown that if the secondary market is perfectly efficient, allowing the government to consolidate its debt in the event of a crisis eliminates the bad equilibrium in which a crisis occurs. This is similar to a suspension of payments during a banking panic, as in Diamond and Dybvig (1983).

There are however two counterarguments, at least in the Italian situation. First, even though the market is much more efficient now than it used to be, it is interesting to recall what happened during the Italian forced consolidation of 1926. At that time, the secondary market price of government debt plummeted by about 30% (even though it later recovered, and debt holders who did not liquidate the consolidated debt did not suffer high losses – see Alesina, 1988, and Confalonieri and Gatti, 1986). This suggests that consolidation is still likely to be very fearsome for private investors. Second, to the extent that the political and economic costs of consolidation are smaller than those of outright repudiation, the panic equilibrium may be made more (rather than less) likely by the option of consolidating the debt. In terms of the model, the parameter α would drop, which in turn makes a crisis more likely.

5 Conclusions

Our theoretical and empirical findings suggest a tentative explanation of the recent difficulties in rolling over the Italian public debt: the fear of a confidence crisis on the debt. If correct, this explanation has some novel policy implications. All of them enhance the chance of surviving a confidence crisis without defaulting on the debt.

First of all, the quantity of debt coming due at each date is more important than the composition of the debt by category of debt instrument. To diminish the perceived likelihood of a confidence crisis, the stock of debt coming due at each date should be minimized. This calls for issuing debt of long maturity and evenly concentrated at all future dates. In the current Italian situation, it also means that the authorities should, up to a point, 'bite the bullet'. They should issue long-term debt even at relatively high interest rates, since accepting a shortening of the average maturity may be counterproductive: by increasing the possibility of a confidence crisis, it may lead to larger risk-premium and a higher average cost of servicing the total outstanding debt.

Second, like in the case of banking panics, there is a role for a lender of last resort. Here this role could be fulfilled by foreign governments or international organizations, through the promise of a credit line to the country hit by the debt panic. Gaining access to such a credit line would increase the chances of surviving a crisis without defaulting, thereby making the occurrence of the crisis less likely. A similar point is raised by Grilli and Alesina (1990) with reference to speculative attacks against the exchange rate.

There is a third option, often used in the past: to rely on financial controls and monetary policy in order to artificially increase the demand for public debt. However, the European accords will severely constrain the use of both instruments. This constraint is more likely to be a blessing than a drawback. It is true that imposing financial controls and monetizing part of the debt would make it easier to withstand a debt run. But on the other hand, resorting to these instruments too frequently distorts the incentives of the government, by hiding the costs of deficit finance and creating a confusion of responsibility between budgetary policy and monetary policy. As often argued in the Italian policy debate, these incentive effects could slow down the process of debt stabilization and thus further undermine the credibility of the government.

NOTES

We are grateful to Silvio Bencini, John Black, Rudiger Dornbusch, Mario Draghi, Douglas Gale, Lars Svensson and several other conference participants for many helpful comments. This paper was revised while Alesina was an Olin Fellow at the NBER: he gratefully acknowledges financial support from the Olin and Sloan Foundations. None of the institutions with which the authors are affiliated bears any responsibility or necessarily shares the views expressed in this paper.

1 First, the lags in the indexation mechanism of CCT determined capital gains as long as inflation and interest rates were falling, but, when they started to increase, the same lags determined capital losses and heavy disinvestments of banks and mutual funds. Second, technical innovations in the newly issued CCT and a change in taxation contributed to the fall of the market price of CCT in the secondary market. Finally, the unusually large redemptions that the mutual funds were facing forced them to liquidate part of their assets.

2 The *ex ante* real returns have been computed by using a survey of inflation expectations published by *Forum-Mondo Economico*, which provides quarterly expected inflation data for the current and following quarter. Naturally, the real return differential in Figure 4.5 should be interpreted with caution, since we are using the same deflator for short- and long-term government debt (we simply analyse the six-months expected inflation from the survey).

3 The shortening maturity and the persisting high real rates indicate that the debt management problems continued throughout 1988; it should be noticed, however, that the demand for government bonds varied largely among the sectors of the economy. In 1988, the disinvestments of the commercial banks (which can in part be attributed to the abandonment of administrative controls, such as the ceiling on loans and the securities investment requirement) and of the mutual funds were compensated by the very large investments of the private sector; the latter, in fact, increased its holdings of government bonds by an amount greater than the net issues.

4 The time series of the differential relative to the 3-month CD starts only in April 1988, since this kind of financial instrument was first introduced at that date.

5 Note that the definition of saving deposits includes the CDs. The interest rate

on saving deposits used to compute the differential in Figure 4.8 is a weighted average of the interest rate on CDs and on other kinds of savings deposits (the CD component will evidently be relevant only since 1984).

6 However, the movements of the differential between TBs and saving deposits correspond quite closely to those of the nominal interest rate. As a consequence, part of the differential can also be attributed to the tax levied on banks by means of the reserve requirement. This tax, in fact, varies together with the nominal interest rate; as long as the banks transfer part of the tax on depositors, the differential with TBs widens when the nominal interest rates increase and it shrinks when they decline.

7 An equilibrium satisfying these two conditions is a sequentially rational Nash Equilibrium, as defined in Persson and Tabellini (1989).

8 Suppose that the government chooses $0 < \theta_{t+1} < 1$. Then it incurs the costs of default as if $\theta_{t+1} + 1$ *and* some remaining debt has to be serviced with distortionary taxation.

9 In principle a third option would be available: consolidation. We will discuss this option below, in Section 4.5. For the moment we rule it out by assuming that the cost α applies to both default *and* consolidation. More fundamentally, this simple model with one-period debt and no uncertainty is not well equipped to handle the issue of consolidation.

10 In this determininistic model a multiplicity of equilibria cannot occur in any period other than the first without violating a rationality condition. In fact if a confidence crisis had to occur at time $t > 0$, nobody would hold debt at time $(t - 1)$, $(t - 2)$ and so on. Thus, the crisis would ravel backward at time zero. Thus, the criticial assumption is that b_0 exists *before* the planning horizon begins.

11 By (5), the cost of repudiation is borne only once. Thus, if $\theta_0 = 1$, then $\theta_1 = 1$ also.

12 If $\bar{\alpha}_s > \alpha$, $s < t$, the confidence crisis unravels to the period immediately preceding that for which $\bar{\alpha}_s > \underline{\alpha}$ for the first time.

13 Remember that given our specification of the costs of default, no value of $\theta \in (0, 1)$ can be a rational expectations equilibrium.

REFERENCES

Alesina, A. (1988). 'The end of Large Public Debts'. In F. Giavazzi and L. Spaventa, eds., *High Public Debt: the Italian Experience*. Cambridge: CEPR and Cambridge University Press.

Banca d'Italia (1981). *Considerazioni Finali del Governatore*, Rome: Banca d'Italia.

Bencini, S. & G. Tabellini (1987). 'Per i CCT una Politica Diversa'. *Il Sole 24 Ore*, July 17th.

(1988). 'Una Ricetta per il Debito'. *Mondo Economico*, December 17th.

Calvo, G. (1988). 'Servicing the Public Debt: the Role of Expectations'. *American Economic Review* **78**, 647–61.

Confalonieri, A. and E. Gatti (1986). *La Politica del Debito Pubblico in Italia, 1919–43*. Bari: La Terza.

Diamond, D.W. and P. Dybvig (1983). 'Bank Runs, Deposit Insurance and Liquidity'. *Journal of Political Economy* **91**, 401–19.

Giavazzi, F. and M. Pagano (1988). 'Confidence Crises and Public Debt Management'. This volume.

Grilli, V. and A. Alesina (1990). 'Avoiding Speculative Attacks in the EMS'. *Il Giornale degli Economisti*, forthcoming.

Lucas, R. and N. Stokey (1983). 'Optimal Fiscal and Monetary Policy in an Economy without Capital'. *Journal of Monetary Economics* **12**, 55–93.

Ministero del Tesoro (1989). *Rapporto sull'attivita del Comitato Consultivo Scentifico sul Debito Pubblico.*

Pagano, M. (1988). 'The Management of Public Debt and Financial Markets'. In F. Giavazzi and L. Spaventa, eds., *High Public Debt: the Italian Experience.* Cambridge: CEPR and Cambridge University Press.

Parcu, P.L. (1986). 'Bank Panics of the Third Kind'. *Moneta e Credito.*

Persson, T. and G. Tabellini (1990). *Macroeconomic Policy, Credibility and Politics.* London: Harwood, forthcoming.

Prati, A. (1989). 'Self-fulfilling Debt Crises'. Chapter 2, Ph.D. dissertation, UCLA.

Spaventa, L. (1988). 'Discussion'. In F. Giavazzi and L. Spaventa, eds., *High Public Debt: the Italian Experience*. Cambridge: CEPR and Cambridge University Press.

Discussion

MARIO DRAGHI

Maturity structure does matter and it should be of particular concern for the management of public debt. The Italian 'authorities should, up to a point, "bite the bullet". They should issue long-term debt even at relatively high interest rates, since accepting a shortening of the average maturity may be counterproductive: by increasing the possibility of a confidence crisis, it may lead to a larger risk premium and a higher average cost of servicing the total outstanding debt' (Alesina *et al.*, in this volume).

Alesina, Prati and Tabellini reach these policy conclusions in their brilliant and provocative paper and support them by two major empirical claims intended to show the reluctance of the Italian authorities to follow this harsh course.

(1) After 1985 the interest rate on the one-year Treasury Bill, to which a good part of the CCT (Certificates of Treasury) are indexed, was – thanks to the type of auction system used – being manipulated so as to keep it

artificially lower than the short-term 3-months Treasury Bill. The authorities, after having kept it higher when the debt was issued, were succumbing to the temptation 'to reduce it once the private sector is locked into an irreversible investment decision, thereby inflicting a capital loss on their debt holders' (ibidem). Therefore they created a time inconsistency and caused an investors' confidence crisis which led to a funding crisis in 1987 and ultimately to the issue of maturities much shorter and/or more expensive.

One could claim that other readings of these data are equally plausible. First, the existence of inverted yield curves is not *per se* a symptom of confidence crisis. They may occur for a variety of reasons, for instance because short-term and long-term inflationary expectations differ, and/or because of tensions on the foreign-exchange market; both examples would fit Italian financial markets during 1985–87. Second, the evidence of manipulation would be a bit stronger if one, like Bencini and Tabellini (1987), could find evidence of a V-shaped yield curve with a minimum at the rate used for indexing public debt. But the last three years data fail to confirm any strong regularity of this kind. This should not be surprising since peaks and bottoms in the yield curves are to be observed in many other countries where no thought is ever given to defaulting on government debt. Third, since March 1989 the method used to auction the Treasury Bills to which the CCT are indexed, has become purely competitive, thus strongly reducing any potential time inconsistency, but returns, contrary to the implication one would draw from the paper, after an initial increase, abated and then followed a path more likely dictated by other considerations. The same thing can be said about investors' subscriptions of CCT after the change in the auction system took place: until very recently they were far from peaking, and in general they did not follow any prior that might be inferred from the paper.

(2) The persistence of a positive and substantial interest-rate differential between the 3-month Treasury Bill and the commercial banks' certificates of deposits having the same maturity, would show that there is indeed a problem of confidence in the paper issued by the government.

Although this evidence cannot be disputed, one could observe that such a differential always existed, even at times when the fiscal policy's soundness was not an issue. Its causes might have a structural character and be related in part to market segmentation, and in part to the placement techniques utilized by the commercial banks. Since they are in the almost unique position of acting at the same time as main agents for the sale of government paper and as issuers of their own paper having similar characteristics, they would use non-price arguments to induce their clients to buy their own paper instead of Treasury bonds. This explanation, as it is entirely based on financial market imperfections lasting for several years, cannot be entirely satisfactory in today's capital markets. But the authors' motivation for the existence of a premium on the government paper is also not fully persuasive, since one could claim that the commercial banks' paper is as sound as that of their major shareholder, the Italian government.[1] The authors could possibly strengthen their point if they were to look into foreign issues by the Italian government, where the domestic placing power of the Italian banking system is not a problem.

The authors present also a thereotical model intended to help the policy maker with 'optimal' advice on how to manage public debt. It is clear and probably unavoidable that some of the results contained in this section depend too closely on certain extreme assumptions like the absence of reputational considerations and the lump-sum nature of the default costs. For example, since reputation is worthless in this model, to defend it would be a waste, and therefore default always comes to be optimal at time zero. One may also conjecture that partial defaults, besides being a more realistic equilibrium, are superior to some of the equilibria described in the paper, but, as the authors themselves observe, they are ruled out by the lump-sum nature of the default costs.

More problematic is this section's treatment of confidence crisis as an exogenous event, when it really should not be so. This approach does not affect as much the theorems' internal consistency, as their interpretation. Consider Proposition 2 saying that an 'equilibrium with a confidence crisis is least likely to exist if only long-term debt is issued, and if the same amount of debt matures in each period'. The authors show that the distortionary costs from having to repay debt under a confidence crisis regime are minimized when debt is only long-term and evenly distributed over time. It is an interesting and useful result, but it does not say that a confidence crisis is least likely to happen under such a circumstance. It does say instead that, *if* you happen to be in a confidence crisis then it costs less to repay a debt having the characteristics just mentioned. This point has a direct bearing on the major policy conclusion reported at the beginning of this discussion. It may well be true that Italian authorities should issue long-term debt at relatively high interest rates in order to avoid a confidence crisis. But such prescription does not follow from the authors' analysis where a confidence crisis is an exogenous occurrence independent of the maturity structure of public debt, and bearing on the costs of such a crisis were it to occur, not on its likelihood.

NOTE

1 Italian commercial banks have always made large investments in their government paper, and, in case of its hypothetical default, they would certainly need a

recapitalization in order to be able to continue their banking activity. But their major shareholder is in the vast majority of the cases the same government which by assumption is unable to service its bonds. The banks would then be sold, and it is not clear that the holders of the banks' CDs would be more protected than the government bond holders.

REFERENCE

Bencini, Silvio and Guido Tabellini (1988). 'Una Ricetta Per Il Debito', *Mondo Economico*, December 17.

Discussion

LARS E.O. SVENSSON

I very much enjoyed reading the paper by Alesina, Prati and Tabellini (henceforth APT), and I feel I learned a lot about both empirical and theoretical aspects of the Italian debt problem.

The paper consists of three major sections: two empirical sections on Italian debt management during the 1980s and on risk-premia on government bonds, followed by a theoretical section with a model of debt runs.

I found the section on Italian debt management most interesting, but I certainly do not have the institutional knowledge necessary to discuss it in detail. In the section with empirical results on risk premia, I was astounded by the big risk-premia reported. Again, lack of institutional knowledge prevents me from discussing to what extent the government and private bonds compared are really otherwise good substitutes, and whether markets are sufficiently competitive for the assets compared to allow for meaningful comparisons of returns.

The theoretical section presents a most interesting model of debt runs, government default, and their relation to the maturity structure of the debt. What is being discussed is outright default on indexed debt, not the more common implicit default on nominal debt via inflation and devaluation. Also, default is modelled as all or nothing: partial default does not occur in the model. This is in contrast to historical experience, where we more often see partial default via renegotiation and rescheduling rather than complete default. Whether any default in the model is complete or partial of course depends on the nature of the cost of default: if the cost is fixed there will be complete default, if any; if the cost is increasing in the amount of default, there may be partial default. I think we all agree that the microeconomics of the default costs are worthy of further study, for instance to clarify which of fixed or variable default costs is a better first approximation.

The main result of the paper, derived in a clear and convincing way, is that issue of long-term debt, and a balanced composition of the debt, reduces the risk of debt runs and defaults. In the model the optimal policy of the government is actually to issue only long-term debt, and no short-term debt at all.

I shall demonstrate that this result can be modified and somewhat strengthened, in that the government may actually reduce the risk of debt runs and default further by *buying* short-term bonds, that is lending in short-term bonds, and increase even further the issue of long-term bonds. That result is reminiscent of a result in a paper by Mats Persson, Torsten Persson and myself (1987), namely that the government in order to reduce the incentive to a surprise inflation should buy nominal assets and issue indexed debt.

The modification of the APT result can be understood as follows: the discounted present value of debt outstanding at the beginning of period t is (from APT equation (24))

$$b = {}_{t-1}b_t + {}_{t-2}b_t + \beta\, {}_{t-1}b_{t+1} \tag{1}$$

Suppose now that a debt crises arises, that is that private agents at t expects the government to default at $t+1$, which we denote ${}_t\theta_{t+1} = 1$ ($\theta^e_{t+1} = 1$ in APT notation). Consequently the government cannot issue any new debt in period t, and has to raise taxes to fulfill

$$\tau_t = {}_{t-1}b_t + {}_{t-2}b_t \tag{2}$$

When period $t+1$ begins, the only outstanding debt is then ${}_{t-1}b_{t+1}$. APT then assumes that the government raises taxes to repay also this debt, and that no new debt is issued. That is,

$$\tau_{t+1} = {}_{t-1}b_{t+1} \tag{3}$$

In the future there is no debt oustanding and taxes will be zero henceforth.

Via these operations the government has tackled the debt crisis and avoided default. It is now straightforward to see that in order to smooth taxes in the event of a debt crises, it is best to choose

$$_{t-1}b_t = 0 \tag{4a}$$

and

$$_{t-2}b_t = {_{t-1}b_{t+1}} = b/(1 + \beta), \quad \text{for all } t \tag{4b}$$

That is, no short-term bonds should be issued, and the composition of long-term bonds should be balanced. This smoothes and minimizes the amount of debt that matures each date.

Note, however, that in the previous reasoning, the government does honour its debt maturing in period $t + 1$ ($\theta_{t+1} = 0$), counter to expectations that it would default in period $t + 1$ ($_t\theta_{t+1} = 1$). Suppose the fact that the government does not default in period $t + 1$ makes private agents believe that the government will honour its debt in periods after $t + 1$, that is,

$$_{t+1}\theta_s = 0 \quad \text{for} \quad s \geq t + 2, \quad \text{when } \theta_{t+1} = 0 \tag{5}$$

This assumption is at least as plausible as the assumption that the private agents continue to believe in future default in spite of the government honouring its current debt.

If (5) holds, the government can actually issue new debt in period $t + 1$, and the optimal tax level is then just to pay the interest on the outstanding debt. Then (3) is replaced by

$$\tau_{t+1} = (1 - \beta)\,_{t-1}b_{t+1} \tag{3'}$$

It then follows from (1), (2) and (3') that tax smoothing requires that

$$_{t-1}b_t = -\beta b < 0 \tag{6a}$$

and

$$_{t-2}b_t = {_{t-1}b_{t+1}} = b > b/(1 + \beta), \quad \text{for all } t \tag{6b}$$

That is, the government should indeed buy short-term bonds and increase further its issue of long-term bonds.

In conclusion, with or without this extension, I find the main result that long maturity and balanced composition of the national debt reduces the risk of a debt crisis convincing and important. It should be emphasized, however, that this result refers to the case of indexed debt only, and there are other aspects to the choice of government debt instruments as well. For instance, long maturities of nominal debt increase the incentive to default by inflation, which provides an argument for issuing indexed or foreign currency debt rather than nominal home currency debt.

Long-term indexed and foreign currency debt may, however, have undesirable risk characteristics. This is an argument for the government's issuing of different assets with more desirable risk characteristics.

It is of interest in this context to note that with a passive monetary policy and flexible exchange rates, nominal bonds have risk characteristics like a share in output. That is, their return is positively correlated with output. This is so since the price level will be negatively correlated with output, and the real return to nominal bonds will be the sure nominal return deflated by the risky price level. Hence, the choice between indexed and nominal debt is to some extent a choice between credibility and desirable risk characteristics, something that has been explored in recent work by Henning Bohn (1988).

We may also recall the result of Robert Lucas and Nancy Stokey (1983) that indexed debt of all maturities is needed to resolve one aspect of the time-consistency problem in a barter economy, and the extension by Persson, Persson and myself (1988) that in a monetary economy both indexed and nominal assets of all maturities are necessary to resolve the time-consistency problem in a monetary economy, including the incentive to surprise inflation.

A synthesis of these different aspects seems most desirable, for instance along the lines suggested in Maurice Obstfeld's Discussion. Before that synthesis is completed, it seems clear that APT have made an important and convincing point about some advantages of long-term government debt.

REFERENCES

Bohn, Henning (1988). 'Why Do We Have Nominal Government Debt', *Journal of Monetary Economics* **21**, 127–40.
Lucas, Robert E. Jr. and Nancy L. Stokey (1983). 'Optimal Fiscal and Monetary Policy in an Economy Without Capital', *Journal of Monetary Economics* **12**, 55–93.
Persson Mats, Torsten Persson and Lars E.O. Svensson (1987). 'Time Consistency of Fiscal and Monetary Policy', *Econometrica* **55**, 1419–31.

5 Confidence crises and public debt management

FRANCESCO GIAVAZZI and MARCO PAGANO

1 Introduction

What maturity structure should the Treasury choose for public debt? When is it advisable to issue indexed bonds? And, in general, is there an 'optimal menu' of debt instruments to be issued by governments? These questions reflect everyday concerns of Central Bankers and Treasury Ministers. Still, until lately economists have provided little help in answering them. The last systematic treatment of the choice of the maturity structure dates back to Tobin's (1963) essay on debt management. Although more work has been done on the choice of debt instruments (chiefly on indexed bonds), Fischer (1983) still concluded that 'there is as yet no satisfactory theory of what types of assets governments should issue' (p. 243).

Recently, however, research interest in this area has been revived by the game-theoretic view of the interaction between government and private sector. The insight is that debt-management issues – such as the choice of maturity structure or the decision on debt indexation – can be seen as a way of altering the set of incentives faced by the government and thus the strategies that the private sector expects the government to play.

For instance, Lucas and Stokey (1983) and Persson et al. (1984, 1987) have shown that a government can choose the maturity structure of debt so as to tie the hands of its successors, eliminating any future incentive to depart from the policy it has optimally chosen (i.e. ensuring time-consistency). Thus, for a particular choice of the maturity structure, the public anticipates that subsequent governments will not deviate from the initial plan, and the latter is not only (*ex ante*), optimal but also credible.

Similarly, a game-theoretic framework has been used by Calvo (1988, 1990) to argue that public debt should be indexed. He produces examples where a government that issues nominal debt is forced to monetize it by the self-fulfilling expectations of the private sector. If debt-holders start fearing debt monetization, they will require a higher nominal rate of interest. To the extent that the government is not willing to pay this premium and accept the implied increase in the future tax burden, it may go for the monetization anticipated by the public. Indexation eliminates the incentive to monetize and thus also the expectations that induce the government to monetize.

The novel element in Calvo's models is that the game between government and private sector may have multiple equilibria, and that some debt management decisions can rule out 'bad' equilibria that imply monetization or repudiation. He captures a phenomenon that economists and business analysts have traditionally called a 'confidence crisis'. A confidence crisis is a critical change in expectations about the behaviour of policy-makers, capable by itself of precipitating a policy regime shift or at least of increasing the chances that it will take place.

The question that we ask in this paper is whether the danger of a confidence crisis can be reduced by acting on the choice of the maturity structure (rather than on the degree of indexation) of public debt. Another novelty of our model is that it relies on the assumption that the public is imperfectly informed about the government's preferences or opportunities, and therefore does not know for sure what is going to happen if a confidence crisis occurs. In Calvo's models, once a confidence crisis explodes, a regime shift occurs – in fact, one can say that a confidence crisis *is* the regime shift (the new regime entailing repudiation). In our setup, instead, a confidence crisis does not necessarily lead to a regime shift, but just to a higher probability of it occurring. In other words, there are chances that the policy-maker will be able to withstand the crisis. The interesting question then becomes what factors determine the policy-maker's chances of resisting the crisis, and if debt management can affect some of these factors.

What the model reveals is that the probability that the authorities will withstand a confidence crisis is critically affected by the extent to which they have to appeal to the market at each given date to roll over public debt. This depends on three factors: the amount of debt outstanding, its average maturity and the time pattern of maturing debt. In a situation where the stock of debt is high, the average maturity is short and maturing debt is concentrated at few dates, the Treasury has to borrow huge amounts from the market at those dates. If on one of those dates a confidence crisis occurs, the Treasury finds itself in the critical situation of refinancing a large portion of its debt on unfavourable terms. This leads the public to expect a higher probability of a regime shift if a confidence crisis occurs.

2   Overview and motivation of the model

The model is set in an open economy context, where the Central bank has embarked on a fixed-exchange regime with free capital mobility. The danger of a confidence crisis is compounded in this context, since a crisis can occur not only if the public is afraid that the government might not honour its debt (monetization or default), but also if it fears that the Central Bank might abandon the fixed parity (devaluation). Here we concentrate on the danger of devaluation and rule out debt monetization or default, although it should be obvious that the model can easily be recast in terms of a closed economy where the regime shift concerns government solvency (as in Calvo). Before motivating this modeling strategy, it is worth offering a quick overview of the analysis to explain how a speculative attack on the currency links up with debt management problems.

Consider the following scenario. Suppose that current and expected monetary policy is consistent with a fixed exchange rate at the current parity, but that occasionally investors launch a speculative attack on the Central Bank (driven by sunspot-type beliefs). The attack raises the conditional probability of a devaluation and thus leads to an increase in the nominal rate of interest through the arbitrage condition between assets denominated in domestic and foreign currency. We assume that the level of reserves is such that the attack can be resisted by the Central Bank, provided the Treasury does not create monetary base at the time of the attack. Consider now what happens if instead the Treasury is entitled to finance part of its current borrowing requirement by money creation.[1] If at the time of the crisis the Treasury has to refinance a large chunk of debt on the market, it has a strong incentive to do so largely by money creation, given that the rate of interest is so high. However, the larger is this injection of monetary base, the lower are the chances that the Central Bank will be able to defend the initial parity.

Investors, on the other hand, know that the higher the refinancing needs of the Treasury at each instant, the higher the probability that a confidence crisis will end in a devaluation. Thus, when a confidence crisis occurs, they require a higher jump in interest rates, and this in turn raises the probability that the crisis will end in a devaluation. In equilibrium, the probability that the Central Bank will successfully resist a speculative attack can be enhanced either by lengthening the average maturity of public debt, so as to diminish the *average* recourse of the Treasury to the market, or by spreading the recourse to the market as uniformly as possible over time, so as to reduce the *variance* of new debt issues by the Treasury. These debt management policies are all the more needed the larger the size of public debt outstanding and the smaller the foreign-exchange reserves owned by the Central Bank.

Other factors that can mitigate the effects of a confidence crisis are the possibility of issuing debt denominated in foreign currencies and the ability to borrow from other Central Banks in the event of a crisis. These factors would enable the public sector to have equal access to world capital markets as the private sector, eliminating the asymmetry between the two implied by our model. Limited access by the public sector to world capital markets is a key prerequisite for confidence crises to materialize: as noted by Obstfeld (1986) in the context of a similar model (where self-fulfilling beliefs can lead to the collapse of *viable* fixed exchange-rate regimes), a regime collapse 'presupposes the existence of some lower bound on central bank reserves, . . . though there is no reason in principle why a central bank facing a perfect international capital market cannot borrow indefinitely to support the exchange rate, provided it raises taxes to service the external debt it incurs' (p. 33). In practice, international lending to the Central Bank has the same role as a loan by the 'lender of last resort' to a commercial bank in models of bank runs – namely enforcing the 'good' Nash equilibrium by stabilizing expectations.

One may ask why we concentrate on the interaction between debt management and the danger of collapse of fixed exchange rates under capital mobility. We do so because this interaction is likely to become very important for a number of European countries in the near future. It is often suggested that EC countries with high public debt will face unsustainable speculative attacks on their currencies if they attempt to liberalize capital movements while maintaining fixed or quasi-fixed exchange rates. Our model suggests that, while this concern is well-founded, it is not only the level of public debt that matters for the viability of fixed rates, but also the way one manages this debt. In a high-debt country, the viability of a fixed rate regime can be enhanced by lengthening the average maturity of debt, spreading maturing issues as uniformly as possible and developing a market for public debt denominated in foreign currency. A relevant historical precedent can be found in the experience of France and Italy in the late 1920s: in both countries, upon returning to full convertibility with the dollar and the pound, the government embarked on a drastic restructuring of public debt. Between 1926 and 1929, the proportion of short-term debt fell from 32% to 12% in France and from 30% to 3% in Italy.[2]

On the other hand, if the model's prescriptions were to be applied today in the high-debt countries of the EC, the overhaul in debt management policy would not be less drastic. As shown by Table 5.1, some high-debt countries such as Belgium, Italy, Greece and Portugal stand out for their relatively short debt maturity (columns 2 and 5). In this group, the last three countries are also characterized by greater reliance on Central Bank loans to finance public debts[3] (column 3); in addition, Italy features very limited recourse to foreign currency debt (column 4). Spain, instead, has a relatively small debt-income ratio, but has the shortest maturity in Europe and uses foreign currency-denominated debt as little as Italy. The case of Ireland is symmetric and opposite to that of Spain, since Ireland has the highest debt-income ratio in Europe, but is characterized by relatively long maturity, no reliance on Central Bank loans and substantial recourse to foreign markets.

As explained above, another qualifying feature of debt management policy is how evenly maturing issues are distributed in the future. Cross-country data on this point are harder to obtain. However, at least as far as Italy is concerned, Figure 5.1 suggests that huge chunks of public debt are going to mature simultaneously at a few dates, especially 1990 and 1991. This suggests that scant attention has been so far devoted to the objective of smoothing out the future pattern of debt issues.

3   The model

There are three agents in the economy: the private sector, the Treasury and the Central Bank. The private sector simply decides what is the probability of a devaluation at each date, and requires an interest rate that compensates debt-holders accordingly. The Treasury decides on the mix of debt and temporary money creation to be used to finance the deficit. It does so by weighting two objectives: (i) to minimize the burden of debt servicing (and thus the deadweight loss associated with future taxes), and (ii) to avoid impairing the ability of the Central Bank to defend the exchange rate. As shown below, there is a natural tradeoff between these two objectives. It is assumed that different governments choose different points along this tradeoff, depending on their preferences, and that the private sector is imperfectly informed about the preferences of the current government. The Central Bank tries to defend the existing nominal exchange-rate parity, and pursues a monetary policy consistent with indefinite exchange-rate stability. Although fundamentals are consistent with the existing parity, in some occurrences the interaction between the private sector and the Treasury can lead to a successful attack on the Central Bank and force it to devalue.

3.1   The private sector

The behaviour of the private sector can be characterized by the state of its expectations concerning a devaluation in the current period. We distinguish

	Total debt as % of GDP	T-Bills and other short-term debt as % of domestic market debt	Central Bank loans to the Treasury as % of total debt	Foreign currency debt as % of total debt	Average residual maturity (years)
	(1)	(2)[a]	(3)	(4)	(5)
Belgium	122.2	21.8	2.8	16.5	3.6
Denmark	59.6	14.5	− 13.7	30.9	3.6
Germany	42.2	1.8	0.0	n.a.	n.a.
Greece	69.0	92.5	14.6	33.5	n.a.
Spain	48.5	60.8	7.2	2.5	1.5[b]
France	24.5	45.3	− 5.3	3.3	4.0
Ireland	124.5	6.5	0.0[c]	39.7	7.8[c]
Italy	92.6	30.3	7.2	2.5	3.5
Netherlands	72.9	9.1	n.a.	n.a.	5.9
Portugal	72.2	62.5	32.8	22.4	n.a.
UK	48.0	30.3	n.a.	9.2	8.2–10.9[d,e]
US	53.1	59.8	0.0	0.2	5.7

Table 5.1. The size, composition and maturity of public debt in Europe in 1987

Notes:
1987 data, end-of-year figures (except for the UK, where they refer to March). Unless otherwise indicated, data for EEC countries are drawn from the report *Evolution récente des finances publiques et implications pour la politique économique*, Comité des Gouverneurs des Banques Centrales des Etats Membres de la Communauté Economique Européenne, 30 June 1988. United States data are drawn from the *Economic Report of the President*, February 1988, Table B-84.
[a]'Domestic market debt' is the sum of T-Bills, other short-term debt, medium and long-term debt. It excludes non-marketable debt, foreign currency debt and other debt.
[b]*Boletìn Economico*, Banco de España, June 1988, p. 67.
[c]*Central Bank of Ireland Quarterly Bulletin*, Winter 1988, Tables D1, D2 and D4. The estimate of average maturity in col. 5 excludes undated government stock (consols).
[d]*Bank of England Quarterly Bulletin*, November 1987, pp. 550–1.
[e]Lowest and highest bound of the estimate. The highest bound refers only to domestic government stock (excluding consols); the lowest bound is based on the extreme assumption that all debt other than government stock (mostly national savings certificates) has zero residual maturity.

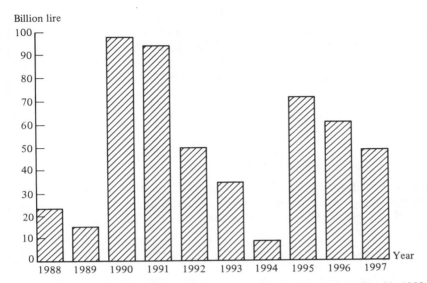

Figure 5.1   Maturing Italian public debt by year, 1988–97, as of August 31, 1988

two such states: a 'normal state' (denoted by N), in which the private sector believes that in the current period the probability of a devaluation π is zero, and a 'confidence crisis' (denoted by C), in which investors believe that there is a positive probability ($\pi > 0$) that the Central Bank will devalue the domestic currency by a fraction d in the current period, d being for convenience a fixed amount. When a confidence crisis occurs, the Central Bank can devalue or resist – how its move is determined will be analyzed below. Crises are serially uncorrelated events: in each period, state C has the same probability q of occurring.[4]

Consider now a 1-period bond issued after the current state (N or C) has been revealed, but before the Central Bank has made its move (for instance, it is known that a confidence crisis is on, but the Bank has not announced yet whether it is devaluing or resisting). If the current state is N, free capital mobility ensures that the return on such a bond is $1 + r^*$, where r^* is the world rate of interest. If instead the current state is C, by international arbitrage the return on a 1-period bond will be $(1 + r^*)/(1 - \pi x)$, where $x \equiv d/(1 + d)$: the return must rise to compensate debt-holders for the expected devaluation, the premium above the world rate being an increasing function of the probability of a devaluation, π, and of its size, d.

Let us now consider multi-period bonds, with a face value of 1 and a fixed coupon c per period. We shall denote their issue price by p_t^N if the bond is issued in state N and by p_t^C if it is issued in state C (obviously the issue price can differ from the face value of 1, since the bond can be issued below or above par). Under risk-neutrality, the expected 1-period return on a multi-period bond must equal that on 1-period bond, in state N as well as in state C, i.e.:

$$1 + r^* = [E(p_{t+1}) + c]/p_t^N \tag{1a}$$

and

$$(1 + r^*)/(1 - \pi x) = [E(p_{t+1}) + c]/p_t^C \tag{1b}$$

where the expected price of the multi-period bond $E(p_{t+1})$ is the same in state N and in state C because of the assumption that confidence crises are serially uncorrelated events. From these two conditions, it is immediate that:

$$(p_t^C - p_t^N)/p_t^N = - \pi x \tag{2}$$

showing that during a confidence crisis the issue price of a multi-period bond falls πx below its normal level: if in the no-crisis state a bond with a fixed coupon c per period is issued at par ($p_t^N = 1$), during a crisis the same bond will have to be issued at a discount of πx below par ($p_t^C = 1 - \pi x$). The magnitude πx thus measures the increase in the burden of servicing each dollar of debt issued during a crisis. This magnitude is independent of the maturity of the bonds issued: the increase in the future tax burden induced by a confidence crisis cannot be affected by choosing a particular maturity for the bonds issued during the crisis. Maturity matters however for another reason: it determines the amount of bonds that mature and must be renewed at each moment in time. As we shall see now, this factor is crucial in determining the probability that a crisis leads to a devaluation.

3.2   The Treasury

Public debt is in the form of B bonds with maturity T. Each of these bonds has face value of 1, pays a fixed coupon c per period and is issued at par ($p^N = 1$) in state N. Goods prices are constant, so B denotes the number of outstanding bonds, as well as their real value. Consider a situation where for T periods a confidence crisis has not occurred, i.e. the economy has been in state N. The government has stabilized debt at a constant level B and has also achieved a uniform distribution of debt issues over time, so that the amount of debt that must be renewed in each period is B/T. The government budget constraint thus requires that the primary deficit $g - t$, *plus* debt servicing on outstanding bonds B, and repayment of maturing bonds B/T, equal new issues B/T:

$$g - t + cB + B/T = B/T \qquad (3)$$

so that the primary surplus must equal the interest payments on outstanding debt. Equation (3) rules out permanent revenue from money creation, i.e. seigniorage. However, we assume that the Treasury can draw from a limited overdraft facility at the Central Bank to meet *temporary* financing needs. After drawing from this credit facility, the Treasury must eventually rebalance its account, so that it can create monetary base up to its overdraft limit but cannot consider money creation as a steady source of revenue.

When a crisis (state C) occurs, the Treasury faces a fall in the issue price of debt from p^N to p^C, equivalent to πx on each dollar of new debt. At this point, it has three options: (i) increasing current taxes or lowering current expenditures; (ii) issuing more debt at the more unfavourable terms offered by the market; (iii) turning to its emergency credit line at the Central Bank. We rule out option (i), for two reasons. First, budgets cannot be revised quickly enough as to react timely to sudden events like confidence crises. Second, if taxes are distortionary, inflicting the entire burden of the distortion on current taxpayers is suboptimal, especially considering that the blip in the cost of debt servicing is temporary. It is instead preferable to finance this blip with debt, and spread the implied tax burden on all future periods (as in Barro, 1979).

Assume then that the government does not change taxes t or expenditures g, and uses only option (ii), i.e. it issues B/T bonds each at the lower issue price $p^C = 1 - \pi x$. The increase in the burden of debt servicing is:

$$\frac{B}{T}(1 - p^C) = \frac{B}{T}\pi x \qquad (4)$$

This increase in future debt service measures the increase in the future tax burden implied by resorting to option (ii) in the event of a confidence crisis. While this expression is independent of the maturity of newly issued bonds, it is decreasing in T, the maturity of the outstanding stock: a higher T means that a smaller amount of bonds has to be renewed at the time of a crisis.

The Treasury, however, has still another option. It can turn to its credit line at the Central Bank to get over the temporary increase in the cost of borrowing from the market. By drawing from this credit facility, the Treasury can compress the increase in debt service below the value given by expression (4). Let α denote the fraction of the increase in debt service that is monetized: for instance, if it sets $\alpha = 1$, the Treasury effectively prevents any increase in debt service, while if it sets $\alpha = 0$ it lets debt service increase by the full amount indicated in (4).

How does the Treasury choose the value of α? Its choice is determined partly by the institutional constraints on the use of the overdraft facility[5] and partly by its preferences. During a crisis the Treasury faces a tradeoff between the welfare of future taxpayers and the objective of exchange-rate stability, to which the Central Bank is fully devoted. The greater the Treasury's withdrawal from the overdraft facility during a crisis, the smaller the subsequent increase in debt service and thus in future taxes, but also the higher the probability that the Central Bank will exhaust its reserves and will be forced to devalue.

We assume that some governments are more conscious of taxpayers' interest (high α) and others are instead more willing to cooperate with the Central Bank (low α). The distribution of the parameter α, $F(\cdot)$, describes the frequency of each 'type' of government. It seems reasonable to assume that the support of α is bounded, and ranges between 0 and some α_{max}.

The private sector does not observe the type of government it faces, i.e. the realization of α that has currently occurred. Due to this informational asymmetry, it regards the current α as a random variable, and can only make a probabilistic assessment about how the Treasury will behave in a confidence crisis.

3.3   The Central Bank

The balance sheet of the Central Bank is elementary. In state N, when the Treasury does not create monetary base by drawing from its credit line, the Central Bank has foreign exchange reserves R on the asset side and currency M^N on the liability side. Thus currency is fully backed by reserves ($M^N = R$). The private sector's demand for currency is assumed to be exponential, with interest elasticity σ. Both these assumptions – the full backing of currency and the functional form of money demand – simplify the analysis, but are not necessary for the qualitative results of the model to go through (see discussion at the end of Section 4).

The rate of interest that is relevant for the money demand function is that on 1-period bonds, i.e. r^* in state N and $r^* + \pi x$ in state C.[6] Money demand in the two states is thus respectively:

$$M^N = Ae^{-\sigma r^*} \tag{5a}$$

$$M^C = Ae^{-\sigma(r^* + \pi x)} \tag{5b}$$

where $A > 0$, $\sigma > 0$. When the state of nature changes from N to C, i.e. a confidence crisis occurs, money demand falls by:

$$M^N - M^C = M^N(1 - e^{-\sigma\pi x}) = R(1 - e^{-\sigma\pi x}) \qquad (6)$$

At the same time, the Treasury injects into the economy an amount of liquidity $\alpha\pi x B/T$, by monetizing a fraction α of the increase in debt service in (4). Thus, the Central Bank is faced with an increase in the monetary base at the wrong moment – when it already has people lining up at its door to convert currency into foreign exchange. If the (algebraic) sum of the fall in money demand (6) and the Treasury's injection of liquidity is larger than reserves R, the Central Bank will have to abandon the current party. The condition for devaluation therefore is:

$$R(1 - e^{-\sigma\pi x}) + \alpha\pi x B/T > R \qquad (7)$$

Rearranging (7), the probability of a devaluation π can be written as:

$$\pi = P(\alpha g(\pi) > 1), \quad \text{where} \quad g(\pi) = e^{\sigma\pi x} \pi x \frac{B/T}{R} \qquad (8)$$

Notice that, if the Treasury always abstained from creating monetary base, the Central Bank would always be able to resist the speculative attack (with x finite, if $\alpha = 0$ the inequality $\alpha g(\pi) > 1$ never holds). In this case, then, the probability of a devaluation would be always zero ($\pi = 0$). What generates the danger of devaluation is precisely the institutional setup that allows the Treasury to create monetary base (i.e. set $\alpha > 0$) in response to a speculative attack: this prevents it from precommitting to set $\alpha = 0$.

4   Confidence crises and average debt maturity

Equation (8) is the condition for a rational expectations equilibrium. It says that the probability of devaluation entering the decisions of investors, π, must be equal to the probability of devaluation resulting from the interaction of the three agents in the economy, $P(\cdot)$. This implies that private sector expectations are consistent with the actual working of the economy.

Analysing equation (8), one can establish that, under certain parameter configurations, for the public it is equally rational to assign a zero probability or a (specific) positive probability to a devaluation in the current period: in the first case, the devaluation will not occur, whereas in the second case it will occur with the probability chosen by the public. Thus both state N and state C correspond to rational expectations equilibria.

Proposition 1: *(Number of equilibria)*
There is always an equilibrium where the probability of a devaluation is zero

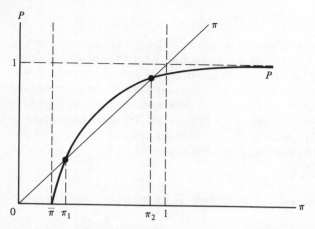

Figure 5.2   The probability of devaluation: rational expectations equilibria with a uniform distribution of government types

$(\pi = 0)$. There can also be other equilibria where the probability of devaluation is positive $(\pi > 0)$.

To prove Proposition 1, recall that equilibria are values of π that solve equation (8). Define a value $\bar{\pi} = g^{-1}(1/\alpha_{\max})$. Intuitively, $\bar{\pi}$ can be interpreted as follows: if the private sector 'plays' a value of π below $\bar{\pi}$, the increase in the burden of debt servicing is so small that even if the government 'plays' the highest possible value of α (i.e. $\alpha_{\max}$), a devaluation cannot occur (i.e. the actual probability $P(\alpha g(\pi) > 1) = 0$ for $\pi < \bar{\pi}$). We then consider separately whether a solution to (8) exists (i) for $\pi < \bar{\pi}$ and (ii) for $\pi > \bar{\pi}$.

(i) For $\pi < \bar{\pi}$, the function $\alpha g(\pi) < 1$ for every possible α, so that $P(\alpha g(\pi) > 1) = 0$. Thus if $\pi < \bar{\pi}$, then $\pi = 0$ is the only solution to (8).

(ii) For $\pi \geq \bar{\pi}$, one can show that the function $P(\alpha g(\pi) > 1)$ is increasing, starts at 0 for $\pi = \bar{\pi}$ and approaches 1 asymptotically for π large (although in equilibrium π cannot exceed 1 of course).[7] Figure 5.2 displays the function $P(\alpha g(\pi) > 1)$ as the locus P, in the special case of a uniform distribution of α: in this case $P(\cdot)$ is concave, so that there are at most two intersections between P and a 45° line from the origin. These intersections are equilibria with $\pi > 0$: in the figure they are indicated as π_1 and π_2. In general, there will be either *no* such equilibria or *multiple* equilibria with $\pi > 0$. The possibility of one equilibrium with $\pi > 0$ occurs only if the P locus is tangential to the 45° line, i.e. for a unique combination of parameters.

The precise location of the P locus depends on the value of $g(\pi)$, that is in turn proportional to $\left(x \dfrac{B/T}{R} \right)$, as shown by equation (8). Thus the P

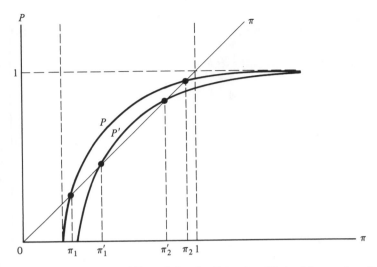

Figure 5.3   The probability of devaluation: the effect of increasing the average maturity of government debt

locus shifts down if there is a *ceteris paribus* increase in T or decrease in B/R and x: for instance, it may shift as shown in Figure 5.3, where the new locus is displayed as P' (the figure is again drawn for the case of a uniform distribution). It is apparent that, whatever the values of the other parameters, there is always a value of T high enough as to rule out any intersection between the P locus and the 45° line, leaving no equilibria with $\pi > 0$. This leads to:

Proposition 2: *(Conditions for the existence of a unique equilibrium with $\pi = 0$)*
For each given value of B/R (the ratio of public debt to reserves) and of x (the size of the expected devaluation), there is a critical maturity T^*, such that for $T > T^*$ only the equilibrium where $\pi = 0$ exists, i.e. confidence crises never occur. This critical maturity T^* is larger the higher B/R and x.

Thus, if the average maturity of public debt is higher than the critical value T^*, a devaluation cannot occur: if people expected it to occur, they would be systematically proven wrong by facts. In other words, state C is no longer a rational expectations equilibrium. The critical maturity T^* is obviously the value of T for which the locus P is tangential to the 45° line, and thus has a slope of 1. Formally, this implies that T^* satisfies both the equilibrium condition (8) and the tangency condition:

$$dP(\alpha g(\pi) > 1)/d\pi = 1 \qquad\qquad (9)$$

Solving equations (8) and (9) for T and π, one finds the critical maturity T^* and the associated probability of devaluation π^*. Differentiating the probability $P(\cdot)$ at $\pi = \pi^*$, it is easy to verify the claim that T^* is larger the higher the debt–reserves ratio B/R and the expected devaluation x:

$$\left. \frac{\partial T^*}{\partial (B/R)} \right|_{\pi = \pi^*} = T^*/(B/R) > 0 \tag{10a}$$

$$\left. \frac{\partial T^*}{\partial x} \right|_{\pi = \pi^*} = T^*/(\sigma \pi^* + 1/x) > 0 \tag{10b}$$

Example. Suppose that $F(\alpha)$ is a uniform distribution: $\alpha \sim U(0, \alpha_{\max})$. Then the equilibrium condition (8) specializes to:

$$\pi = 1 - \frac{1}{\alpha_{\max} g(\pi)} ,$$

and the tangency condition (9) becomes:

$$\frac{\frac{1}{\pi} + \sigma x}{\alpha_{\max} g(\pi)} = 1$$

These can be solved to yield

$$\pi^* = \frac{1}{2} - \frac{1}{\sigma x} + \left[\frac{1}{4} + \left(\frac{1}{\sigma x} \right)^2 \right]^{1/2}$$

and

$$T^* = (1 - \pi^*) \tau^* x e^{\sigma \pi^* x} \frac{B}{R} \alpha_{\max}$$

Setting the elasticity of money demand σ at 0.05, the expected devaluation at 10%, the debt–reserve ratio B/R at 39 (the actual value for Italy) and $\alpha_{\max}$ at 1 (so that at most the Treasury monetizes the whole increase in the interest burden), one finds that $T^* = 0.98$. If the time unit (implicit in the choice of x) is 1 year, in this example the confidence crisis equilibrium can be ruled out if the average maturity of public debt is at least 1 year.

The results in Proposition 1 and 2 generalize in at least two directions. *First*, they easily extend to the case in which currency is not fully backed by foreign exchange reserves. Predictably, it turns out that the lower the share of currency backed by foreign exchange rather than by domestic credit, the larger is the critical maturity T^*: the lower are foreign-exchange reserves relative to currency, the less likely is the Central Bank to withstand speculative attacks, so it is even more important to avoid conflicting behaviour by the Treasury in such occurrences. *Second*, the results do not hinge on the exponential form assumed for the money demand function: they go through also with a linear demand function (provided money demand is restricted to be non-negative).

5   Smoothing out maturing debt and other policy implications

The policy prescriptions that can be drawn from this simple model extend beyond those on the average maturity of public debt. There are *three* additional ways to increase the Central Bank's ability to withstand a confidence crisis.

First, the Treasury should *avoid concentrating bulges of maturing debt at specific moments* in time, and play instead with debt maturities so as to smooth out the time pattern of maturing debt. So far this point has not emerged from the analysis because the Treasury has been assumed to inherit from the past a constant amount B/T of maturing debt per unit time. If instead we suppose that the amount of debt that matures per unit time changes over time in a known fashion, the equilibrium probability of devaluation (conditional on a confidence crisis) will also shift around, rising and falling together with the amount of maturing debt. Formally, this is because in the function $g(\pi)$ of equation (8) the constant amount of maturing debt B/T would be replaced by a time-varying magnitude. Graphically, this translates in the locus P shifting up when maturing debt is high and down when it is low. Intutively, the private sector anticipates the Central Bank to be weakest if the confidence crisis takes place at a time when the Treasury is forced to re-issue a large portion of public debt, and in equilibrium this is indeed the case.

Second, the Treasury can further improve the system's resilience to confidence crises by *developing a well-functioning market for public debt denominated in foreign currencies*. This in fact provides the government with another way to bridge the gap of a speculative attack on the currency without paying abnormally high interest rates. To be able to absorb large amounts of debt in such circumstances, however, the market for foreign-denominated debt must be deep enough, which requires that the Treasury must feed it with substantial issues at regular intervals. This prescription is particularly relevant for countries such as Italy and Spain, that are characterized by negligible amounts of foreign currency debt (see Table 5.1, col. 4).

Third, the Central Bank can itself strengthen its position against specula-tors by *ensuring that foreign Central Banks will cooperate by lending foreign exchange in the event of a crisis*. If, for instance, foreign Banks open an emergency credit line in foreign currency up to a maximum amount L, the condition for devaluation (7) must be rewritten by adding

L to the RHS, and correspondingly the equilibrium condition (8) becomes:

$$\pi = P(\alpha g(\pi) - e^{\sigma \pi x} L/R > 1) \tag{8'}$$

This implies a downward shift in the P locus relative to the case with no cooperation from foreign Central Banks ($L = 0$), and thus also a fall in T^*, the minimal average debt maturity required to avoid confidence crises.

The latter two prescriptions both go in the direction of eliminating the asymmetry between the private and the public sector in the access to international financial markets. As explained in Section 2, (p. 128), such an asymmetry is crucial for speculative attacks to have a chance of success. Thus it is not surprising that reducing this asymmetry also reduces the danger of successful attacks.

A final word must be said on transitional problems. Up to this point, we have kept inflation out of the picture, assuming essentially that all debt is real debt. In reality, very few countries issue substantial amounts of indexed debt (the UK being one of the few exceptions). In fact, the reason why in high-debt countries the authorities are reluctant to lengthen the average maturity of debt is precisely that they expect the private sector to demand very high returns on long-term nominal debt, because of the implied risk of real capital losses due to inflation and because of the incentive that the government has to inflict such losses on the private sector. This problem can obviously be overcome by issuing long-term debt indexed to the price level or denominated in a foreign currency. Thus the choice from the debt menu – the mix of nominal, real and foreign currency debt – is crucial in making the transition to a more balanced maturity structure.

In this sense, the results of this paper connect with those obtained by Calvo on the desirability of indexed versus nominal debt. Indeed our model provides the opportunity of performing another comparison, that between indexed and foreign currency debt. While both types of debt can in fact ease the transition towards a longer average maturity, foreign currency debt turns out to have an additional advantage – that its real return is totally insensitive to expected exchange-rate changes, and thus to confidence crises.

6   Conclusions

In several European countries, there is growing concern over the combination of free capital mobility and fixed exchange rates that EC treaties have planned for the 1990s. This concern is often motivated by remarking that some member countries are entering the process of liberalization with a comparatively high level of public debt. It is feared that defending a fixed parity from speculative attacks may prove particularly arduous for high-debt countries, and may eventually force them to restore capital controls or to opt out of the fixed exchange-rates system.

In the paper we argue that, although there *is* reason to worry, there are steps that high-debt countries in the EEC can take to face the odds of the 1990s in a better position. These steps concern the way in which these countries should manage their debt, and are summarized by three simple rules: (i) lengthen the average maturity, (ii) smooth out the time pattern of maturing debt and (iii) develop a well-functioning market for foreign-currency debt. For Italy, Spain, Portugal and Greece, the adoption of these policies would imply a sharp turnaround relative to the practice so far prevailing in their debt management.

NOTES

We thank Willem Buiter, Daniel Cohen, Enrica Detragiache, Vittorio Grilli, Maury Obstfeld, Torsten Persson, Luigi Spaventa and Guido Tabellini for insightful comments and discussions. Seminar participants at the London School of Economics (Financial Markets Group), at the Centre for Economic Policy Research (London), at the Séminaire d'Economie Internationale (Paris) and the NBER–CEPR Conference on 'European Economic Integration: Towards 1992' (Cambridge, Mass.) also provided useful suggestions.

1 In Italy, for instance, the Treasury can draw from an account at the Central Bank up to 14% of public spending in the current fiscal year.

2 See Eichengreen and Giavazzi (1984), Tables 2–3. Short-term debt is defined as debt with 1 year to maturity or less.

3 Recall that in our model the easy access of the Treasury to Central Bank financing is crucial in determining the chances of success for a speculative attack on the currency.

4 The probability q of a confidence crisis (state C) should not be confused with the probability π of a devaluation: the first is the probability that a *confidence crisis* will occur in some *future* period, whereas the second is the probability that a *devaluation* is going to occur in the *current* period. The two are obviously related: since a confidence crisis is defined as a state in which $\pi > 0$, q is the probability of observing $\pi > 0$ in some future period. As we shall see below, there are sets of parameter values for which confidence crises can never occur under rational expectations, i.e. it is always $\pi = 0$: obviously for those values the probability of state C occurring is zero as well ($q = 0$). When instead the parameters are such that confidence crises can occur, in general there can be several rational expectations equilibria, each characterized by a different positive value of π. Thus, to be rigorous, we should have attached a distinct probability q_i to each of the rational expectations equilibria with a positive probability of devaluation, and denote each of the latter by π_i. We have opted for the simpler notation in the text to avoid confusion to the reader at this early stage in the presentation of the model. It should be clear that nothing of

substance would change in the derivations and results of the model by making use of the more rigorous notation.

5 Obviously the two key institutional constraints are the overdraft limit and the time allowed to rebalance the account. The effect of these two constraints on the recourse to the overdraft facility will depend on the frequency of confidence crises. For instance, the shorter the time allowed to rebalance the account and the higher the frequency of confidence crises, the lower will be the optimal value of α, *ceteris paribus*: the Treasury will not risk being caught by another crisis just at the time when it must rebalance a large overdraft at the Central Bank. In the model of this paper we do not provide a formal analysis of the effect of these constraints on the choice of α by the Treasury.

6 Approximating the rate of interest on a 1-period bond issued in state C by the logarithm of the corresponding return, $(1 + r^*)/(1 - \pi x)$.

7 To show that P starts at 0 for $\pi = \bar{\pi}$, notice that at $\alpha g(\bar{\pi}) = \alpha/\alpha_{max} \leq 1$, and therefore $P(\alpha g(\bar{\pi}) > 1) = 0$. Similarly, to prove that P has an asymptote at 1 for π large, notice that $\lim_{\pi \to \infty} \alpha g(\pi) = \infty$, implying $\lim_{\pi \to \infty} P(\alpha g(\pi) > 1) = 1$. Finally, the proof that P is increasing goes as follows: the probability $P(\alpha g(\pi) > 1) = 1 - F(1/g(\pi))$, and its first derivative with respect to π is:

$$P'(\cdot) = F'(1/g(\pi))[(\sigma x + 1/\pi)/g(\pi)] > 0$$

The second derivative of $P(\alpha g(\pi) > 1)$ is:

$$P''(\cdot) = - F'(1/g(\pi))[(\sigma x + 1/\pi)/g(\pi)]^2 \\ - F'(1/g(\pi)[1/\pi + (\sigma x + 1/\pi)^2]g(\pi)$$

whose sign is in general ambiguous because $F''(\cdot)$, the slope of the density function, can be either positive or negative. $P''(\cdot)$ is however unambiguously negative for π large, when $F''(\cdot)$ becomes positive. In the special case of a uniform distribution for α, $F''(\cdot) = 0$, so that $P''(\cdot)$ is negative for *all* values of π, so that the function $P(\cdot)$ is concave.

REFERENCES

Barro, Robert J. (1979). 'On the Determination of Public Debt', *Journal of Political Economy* **87**, 940–71.

Calvo, Guillermo (1988). 'Servicing the Public Debt: the Role of Expectations', *American Economic Review* **78**, 647–61.

(1990, forthcoming). 'Controlling Inflation: The Problem of Non-Indexed Debt', in S. Edwards and F. Larrain, eds., *Debt Adjustment and Recovery: Latin America's Prospects for Growth and Development*, New York: Basil Blackwell.

Eichengreen, Barry and Francesco, Giavazzi (1984). 'Inflation, Consolidation or Capital Levy? European Debt Management in the 1920s', paper presented at the Annual Meetings of the American Economic Association, December.

Fischer, Stanley (1983). 'Welfare Aspects of Government Issue of Indexed Bonds', in *Inflation, Debt and Indexation*, edited by Rudiger Dornbusch and Mario Simonsen, Cambridge, MA: The MIT Press, 233–56.

Lucas, Robert E., Jr. and Nancy L. Stokey (1983). 'Optimal Fiscal Policy and Monetary Policy in an Economy without Capital', *Journal of Monetary Economics* **12**, 55–93.

Obstfeld, Maurice (1986). 'Rational and Self-Fulfilling Balance-of-Payments Crises', *American Economic Review* **76**, 72–81.

Persson, Torsten and Lars E.O. Svensson (1984). 'Time-Consistent Fiscal Policy and Government Cash Flow', *Journal of Monetary Economics* **14**, 365–74.

Persson, Mats, Torsten Persson and Lars E.O. Svensson (1987). 'Time Consistency of Fiscal and Monetary Policy', *Econometrica* **55**, 1419–31.

Tobin, James (1963). 'An Essay on the Principles of Debt Management', in *Fiscal and Debt Management Policies*, Englewood Cliffs, NJ: Prentice Hall, 143–218.

Discussion

ENRICA DETRAGIACHE

A small open economy in a regime of fixed exchange rates and free capital mobility with a large stock of government debt that is rolled over every period is vulnerable to 'confidence crises'. Such crises are brought about by exogenous changes in the expectations about the future value of the exchange rate that are self-fulfilling. Even when the level of the exchange rate is sustainable, that is there is a rational expectations equilibrium in which no devaluation occurs, there may be other equilibria, supported by 'pessimistic' expectations, in which the Central Bank is forced to devalue the currency. The goal of the paper is to demonstrate how appropriate public debt management, especially a lengthening of the average maturity of debt, can greatly reduce and indeed completely eliminate the possibility of such crises.

Let us first go over the mechanics of a confidence crisis, as described by Giavazzi and Pagano. A crisis occurs when agents expect a devaluation to occur in the next period. Such a change in expectations raises the domestic interest rate through the uncovered interest parity equation. This in turn generates an additional fiscal burden equal to the increase in the interest rate times the amount of debt rolled over in the period. The Treasury can finance the extra burden either by increasing borrowing from the private sector or by drawing from a temporary credit line with the Central Bank. The public, not knowing the Treasury's preferences, assigns some positive probability to the latter alternative. If it withdraws from the credit line, the Treasury increases the money supply, and it does so at a time in which money demand decreases because of the increase in the nominal interest rate. To preserve money-market equilibrium and maintain the exchange rate parity the Central Bank must seek foreign exchange reserves. In practice, the additional fiscal burden imposed by the increase in the interest rate is paid off through a sale of reserves, that is a reduction in the stock of foreign assets in the economy. When reserves are not sufficient to close the gap in the money market, however, a devaluation must follow, and expectations are validated. Thus, confidence crises are rational expectations equilibria of the model, and these equilibria are Pareto-dominated by the equilibrium in which agents expect no devaluation.

A role for the maturity structure of public debt immediately emerges from this picture: the shorter the average maturity, the larger the amount of debt that needs to be rolled over at any time, the larger the cost for the Treasury of a change in expectations. With a larger additional fiscal burden, the more likely is the Treasury to monetize an amount that forces the Central Bank to devalue. The authors prove that there exists a crucial maturity beyond which no self-fulfilling confidence crisis can arise for a given amount of reserves and given the public's beliefs on the behaviour of the Treasury. Hence the policy prescriptions of lengthening the average debt maturity and spreading the amount of debt to be rolled over evenly through time.

To evaluate the proposed policies it is important to notice that it is not true in this model that lengthening the average debt maturity always reduces the probability of a confidence crisis. As Figure 5.3 shows, it is possible that with a longer maturity the economy will move to an equilibrium in which the probability of a self-fulfilling crisis is higher. This can happen if the equilibrium with a shorter maturity was π_1 corresponding to curve P, and the new equilibrium is π_1 corresponding to curve P' in Figure 5.3. This counterintuitive implication raises some doubts on the ability of the model to capture what the authors really have in mind. It also suggests that lengthening debt maturity may even be counterproductive if it is not done drastically enough. But how much is enough? The answer unfortunately depends on the probability distribution that the public has about the preferences of the Treasury (see Proposition 2).

The authors take the existence of the Treasury's overdraft facility with the Central Bank as an institutional feature. In reality, such a facility can be regulated through legislation, and it is therefore a policy instrument. When this is accounted for, it is easy to see that confidence crises can be eliminated for instance by making the maximum amount that the Treasury can borrow from the Central Bank depend on the size of reserves. By rearranging equation (7) in the paper, a devaluation occurs with positive probability if and only if

$$\alpha x \pi \frac{B}{T} > R e^{-\sigma \pi x}$$

The left-hand side of this inequality is the amount that the Treasury borrows from the Central Bank. Suppose that $\bar{B}$ is the maximum that the Treasury is allowed to borrow from the Central Bank in any given year. Clearly no devaluation can ever occur if

$$\bar{B} \le \max_{\pi} [R e^{-\sigma \pi x}] = R$$

By setting the maximum of the overdraft facility equal to the amount of reserves confidence crises could be ruled out. This threshold does not depend on the functional form of the probability distribution of beliefs, so it should be easier to evaluate than the critical debt maturity.

In general, eliminating the possibility for the Treasury to monetize increases in debt service would completely rule out the possibility of the type of confidence crises analyzed here. The authors suggest that an overdraft facility may be beneficial since it can avoid burdening future taxpayers with the costs of additional debt service. This argument is not completely convincing since the credit line must be quickly rebalanced, so that an increase in debt or a decrease in current expenditure must take place in the nearby future, although this is not modeled in the paper. To show that maintaining a large overdraft facility and lengthening maturity is a better policy option than eliminating the facility altogether, the analysis should show that there are benefits in temporarily financing budget needs through Central Bank reserves rather than with increases in indebtedness.

On the other hand, if the Treasury needs a credit line with the Central Bank to finance part of the deficit through the inflation tax, lengthening maturity is not feasible unless a risk-premium is paid, as the authors point out in their final comments. Investors will demand a premium equal to expected inflation, otherwise they will buy foreign assets. With rational investors that have access to the international capital market, the maturity structure of debt does not affect the cost of financing any given deficit.

The authors also suggest that creating a market for public debt denominated in foreign currency would help the Central Bank defend the parity in countries with a large government debt. In a world of free capital mobility, government bonds denominated in foreign currency may attract foreign investors, and open the way to financing public deficits with foreign savings. As Latin American experience suggests, this is not always a desirable outcome. From this perspective, one may be tempted to conclude that to the extent that confidence crises are a way to impose some fiscal restraint on governments that have none of their own, they should be the welcome. In any case, the authors also consider instituting emergency credit lines among Central Banks. This option seems to be the most desirable, since it provides a good instrument to withstand speculative attacks on the exchange rate, while at the same time preventing the Treasury from increasing its foreign borrowing.

Discussion

MAURICE OBSTFELD

Francesco Giavazzi and Marco Pagano have written a stimulating paper that identifies the maturity structure of the public debt as a key influence on the probability of financial crisis. In these comments I will question aspects of the authors' modeling strategy and even take issue with their explanation of why maturity structure matters. I hope these criticisms will not obscure my basic message: Giavazzi and Pagano have raised a pertinent and challenging policy question worthy of much future research effort.

In the Giavazzi–Pagano model, a government wakes up to find that the public has temporarily lost confidence in the existing exchange-rate parity. Domestic-currency interest rates rise as a result, and the government must decide whether to borrow on harsher terms or spend some foreign reserves and thereby imperil the exchange-rate peg's survival. Governments differ in their propensities to draw down reserves, and the current government's 'type' in this regard can only be guessed by the public. In a rational-expectations equilibrium, the probability that the government weathers the crisis is accurately reflected in the market's expectation of currency depreciation.

On its face the story is a plausible one, but closer scrutiny raises questions about the properties of the equilibrium studied and the model's policy implications. I take up several of these questions in turn.

What kind of crisis?

Giavazzi and Pagano make the case that a confidence crisis is most likely when the maturity structure of public debt is uneven. With an uneven maturity structure, there will be dates on which the Treasury must approach the market to refinance a disproportionate share of the public debt. If public confidence is low on those dates, however, refinancing will take place on terms unfavourable to the government. The desire to somehow circumvent these unfavourable market terms lies behind the Giavazzi—Pagano confidence crisis.

It is important to distinguish the type of crisis Giavazzi and Pagano describe from the different situation in which the government is suddenly unable to borrow or even refinance existing debt on *any* terms. In that situation a government with a large chunk of maturing debt would simply be unable to roll it over, and would need to come up with enough cash to repay creditors immediately.

The government is not completely credit-constrained in Giavazzi and Pagano's account: it can still borrow in domestic currency, albeit at unpleasant money interest rates. Public-sector borrowing in foreign currency is ruled out by assumption, but the government's option to roll over its domestic-currency debt changes the way we should think about the problem of uneven debt maturity structure.[1] The problem is not simply to find the money to pay creditors off today. Instead, the problem is an intertemporal one that certainly involves today's maturing debt, but also involves other factors.

The essentially static nature of Giavazzi and Pagano's model, as well as their explanation that maturity matters because 'it determines the amount of bonds that mature and must be renewed at each moment in time', might lead careless readers to misinterpret the government's problem. I therefore found it illuminating to adopt the following alternative perspective, which reveals intertemporal considerations that the authors have on the whole left implicit.

An explicitly intertemporal interpretation

A nonmonetary model with two periods (called 0 and 1) captures most features of the economic problem. The government's objective is to minimize the distortion burden of taxes levied and subsidies paid, subject to the constraint of public solvency. Specifically, let τ_i denote net taxes levied on date i, b_i the net government payment (principal plus interest) due to the public on date i, and g_i government purchases on date i ($i = 0, 1$). All these variables are measured in real terms, as is the market interest factor between dates 0 and 1, denoted R. The problem

$$\text{minimize} \quad (\tau_0)^2 + \beta(\tau_1)^2 \quad (0 < \beta < 1) \tag{1}$$

$$\text{subject to} \quad \tau_0 + (1 + R)\,\tau_1 \geq (b_0 + g_0) + (1/R)(b_1 + g_1) \tag{2}$$

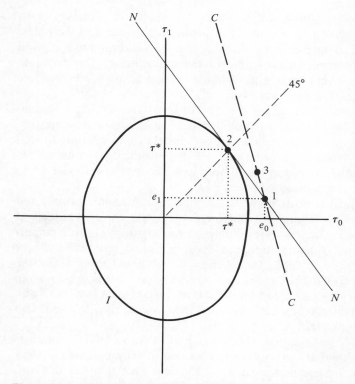

Figure 5A.1   The effect of a rise in the interest rate on the government's intertemporal budget constraint

suffices to generate the intertemporal tax-smoothing behaviour assumed by Giavazzi and Pagano. The time profile of government purchases is exogenous to the model.

Figure 5A.1 shows how the government solves it problem when the interest factor is $R^N = 1/\beta$, equal to the slope of budget line NN. The government's period 'endowments' are $e_0 = b_0 + g_0$ and $e_1 = b_1 + g_1$, so NN passes through point 1 and the optimum is at point 2, where NN is tangent to the smallest attainable isocost contour I. The best intertemporal tax pattern is flat with $\tau_0 = \tau_1 = \tau^*$.

How does the maturity structure of the debt fit into this framework? The maturity structure is fully described by the time profile of government payments to the private sector, (b_0, b_1), relative to the time path of government purchases, (g_0, g_1). These payments are all predetermined from the perspective of date 0, but a hypothetical debt rescheduling *prior* to date 0 could result in a government endowment point anywhere along

NN. Such a rescheduling changes the maturity structure of debt that the government inherits on date 0, but not the debt's present value when calculated using the interest factor R^N.[2] In the case shown, the debt's maturity structure is skewed toward the short end in the sense that the government desires to go to the market and borrow to meet its period-0 bills (which could include principal repayments).

To see why this skewness may matter *ex post*, imagine that there is a second equilibrium interest factor R^C relevant in crisis states and equal to the slope of CC. Given the predetermined endowment point 1, the government ends up choosing point 3, on an isocost contour inferior to I, if a crisis occurs. Prior decisions on maturity structure have made the government a market borrower in period 0, so it suffers an unfavourable shock to its intertemporal terms of trade if R^C rather than R^N materializes. Clearly if the government held some 'foreign' assets, as in Giavazzi and Pagano's story, it might now have an incentive to run them down; but to discuss this possibility rigorously we would have to incorporate such additional government resources into the model from the start.[3]

Implications for debt management

The effect of an interest-rate rise is naturally different if the government starts out at an endowment point other than point 1. Notice in particular that if the government had inherited instead endowment point 2 on NN, where $b_0 + g_0 = b_1 + g_1 = \tau^*$, it would be insulated from the shift in the intertemporal terms of trade that a crisis entails, in the sense that the original optimum would remain feasible. (Indeed, a very small change in the interest rate now has essentially no budgetary impact.) With these more favourable initial conditions, total government payments on each date just equal the optimally smoothed tax level for the noncrisis state; and since the government need not enter the bond market to implement its tax plan, it is not hurt by a change in market interest rates. If the goal of debt management is to neutralize the damaging budgetary effects of crises, policymakers acting before date 0 should ensure that point 2 is the date-0 endowment point.

The resulting debt-management rule does *not* prescribe evening out the debt maturity structure (that is, setting $b_0 = b_1$). The rule requires instead that overall government outlays equal planned taxes period by period, or, in the terminology of Persson and Svensson (1984), that government 'cash-flow' is zero on every date. Only in special cases would a flat maturity structure emerge, for example, when taxes are constant over time absent a crisis (as here) and government purchases g are also constant. In general, unusually high government purchases on any date would make unusually *low* government debt payments desirable. Conversely, there may be nothing wrong with a large debt coming due on a particular date if government purchases are sufficiently low then.

Figure 5A.1 might seem to imply that it would be even better for the government to be a net lender in period 0; but this is where the two-period setup becomes misleading. In an infinite-horizon model with no final period, the future eventually becomes the present, and a zero cash-flow rule therefore emerges. To see this in the simple case where the noncrisis interest factor is constant at $1/\beta$, write the government budget constraint as

$$\sum_{i=0}^{\infty} (1/R^N)^i \tau_i \geq \sum_{i=0}^{\infty} (1/R^N)^i (b_i + g_i) \tag{3}$$

and let τ^* again denote the constant tax rate satisfying this constraint. Then the debt structure $b_i^* = \tau^* - g_i$, if put in place before period 0 and subsequently maintained, immunises the government from a sudden shift in the interest factor on date 0 or a later date.

An implication of the infinite-horizon perspective is that more is involved in generating confidence crises than the amount of debt the government must redeem on any particular date. What is at issue is the effect of interest-rate shifts on the entire feasible set of government fiscal policies. In general, any debt maturity structure that leaves the government vulnerable to adverse movements in its intertemporal terms of trade could admit the possibility of a Giavazzi–Pagano crisis.[4]

Alternative models of crisis

The Giavazzi–Pagano model is an intriguing attempt to apply Calvo's (1988) analysis of debt default to devaluation. Like Calvo's model, theirs is driven by a rise in domestic interest rates that induces the government to validate market fears *ex post*. The authors' account of devaluation crises is, however, incomplete in several respects. I have already mentioned the model's essentially static nature, which leaves implicit the government's incentive to smooth taxes over time. Also implicit are the ways devaluation affects government finance, the sense in which devaluation carries utility costs, and the factors that enable the authorities to peg the exchange rate anew after devaluation has occurred.

The Giavazzi–Pagano model shares with others in this area, however, the central insight that crises may result from a government's inability to precommit its policy choices with credibility. As Enrica Detragiache observes in her comments on the model, crises would never arise in it if credible restrictions on monetary financing of the deficit were possible.

Private expectations are central to these stories, of course, and I have some doubts about the way 'rational' expectations are modeled here. In particular, it seem unrealistic to assume that market expectations of the probability of a crisis and of the *ex post* extent of a devaluation are not influenced by variables like the level of central-bank reserves, which clearly matter in practice. In Obstfeld (1989) I report some progress on developing a model in which private agents as well as the government maximize, and in which expectations are rational but depend on the economic state variables that enter the government's budget constraint. The dynamics implied are more complex (and more compelling, I think) than those derived using simpler 'open-loop' expectations assumptions.[5]

Giavazzi and Pagano have taken up one important aspect of public financial crisis, but as they acknowledge, a broader analysis of confidence would require consideration of debt monetization and questions of seigniorage in general. This broadening could change some of the policy conclusions reached in the paper. Blanchard, Dornbusch and Buiter (1986) argue, for example, that in a world with a sticky general price level, a shortening of the public-debt maturity structure is likely to reduce the 'capital-levy' motive for inflation. This argument, if valid in practice, supports a case for short-term public debt. In contrast, the Giavazzi–Pagano model makes a case for consols.[6]

Giavazzo and Pagano suggest that a greater scope for official foreign-currency borrowing – more broadly, debt indexation – could help governments avoid currency crises. The recommendation is very much in the spirit of Tobin (1963), who argued long ago that indexing government debt would reduce the attractions of inflation. Debt denomination becomes less relevant, however, when the government's solvency comes into question; and country risk itself leads to currency risk by raising incentives to devalue and inflate.

In this connection, official EMS undertakings to lend *à outrance* for exchange-rate support raise potential fiscal problems that could undermine the credibility of fixed parities. Suppose, for example, that Germany is lending intervention marks to Italy, and simultaneously sterilizing the expansionary effect on the German central-bank money stock. This set of operations amounts to loans from the German public to the Italian government through a financial intermediary, the Bundesbank, which sells domestic-currency debt to Germans and acquires counterpart claims on the Banca d'Italia. In lending Italy reserves, however, the Bundesbank is taking risks that make Germany's public finances dependent in part on Italian credibility. One wonders how long this process would continue in the face of a sustained attack on the lira–mark parity.

152   **Discussion by Maurice Obstfeld**

NOTES

Research support from the National Science Foundation is gratefully acknowledged. These comments were first sketched out during a visit to the International Monetary Fund's research department, which I thank for its hospitality.

1 Since there is no sovereign risk in the model – only currency risk – it is unclear what prevents the government (including the central bank) from issuing debt denominated in foreign currency. After all, why should people expect the government to make payments on domestic-currency debt but not foreign? Notice that the government effectively 'borrows' foreign currency when it runs down its foreign reserves through the act of money creation.
2 Whether a rescheduling of the type described is feasible prior to date 0 is actually a subtle question, since alternative maturity structure will affect the probability of crisis and thus the interest rate the market expects to prevail on date 0. Thus, rescheduling will not generally move the endowment along a straight line like *NN*. I am ignoring this problem for expository purposes, although it clearly would be central to a more complete model of crisis prevention through debt management.
3 Indeed, income from foreign reserves should appear somewhere in the government budget constraint specified by Giavazzi and Pagano.
4 The simple guidelines for optimal debt management suggested here are closely related to the conditions ensuring the time consistency of optimal fiscal policy in similar models. See Persson and Svensson (1984).
5 As an example, my (1988) paper presents an intertemporal monetary model of devaluation crises based on open-loop expectations formation. In that model the money-stock component of the inflation-tax base is central to the crisis mechanism.
6 In their contribution to this volume, Calvo and Guidotti study how the possibility of inflation affects the optimal maturity (and indexation) structure of government debt.

REFERENCES

Blanchard, Olivier, Rudiger Dornbusch and Willem Buiter (1986). 'Public Debt and Fiscal Responsibility'. In Olivier Blanchard, Rudiger Dornbusch and Richard Layard, editors, *Restoring Europe's Prosperity*. Cambridge, MA: MIT Press, pp. 125–33.
Calvo, Guillermo A. (1988). 'Servicing the Public Debt: The Role of Expectations'. *American Economic Review* **78**, 647–61.
Obstfeld, Maurice (1988). 'A Theory of Capital Flight and Currency Depreciation'. Unpublished manuscript, August.
   (1989). 'Dynamic Seigniorage Theory: An Exploration'. Working paper no. 2869, National Bureau of Economic Research, February.
Persson, Torsten and Lars E.O. Svensson (1984). 'Time-Consistent Fiscal Policy and Government Cash-Flow'. *Journal of Monetary Economics* **14**, 365–74.
Tobin, James (1963). 'An Essay on the Principles of Debt Management'. In *Fiscal and Debt Management Policies*. Englewood Cliffs, NJ: Prentice-Hall (for the Commission on Money and Credit), pp. 143–218.

6 Funding crises in the aftermath of World War I

GAIL E. MAKINEN and G. THOMAS
WOODWARD

The problems encountered by governments facing large budget deficits arise frequently in economic history. Yet, even when these deficits are reduced and the budget balanced, they still leave a legacy of debt that lingers well afterward. And the inability to roll over this debt can present essentially the same dilemma as the deficits that gave rise to it.

The problem of rolling over existing debt is the focus of this study. It is distinguished from the problem of borrowing to cover a deficit in that it is not concerned with financing a current shortfall of revenues below expenditures, but with refinancing already-incurred indebtedness. When this phenomenon manifests itself in an unwillingness of the public to purchase new government securities as old ones mature, we refer to it as a 'funding crisis'.

We turn to war-time to start our examination. Wars, Brown (1990) reminds us, are a major reason for the growth of public debt. This was especially true of the 1914–18 War. Among its legacies were major additions to the public debt in all belligerent countries, due both to the costs of waging war and for reconstruction afterwards. Some of these nations escaped their large internal debts as a consequence of hyperinflation. Others were faced with having to manage much-enlarged public debts, a high proportion of which consisted of short-dated maturities – the so-called 'floating debt' – which required treasuries to return frequently to the market for funds.

Several countries encountered difficulties in the 1920s when large numbers of creditors failed to renew subscriptions to the outstanding debt as it matured. They first responded to these funding crises by monetizing the debt as it fell due, igniting potentially serious inflations. The inflations were ultimately brought under control when the countries consolidated their floating debt.

This paper discusses three of these funding crises in detail: those in France, Belgium, and Italy. Each occurred during the summer of 1926

153

when the respective budgets were either in surplus or very near being balanced.[1] In addition, we also examine the funding crises in Greece and Portugal, episodes that occurred a few years earlier than the other three and in the presence of persistent budget deficits.

We analyse why these funding crises occurred when they did, their causes, and what lessons they hold for the present. We conclude that they resulted from a *debt management policy* of paying less than the equilibrium interest rate on government securities. Such a policy is equivalent to a *monetary policy* of pegging interest rates, a policy that is known to yield an endogenous and unstable money supply. Our conclusion contrasts with the view that these funding crises resulted from a *lack of confidence* among creditors in the respective governments, due, among other things, to protracted budget deficits or to *fiscal policy*.

We proceed as follows. In Section 1 we outline the events that occurred in France, Belgium, and Italy, analysing what took place in each episode. In Section 2 we more briefly discuss the cases of Greece and Portugal. In Section 3 we draw conclusions and discuss the relevance of these historical episodes for contemporary policy.

1   France, Belgium and Italy

France, Belgium, and Italy all had large budget deficits in the period immediately following World War I. Each made great strides in reducing these deficits over several years. Yet all experienced a funding crisis in the spring and summer of 1926 when their budgets were nearly balanced.

1.1   France

Like all belligerents in World War I, France relied heavily on deficit finance during the conflict. Moreover, when the hostilities ended, French budget deficits did not. The northern part of France, as the major battleground of the western front, evidenced the extent of devastation that could be wrought when all the resources of a modern economy were engaged in the task of physical destruction. Expecting that the Germans would pay for this damage, France in the early 1920s borrowed considerable sums to restore the area.

1.1.1 Fiscal and economic performance, 1920–25

Substantial progress was nevertheless made toward achieving fiscal balance in this period. As Table 6.1 shows, no matter which measure of deficit is used, by 1926, the eve of the funding crisis, the French budget was in virtual balance if not surplus.[2] In addition to the budgetary

	1920	1921	1922	1923	1924	1925	1926
Dulles	38.0	28.0	27.7	18.1	9.1	4.7	−0.2
Haig	37.7	24.9	17.4	15.8	6.8	4.4	1.5
Official	17.1	9.3	9.8	11.8	7.1	1.5	−1.1

Table 6.1. Alternative measures of the French budget deficit, 1920–26 (billion francs)

Note: − indicates surplus.

Sources: Dulles (1929), Haig (1929), and Ministère de l'Economie et des Finances (1966).

improvement, real growth, inflation, and the efforts made to balance the budget reduced the ratio of internal debt to NNP from 1.74 in 1922 to 1.4 in 1926. In real terms the internal debt declined nearly 50% in these four years.

The method used to sell the internal debt was common among countries at the time. For longer-term debt, the treasury would announce the interest rate to be paid on the issue and then hold open the subscription list for a fixed period. Treasury bills, on the other hand, were on sale continuously (or on 'tap') at fixed rates of interest.

Long-term bonds were sold primarily to raise funds to restore the areas damaged by the war. As shown in Table 6.2, the major means of financing the budget deficits and managing the debt was through issuing short-dated

Year	Short Term Bonds	Long Term Bonds	Advances	National Defense Bills	Deposits with Treasury	Total Internal Debt	External debt [a]	[b]
1920	0.4	133.2	30.6	50.9	4.1	219.2	36.0	105.1
1921	10.3	138.4	28.7	60.4	3.6	241.4	35.7	84.0
1922	26.8	134.0	28.0	59.1	6.5	254.4	35.4	98.0
1923	39.9	143.8	27.9	57.7	5.9	275.2	35.7	140.9
1924	46.6	146.5	27.5	56.4	8.5	285.5	36.5	142.9
1925	39.5	153.2	41.2	48.1	9.6	291.6	36.5	213.9
1926	38.8	156.9	41.6	44.5	10.1	291.9	36.7	205.3

Table 6.2. France: distribution of the national debt, 1920–26 (billion francs)

Sources: Rogers (1929) and Haig (1929).
[a]Measured in billions of gold francs.
[b]Converted to nominal francs.

	1920	1921	1922	1923	1924	1925	1926
Notes	38.1	37.7	36.4	37.4	39.9	44.1	53.4
% change		1.1	−3.5	2.8	7.3	11.1	20.1
M1	63.2	62.4	62.0	64.1	69.4	76.6	95.3
% change		−1.3	−0.6	3.4	8.3	10.4	24.4

Table 6.3. The French money stock, 1920–26 (billion francs)

Note: Averages of monthly data.
Sources: League of Nations (1920–27) and Rogers (1929).

securities and obtaining advances from the Bank of France. Especially important were the National Defence Bills issued in maturities of 1, 3, 6, and 12 months. Between January 1, 1919 and mid-July 1926, the rates of interest on the bills were changed only twice: in March 1922 the rates were lowered approximately 0.5%; in February 1923 the rates on the three longer-term maturities were raised back again.

By means of Bank of France advances to the government, the supply of notes increased roughly five-fold from the beginning to the end of the war. Further increases occurred in 1919. But by the end of 1919 total advances had stabilized. A ceiling was placed on the total note issue of the Bank of France, and the government (under the François-Marsal Convention) was required to reduce its advances from the Bank by Frs. 2.0 billion per year for all years after 1920. Growth of notes and the money supply is shown in Table 6.3.

Economic performance during the post-war period was impressive. After a short but brief economic downturn during 1920–21, real national income through 1926 grew at an average annual rate of 6.8% per year (see Table 6.4). Industrial production evidences a similar pattern of growth. By 1923 national income had surpassed pre-war levels.

	1920	1921	1922	1923	1924	1925	1926
National Income (billions of 1938 francs)	270	250	304	329	381	384	401
Industrial Production (1913 = 100	65.5	54.4	81.5	91.7	110.2	109.0	125.3

Table 6.4. France: real national income and industrial production, 1920–26
Sources: Ministère de l'Economie et des Finances (1966) and League of Nations (1920–27).

	1920	1921	1922	1923	1924	1925	1926
Wholesale prices	520	352	334	428	499	561	718
% change		− 32	− 5	28	17	12	28
Exchange rate*	7.04	7.46	8.20	6.08	5.24	4.77	3.24
% change		6	10	− 26	− 14	9	32

Table 6.5. France: prices and the exchange rate, 1920–26

*US cents per franc.
Sources: Rogers (1929), League of Nations (1920–27), and Board of Governors (1943).

The French experience with inflation during the period was irregular. Prices moved up with the note circulation during the war, and burst forward to a peak in 1920 as import prices responded to the unpegging of the exchange rate. The price level then declined during the 1920–21 downturn (see Table 6.5). Once the recovery got under way, inflation took hold again, with a burst in late 1923–early 1924. Again prices receded only to move upward, accelerating rapidly in 1926.

A dominant political concern of France in the early 1920s was extraction of reparations from Germany. After Germany failed to make a required payment late in 1922, the French occupied the Ruhr and tried to extract the payments in kind. While the policy was judged a failure, it did lead to the Dawes Plan which regularized the payments Germany made to both France and Belgium. For the first three Dawes Plan years 1924–27, France received slightly over Frs. 10 billion in reparations.

Between September 1923 and February 1924, the foreign exchange value of the franc fell from 6.2 to 3.8 US cents. The government showed few signs of having any trouble selling its debt, and advances from the Bank of France were relatively steady. But the runup was taken as a sign that something more serious had to be done about the budget deficit. Premier Raymond Poincaré moved to push through parliament a 20% increase in most taxes ('double decime'), something he had failed to accomplish in the months before. On the strength of this increase, France borrowed $100 million from J.P. Morgan and £4.0 million from Lazard-Freres. The funds were used to engineer a successful 'bear squeeze' against those who had sold the franc short. The franc recovered and the foreign exchange expended in its defense was also recovered and held in reserve for future contingencies.

In the fall of 1924, Poincaré's *Bloc National* coalition of right-center parties gave way to a centre-left coalition known as the *Cartel des*

Gauches. The parties of the *Cartel* put forth several different debt management strategies. Among them were (1) a forced consolidation of short- for long-term debt, (2) a capital levy, and (3) the monetization of the short-term debt. Short on votes, the *Cartel* never had any real chance of passing any of these schemes into law.[3] Between June 1924 and July 1926, France had seven premiers and nine ministers of finance. Of particular note was the fall of the Herriot government in 1925 when it was discovered to have induced the Bank of France to conceal that it had exceeded the statutory limit on note issue and advances to the government.

1.1.2 The funding crisis of 1925–26

In 1925 the treasury had to roll over some Frs. 40 billion in bills as well as refinance Frs. 22 billion of longer-term debt that was set to mature. In the second quarter of the year, many creditors refused to renew their subscriptions to the maturing debt. Three times in 1925 the statutory limits on advances by the Bank of France to the state and on its note issue were raised as the government monetized the maturing issues. While the longer-term issues that were sold in 1924 and 1925 carried higher rates of interest, yields on the short-term debt were not raised at all.

As the note issue and money supply rose at a more rapid rate, so did the price level. This was matched by a depreciation of the franc. For the periods May-June and June-July 1926, the annualized rate of inflation (measured by wholesale prices) was 136% and 346% respectively. Between May and July 1926, the dollar rose in Paris at a 490% annual rate. In the midst of this crisis, on July 1926, Poincaré was called again to be premier when no candidate from the *Cartel* parties could command a majority.

Poincaré moved quickly. The remaining Morgan loan of 1924 was used to support the franc on foreign exchange markets. Next, to give the treasury a working balance, a billion franc loan was secured from private banks in France. Finally, additional revenue was secured through changes in the tax system, a large portion of which was pledged to a newly created sinking fund whose purpose was to retire and refund the short-term debt.

1.1.3 Assessment

The situation in France is illustrated clearly by the data in Tables 6.1 and 6.3. As the deficit fell, money growth rose. Indeed, in 1921 and 1922, the government, even though it ran a large deficit, was able to repay advances in accordance with the François-Marsal convention. But by 1925–26 the government had to obtain advances in excess of its deficit. This was not an inflation that grew worse as the government sought to finance its budget deficit through money creation. It was a funding crisis rooted in the problem of rolling over existing debt. Unable to roll over debt, money was created to fill the gap. With more money the price level rose. The inflation made debt less desirable and harder to sell. And the process repeated itself with higher and higher rates of inflation and money growth.

What caused a funding crisis in 1925–26? The budget was better than before, the burden of the debt no greater. The reparations question was largely settled and the parties of the left were proving repeatedly that they posed little threat to the owners of capital. Many observers therefore point to 'loss of confidence', by which they apparently mean growing doubts about whether the government would service its debt.[4] Such doubts need not be founded in a rational assessment of the government's fiscal situation. They might have been engendered by an event that has little direct relevance to domestic economic problems merely because people regard it as worrisome. As a result, the public's willingness to hold government securities may shift in a fleeting, volatile, and mercurial fashion. And all that would be needed is a belief that others might not renew their holdings of debt. As in a bank run, one need not have a good reason for believing the bank to be unsound, the importance of not being last in line for one's money is enough to get you to stand in one.

Yet, if repudiation was feared by inflation, consolidation, or levy, debt might still have been sold at a higher interest rate. Of course, there are rates so high that they make default more likely. But clearly that was not the case in France.[5] And at the rates of inflation experienced in 1925 and 1926 is there any wonder that holders of the debt were abandoning it?

Because money creation filled the financing gap left by maturing debt, France was essentially pegging the interest rate. The rate wasn't held strictly constant, but clearly it was not keeping up with reasonable expectations of inflation. As long as this debt management/monetary regime continued, accelerating inflation and debt runoff would continue as well. Consolidation of the debt made it possible to change this regime. This regime change, as embodied in the sinking fund created by Poincaré, was the necessary condition for stopping the inflation, irrespective of any tax increases.

1.2 Belgium

The economic history of Belgium after the war parallels that of France. It sustained heavy war damage, on which it spent large sums for restoration in anticipation of German reparations. Unlike France, it was mostly under German occupation during the war. Consequently, it did not bear

	1920	1921	1922	1923	1924	1925	1926
League of Nations	5.8	3.2	2.4	1.7	2.0	1.2	0.8
Shepherd	5.7	2.9	2.4	1.5	1.5	5.2	3.9
Changes in debt	5.8	4.9	1.8	1.9	0.1	2.5	−1.8

Table 6.6. Alternative measures of the Belgian budget deficit, 1920–26 (billion francs)

Note: − indicates surplus.

Sources: League of Nations (1927b), Shepherd (1978), and Ministère de l'Interieur et de l'Hygiene (1920–27).

as great a burden of the military outlays and did not accumulate the war-time deficits that France had. However, during the course of the occupation, the Germans issued their own currency. In 1919 the Belgian government retired this currency and replaced it with its own. To do this, the central bank advanced the state some 5.8 billion Belgian francs. Although it expected to be reimbursed for this sum by Germany, the negotiations bogged down. Hence, the war left Belgium, like France, with a swollen stock of currency, a large debt, and continuing deficits.

1.2.1 Fiscal and economic performance

By all three alternative measures of the deficit shown in Table 6.6, Belgium made considerable progress in bringing its budget into balance through 1924. In 1925, the deficit rose by two of the three measures, but using information available at the time (1925), the budget must have appeared to be near balance for two consecutive years.[6]

Belgian efforts to finance the deficit and manage the debt consisted of using both long-term loans and short-term treasury bills. The average maturity of the debt was increased, but as late as 1924, nearly one-half the debt was still short-term or floating (see Table 6.7).

Belgium marketed its debt in the same manner as France. Long-term debt was sold by subscription and treasury bills were on sale continuously at fixed interest rates. These rates were changed more frequently than in France. The bulk of the treasury's financing requirements were met from domestic resources. The government did float several large loans abroad in 1924–25, raising some $93 million, most of which was to be used as a reserve for stabilizing the currency as Belgium prepared to return to the gold standard.[7]

Unlike France, in Belgium there was no recourse to advances from the central bank until the funding crisis in 1926.[8] The behaviour of the money

Year	Internal (billion francs) Funded	Floating	Total	External (in millions) £	$	FrFr[a]	Flor[b]	SwFr[c]	SwKr[d]	Total (in billions)[1]
1919	6.3	12.4	18.7	17.5	213	334				22.1
1920	8.7	14.2	22.9	24.0	294	334				29.4
1921	11.1	16.3	27.5	25.9	316	334				33.3
1922	12.8	17.0	29.8	20.0	306	334				36.2
1923	14.0	17.2	31.2	18.3	302	697	45			40.8
1924	15.9	15.3	31.3	18.3	302	697	42	10		40.2
1925	17.2	14.7	31.9	17.3	607	641	40	32		48.0
1926	22.1	5.0	27.1	25.5	650	400	43		9	56.4

Table 6.7. Belgium: distribution of the national debt, 1919–26

[1] Converted to nominal francs.
[a] French Francs; [b] Dutch Florins; [c] Swiss Francs; [d] Swedish Kroner.
Source: Ministère de l'Interieur et de l'Hygiene (1920–27).

	1920	1921	1922	1923	1924	1925	1926
Notes	6.0	6.3	6.7	7.3	7.6	7.6	9.5
% change		5.0	6.3	9.0	4.1	0.0	25.0
M1	14.3	14.8	16.2	17.5	17.4	18.8	23.8
% change		3.5	9.5	8.0	−0.6	8.0	26.6

Table 6.8. The Belgian money stock, 1920–26
(billion francs)

Data on notes are averages of monthly data. M1 adds sight deposits which are
year-end numbers.
Sources: Banque Nationale de Belgique (1923–27) and League of Nations (1927a).

stock is shown in Table 6.8. In contrast to France, in which the money
supply was relatively stable through 1923 and increased mostly from 1924
on, in Belgium almost the reverse occurred; moderately rapid rates of
growth were experienced through 1923 while virtual stability was
achieved in 1924–25; all the rapid growth came suddenly in 1926.

Belgium also experienced rapid economic growth after the war. Initially,
however, it shared in the world-wide contraction of 1920–21. But the next
three years were ones of expansion, with industrial production in 1924
surpassing pre-war levels. While production declined somewhat in 1925,
by 1926 it reached its highest level in the post-war era. A similar pattern
emerges from the unemployment date.

As in France, the rate of inflation in Belgium was irregular. As shown in
Table 6.9, while 1921 and 1922 were years of price stability, they were
followed by two years of relatively high inflation. Price stability was
achieved again in 1925 with wholesale prices actually declining. But

	1920	1921	1922	1923	1924	1925	1926
Wholesale prices	n.a.	43	43	58	67	66	87
% change	—		0	35	16	−2	32
Dollar exchange rate*	7.38	7.45	7.68	5.22	4.64	4.76	3.37
% change		1	3	−32	−11	3	−29

Table 6.9. Belgium: prices and the exchange rate, 1920–26

*US cents per franc (average for 1926 runs through October 25th).
Sources: Mitchell (1975), Franck (1927) and Board of Governors (1943).

during 1926, the year of the funding crisis, the rate of inflation reached a near high for the post-war period.

The major political development was the national election of April 1925 in which the so-called 'slide to the left' took place, reflecting the enhanced position of the socialist party. The new center-left coalition headed by Poullet named Albert Janssen Minister of Finance. Following a funding agreement with the United States, the regularization of reparations under the Dawes Plan, and the presentation of a balanced budget, the Poullet/ Janssen government believed the time was opportune for stabilizing the franc.

While this curious *de facto* stabilization plan was not enacted into law until February 26, 1926, the central bank, acting as a fiscal agent for the government, began to support the franc possibly as early as mid-September 1925.[9] For the next six months the franc was held steady at 107 per pound and 22 to the dollar.

To support the franc, the government had at its disposal what remained (probably about $50 million) of the proceeds of two loans from the US which had netted $93 million, and a short-term line of credit of $54 million arranged late in 1925 with various foreign bankers.[10] The operation in support of the franc was not successful.

1.2.2 The funding crisis of 1925–26

Once the central bank started to support the franc, it was faced with an immediate loss of foreign exchange that soon became a haemorrhage. Between mid-September and December 31, 1925, the loss of foreign exchange was $65 million. From January 1 through March 9, the loss was $25 million, and in a climatic three-day period from March 10 to March 13, an additional $20 million was lost. The government abandoned the support program.[11]

If $100 million had been spent to stabilize the franc at 22 to the dollar, 2.2 billion francs should have been removed from circulation. But money supply figures for the period show at most a reduction in notes of only Frs. 279 million. Some of the purchased francs were undoubtedly held in reserve by the treasury for additional operations but shown on the balance sheet of the central bank as still outstanding. But the fact that the treasury soon had to get advances from the bank once the runoff began (and calculating from the amount of debt ultimately converted and how much the money supply actually increased) one must assume that much that was collected in the exchange operations was soon spent. Apparently, in the process of supporting the franc, the government was exchanging dollars for francs which were then used to finance its current expenditures. Thus, the foreign loans were being used to finance a budget deficit.

The reduction in the stock of outstanding notes meant a period of tightening credit. The central bank discount rate was raised in a series of steps from 5.5% in October to 7.5% in March (it was lowered to 7.0% in late April). The treasury responded by raising the rate paid on six-month bills. For the first 10 months of 1925, 3- and 6-month bills were issued at 4.75% and 5.0%. On November 30, 1925, in the wake of two increases in the discount rate, the rate on 6-month bills was raised to 6.0%. There it remained until March 1926. By February 1926, the market discount rate on treasury bills of 1-, 2-, and 3-months maturity had risen to 5.86%, 6–6.25%, and over 7.0%.[12]

The funding crisis began as creditors refused to renew their subscriptions to maturing treasury bills. It was the large denomination bills that were presented for payment, suggesting that they came primarily from financial institutions.[13] As the bills ran off, treasury coffers emptied. Monetizing the public debt led to a rapid increase in high-powered money and the price level, and a depreciation of the franc. Between April and July, notes in circulation increased at an annual rate of 73% and during June-July at an annual rate of 110%. During these same two periods, wholesale prices rose and the franc depreciated at annual rates of 296% and 81% and 441% and 91% respectively.

On May 7, 1926, the centre-left coalition gave way to a centre-right government of 'National Union' headed by Henri Jasper, in which Emile Franqui, to be called the 'saviour of the franc', was given the position of Minister without Portfolio. In the interim between the two governments, on May 19, a law was approved authorizing the central bank to grant additional advances to the government in an amount not to exceed Frs. 1.5 billion.[14]

The new government voted Frs. 1.5 billion in new taxes. The revenue was earmarked for a newly established sinking fund for debt retirement. But it was not sufficient to stop the funding crisis. Not only did the runoff of treasury bills continue, but during the second half of 1926 some Frs. 6 billion additional bills and long-term debt were scheduled to mature as would about $50 million in external debt.

On July 16, the King was given the power for 6 months to issue decrees deliberated in ministerial council in pursuit of the 'financial improvement of the country'. Thus, the stabilization plan worked out by Franqui would become law without parliamentary debate or approval. A forced conversion was decided upon. A new National Railway Company was formed and it was authorized to issue preferred shares bearing interest at 6% plus a dividend based on one-half its net earnings after interest payments (the 6% interest payment was guaranteed by the government). All holders of maturing debt could, at their option, convert to the preferred shares.

Those who did not wish to convert were given a special issue of treasury bonds bearing interest at 5% and redeemable as the resources of the sinking fund permitted. For banks and other institutions for whom liquidity was important, a special treasury bond bearing 7% and amortizable over three years was authorized.

1.2.3 Assessment

The stories of France and Belgium are intertwined. They would experience much the same fate because they suffered from much the same problems. They both suffered damage from the war that they felt would be paid for by the Germans. Yet one big difference is that France slowly built to a crisis over the period late 1924 through mid 1926. Belgium appeared to have achieved stability in 1924 and 1925. The crisis came on suddenly.

That is the hardest part of the Belgian story to explain. In both cases the combination of floating debt, fiat money standard, and slowness in adjusting interest rates offered on government securities made the money supply endogenous and potentially unstable. The explosion of this potential instability into rapid inflation and massive runoff of debt depended on holders of the debt coming to understand the nature of the debt management/monetary regime and that the natural rate of interest had risen above the level that the government offered on its securities.

In France, the slow evolution of the runoff seemed the likely consequence of this process. Savvy investors understood in late 1923–24 what was happening, but by themselves could not force the crisis in the first Poincaré ministry. Over the next two years, others came to understand as well. By increments, holders deserted government securities, forcing more money creation and inflation, which put a greater wedge between the rates offered by the government and the natural rate. The bigger the wedge, the larger the fraction of the public that caught on.

While this seems a reasonable interpretation of events in France, unless one accepts an extreme version of rational expectations, the Belgian episode evolved too quickly for such a gradual learning process to take place. Up to winter 1926, it had avoided a runoff of debt. When the runoff finally occurred, it came suddenly and on a large scale.

Belgium had already reduced its deficit substantially by 1924. In addition, it seemed far more flexible in adjusting the interest rates it offered on its debt. It was not until the winter of 1926 that it could have been clear that it had a potentially endogenous money supply. But by then events were well under way in France. Linked by common circumstances it is reasonable that concerned parties in Belgium could have learned in a few weeks from the French example what it took the French two years to

	1920	1921	1922	1923	1924	1925	1926
Budget documents	12.4	18.2	17.2	4.9	0.6	− 0.4	− 1.5
Cash budget	11.9	12.6	6.2	2.0	− 2.7	− 2.1	− 2.8
Changes in debt	14.3	12.0	6.4	2.7	− 2.4	− 2.3	0.5

Table 6.10. Alternative measures of the Italian budget deficit, 1920–26 (billion lire)

Note: − indicates surplus.

Source: McGuire (1927).

understand. Unfortunately, bondholders in Belgium learned the lesson faster than the government.

1.3   Italy

Italy, like France and Belgium, came out of the war with large budget deficits. Unlike Belgium and France, it went into the war with relatively large deficits caused by its war to conquer Libya in 1912–13. In addition, nothing comparable to France or Belgium was required for reconstruction, although reparations were expected.

1.3.1 Fiscal and economic performance

Of the three countries, Italy had dealt most effectively with its budget problem. Shortly after the accession of Mussolini in 1922, Albert De' Stefani became Minister of Finance. He moved quickly to restore balance largely by draconian cuts in expenditures. Measuring the deficit either by changes in the national debt or the cash budget, the data in Table 6.10 show that the fiscal imbalance was eliminated by 1924.[15]

The large deficits during the war and immediate post-war period added greatly to Italy's national debt. The government gradually lengthened the maturity of the debt. But as late as 1925 about $\frac{1}{3}$ of the internal debt consisted of short-dated obligations. As a fraction of GNP, the internal debt fell from 75% in 1921 and 1922 to 48% in 1926 (see Table 6.11).

Italy, like Belgium, was successful in selling its debt to the private sector. While some of the debt was purchased by private banks, it was not monetized by the Banks of Issue.[16] In fact, as shown in Table 6.12, the period between 1920 and 1926 was one of moderation in monetary policy. The outstanding notes of the Banks of Issue rose from 19.9 billion lire in 1920 to 20.2 billion in 1926 – a growth of 1.5% spread over 6 years. The money supply measured akin to M2, however, grew more rapidly.[17]

	1914	1919	1920	1921	1922	1923	1924	1925	1926
Funded	14.8	34.4	53.3	55.0	56.6	60.1	60.5	63.2	63.4
Floating	0.9	25.8	22.2	31.5	36.2	35.5	32.7	27.6	27.9
Total	15.8	60.2	74.5	86.5	92.8	95.5	93.2	90.8	91.3
% of GNP	66	74	60	75	75	70	65	51	48

Table 6.11. Distribution of Italy's internal debt, 1914–26
(billion lire)

Source: McGuire (1927).

The economic performance of Italy in this period was as robust as that of France and Belgium. There was a downturn in the period of demobilization; as shown in Table 6.13, real GNP fell by 4.1% in 1919. An expansion during 1920 was followed in 1921 by the same downturn that was experienced in France, Belgium, and other countries. But with the implementation of high-growth policies of the new fascist government, the economy grew rapidly in the years to follow. Real GNP rose at an average rate of about 3.5% between 1921 and 1926. There was also a steady reduction in unemployment from nearly 500,000 in late 1921 to 80,000 in both 1925 and 1926.[18] The Italian inflation experience was better than that of France and Belgium. Except for 1919–20 and 1925, Italy had either deflation or a very low rate of inflation (see Table 6.14). The exchange value of the lira mirrored the inflation rate, losing more

	1920	1921	1922	1923	1924	1925	1926
Notes	19.9	20.7	20.3	19.4	19.7	20.8	20.2
% change		4.0	−1.9	−4.4	1.5	5.6	−2.9
M2	49.6	54.7	*	51.0	56.0	59.1	59.7
% change		10.3	—	—	9.8	5.5	1.0

Table 6.12. Measures of the Italian money stock, 1920–26
(billion lire)

Notes are averages of monthly data. M2 derived by adding deposits which are on an end-of-year basis.
*Late in 1921 the large Bank d'Sconto failed. Because of this, a deposit figure for commercial banks is unavailable for 1922. During that year, the savings deposits at the post office and all other banks totalled 17.2 billion lire.
Sources: League of Nations (1920–27), Young (1925), and Mitchell (1975).

	1918	1919	1920	1921	1922	1923	1924	1925	1926
GNP	109.1	104.6	110.8	106.7	113.0	118.3	118.3	125.8	126.7
(billions of 1938 lire)									
Industrial production	107	104	104	95	107	116	128	146	146
(1913 = 100)									

Table 6.13.. Italy: real GNP and industrial production, 1918–26
Source: Mitchell (1975).

than half its value relative to the dollar from 1919 to 1920.[19] From 1920 to 1926, the lira depreciated another 20% against the dollar, with 1920 and 1925 showing the biggest declines.

Although the fascist party ascended to power in 1922, during the period from 1922 to 1926, the focus period of this study, Italy still had a semblance of parliamentary democracy and an economy that was not yet organized along the lines of the corporate state. Indeed, De' Stefani's first moves were along the lines of liberalization. Besides cutting the budget deficit, he reformed taxes, removed considerable government intervention from commerce, began a number of productivity enhancement schemes, privatized several industries, and eliminated various barriers within finance markets to promote investment.

The result was an investment-led business boom. Unfortunately, not all the investment that occurred was sound. Many of the reforms was also conducive to speculation. This put considerable pressure on credit markets, with stock prices and bank credit rising accordingly. As the economy threatened to overheat, upward pressure on prices was felt by 1925. Real GNP grew 6.3% and unemployment declined from 156,000 in January to 72,000 in August.

	1919	1920	1921	1922	1923	1924	1925	1926
Wholesale prices	461	787	727	709	724	737	869	896
% change		70.7	−7.5	−2.6	2.1	1.8	17.9	3.1
Exchange rate*	11.4	5.0	4.3	4.8	4.6	4.4	4.0	3.9
% change		−56	−14	12	−4	−4	−9	−3

Table 6.14. Italy: prices and the exchange rate, 1919–26
*US cents per lira.
Sources: League of Nations (1920–27) and Board of Governors (1943).

Inflation accelerated and the lira depreciated with both the price level reaching a peak and the lira a low point against the dollar in August; the annualized rate of inflation varied from 28% to over 50% while the lira depreciated against the dollar at a rate that varied from 3% to 35%. The growth in the notes outstanding of the Banks of Issue rose at an annual rate of 28% from April through August and 39% from May through August. Increases in the money supply also came from deposits.

1.3.2 The funding problems of 1925–26
De' Stefani moved to slow speculative activity. He imposed restrictions on brokers and established a 25% margin requirement on securities purchases. The Banks of Issue raised the discount rate from 5.5% to 6.0% in March, to 6.5% in June, and to 7.0% in June.[20] Market interest rates also increased. The private discount rate rose from 5.47% in February to 8.5% in September.[21] Interest rates on treasury bills were raised twice in June, to 5.25%. 5.75%, and 6% for 3- and 5-month, 6- and 8-month, and 12-month securities.[22] De' Stefani lost favour with the business community. In July he was replaced by Giuseppi Volpi.

During the remainder of 1925, the economy appeared to cool in response to the tightening of credit. Bank notes outstanding declined slightly, the wholesale price index fell from 921 in August to 901 in December, the lira rose from a low of 3.66 cents in August to 4.03 cents in December, and over the same period unemployment rose to 122,000.

But funding problems had arisen in the process. A harbinger of things to come occurred during the second half of the year. The 5th, 6th and 7th issues of nine-year lottery bonds, each in the amount of 1.0 billion lire, were issued. The 5th and 6th were issued at par and bore interest at 4.75% and 5.0% respectively. The 7th was issued in August at a price of 97 with interest at 5.0%. By December 31 the three issues had garnered subscriptions of only 2.175 billion lire, slightly in excess of $\frac{2}{3}$ of the hoped-for amount.

Volpi set about reorganizing the foreign debt. He settled accounts with the US in November 1925 and the UK in January 1926. He arranged a $100 million loan from Morgan for stabilization at the same time. Finally, in May 1926 he limited the right of issue to the Bank of Italy.

The summer of 1926 was a repeat performance of 1925 with the price level reaching a post-war high and the lira a post-war low in August. The rate of inflation varied between 17% and 30% and the rate of depreciation of the lira between 17% and 47%. Amazingly, these developments took place in a period when the outstanding notes of the Banks of Issue actually declined – from 20.8 billion lire in January to 20.0 billion in August. Market interest rates rose sharply with the private discount rate, which had declined from 8.5% in December to 8.0% in May, rising to a high of 9.25% in November.

In July, funding problems emerged. Of the 7.5 billion lire of short-term debt that matured, only 5.0 billion was renewed, leaving a net run-off of 2.5 billion lire. Since the shortfall was not made up by advances from the Bank of Issue, one can surmise that treasury cash balances built up by the budget surpluses of 1924 and 1925 were used to avert a crisis.[23] Nonetheless, officials knew that during the remaining five months of the year an additional 10.0 billion lire of debt would mature and have to be refinanced.

Since the government was determined to halt the depreciation of the lira at the time the funding problem emerged, monetizing the maturing debt was not a viable option.[24] Rather than raise interest rates further, the government decided to deal directly with the floating debt problem by means of a forced consolidation. On November 6, the so-called 'Littorio Loan' was announced which obligated all holders of treasury bills and five and seven-year bonds to take in their place long-term securities (payable starting in 1937). Within a year and a half, Italy's floating debt ceased to exist.

1.3.3 Assessment

The Italian experience is difficult to interpret at times. The rates of inflation, depreciation, and money growth are relatively low on a year-to-year basis. The monthly changes, therefore, while large on an annualized basis, are not always distinguishable from random noise and seasonal movements.

In many respects the Italian story resembles the Belgian episode. By the beginning of 1925 stability seems to have been largely achieved. But control over the floating debt was ultimately disrupted by moves taken to stabilize the lira. The exchange rate set for the lira was too high to achieve without contraction. Restriction of credit generated market interest rates that the government was unwilling to pay on its own debt.

The Italian experience with inflation was better than in France and Belgium because the cumulative process never really got under way. Consequently, there is little hint that the situation was about to explode into an inflationary episode of the sort that characterized the other two cases. Volpi no doubt understood that if the debt problem was not resolved the stabilization would be at risk. The move to a forced consolidation ended the whole episode before it really got out of hand.

2   Portugal and Greece

The involvement of Greece and Portugal in the war differed substantially from each other as well as from the three countries just examined.

	1921–22	1922–23	1923–24	1924–25	1925–26
Expenditure	577	1,045	1,072	1,608	1,492
Revenue	388	544	842	1,365	1,369
Deficit	189	501	230	243	123

Table 6.15. Portuguese budgets, 1921–26
(million escudos)
Sources: League of Nations (1927b) and Mitchell (1975).

Portugal joined the war in 1916. Its contribution of men and material was minor relative to other beligerents. Greece was in a state of war off and on from 1912 through 1923, fighting first the Turks, then the Bulgarians before World War I. A period of internal turmoil involving its stance in the war culminated in the abdication of the king and joining the Allies in 1916. It won substantial gains from Turkey in the 1919 treaty of Sèvres. But renewed fighting with Turkey resulted in a humiliating defeat for the Greeks and the far less favourable 1923 Treaty of Lausanne.

Like the other belligerents covered in this study, Greece and Portugal mounted up large debts and expected reparations from the Central Powers. Unlike the others, important data on output, employment, and industrial production are not available. Figures on money, prices, and budgets are, at best, sketchy.

2.1 Portugal

During its history as a republic (1910–26), Portugal had 48 governments, seven presidents (only one of whom served a full term), and at least 25 attempted coups. And its public finance practices were as chaotic as its political situation.

Deficit finance became a way of life beginning with fiscal year 1914–15[25] and remained so even after peace returned in 1918. As shown in Table 6.15, during fiscal year 1922–23, the deficit in the 'gerencia', or cash transactions budget, was 501 million escudos or nearly 50% of all cash expenditures, and would have been larger had Portugal serviced its substantial war debt to Britain.

A major tax reform enacted in September 1922 laid the groundwork for a substantial increase in revenue, although it was slow to materialize. Progress was made during fiscal 1923–24, with the cash deficit falling by more than one-half. It then remained virtually unchanged in 1924–25.[26] In

	1921	1922	1923	1924	1925
Notes	0.66	0.86	1.24	1.61	1.69
% Change		30	44	30	5

Table 6.16. The Portuguese money stock, 1921–25
(billion escudos)
Sources: League of Nations (1920–27), Banco de Portugal (1927–27).

real terms, however, the deficit fell substantially over the period 1923–26, given the high rate of inflation experienced by Portugal during much of the time.

Financing these deficits and managing the resulting national debt would have been a formidable task for any treasury, but especially for Portugal with its underdeveloped financial markets. Consequently, Portugal resorted to the printing press to finance a high proportion of each deficit, a fact reflected in its money stock figures (see Table 6.16). Between July 1921 and June 1924, the note issue of the Bank increased by 970 million escudos, of which over 800 million or about 82% arose through various loans to the government.

Some portion of the cumulative deficits was financed by borrowing from the private sector, primarily through the medium of treasury bills. They were issued in maturities of 3, 6, and 12 months, and (apparently) throughout the period 1919–25, bore interest at unchanged rates of 7%, $7\frac{1}{2}$%, and 8%, respectively.[27] The total floating debt on June 30, 1923 stood at 591 million escudos, of which 310 million was in treasury bills – slightly in excess of the budget deficit for 1922–23.[28]

Unfortunately, Portugal does not have a price index computed monthly for this period. Rather, a cost-of-living index was computed in July starting with 1922. Based on this index, prices rose 52% and 54% during 1922–23 and 1923–24, respectively. During 1924–25 and 1925–26 Portugal had deflation, with the price level falling 14% and 6%, respectively.

Paralleling the rise in prices, the exchange value of the escudo fell from 12.1 cents in July 1921 to 2.8 cents in July 1924 (see Table 6.17). After that it rose and remained in the 4 to 5 cent range for the remainder of the decade. The fall in the value of the escudo from July to July 1921–22, 1922–23, and 1923–24 was 41%, 41%, and 34%, respectively. Between July 1924 and July 1925, it rose 83%, and declined by 2.5% during 1925–26.

In an ineffectual manner, the central bank attempted to stem the

	1922	1923	1924	1925	1926
Price level	1128	1720	2652	2286	2148
% change		52	54	− 14	− 6
Exchange rate*	6.67	4.25	3.39	5.04	5.13
% change		− 41	− 34	83	− 2

Table 6.17. Portugal: prices and the exchange rate, 1922–26

*US cents per escudo.
Sources: League of Nations (1929) and Board of Governors (1943).

inflation by raising the discount rate. In May 1923 the rate was raised to 8% from the 7% at which it had been held for the preceding 16 months. In September 1923 it was raised to 9%. It was reported that private sector interest rates rose during 1923 and that by December they stood as high as 24% for discounts of commercial paper. This same account states that 'there was little demand for treasury bills during the year and none towards the close.'[29]

Thus, it was in this maelstrom of budget deficits, rising national debt, and inflation that Portugal experienced a funding crisis. Between June 30, 1923 and June 30, 1924, the domestic floating debt fell by 102 million escudos (of which treasury bills declined 74 million). Combined with the fiscal year deficit of 230 million escudos, this required the treasury to make up a 332 million escudo shortfall. The wherewithal was obtained from the Bank of Portugal. During this period the Bank advanced notes to the State in the sum of 325 million escudos, meaning that both deficit and debt run-off were monetized. The monetization was not uniform throughout the fiscal year but occurred during September-December 1923 (164 million escudos) and March-June 1924 (161 million escudos).[30]

In late 1923 and early 1924, the government bought the silver reserve of the central bank at par, demonetized it, and sold part of it abroad (using the rest as collateral for a foreign loan). An additional internal loan of 173 million escudos was floated about the same time (a $6\frac{1}{2}$% gold loan that the government apparently had little trouble selling). Exchange and capital controls were tightening in June, and by decree, domestic holders of the 3% sterling loan of 1903 were given no choice but to accept their interest payments in escudos (saving approximately £700,000 needed for service). This enabled the government to enter the exchange market to raise the value of the escudo.

For the first few months while the escudo appreciated, note circulation

	1919–20	1920–21	1921–22	1922–23	1923–24	1924–25	1925–26
Expenditure	1,146	1,354	1,683	2,476	3,460	5,000	5,498
Receipts	516	586	725	978	1,895	3,712	5,091
Deficit	930	768	958	1,498	1,565	1,285	407

Table 6.18. Greek budgets, 1919–26*
(million drachma)
*The Greek fiscal year runs from April 1 to March 31.
Source: Mitchell (1975).

still increased. But the success of the operation to raise the exchange rate led to a decline in the domestic price level.[31] The deflation during 1924–25 was substantial enough to raise the *ex-post* real yield on treasury bills to the 20% range. The government found a ready market for its debt, and private holdings of bills rose by 170 million escudos during that fiscal year.

2.2   Greece

Greece not only had to contend with financing war for a decade, but by the terms of the final treaty with Turkey, had to resettle roughly $1\frac{1}{4}$ million refugees – a number equal to nearly $\frac{1}{3}$ of her population. As a result the Greek budget, shown in Table 6.18, was in a constant state of deficit.

Financing of the deficit after the war consisted primarily of domestic sources, with only one major foreign loan, of £12.3 million for refugees in 1924, floated prior to 1925. The primary financing medium for tapping internal sources was treasury bills. These were issued in maturities of 3, 6, and 12 months. At the beginning of 1918 interest on the three maturities was fixed at 4%, 4.5%, and 6%, respectively. In late 1920 these were raised to 5%, 5.5%, and 6%, respectively. Finally in 1923 the rates were raised again to a range of 5.5% to 7.5%.[32] These bills were sold both to the private sector and to the central bank. In the depressed circumstances of the early 1920s, they were a major means of holding the liquid wealth of the country, as well as a favourite investment medium for banks. This made them relatively easy to sell. Nevertheless, a large portion of each deficit was monetized.

Prior to the funding difficulties of 1924–25, the Greek government used one other device to finance its budget deficit (that of 1922–23): a forced loan. On April 1, 1922, the government decreed that one-half of all bank notes would have to be surrendered and exchanged for 6.5% bonds

	1919	1920	1921	1922	1923	1924	1925
Notes	1,382	1,508	2,161	3,149	4,681	4,866	5,339
% change		9.1	43.3	45.7	48.7	4.0	9.7
M1	2,018	2,305	3,214	4,287	6,350	6.970	7,571
% change		14.2	38.4	33.3	48.1	9.8	8.6

Table 6.19. The Greek money stock, 1919–25
(million drachma)

Deposits included in M1 are nonsavings deposits of the five main commercial banks.
End of year figures.
Source: League of Nations (1920–27) and (1927a).

payable in lots up to 1943. The banknotes were literally cut in half and the portions bearing a picture of the Greek crown were exchanged for bonds while the other half was exchanged for a new issue of central bank notes (at half the original value). The forced loan raised 1.6 billion drachma, about the size of the deficit.[33]

The monetization of treasury bills caused a rapid increase in the money supply during the period 1919–25. This is shown in Table 6.19. In an effort to restrain the inflation rate, the central bank raised the discount rate to 7.5% in January 1923 (it had been 6.5% during 1921 and 1922), to 8.5% in February 1925, and to 10% in August 1925. Rapid money growth led to a high rate of inflation and a more or less continuous depreciation of the drachma as shown in Table 6.20.

The continuous budget deficits and their financing using treasury bills

	1919	1920	1921	1922	1923	1924	1925
Retail prices	17	18	21	33	61	64	74
% change	—	5.9	16.7	57.1	84.8	4.9	15.6
Exchange rate*	n.a.	n.a.	5.03	3.31	1.71	1.79	1.56
% change	—	—	—	−34.2	−48.3	4.7	−12.8

Table 6.20. Greece: prices and the exchange rate, 1919–25

*US cents per drachma. No quotations exist during Jan. 1919–May 1921.
Prices as of July of each year, exchange rate as annual average.
Source: Mitchell (1975) and Board of Governors (1943).

nearly doubled the floating debt between 1921 and 1924. On March 31, 1924, of a domestic debt of 7.6 billion drachma, over 25% consisted of short-dated maturities. The issuance of treasury bills also directly involved the central bank in that it not only marketed the bills for the treasury, but guaranteed their payment in notes (as well as standing by to discount them if the holder desired cash before maturity).

During the last six months of 1924 Greece was beset with funding difficulties when 300 million drachma of treasury bills were presented for redemption. During this same period the note circulation of the central bank rose by 323.6 billion drachma.[34] The redemptions continued into 1925 as another 311 billion drachma apparently ran off. The government then decided to deal directly with the floating debt. The 10% surtax of 1922 was increased to 20% and all proceeds were to be used to redeem the treasury bills which the central bank had been presented. Next, another forced loan was enacted in which one-fourth of all banknotes in circulation (of over 25 drachma in value) were converted into 6% 20-year bonds (the proceeds of which were to be used to redeem treasury bills). Finally, of the remaining bills that were to fall due up to April 1, 1927, one-half were to be paid off in cash and the other half were forcibly converted into 8% 10-year bonds. Thus, in a very short time, Greece removed the floating debt that had been the source of its monetary instability.

2.3   Assessment of Greece and Portugal

In Greece and Portugal the funding problems encountered are difficult to disentangle from deficit financing problems. Yet, these two cases have all the earmarks of funding crises generated by holding rates of interest too low. In each the central bank was forced to monetize debt in excess of what was required to fund the deficit. In each the evidence is strong that interest rates in general increased faster than the rates offered by the government on its own securities. There is little in either experience to suggest that a sudden crisis of confidence gave rise to the funding problems that occurred.[35]

Greece addressed its funding crises with what amounted to a forced consolidation, albeit a more imaginative one than either Belgium or Italy. Portugal's approach was unique among the episodes studied. Instead of directly addressing the problem of rolling over its debt and thus stopping the monetization that generated inflation, it moved against inflation/depreciation and let the funding crisis solve itself as real rates of interest rose. It was able to do this because it had the wherewithal to move successfully on the foreign exchange market, the economy was open enough for exchange-rate movements to significantly affect the price level, and the nominal rates of interest on the government's debt were apparently high enough for the government to sell debt once the inflation rate (and inflation expectations) came down.

3   Extensions and conclusions

Governments carry large debts virtually all the time. In today's world at least, few have any intention of paying them off. For many of these countries, the maturity of the debt is relatively short. We note that the US government, the world's largest debtor, has marketable debt well in excess of one and a half trillion dollars. The debt has an average maturity of less than six years. A third has a maturity of less than a year. Rolling this debt over is essential, even in the presence of a balanced budget.

We therefore find it reassuring that inability to roll over internal debt seems to be rare. Undoubtedly, there are examples other than those presented here, but these few were the only episodes we examined that turned out to be true funding crises. Moreover, in each of these cases the public became unwilling to hold securities because the governments in question did not pay competitive interest rates on them. Theoretically, a funding crisis can be generated spontaneously: expected refusal of some investors to hold debt will beget refusal by others. Yet, with all the potential instances in which a spontaneous 'debt run' could happen, as far as we know, it has not. Hence, it would seem that such problems can be avoided by the simple expedient of offering sufficiently high yields on one's debt.

In another respect, however, some of these cases are cautionary. In France and Belgium, unwillingness to pay a high enough interest rate on government securities led to serious inflation problems. One cannot therefore assume that major inflations are always associated with money-financed deficits. As these examples show, even in the presence of a balanced budget, it is possible to get a significant inflation going by means of pegging interest rates – which is essentially what France and Belgium were doing.

An interesting historical question is why did all these cases occur in the period after the war? To those who participated in it, the Great War of 1914–18 was just that: great. No one expected the events in Sarajevo to degenerate into such a long, expensive, and destructive slugfest. The world emerged from this affair dazed, countries were heaped with debt accumulated in the war, obliged to repair what had been destroyed, and armed to face it with the financial techniques, institutions, and knowledge of the nineteenth century.

In concrete terms, this meant, first, that governments were carrying debts of a magnitude previously unknown. To find another instance in which debt was so high relative to income, one has to go back to the Napoleonic wars. Second, the exchange system had been cut loose from gold so that resort to the printing press was easy and any inflation rate possible. Third, financial markets in most of the countries were probably still not sophisticated enough to support well-functioning auctions in new government securities.

Together this meant that large amounts of debt had to be brought to market repeatedly by treasury officials who had to guess at the interest rate that would clear the issue. Accustomed to a world of relatively stable prices but operating in a new world of fiat money standards, they could not at times have imagined what nominal interest rate it would have taken to sell their debt once the public came to expect inflation. We can only conjecture that late 1925 and early 1926 were especially challenging to them as world-wide expansion pushed up interest rates and required them to pay yields much higher than they ever could have thought was appropriate for a sovereign government to pay. It is little wonder that commentators of the period thought it all a matter of public confidence; what else but doubt could have led the public to demand of governments interest rates that would have been required of only the riskiest of ventures in the past?

If the amounts that the governments had to re-fund had been smaller so as to have given them more time to adjust to what financial markets were telling them, or had officials been more accustomed to what inflation expectations could do to nominal interest rates, or if the securities could have been sold in an auction process, the funding problems probably could have been avoided. For the most part, funding crises emerged only in those belligerent countries in which they could emerge. Both the US and the UK avoided the problem. The US re-funded its short-term debt as the war progressed, and the UK re-funded its debt after the war and substituted an auction for the tap method of selling treasury bills.[36]

It was probably not easy to conceive of just how high interest rates had to rise in a potentially inflationary environment. It is worth reflecting on the experience in the US in the late 1970s. It became accepted wisdom by that time among US monetary authorities that the economy would have to be slowed down to arrest inflation. Yet, focusing on interest rates as the target for monetary policy, the Federal Reserve repeatedly aimed for interest rates too low to slow the economy down. They, like the debt management officials of the 1920s, could not imagine that interest rates had to rise as high as they eventually did to bring about real rates of interest consistent with long-run equilibrium. Such is the power of an inflation premium to confuse even those who presumably have an understanding of the phenomenon.

A major difference between the episodes under study in this paper and the experience of the US in the late 1970s is that in the 1970s the US auctioned its securities. Thus it never encountered a funding problem. Of course, the monetary dynamics were no different. To keep the interest rate down, the Federal Reserve bought up existing securities on the open market, thereby injecting money into the economy. For countries studied here there was an inability to sell debt, with the central bank financing the shortfall in a way that led to the same outcome: fewer securities in the hands of the public, more money, and ultimately a higher price level. The funding crises were merely the outward manifestation brought about by the particular institutional arrangement.

NOTES

The authors wish to thank James Brennan, Michael Steinbeisser, and Alfred Reifman for assistance in obtaining and interpreting data, and Robert Anderson for comments on a draft of the paper. The views expressed in the paper should be read as those of the authors and not those of the Congressional Research Service or the Library of Congress.

1 Budget practices of the period make it difficult to say anything meaningful about the budget deficit. Multiple budgets were common. Figures often consisted of tax assessments and outlay authorizations instead of realized receipts and expenses. Debt service expenditure included outlays for debt retirement. Thus, there are different deficit numbers attributed to the same year by different authors. Two measures are especially relevant in our minds. First, is the difference between flows of actual receipts and outlays excluding debt redemption, asset sales, and liability swaps. This would indicate the effect of the government's fiscal posture on interest rates, aggregate demand, and prices. Second, are the measures of the budget at the time, indicating what the public knew of the government's fiscal circumstances and any psychological effect that may have stemmed from that.

2 The Dulles and Haig figures reflect information available at the time. Dulles's 1926 figure was the budget submitted in late 1925. The debt statements on which Haig based his figures were available monthly. In addition, a committee of experts summoned in the spring of 1926 reported on July 3 that the budget was in balance. The official measure, compiled after World War II, may come closer to reflecting the true fiscal impact.

3 Lacking a majority in the Chamber of Deputies, the *Cartel* depended on non-*Cartel* parties to govern. Moreover, the Senate, no mere debating society, was controlled by parties of the right (it was the Senate that blocked Poincaré's first attempt to pass the double decime, and it was the Senate's no confidence vote that ousted the Herriot government).

4 See Makinen and Woodward (1989) for a fuller account of earlier interpretations and the role they ascribe to confidence. The theme is repeated in analyses of the other episodes as well (e.g., Shepherd, 1988, and Yeager, 1981).

5 See Makinen and Woodward (1989).

6 The League of Nations measure reflects information available to the public at the time. The same is true of figures on the size of the national debt. Shepherd

used official sources published in the period 1930–35. The third measures the change in the national debt. The deficit of 1925 is of some importance and should be explained. A large part of the increase resulted from an expenditure to pay off certificates for war damage. It shows in the Shepherd measure for 1925 but not in the deficit measured by the change in the national debt because one form of debt was simply exchanged for another. The remaining deficit for 1925 was from the $93 million stabilization loan from the US arranged in two parts in late 1924 and 1925. It caused the deficit for 1925 to be overstated since much of the sum was not actually spent until 1926.

7 The increase in the dollar portion of the external debt in 1925 of over $300 million comes from two sources. The first is the $93 million borrowed abroad in that year while the second represents the recognition of loans made by the US to Belgium during and immediately after the war. When a funding agreement was concluded with the United States in 1925, they were recognized in the statement of public debt for the first time. No new borrowing was involved. This latter amount was excluded from the change in debt measure of the budget deficit in Table 6.6.

8 The law forbade the central bank to make advances to the government (the retirement of German currency was an exception).

9 It was curious in the sense that it did not define the gold content of the Belgian franc. Thus, market participants did not know at what value it would be supported.

10 See Shepherd (1978).

11 See Fournier (1927).

12 See Bagge (1926) and (1927) and Davin (1950). Other private sector rates were raised during the period. The Banque de Bruxelles, a leading commercial bank, raised its rates on 15-day time deposits in a series of steps from 4.5% in 1924 to 6.25% in 1926 and on its 3, 5, and 12 month time deposits from 4.5% to 6% during the same period (Banque de Bruxelles, 1989).

13 See League of Nations (1927b).

14 The government had been obtaining advances from the central bank. It held that this did not violate the law because the bank was merely returning part of the Frs. 600 million the government had paid to the bank to reduce the original advance of Frs. 5.8 billion that had been made when the German marks were converted into francs in 1919.

15 The cash budget measures the actual money flows per year and does not include accruals. In historical data published after World War II, the Italian deficit, based on closed accounts after all revenue was collected and all expenditures made and allocated, declined considerably in the period 1923–26. A surplus does not, however, emerge. The deficits according to this series for 1924 through 1926 are, in billions of lire, 3.6, 1.5, and 1.8 respectively. See Mitchell (1975).

16 Until May 6, 1926, there were three banks whose notes were legal tender: the Banks of Italy, Naples, and Sicily.

17 Which component of the money multiplier is responsible for this rise is unknown.

18 See League of Nations (1920–27). Also accounting for the fall in unemployment was the exodus of Italian labor to other countries in Europe.

19 See Board of Governors (1943).

20 See League of Nations (1920–27).

21 See Board of Governors (1943).
22 They had been decreased earlier in February, April, and May 1922. See Henderson and Carpenter (1922).
23 See Rawlins and Carpenter (1927).
24 Volpi's policies during the end of 1925 and beginning of 1926 look like preparations for a stabilization. In August 1926, Mussolini gave his famous speech in which he vowed to defend the lira to the 'last drop of blood'.
25 The fiscal year ran from July 1 to June 30.
26 The deficit figures reflect 167 million escudos received in 1924–25 from the sale of the Bank of Portugal silver reserve and 173 million escudos received in 1925–26 from a long-term loan floated domestically. Had these events not occurred, the deficit for the two years would have been 414 and 301 billion escudos, respectively. The public finance practices of Portugal are detailed in Cunningham and Copp (1927).
27 See League of Nations (1929).
28 This is the floating debt held by private sources. The debt to the central bank was treated by government as a part of the funded debt.
29 See Irving (1926).
30 See League of Nations (1924) and (1925).
31 By some accounts this success led to a repatriation of capital that reinforced the operation. We can find no evidence in the data to confirm or refute this claim. See Yeager (1981).
32 See Mood (1925).
33 At the same time all existing direct and indirect taxes and other dues were increased by 10% and the revenue raised was paid into a sinking fund to retire bonds.
34 See League of Nations (1925).
35 It was the opinion of the head of the central bank that the redemptions came primarily from commercial banks who wished to make loans in the then booming Greek economy and that they did not reflect a lack of confidence in the public finance practices of the government. See National Bank of Greece (1926).
36 See Gilbert (1970) and Hicks (1970).

REFERENCES

Bagge, J. Picton (1926). *Report on the Economic Situation in Belgium* (February), Department of Overseas Trade, London: H.M. Stationery Office.
   (1927). *Report on the Economic Situation in Belgium*, Department of Overseas Trade, London: H.M. Stationery Office.
Banco de Portugal (1921–27). *Relatorio do Conselho de Administracao* (Annual Report), Lisboa: Imprensa National.
Banque de Bruxelles (1989). Personal correspondence arranged through Mr. Michael Steinbeisser (May).
Banque Nationale de Belgique (issues 1923–27). *Rapport Fait Par Le Gouverneur* (Annual Report), Bruxelles.
Board of Governors of the Federal Reserve System (1943). *Banking and Monetary Statistics 1914–1941*. Washington, D.C.
Brown, E. Cary (1990). 'Episodes in the public debt history of the United States', this volume.

Cunningham, Charles H. and Copp, Philip M. (1927). *Portugal: Resources, Economic Conditions, Trade, and Finance* (February), United States Department of Commerce, Bureau of Foreign and Domestic Commerce. Trade Information Bulletin No. 455. Washington, D.C., pp. 29–37.

Davin, Louis E. (1950). *La Politique de la Dette Publique en Belgique de 1919 a 1939* in *Histoire des Finance Publiques en Belgique*, edited by E. Bruylant. Bruxelles: Institut Belge de Finance Publiques.

Dulles, Eleanor Lansing (1929). *The French Franc 1914–1928*. New York: Macmillan Co.

Fournier, Henri (1927). *La Reforme Financiere et Monetaire en Belgique*. Paris: Giard.

Franck, Louis (1927). *La Stabilisation Monetaire en Belgique*. Paris: Payot.

Gilbert, Charles (1970). *American Financing of World War I*. Westport: Greenwood Publishing.

Haig, Robert Murray (1929). *The Public Finances of Post-War France*. New York: Columbia University Press.

Henderson, J.H. and H.C.A. Carpenter, (1922). *Report on the Commercial, Industrial, and Economic Situation in Italy* (December), Department of Overseas Trade. London: H.M. Stationery Office.

Hicks, Ursula K. (1970). *The Finance of British Government 1920–36*. London: Oxford University Press.

Irving, Stanley G. (1926). *Report on the Commercial, Financial and Economic Conditions in Portugal* (March), Department of Overseas Trade. London: H.M. Stationery Office.

League of Nations (issues 1920–27). *Monthly Bulletin of Statistics*. Geneva.

(1924). *Memorandum on Central Banks 1913, 1918–1923*. Geneva.

(1925). *Memorandum on Currency and Central Banks 1913–1924*. Volume II. Geneva.

(1927a). *Memorandum on Commercial Banks 1913–1926*. Geneva.

(1927b). *Memorandum on Public Finance 1922–1926*. Geneva.

(1929). *Memorandum on Public Finance 1926–1928*. Geneva.

Makinen, Gail E. and G. Thomas Woodward (1989). 'A Monetary Interpretation of the Poincare Stabilization of 1926'. *Southern Economic Journal*. Vol. 55, July.

McGuire, Constantine E. (1927). *Italy's International Economic Position*. Institute of Economics. New York: Macmillan Co.

Ministere de l'Economie et des Finances (1966). *Annuaire Statistique de la France, Reseme Retrospective*. Paris.

Ministere de l'Interieur et de l'Hygiene (issues 1920–27). *Annuaire Statistique de la Belgique*. Bruxelles.

Mitchell, Brian R. (1975). *European Historical Statistics 1750–1970*. New York: Columbia University Press.

Mood, James R. (1925). *Public Debt of Greece* (February). U.S. Department of Commerce, Bureau of Foreign and Domestic Commerce. Supplement to Commerce Reports. Trade Information Bulletin No. 321.

National Bank of Greece (1926). *Report of the Governor of the National Bank of Greece*. Athens: Printing Office 'Hestia'.

Rawlins, E.C. Donaldson and Carpenter, H.C.A. (1927). *Report on the Commercial, Industrial, and Economic Situation in Italy* (March), Department of Overseas Trade. London: H.M. Stationery Office.

Rogers, James Harvey (1929). *The Process of Inflation in France 1914–1917.* New York: Columbia University Press.
Shepherd, Henry L. (1978). *The Monetary Experience of Belgium.* Reprint. New York: Arno Press.
Yeager, Leland B. (1981). *Experiences with Stopping Inflation.* Washington, D.C.: American Enterprise Institute.
Young, John Parke (1925). *European Currency and Finance.* Foreign Currency and Exchange Investigation. Washington D.C.: Government Printing Office.

Discussion

ALBERTO GIOVANNINI

This well documented paper discusses the difficulties that several European governments faced in managing their debts accumulated after World War I. The authors assemble convincing evidence to discriminate between alternative explanations of the common experiences of France, Belgium, Italy, Portugal and Greece.

In my remarks, I argue that the phenomenon discussed by Makinen and Woodward is just an example – but a very interesting one – of the consequences of financial repression. Viewed in this light, the interwar experience helps to emphasize the way financial repression works, and its limitations as a policy for raising tax revenue.

1   Funding crises: equilibrium or disequilibrium?

The common problem faced by the European governments was the inability to roll-over debt. In France buyers refused to renew subscriptions to maturing long-term debt in the Spring of 1925, in Belgium apparently financial institutions refused to renew large-denomination Treasury bills, in Italy issues of nine-year bonds went undersubscribed by 30 percent in 1925, and similarly, in the July of the following year, only 60 percent of maturing short-term debt was renewed, in Portugal the government could not stem a sharp fall of floating debt between June 1923 and June 1924, and, finally, in Greece the government was unable to roll-over Treasury bills in the second half of 1924.

Pursuing the arguments of the two authors, one might identify two alternative explanations of funding crises, which might be labelled 'equilibrium' and 'disequilibrium'. According to the equilibrium view, funding crises are just a reflection of the public's assessment of governments' ability to repay debt. A funding crisis occurs whenever the public regards the government as unable to satisfy its intertemporal budget constraint, relating the present discounted value of tax revenue to the present discounted value of spending plus the level of current liabilities. If the budget deficit is expected to grow 'too fast' current government liabilities are worthless. In this sense the funding crisis is an equilibrium phenomenon, which could occur even with perfectly functioning financial markets.

The alternative theory states that, by contrast, funding crises occur when governments attempt to fix both prices and quantities of their liabilities, without taking account of market conditions. The attempt to fix prices and quantities at levels that do not take account of the conditions of demand might be due to errors of estimation by the government, or might result from conscious attempts to tax the holders of government debt. Such attempts might fail when the public perceived the tax rate to have increased excessively.

It is the latter explanation of funding crises that the authors find more appealing, and I concur. The basic fact bearing on their conclusion is that, in most of the countries in the study, budgetary problems were solved – and known to be solved – years before. Hence the funding crises of the interwar were failed attempts to tax domestic residents by paying below-market interest rates on government securities, and, interestingly, were solved with analogous, but extraordinary, forms of taxation.

2   Financial repression and public finances

Financial repression is a source of revenue to governments, and works by delinking domestic financial markets from the rest of the world. In the absence of the arbitrage opportunities offered by international financial markets, domestic residents may be forced to hold portfolios with artificially low returns. Governments with liabilities in financially repressed markets are able to obtain a source of finance at low rates. The tax revenue is represented by the difference between the opportunity cost of funds (measured by the interest rates paid by the government in the world financial markets) and the cost of domestic financing times the stock of domestic debt. How much revenue governments are able to raise with this form of distortions is, however, not known in general. Recent estimates by myself and Martha de Melo (1989) suggest that, at least among developing countries in the last twenty years, financial repression can account for as much as 20 percent of total revenue, and that the implicit tax rates (the differentials between domestic and foreign costs of funds) are as high as 50 percent (in the presence of large exchange-rate devaluations) and average around 15–20 percent.

The interwar funding crises confirm the basic mechanics of the taxes from financial repression which are also found in the current experience of LDCs: governments keep nominal interest rates artificially low, but at the same time they allow inflation to increase and the currency to depreciate. Thus most of the variation of the taxes from financial repression arises from exchange-rate depreciations which are not reflected by the low nominal interest rates in the domestic financial market.[1] Indeed, the interwar funding crises were plausibly caused by the public expectation of large exchange-rate depreciations.

Yet, the findings of Makinen and Woodward also suggest that there might be a limit to the amount of revenue that can be raised by financial repression, especially as long as governments rely on semi-voluntary subscriptions of public debt. At low rates of inflation and currency depreciation financial repression and the inflation tax are likely to be complementary. Capital controls restrict the public's portfolio choices and increase money demand, thereby, other things equal, increasing the revenue from inflation. At the same time, capital controls and moderate inflation allow governments to pay below-market interest on their domestic liabilities. At high rates of inflation, however, financial repression and the inflation tax are likely to become substitutes. The real return on domestic securities is so heavily depressed that there is a flight towards safety, even if it entails substantial transactions costs.

NOTE

1 The mirror image of the financial repression tax is the peso problem, whereby the government pays high *ex-post* interest rates at home whenever the market expects exchange-rate devaluations that do not materialize. The experience of Italy in late 1988–early 1989 might in part fit this description.

REFERENCE

Giovannini, A. and M. de Melo (1989). 'Government Revenue from Financial Repression' mimeo, Columbia University, September.

Discussion

ANDREA RIPA di MEANA

The focus of Makinen and Woodward's paper is on the mechanisms that made the maturity of the public debt a source of financial instability in some of the countries that had accumulated large stocks of debt during WWI.

The lion's share of the studies on the economic history of the interwar years analyses the dynamics of hyperinflations and the policies that were devised to end them (Dornbusch, 1987). No country in Makinen and Woodward's sample was hit by extreme inflation in the 1920s.

However, all of them experienced what was then called the 'floating debt problem', that is the difficulties posed to debt management by the over-hang of a large stock of debt, which was of extremely short maturity by the standards of the time.

There are basically two views of the stabilization policies undertaken in the 1920s by these moderate-inflation countries. One view is that the key to success was a credible and well publicized fiscal reform (Sargent, 1984). The 'Poincaré miracle' of 1926, for instance, was simply the result of the reversal of an unsustainable fiscal policy.

A second, very different view, which is shared by the authors and can also be traced back to the League of Nations report (1946) on interwar stabilization, highlights the importance of the elimination of the floating debt. It was the potential loss of control over the monetary composition of the debt that created the problem, rather than the deliberate excess of money creation.

On the whole, I find this second interpretation quite convincing and the authors' reconstruction of the evidence quite accurate. Hence, I have only two sets of comments on their work. First, I would like to add a few specific elements on the Italian episode that change the picture somewhat, even if they lend overall support to their interpretation. Second, I would like to offer some remarks on why debt management policies that contributed to financial instability were actually followed in the 1920s, and on the lessons for current debt management policies.

1   Italy: floating debt as a potential threat[1]

The case of Italy is interesting from a funding crisis perspective because apparently there was not much to stabilize at all by 1925. Public expenditure had been chopped three years earlier by 60%; the Fascist regime was fully in control and political instability was virtually nil, as all opposition was about to be outlawed. It is quite clear that financial instability *followed* fiscal adjustment by several years, not the other way around.

On the other hand, the redemption-monetization-devaluation link is *less* clearcut than in contemporaneous French and Belgian cases. The exchange rate data show that the speculative attack on the Lira started in April and ended in July 1926, when the Pound reached a peak (Einzig, 1961). However, the wave of net redemptions was most substantial in the months from July to October, when the market refused to roll-over about 12% of the outstanding stock of floating debt.

There is some overlap between the two periods, but one can hardly fail to notice that the most severe phase of the funding crisis came mostly *after* speculation against the Lira had ended. Hence the benefit and the purpose of the forced debt consolidation, which was decided in November 1926 and took the market by surprise, are not immediately obvious.

In spite of this peculiar timing of events, it remains true in my opinion that the forced consolidation was an essential step towards the return to gold in 1927. In essence, consolidation was meant to counter *potential*, rather than actual speculative pressure on the currency and to prevent sterilization of domestic monetary contraction.

Without going into too much detail, let me just recall three facts which bear out this interpretation.

First, note that exchange rate developments beyond the attack of the summer of 1926 followed two distinct phases. Between October 1926 and March 1927, the parity essentially fluctuated around, but not below, the same average value as the previous years (1924–25). Phase two only began in the spring of 1927, when capital started massively flowing into the country and the Lira appreciated by 25%. This pattern shows that the return to gold became a *fait accompli* only after phase two, that is several months after the debt consolidation.

The second relevant fact is the so called 'bloc of circulation', an expression coined by the contemporary financial press. The public belief was that monetary authorities were imposing a credit crunch in order to prepare the ground for the intended peg of the currency. This belief led many investors to liquidate their holdings of short bonds to eschew the perceived crunch. The perception was right, because note circulation actually remained almost constant from July to October, *in spite* of the massive (2.5 billion) note creation resulting from failure to roll-over maturing bonds during the same months.

The last relevant fact, which is also referred to by Makinen and Woodward, is that a very large chunk of debt was scheduled to mature between November 1926 and March 1927. This meant that a funding crisis taking place in those five months could have increased note circulation by no less than 40%.

Putting these facts together, we have a fairly straightforward story. In the midst of a long-sought process of currency stabilization, the roll-over of the floating debt was preventing effective control of the monetary base. By October 1926, undesired sterilization of the credit contraction had already been observed for several months. The very real threat was to have more of the same at the turn of the year, with the chance of a new round of speculation against the currency and the collapse of the preannounced return to gold. The very timely consolidation, decided in November, diffused this threat once and for all.

The last remark I wish to make on the Italian debt consolidation is that it actually benefited bondholders, contrary to widespread opinion (found, for example, in Confalonieri, 1986). A simple glance at bond prices corrected for inflation, shows that the market realized within a few months that this was the case. Real bond prices bottomed *before*, not after November and rose by 20% in 1927. The real share prices of bank equity, which were allegedly hurt by the loss of value of their bond holdings, followed a similar pattern.

Considering the very sizeable deflation that persisted for many years after 1926, this should come as no surprise. Investors realized pretty soon that the Treasury had locked them into long-term bonds that were paying a very hefty real rate. There was not much to be displeased about being paid more than the holders of equivalent British paper.

Some general remarks on funding crises and pegging policies

Another comment I wish to make is that many contemporary observers drew an analogy between funding crises and bank runs.[2]

The bank run analogy confirms a point that is made in the paper as well. Namely, that debt maturity does not make refinancing harder *per se*, but only when at the same time the interest rate on new issues is subject to some form of pegging. It was not so much a question of paying an inadequate nominal rate, as much as the fact of *non-auctioning off* the bonds that turned the floating debt into a problem.

In principle, with perfectly flexible nominal interest rates, the run equilibrium does not exist. For if the Treasury is willing to compensate bondholders against *any* expected devaluation, roll-over should never fail. But then forced monetization never takes place, nor does devaluation. The only confirmed expectation is one of customarily low nominal interest rates and no devaluation.

All this was clear at least to Minister Caillaux, one of the seven Finance

Ministers of the Cartel des Gauches, who had a reputation for financial wizardry. In 1925, he floated an issue of Treasury bonds that were indexed to the external value of the French Franc. Unfortunately, not enough information was provided to the market on this financial instrument, which must have been novel at the time. This probably explains the failure of his remarkable initiative.

If interest-rate pegging, rather than the large floating debt itself, is at the root of the funding crises of the mid-1920s, one might wonder *why* such policies were chosen in the first place.

On this point, I basically agree with Makinen and Woodward's final remarks. The simple answer is that inflation was predictable during the gold standard, so that there was no need of repricing new bond issues very often, or of actively managing the maturity structure of the debt. The stickiness of interwar nominal interest rates in non-hyperinflationary European countries is well documented.

The policy was so ingrained that we have a somewhat *paradoxical situation* in the mid-1920s. All countries were enormously concerned with the value of the currency and strove to restore the gold standard system at great economic cost. At the same time, quite a few countries were sticking to old debt management policies that did not stop huge portfolio shifts across currencies. Those countries recurred to the extreme choice of debt consolidation, instead of trying the easy solution first, i.e. letting interest rates loose.

In closing, let me go back to the final point of the paper, namely whether we should worry about a short maturity of the public debt in the current environment.

Of course we should, if the fiscal regime is unsustainable, but that is another matter. The relevant question is whether the *pure refinancing aspect* of debt management could be much complicated by a short average maturity. Should a country like Italy, with a large debt of short average maturity, be concerned about the roll-over of its debt, *even if* the fiscal regime were perceived to be fully sustainable? I think the answer is no, especially now that the procedure for selling bills has evolved into a full auction system. Any refinancing difficulty must ultimately be due either to the perception of fiscal insolvency, or to the practice of interest-rate pegging. Barring any of these circumstances, whatever the reasons for aiming at a long average maturity, the threat of total shutouts of the Treasury from the capital markets is probably not one of them.

NOTES

1 All facts and figures referred to in this section are drawn from a paper of mine, 'The Mussolini stabilization' (1988).

2 Cf. Dulles (1929).

REFERENCES

Confalonieri, R. (1986). 'La politica del debito pubblico in Italia e in alcuni Paesi Europei', in A. Confalonieri and E. Gatti, eds., *La Politica del Debito Pubblico in Italia 1919–1943*, Rome: La Terza.

Dornbusch, R. (1987). 'Lessons from the German Inflation Experience of the 20's', in R. Dornbusch, S. Fischer and J. Bossons (eds.) *Macroeconomics and Finance, Essays in Honor of Franco Modigliani*, M.I.T. Press, Cambridge.

Dulles, E. (1929). *The French Franc 1914–1928*, Macmillan, New York.

Einzig, P. (1961). *A Dynamic Theory of Forward Exchange*, Macmillan, London.

League of Nations (1946). *The Course and Control of Inflation*, Washington D.C.

Ripa di Meana, A. (1988). 'The Mussolini Stabilization', chapter III of Ph.D. dissertation, M.I.T., unpublished.

Sargent, T. (1984). 'Stopping Moderate Inflation: the Methods of Poincaré and Thatcher', in R. Dornbusch and M.H. Simonsen (eds.), *Inflation, Debt and Indexation*, M.I.T. Press, Cambridge.

7 The capital levy in theory and practice

BARRY EICHENGREEN

1   Introduction

Debt management is a topic of considerable concern in Europe today. Italy, Belgium and Ireland all have debt-to-GDP ratios of around 100 per cent. Debt service consequently absorbs a significant share of government revenues, and shocks to real interest rates or economic growth threaten to launch debt-income ratios onto an explosive path. Substantial attention is devoted to alternative strategies for minimizing these dangers and costs (Giavazzi and Spaventa, 1988). These include budget surpluses designed to retire debt, inflationary policies designed to erode its real value, and capital levies designed to eliminate the debt burden at the stroke of a pen.

A capital levy in which a one-time tax is levied on all wealth holders with the goal of retiring public debt is the most controversial solution to the problem.[1] The reasons for controversy are clear. A capital levy has prominent distributional consequences. It transfers wealth from asset holders to taxpayers who pay in the monies used to service the debt or to the beneficiaries of public programs that are crowded out by debt service costs. Alternatives such as inflation, forced conversion and debt retirement have distributional implications as well, but those consequences are usually less pronounced and hence not so hotly contested.

Moreover, it is not even clear that a capital levy can succeed in lowering the cost of debt service, properly measured, or enable the government to achieve its other objectives. On the one hand, by reducing the debt overhang a capital levy indisputably lowers short-run debt service costs. If it leaves other taxes unchanged, the government is able to expand the provision of services. If spending on items other than debt service remains unchanged, the authorities are able to lower taxes, which permits increased private-sector consumption and saving. On the other hand, if it is believed that the exceptional tax on wealth will be repeated, the capital levy will discourage saving. Governments which utilize the capital levy may develop a reputation for doing so repeatedly, encouraging capital flight, eroding the domestic tax base and undermining their capacity to service debt and finance social programs.

Two recent literatures, one theoretical and one empirical, bear directly on these questions.[2] On the empirical side, there is a growing literature on LDC debt. Two conclusions of this literature are that the debt overhang of the developing countries has significantly undermined their growth performance, and that sovereign default has often failed to bring about a significant rise in the subsequent cost of borrowing. Both conclusions have favourable implications for the efficacy of a capital levy. They suggest that there are conditions under which benefits of reducing a domestic debt overhang are substantial, and that there are plausible circumstances in which the damage to capital market access is minimal. On the theoretical side, recent work on time consistency highlights the fundamental problem with a capital levy. If governments could make a credible commitment not to repeat it, a one-time levy would be unambiguously beneficial, since it would eliminate the deadweight burden of the debt without discouraging saving. In the absence of a commitment mechanism, however, the government will have an incentive to renege on its promise not to repeat the levy. Official statements that the levy is nonrecurrent will not be credible. The optimal policy will be time-inconsistent.[3]

A recent article by Grossman and Van Huyck (1988) has begun to bring these two literatures together. Grossman and Van Huyck treat sovereign debt as a contingent claim. They suggest that bondholders recognize that if certain contingencies arise, governments will be forced to reduce or suspend debt service. Investors demand *ex ante* risk premia as compensation. If the contingencies are widely understood and readily verified, then the government will be able to default partially or completely in response to an unfavourable state of the world without violating its implicit contract with the creditors or damaging its capital market access. An obvious example is public debt issued in time of war. Purchasers presumably realize that the government's ability to honour this debt depends on whether the country emerges from the war victorious. If it triumphs, then the debt will be serviced in full out of domestic or foreign resources. If it is defeated or suffers extensive damage, then the debt will be repudiated or fall into default.[4]

It is tempting to conceptualize capital taxation analogously. Capital taxes could be modeled as a contingent claim, whose value is high in states of the world where the government's obligations for items other than programatic spending are unusually large, the social returns to spending are unusually high, or conventional revenues are unusually low. It is in response to such contingencies that one should expect to observe a capital levy. If the contingencies in response to which the capital levy is imposed are widely understood, readily verifiable and not subject to government control, then saving and investment should not fall following the adoption of the levy.[5]

It turns out to be straightforward to reinterpret the historical debate over the efficacy of the capital levy in this light. Yet when one turns to evidence on the operation of such levies, one encounters a most disconcerting fact. One finds virtually no examples of successful peacetime capital levies. I argue that this is no coincidence. In a democracy, there is no independent authority to verify to the satisfaction of savers that the realization of the state of the world in fact justifies a capital levy. Even if savers recognize that capital taxation is a contingent claim, they retain the incentive to dispute that the relevant contingency has arisen. Neither is there a mechanism to prevent the government from pursuing policies that strengthen the case for capital taxation – for example, increasing ordinary expenditures as levy receipts roll in. Savers will accuse the government of succumbing to moral hazard and resist the levy on those grounds. They will continue to oppose the levy for distributional reasons. If the levy is imposed at all, typically this will occur only at the end of a protracted and divisive political debate. Since, by the time the levy is adopted, the exogenous shock providing the justification has receded into the past, investors will feel entitled to evade it.

Equally important, time will have permitted investors to shelter their assets. Even in a contingent capital taxation setting, investors have an incentive to move their capital abroad if they can anticipate the timing of unusually high capital taxes. If there is an extended delay between proposal and implementation of the levy, capital flight is likely to render the measure ineffectual. I argue that such delay is an intrinsic characteristic of tax policy in a democracy.

I point to some measures governments have adopted in an effort to circumvent these obstacles. Exchange controls have been utilized to minimize capital flight. Statutes segregating levy receipts from ordinary tax revenues and mandating that they be devoted to debt retirement rather than ordinary expenditure have been utilized to minimize moral hazard. The story is analogous to Sargent's (1982) emphasis on statutes strengthening central bank independence in bringing post-World War I hyperinflations to a halt. Such fiscal restrictions, like Gramm-Rudman, can be thought of as an investment in precommitment on the part of government. If the authorities promise to devote levy receipts to debt retirement but fail to do so, they suffer embarrassment, which is supposed to serve as a deterrent to fiscal profligacy. But in contrast to the episodes with which Sargent is concerned, I find these investments in precommitment to have been largely ineffectual.

The body of the paper is organized into four sections. Section 2 formalizes the notion of capital taxation as a contingent claim. Section 3 then reinterprets the historical debate on the capital levy in terms of theories of time consistency and excusable default. This literature reached its most sophisticated stage in Britain in the 1920s. Contributors constitute a galaxy of economic stars: Edgeworth, Hicks, Hobson, Keynes, Pigou and Stamp, to name a few. Hence my examination of the literature focuses on the British debate in the 1920s.

Section 4 then provides a catalogue of failed capital levies, mainly from the aftermath of World War I. In each case, I argue, the capacity of governments to utilize the capital levy as an instrument of contingent taxation was hindered by the difficulty of verifying that the relevant contingencies obtained. The decision was reached via a political process which provided scope for political resistance motivated by distributional interests. The longer the levy was delayed, the less compelling the exogenous shock providing the justification appeared, the greater the scope for capital flight, and the less successful the impost.[6]

Section 5 analyses the exception that proves the rule: the Japanese capital levy after World War II. This is the single example of a major, successful peacetime capital levy of which I am aware. The Japanese case, in which a levy was imposed in a period of foreign military occupation when domestic distributional conflicts were totally suppressed, reaffirms the importance of political impediments to successful implementation.[7]

2   A positive theory of the capital levy: capital taxation as a contingent claim

In this section I analyse capital taxation as a contingent claim. The approach parallels Grossman and Van Huyck's (1988) analysis of foreign borrowing and sovereign default.

I assume that the government's objective in period j is to maximize the expectation of present and future utility from government spending g.

$$U_j = u(g_j) + E_j \sum_{i=j+1}^{\infty} u(g_i) \tag{1}$$

where $u' > 0$, $u'' < 0$, and $u'(0) = \infty$.

The benevolent interpretation is that government provides a public good, the malevolent one that the government is maximizing its own consumption. For simplicity, I assume no discounting.

In addition to capital taxes, the government receives lump-sum revenues q. An example is oil reserves like those discovered in the North Sea by Britain and Norway. q depends on the state of the world z (assumed stationary). The government cannot borrow, lend, or print money. Its budget constraint is:

$$g_j = q(z_j) + trK \tag{2}$$

where K is the amount of capital subject to taxation, r is the gross domestic rate of return, and t is the *ad valorem* capital tax rate.

I abstract from the consumption and savings decisions of households, focusing exclusively on their decision of whether to invest their savings at home or abroad. (This enables me to ignore the opportunity costs of government spending.) I assume that the quantity of accumulated savings (capital) is fixed at $\bar{K}$.[8] Capital invested abroad yields a rate of return r^*. (Precisely, r^* is one plus the foreign rate of return.) The domestic government cannot tax capital invested abroad. (I assume that the foreign government imposes no taxes either.) This extreme assumption is designed to capture the notion that the foreign investments are more difficult to tax than domestic ones. The gross rate of return on capital invested at home exceeds the return on capital invested abroad ($r > r^*$).[9] After domestic capital taxes are imposed, the net return is $(1 - t)r$. The rate of domestic capital taxation t depends on the state of the world ($t = t(z)$).

Savers decide in period $j - 1$ whether to invest at home or abroad in period j. I assume a large number of risk-neutral savers. They will invest all of their savings abroad unless the expected value of the after-tax return on domestic capital in period j conditional on information available in period $j - 1$ at least equals the (expected) alternative risk-free return r^*.

$$\sum_z p(z_j)r[1 - t(e(z_j))] \geqq r^* \tag{3}$$

where $r[1 - t(e(z_j))]$ is the net-of-tax rate of return that savers in period $j - 1$ expect to receive in period j as a function of the realization $z(j)$. (Note that $t(e)$ denotes the expected tax rate.)

2.1   Contingent capital taxation with commitment

Imagine that the government can commit irrevocably in period $j - 1$ to a state-contingent capital tax policy for period j, given by:

$$t_j = T_{j-1}(z_j) \tag{4}$$

Because of the commitment, taxpayers' expectations of capital taxes will be verified:

$$T_{e,j-1}(z_j) = T_{j-1}(z_j) \tag{5}$$

The government has no effective choice regarding the level of spending in the current period, which is given by the sum of its state-contingent capital tax revenues plus its lump-sum revenues $q(z)$.

The government maximizes its objective function (1) subject to its budget constraint (2), the constraint that after-tax capital income at home not fall short of the rate of return available abroad (3), and the rationality of expectations. Given the form of the objective function (separability and no discounting), government spending is the same in each period. (3) holds as an equality. Capital taxes are high in states of the world in which alternative revenues are low. In bad states, capital taxes can reduce the domestic net return below the return available abroad, so long as in good states the domestic return exceeds that available abroad by a sufficient margin that (3) holds as an equality.

This analysis assumes that savers must decide in period $j - 1$ whether to invest at home or abroad in period j, after which the government selects the current rate of capital taxation in light of the realization of $q(z_j)$. What happens if instead there are lags in the authorities' response, or if savers are able to redeploy their capital after the government announces current tax policy? Savers will move their capital abroad in any period when $r(1 - t) < r^*$, even if (3) holds over time. The authorities' ability to utilize the capital levy, even in the presence of a commitment technology, will be vitiated by delays in implementation that facilitate capital flight.

2.2   Contingent capital taxation without commitment

As the historical analysis below will remind us, governments cannot irrevocably commit to a sequence of state-contingent capital taxes. What are the implications in the present context?

Assume that the government ignores any effect of its current actions on expectations of its future actions. (This assumption will be relaxed shortly.) Then the optimal tax policy for the current period is a capital levy at a rate of 100 per cent. This maximizes government expenditure in the current period and, absent any impact on expectations of future policies, has no damaging repercussions. Specifically, the capital levy does not reduce the government's anticipated ability to finance its expenditures in the future.

It is unrealistic, of course, to assume that the government can ignore the effect of its current actions on expectations of its future actions. If savers correctly perceive that the government will face the same problem and arrive at the same solution in the next period, they would anticipate that the capital levy would be repeated. They would shift their capital abroad, where it is free of taxation, and government spending in all subsequent periods would be $q(z)$. The government would be unable to smooth its spending over time. The outcome is suboptimal in the sense that a policy that involved capital taxes at rates somewhat lower than a 100% capital levy in bad states of the world and taxes much lower than a 100% capital levy in good states would yield higher expected utility, if only savers could be convinced to expect such a policy.

2.3   Contingent capital taxation in reputational equilibrium

Subsection 2.1 treated expectations as a control variable. Subsection 2.2 treated them as a given. This section treats them as determined by government policy. I consider reputational equilibria in which the capital taxes that savers in period $j - 1$ expect the government to impose in period j are self-confirming. Whatever the realization of z_j, the expected present value of the government's utility is at least as large if the government validates savers' capital tax policy expectations as it would be if the government imposes a 100% capital levy. Given the setup, the equilibrium state-contingent tax policy, $T^*(z_j)$, is time-invariant.

Assume that if government policy does not confirm savers' expectations, capital flight results. Savers refuse to repatriate their capital so long as memory of the violation of expectations lingers. This memory lingers for f periods. $f = \infty$ is the well known 'grim trigger strategy'.[10] Experimental studies like Axelrod (1984) have shown more forgiving strategies ($f < \infty$) to perform better. An alternative rationale for $f < \infty$, adopted by Grossman and Van Huyck, is that the current generation of savers has limited memory and recalls the violation of expectations for only f periods.[11]

If the government does pursue policies in violation of expectations, it will impose a value of $t = 1$. Whether the government benefits from this policy depends on whether or not:

$$U(q(z_j) + r\bar{K}) - U(q(z_j) + T^*(z_j)r\bar{K})$$

$$< \sum_{i=j+1}^{j+f} E(i)[U(i)(q(z_i) + T^*(z_i)r\bar{K}) - U(i)(q(z_i))] \tag{6}$$

Thus, the government will have no incentive to violate investors' expectations if the benefits of increased government spending in the current period due to a rate of capital taxation in excess of that anticipated given $z = z_j$ falls short of the costs of inability to tax capital for the next f periods. In this case, the reputational equilibrium is sustainable.

In summary, if other sources of revenue (alternatively, other government commitments or the benefits of government spending) vary randomly over time, it will be optimal for capital taxes to vary with the realization of the random shock. Ideally, the government would precommit to a sequence of capital taxes whose average level was constrained by the differential between the gross rate of return domestically and the return available in foreign tax havens. In exceptionally bad states of the world, exceptionally high capital taxes would be levied, and conversely in exceptionally good states. In reality, no commitment technology is available. Government will have an incentive to renege on its commitment, assuming no reputational effects. Knowing this, savers will shift their capital to tax havens, and the government will be unable to utilize capital taxes. If reputational effects are sufficiently powerful, it may be possible to sustain contingent capital taxes in the absence of a commitment mechanism. But even in the presence of reputational effects or a commitment technology, delays in implementation may render a capital levy ineffectual.

3   The debate over the capital levy

It is straightforward to reinterpret the historical debate over the capital levy in this light. Here I focus on the British debate between the wars.

The stated rationale for a capital levy in Britain after World War I was to reduce the economic costs of the debt overhang. Britain had accumulated a substantial public debt as a result of the war (see Section 4 below). The debt burden was seen as having a variety of depressing economic effects. J.A. Hobson (1920, p. 197), for example, focused on the tendency of the debt overhang to raise the rate of interest, which slowed postwar reconstruction, impeded the expansion of industry and commerce, and depressed the housing industry. He advocated a one-time levy which, by drastically reducing the costs of debt service and levels of income and profit taxation, promised to stimulate saving, investment and economic growth. A further cost was the need to constrain spending on the provision of public goods in order to devote scarce resources to debt service. 'Expenditure . . . upon new enterprises such as assistance to housing schemes, and on the development of existing services, such as education, is inevitably restricted,' read the Minority Report of the Colwyn Committee (1927, p. 358). The young economist Hugh Dalton (1923, pp. 11–2), soon to rise to greater fame, put the case as follows:

> To pay away a million pounds of taxation a day for education, health and housing would be a bold and hopeful adventure. To pay it away for capital development in our fundamental home industries – coal-mining, transport, electric power, etc. – or even in new sources of supply of

foodstuffs and raw materials in distant lands, might be a defensible scheme of investment in the social interest ... but what we are now doing is to pay it away for nothing, as a permanent annual tribute to the holders of War Loan and other public securities. The sums thus paid away are, indeed, partly reinvested, but are largely spent on the immediate enjoyments of the recipients, who are rendering no present service in return for what they receive and who, just because they have this assured source of future income, are in many cases the less inclined to work and save.

Finally, a heavy debt burden increased the fragility of the government's fiscal position and heightened the difficulty of financing budget deficits. A one-time levy, by eliminating the overhang, could actually enhance the government's subsequent ability to borrow. This was the position argued by Pigou in his testimony to the Colwyn Committee (1927a, p. 266).

Much of the debate revolved around the question of whether saving and investment would be discouraged by the imposition of a capital levy or encouraged by subsequent tax reductions. According to Edgeworth (1919, p. 121), 'I am inclined to think that the check to accumulation would be considerable.' Still, this did not necessarily render a levy undesirable. 'The advantages of a capital levy, less by its attendant dangers, are to be weighed against the continuance of the present regime with all its evils.'

As the discussion evolved, observers began to distinguish different types of levies and different circumstances. 'All the economic effects of a levy would depend a great deal on the psychological reactions,' reminded the Colwyn Committee (1927a, p. 259). Much hinged on whether or not investors expected the levy to be repeated. 'The possibility of a periodic levy on capital', admitted even Philip Snowden (1920, p. 79), a staunch advocate of the policy, 'would discourage saving, it would keep the commercial world in a continual state of uncertainty, and it would arrest trade enterprise'. But, he continued, these evils would follow only if the levy was repeated periodically. Such fears 'need not be entertained in regard to a special levy on capital *once and for all* for the purpose of reducing the National Debt'. (Emphasis added.)

Some described the capital levy using phrases that sound suspiciously like contingent capital taxation. In the words of the Minority Report of the Colwyn Committee (1927a, p. 406), 'the effect of a levy on future savings clearly depends to a considerable extent upon the confidence of levy payers that the Capital Levy is an exceptional operation designed to meet exceptional circumstances and not to be forthwith repeated'. The majority (pp. 295–6) concurred that 'exceptional circumstances are required to reconcile the owner of capital wealth to the levy idea'. Hicks, Hicks and Rostas (1941, p. 180), reviewing the implications of the post-WWI debate for post-WWII policy, concluded that 'A capital levy is not capable of being adopted as a regular part of a fiscal system; it is only suitable for use in special emergencies.'

Proponents distinguished the likely effects of a one-time levy in the exceptional circumstances of the postwar world from high levels of recurrent capital taxation. Because it was imposed as a result of independently verified, well understood contingencies, the post-war levy would not discourage saving and investment. There was no reason to anticipate that the public would regard a levy as an abrogation of their contingent claims, or anticipate that the government would utilize it repeatedly in the future.[12] In the exceptional circumstances of the early 1920s, there was no reason to expect that imposition of a levy would increase the perceived probability of its future repetition. Hence individuals would have no reason to reduce their saving or to engage in capital flight. It was essential, therefore, that informed discussion distinguish an exceptional levy imposed under extraordinary circumstances from recurrent capital taxation. '[T]his recognition of the obvious folly of failing to distinguish between this unprecedented emergency and the ordinary needs of state finance will remove the apprehension of future raids from operating on the minds of the saving classes so as to prevent them from saving. . . . It is reasonable to regard this war-emergency as so exceptional and so severe that nothing resembling it is likely to recur in our time.'[13]

Some proponents of the policy admitted that the kind of levy under contemplation exceeded the levels of capital taxation justified by the contingencies that had arisen. They insisted, however, that a nonrecurrent levy at rates exceeding those implicit in the social contract between government and taxpayer, by eliminating the debt overhang at one fell swoop, could enhance national welfare so long as savers were guaranteed that the exceptional levy would not be repeated. (This is the case of binding commitment in Subsection 2.2 above.) To the objection that a capital levy would discourage saving and enterprise, Hobson (1920, pp. 209–10) responded, 'I do not admit that a graduated emergency levy on capital will carry any appreciable danger of this sort', so long as it was not repeated. 'For this reason the advocates of a levy insist strongly on its emergency character, and the opponents on the apprehension of its repetition.' As Stamp (1924, p. 235) put it, when the 'no-repetition of the levy has been fully guaranteed', saving is likely to be encouraged, since the subsequent tax burden will fall. 'The satisfactory economic consequences of a levy would be at their maximum possible point.' (This is the case where commitment permits a higher level of social welfare to be achieved than in the absence of a guarantee, as in Fischer, 1980.) But, Stamp went on, 'It is equally clear that where the right to repeat the levy is expressly left open, and where there is to be no relief to the future taxation of those who have paid it, the consequences are at the point of minimum advantage.' (This is the case, in Subsection 2.2 above, where absence of a commitment technology and of reputational effects prevents government from smoothing its expenditure.)

All too many advocates of a levy, while acknowledging the importance of insuring nonrecurrence, failed to recognize the time-consistency problem. Dalton's solution was to have the present generation of politicians pledge themselves against repetition. No mention was made of the incentive to renege, or of the incentive of the private sector to adapt its behavior accordingly. The Co-operative Congress thought it sufficient for all parties to aver their commitment that the levy 'would not be repeated within any conditions that could now be foreseen'. The Trades Union Congress embraced Sir Josiah Stamp's suggestion that receipts be issued to those who paid the levy and that these be imprinted with a solumn oath that the tax would not be repeated for 25 years.[14] Hobson (1920, p. 210) similarly failed to acknowledge the time-consistency problem. 'If the State discovers that it can once "raid" capital advantageously, will it not recur periodically to this method? The answer is "No, not if you accredit it with any true regard to the economic interests of the nation, or even to the future interests of public revenue." It will not do so, precisely because of the soundness of the objection that is raised to such recurrence.'

Opponents of the levy, such as the majority of the Colwyn Committee (1927a, p. 259), rejected the argument that the sort of capital levy under consideration would be received as the consequence of an independently verified, fully anticipated contingency, concluding that a levy, 'unless it were accompanied by some kind of guarantee, would give rise in greater or less degree to the fear of repetition'. The problem was that there existed no commitment technology, or guarantee, to insure nonrepetition of the levy. Even Hugh Dalton (1923, pp. 65–66) admitted, 'There can, in the nature of the case, be no such guarantee. If the Levy were once made, and if it were subsequently proposed to repeat it, that proposal would have to be considered on its merits in the light of the subsequent situation. . . .' Similarly, representatives of the Trades Union Congress (Colwyn Committee, 1927b, p. 587) reluctantly admitted, 'We are aware that no guarantee of non-repetition can be absolutely secure'. The Colwyn Committee (1972a, p. 259) concluded that 'an absolute guarantee against the repetition of a levy would be constitutionally impossible in this country'.

In the absence of a commitment mechanism, governments were advised to heed the reputational effects of a levy.[15] The Colwyn Committee (1927a, pp. 295–6) referred to the 'political suspicion' to which a levy would give rise – suspicion presumably of repetition. Pethick-Lawrence

(1918, pp. 52–3) emphasized reputational effects when contrasting the capital levy with debt cancellation. All this was an argument against imposing a capital levy in excess of that which could be justified on the basis of independently verified, fully anticipated contingencies. Larger levies would undermine the government's ability to utilize capital taxes in the future.[16]

Finally there was the danger that delays in implementation would render the levy ineffectual. Anticipating exceptionally high rates of capital taxation, savers would move their assets abroad. In addition to disturbing domestic financial markets, this would reduce the yield. The obvious solution was for governments to adopt the levy quickly. But as time wore on and the debate remained dedlocked, the policy lost its attractiveness in the eyes of some observers. The probability of compliance declined with the passage of time.[17]

Some advocates of the levy minimized the danger of capital flight. Dalton (1923, p. 62) argued it could not reduce the burden of the levy, since the levy would be applied to all wealth wherever its domicile. Others such as Scott (1918, p. 250) and Pigou (918, p. 143) acknowledged the difficulty of identifying and taxing flight capital. The solution of Pethick-Lawrence (1918, p. 79) was to coordinate capital levies internationally.

4   The history of the capital levy

Levies on capital have been contemplated ever since governments existed to exploit the power of taxation.[18] The ancient Greeks used periodic capital taxes at rates varying from one to four per cent. It is said that these levies were phenomenally successful because property owners, out of vanity, overstated the value of their assets! In modern times, capital levies have come under consideration following every period of major military expenditure and rapidly rising debt-income ratios. Archibald Hutchison, a British Member of Parliament, proposed a 10 per cent levy on all property in 1714. Ricardo urged the adoption of a levy following the Napoleonic wars.[19] Following the Franco-Prussian war, Menier suggested that the French public debt be retired through the adoption of a one per cent capital levy. In the 1890s, a capital levy was discussed in Germany as a way of financing the expenditures needed to achieve naval parity with Britain.

None of these proposals was adopted. For examples where capital levies were actually implemented, we must turn to the 20th century. The high point of the capital levy debate came after World War I. Not only had debt-income ratios reached high levels as a result of the war, but returning to the gold standard at prewar parities implied deflation and hence even heavier real debt burdens. Many of the new states of Central and Eastern Europe found themselves saddled with public debt but endowed with few resources out of which to service it. Finally, the distribution of the tax burden, and of income and wealth in general, was up in the air, particularly so long as the prospect of socialist revolution loomed, as it did throughout the European Continent in the immediate aftermath of the war, and as new political entities representing the working class vied with established parties for control.

4.1   Italy

The Italian capital tax of 1920 is the closest approximation to a successful capital levy in the 1920s. Italy emerged from the war with a significant debt burden. Fiscal capacity was strained by the ambitious spending programs of the postwar Socialist Government, which wished to maintain its wartime subsidies on foodstuffs and other consumer goods and to initiate a variety of new social programs. Thus, the source of the fiscal problem was not simply extraordinary wartime expenditures but a permanent rise in the state's fiscal needs. This rendered less than credible assurances by the advocates of a levy that it would both eliminate the fiscal problem and be nonrecurrent.

In the summer of 1919, shortly after coming to power, the Nitti Government appointed a commission of experts to study the levy idea. Its charge was to design 'an extraordinary tax on property'.[20] The commission's proposal was for a one-time tax on the increment to wealth since 1914, plus a forced loan bearing interest at one per cent and repayable in 60 years, to be allocated to taxpayers on the basis of property values. The rates of this proposed increment levy, which depended on the value of property before and after the war, ranged from 3.33 per cent on small properties with no increment to 53.33 per cent on large estates accumulated since 1914. Payment in full was to be due on January 1, 1920, with provision for deferral by owners of illiquid assets for up to eight years.

When in the autumn of 1919 these details became known, 'the usual storm of abuse and panic immediately arose'.[21] The strongest opposition came from owners of real estate who might be forced to resort to distress sales. Bankers feared a run on deposits. Spokesmen for joint stock companies warned of a stock market crash. Proponents of the plan found it difficult to counter their opposition because of the complexity of the commission's scheme, in particular the difficulty of determining the wartime increment to wealth.

In 1920, the initial proposal was superceded by a straightforward capital levy, or 'extraordinary tax on capital'. The rates, graduated from 4.5 to 50 per cent, looked impressive. But payment could be stretched out over 20 years, which reduced annual rates to 0.225–2.5 per cent, little different from a modest tax on dividends and capital gains. Thus, the one-time capital levy was transformed into a permanent increase in rates of capital taxation, reflecting the permanently higher levels of government expenditure which created the need for the measure. Rates of taxation were adjusted to circumstances: they were raised temporarily in 1921, to finance increased government spending on subsidies, and reduced to previous levels in 1922; the valuation of property was revised repeatedly with changes in the price level and in the profitability of different sectors, thus altering the effective tax rate. Capital taxation made a useful contribution to the public sector's revenue needs throughout the interwar years, but to call these policies a capital levy rather than capital income taxation would be misleading.

4.2   Czechoslovakia

Czechoslovakia provides the other marginally successful example of a capital levy after World War I. The levy law was passed by the National Assembly in April 1920. Two distinct taxes were adopted: a levy on all property, and a surtax on the wartime increment. Both were progressive, with rates for the capital levy ranging from 3 to 30 per cent and rates for the increment tax reaching 40 per cent. A separate levy with rates ranging from 3 to 20 per cent was imposed on corporate property. Collection was to be complete within three years.

The success of the levy was mixed. The authorities met with resistance in 1920–21, but significant amounts of revenue were raised in 1922–23. In these years the two levies provided the majority of direct tax revenues.[22] But then new concessions were introduced, especially once financial instability in Central Europe began to disrupt foreign trade. Taxpayers were allowed to pay in installments over many years without additional interest charges. In 1924 levy receipts fell to a third of direct tax revenues and declined steadily thereafter.

What accounts for the unusual success of the Czech levy? First, the levy fell mainly on a small ethnic German minority that was unable to mount effective political resistance or to delay adoption. With political opposition minimized, the authorities were able to move quickly toward implementation.

Second, the government succeeded in minimizing capital flight. In March 1919, when property values were assessed, financial relations with other countries were effectively severed.[23] Assessment followed immediately upon the conclusion of hostilities and preceded by more than a year passage of the levy law. Other countries attempted to pursue a similar strategy but failed. Czech experience reveals a further advantage of initiating the process in the immediate aftermath of war: with rail and road transport still disrupted, shifting assets abroad was more difficult than it was to become subsequently. Capital flight still reached significant levels, as Van Sickle (1931, p. 176) notes, but it was not as debilitating as in subsequent cases.

Third, it seems likely that the way the Czech authorities structured their budget encouraged compliance. The administration of the levy was completely sequestered from the day-to-day operations of the Ministry of Finance. Levy revenues were explicitly allocated to the special costs of establishing a newly-independent nation. They were used to extinguish obligations taken over from the Austro-Hungarian Bank and to meet 'the most pressing needs of the Czechoslovak State arising from the establishment of its independence. . . .'[24] The government was prevented from using levy receipts to defray current state budget deficits. This lent credibility to claims that the levy was an extraordinary tax whose repetition was unlikely.

4.3   Austria

The Austrian levy was an abject failure. It had been under discussion since 1917. Gustav Stolper wrote a series of articles in which a levy figured in his plan for postwar reconstruction. Joseph Schumpeter, in his capacity as finance minister, included a modest levy in his 1919 budget proposal.[25] But political wrangling over the levy and over the general question of who should defray the costs of postwar reconstruction and adjustment led to fatal delays in implementation. Feuding between the Social Democrats, representing urban labourers, and the Christian Socialists, representing small farmers and shopkeepers, left postwar tax policy deadlocked. The Social Democrats were understandably more supportive of the levy idea than the Christian Socialists. Even when the two parties formed a coalition government, they found it difficult to resolve the issue.[26]

Political sparring dragged on for more than a year until property values were assessed in the summer of 1920. Except for the decision to drop the distinction between total property and the post-1914 increment, the plan was virtually identical to its Czech predecessor. But by the time assessment took place, asset holders had had more than a year to prepare. Reconstruction of the transportation and communication networks had faciliated capital flight. Anti-evasion legislation, including laws requiring those taking assets out of the country to declare their intention to the authorities a month in advance and to pay a 30–50 per cent tax, proved ineffectual. Capital flight heightened objections to the levy on grounds of equity, leading to further resistance and evasion. Small savers and agriculturalists ill placed to engage in capital flight demanded and received favourable treatment by tax assessors. The valuation process was reduced to a 'joke'.[27] The Christian Socialists secured exemptions for Church property, while the Social Democrats obtained exemptions for newly-created public utilities. Moreover, the authorities failed to segregate levy receipts from ordinary revenues and expenditures of the state, casting doubt on their characterization of the measure as extraordinary and nonrecurrent.

With capital flight and erosion of the tax base came financial instability and, ultimately, hyperinflation. The effects of the hyperinflation are the subject of an extensive literature. One effect was to liquidate levy obligations. As soon as they were established, property assessments were outdated. By delaying payment, taxpayers could virtually eliminate their obligations. In addition to liquidating the tax base, hyperinflation undermined the very rationale for exceptional capital taxation. The burden of public debt which provided the justification for a levy was effectively eliminated by inflation. By 1922, the levy had been written off. As part of the League of Nations stabilization agreement, it was converted into an annual property tax at extremely low rates. The revenues raised by the levy, over its 2½ years of operation, amounted to little more than a third of the ordinary tax revenues collected in the first six months following the stabilization.

4.4   Hungary

Hungary also attempted, in 1920–1, to impose a levy along Czech lines. As in Austria, implementation was impeded by postwar political instability, including a short-lived Communist experiment. Once a semblance of political stability was restored, the government attempted to impose a levy. All property was blocked and registered, to be reacquired by payment in cash or kind, at rates ranging from 5 to 20 per cent. The Hungarian levy differed from its Czech and Austrian counterparts by taxing different assets at different rates. The advantage was administrative ease: individuals were simply required to cede a given percentage of each type of security, or a certain share of their land, without complicated assessments. The disadvantage was the perception of inequity; one person who held foreign exchange might be required to cede 20 per cent, while another who held domestic bank deposits might pay only 5 per cent.

As in Czechoslovakia, levy receipts were initially segregated from other government revenues and earmarked for debt retirement. As the budgetary crisis deepened, however, the distinction was eliminated, and levy receipts were used to finance ordinary expenditures. Arguably this failure to earmark receipts for debt retirement weakened the argument that the levy was an extraordinary tax.

The Hungarian levy was actively resisted by the landowners, who utilized delaying tactics. The large landowners had long dominated local politics.[28] Because their assets were largely illiquid, rendering capital flight impractical, they had the most at stake. Some capital flight surely took place, mainly by urban wealthholders with liquid assets, but it probably was less important than in Austria. In any case, the Finance Minister's decision to include the levy as part of his 1920 budget, thereby provoking capital flight, was widely cited as a cause of the hyperinflation. Thus, when the Finance Minister was forced to resign as a consequence of the inflationary chaos, the levy was revoked. As one of the fiscal reforms adopted in conjunction with the 1924 League of Nations stabilization agreement, remaining vestiges of the levy were converted into a regular property tax at low rates.

4.5   Germany

The outcome in Germany was the same; only the political cleavages differed. Germany had attempted to employ various forms of nonrecurrent capital taxation to finance the war. The euphemistically-named National Distress Contribution of 1920 was only the latest in this series of supposedly nonrecurrent levies; hence assurances that it was not to be repeated were received skeptically. In addition, much of the support for the levy by the parties of the Left was based not merely on the need to finance extraordinary expenditure, but on the desire to achieve a more equal income distribution. Thus, the equity issues that inevitably complicate use of the instrument were especially prominent in the German case.

The most effective opposition to the measure came not from landowners but from business. Economists added their voices to the chorus of those questioning the measure's practicability.[29] As in Austria and Hungary, opponents relied on delaying tactics. Capital flight provoked by the levy did not play a direct role in the German hyperinflation of 1923, for the levy was effectively abolished by the end of 1921, although its failure may have played a role in the fiscal crisis facing the state in 1922. But imposition of the levy surely encouraged capital flight in 1920, which well may have contributed to the 70 per cent rise in the price level between May 1919 and May 1920. Since property values were to be assessed on December 31, 1919, the tax base was quickly eroded. Nominal rates ranged from 10 per cent on small properties to 65 per cent on the large estates.

In order to overcome opposition to the levy idea, its supporters acceded to demands that payment be spread over 30 years (as long as 50 years for landowners). Only 5 per cent interest was charged on arrears. Thus, the levy as implemented did little to resolve the fiscal crisis. As an unindexed tax, it created a natural constituency for policies with an inflationary bias. By the end of 1921 inflation was under way. The real value of receipts diminished rapidly, both because of the erosion of the tax base and because of the increased incentive to delay payment. In early 1922 the government enacted new measures to accelerate payment of small liabilities, but these proved inadequate to offset the effects of continued inflation. Levy receipts fell to negligible levels. In April 1922 the capital levy was converted into a conventional property tax at low rates.

4.6   France

The capital levy was intensely debated in France and Britain but adopted in neither country. In France, exceptional political fragmentation stood in the way. Parliament was fragmented into an unusually large number of parties, intensifying the difficulty of forming a coalition in support of a levy. Income distribution, while only one of a range of issues on which parties disagreed, figured prominently in political manoevering. Although there existed a broad range of opinion in agreement that contingencies justifying extraordinary taxation had occurred, parties disagreed on the appropriate tax base, some pushing for exceptional income taxes, other for exceptional excise duties on consumption, still others for a capital levy. For more than half a decade, consensus proved impossible to achieve.

On fringes of the political spectrum, there was dissent from the view that the relevant contingencies had in fact occurred. It was argued, particularly on the Right, that extraordinary taxes to finance postwar reconstruction were superfluous because Germany would pay. Budget deficits had the desirable effect of keeping the pressure on Germany and the Reparations Commission. Thus, there was a natural incentive to delay resolution of the fiscal crisis. The longer delay persisted, the further the events justifying extraordinary taxation receded into the past.

The extremity of the budgetary crisis was the central factor favourably inclining Frenchmen toward some form of exceptional taxation. In 1920, for example, when a capital levy was first seriously contemplated, the central government budget deficit amounted to 150 per cent of revenues. In part this reflected the extraordinary reconstruction needs of the economy, but it also reflected political exigencies. Government expenditures were segregated into a nonrecoverable budget, whose deficit was about 33 per cent of revenues, and recoverable expenditures on special account, all of which were to be financed out of German reparations. In the meantime, bonds were issued to finance recoverable expenditures, adding to the debt overhang.

The outgoing Clemenceau Government's 1920 budget projected substantial amounts of new revenue, to be raised in part through two new levies on the increment to wealth. The first would have imposed a progressive tax on the increment to wealth between 1914 and 1919. The second would have imposed a special tax on increases in the value of real estate and business concerns accruing over the last 25 years. Rates would have averaged around 20 per cent. The incoming Millerand Government regarded these levies as impractical and eliminated them from its program. Its Finance Minister, François-Marsal, a banker, noted that a levy on accumulated savings penalized the frugal, rewarded the spendthrift, and was likely to discourage saving.[30]

The French finances staggered on through 1926, with one finance minister replacing another on average at four-month intervals. The reparations tangle remained at the root of the problem: reinforcing the unwillingness to compromise of the proponents of indirect tax increases, expenditure reductions and the capital levy was blind faith that German transfers would eventually fill the budgetary gap. Only with the failure of the Ruhr occupation and the acceleration of inflation did politicians begin to acknowledge that the solution had to be found at home.

This realization was one factor underlying the formation of the Cartel des Gauches, a coalition of left-of-centre parties all of which preferred a capital levy to indirect tax increases and expenditure reductions. The Bloc National of centrist parties had obtained breathing space in early 1924 by adopting modest expenditure economies and raising taxes by 20 per cent. Its defeat at the polls in May of that year and the accession to power of the Cartel des Gauches are widely ascribed to the unpopularity of these fiscal measures. Compared to the Bloc National, the Cartel was less virulently anti-German and hence more inclined to seek a solution to the fiscal deadlock at home. The capital levy was its official policy. Unfortunately, the Cartel did not possess a Parliamentary majority and some of its own members opposed extraordinary capital taxes. Clementel resigned as finance minister in April 1925 when the Cabinet rejected his proposal to increase income taxes by 50 per cent, preferring a 10 per cent levy on all wealth to be payable over no more than 10 years. His successor de Monzie, to subdue the most fervent opposition, recast the levy as a forced loan but was no more successful securing adoption.[31]

By the autumn of 1925 inflation and exchange-rate depreciation were threatening to run out of control. Endless discussion of a levy, unaccompanied by decisive action, provoked capital flight and rendered investors hesitant to absorb new bond issues, fueling the monetary inflation.[32] The current Finance Minister, Painleve, embraced both the income tax increase favoured by the centre and the capital levy favoured by the Left. To minimize problems of valuation, the levy was to be assessed mainly on income from assets rather than their capital value: 150 per cent of the rental value of real estate, 50 per cent of average annual profits of businesses, 15 per cent of annual income on securities. Payment would extend over as many as 14 years. Inclusion of the levy in the fiscal package is sometimes ascribed to the need to buttress support on the Left. It met with understandable opposition from business and the Right, who referred to it as 'an infringement of the right of property . . . pure collectivism'.[33] In addition there was dissent within the Cartel; combining the levy with an income tax increase did not defuse the opposition of its more moderate members.[34] The stability of the Government was called into question. The occasion for its fall was Painleve's proposal to temporarily suspend amortization of government bonds, a drastic step to which he was led by inability to make more rapid progress on the fiscal front. This ended serious discussion of the capital levy.

4.7   Britain

Great Britain emerged from World War I with a greatly increased internal debt burden. Interest payments as a share of budgetary receipts rose from less than 10 per cent in 1913–14 to 22 per cent in 1919–20. Not only might the taxation required to service this debt hinder recovery from the war, but the overhang posed a challenge to policies designed to restore the prewar sterling parity. Returning to gold at $4.86 required deflation; as the price level fell, the debt burden rose, to 30 per cent of budgetary receipts in 1922–23 and as much as 36 per cent in 1925–26.

The capital levy was Labour's preferred solution to the problem. As early as 1916, the Fabian Research Society, in a pamphlet authored by Sidney Webb, proposed a 10 per cent levy on capital. In 1918 Sydney Arnold, a Labour MP, raised the issue in the House of Commons. Pethick-Lawrence (1918) published an articulate statement of the Labour case for the levy. By 1920 the levy had become a plank in the financial platform of the Labour Party.

The ruling coalition, which drew support from property owners, had only limited sympathy for the idea. Chancellor of the Exchequer Austen Chamberlain rejected the levy in 1919 as a fatal deterrent to saving.[35] Private parties reiterated his warning. The Manchester Chamber of Commerce adopted a resolution in March of 1920 warning that 'confiscation of capital' would severely disrupt the expansion and development of industry.[36]

Significantly, Labour advocated a levy not only to eliminate the debt overhang but also as a means of effecting a socially desirable redistribution of income. It envisaged a revolution not merely in the national finances but in the distribution of income and wealth.[37] Labour could point to large fortunes acquired through war profiteering as a source of particularly unjustifiable income inequality. To cultivate support for the levy by focusing attention on these cases, Labour MPs modified their proposal in 1920 from a levy on all property to a special tax on war wealth. Unfortunately, limiting the tax base to the wartime increment greatly reduced the prospective yield. This fueled the argument that the administrative costs of a levy might swamp the benefits. The ruling Liberal-Conservative coalition was nonetheless sufficiently attracted to the idea of a limited levy to appoint a Parliamentary committee, which in 1920 submitted a plan for a special tax on war wealth, to be applied to the 1914–1919 increment to property values.

Among the submissions to the committee were memoranda from the Board of Inland Revenue. The Revenue Authority expressed skepticism about the practicability of a levy, warning of disruptions to financial markets if property owners were forced to liquidate assets. It recommended stretching out payments over ten years, so that the levy could be paid out of income rather than principal. Supporters of the levy, such as Pigou, objected that this would effectively transform the levy into a recurrent income tax with serious disincentive effects.

Talk of new taxes was deferred by the 1921 recession. Proposals for a levy were then subjected to electoral debate. The First Labour Government made no attempt at implementation upon taking office in 1923, however. It shunned the levy for the same reasons that it embraced the gold standard. First, Labour was concerned to reassure the financial community and demonstrate its ability to govern. Second, as a minority government, it relied on the support of the Liberals, who were firm believers in laissez faire and staunch opponents of the levy.

With the passage of time, support for the levy idea began to dissolve. Conservatives and Liberals, who opposed the Labour notion that income redistribution was desirable, succeeded in delaying implementation. As World War I receded into the past, the contingency providing the justification for extraordinary capital taxation became increasingly remote, and the perceived likelihood of active resistance grew. By the mid-1920s, Britain had lived with the war debt for nearly a decade, without overly disastrous consequences.[38] Property owners pointed to this when challenging the notion that exceptional circumstances justified extraordinary capital taxes. Moreover, with Britain's restoration of gold convertibility in 1925, the last barrier to international capital mobility was removed. No longer was there any impediment to capital flight by investors potentially subject to the levy. Not only did this threaten to greatly reduce the yield, but capital flight might bring down the gold standard edifice that had been so laboriously reconstructed. Keynes, initially a proponent of the levy, had by the 1923 General Election become an opponent. Sir Josiah Stamp, also an early advocate, concluded by 1924 that the nation was no longer willing to tolerate the compromises in equity that might have been justified earlier by extraordinary wartime contingencies.[39]

The last gasp of the levy campaign was the Minority Report of the Committee on National Debt and Taxation (the Colwyn Committee). Though approving the levy in principle, the minority suggested substituting, on grounds of practicability, a surtax on investment incomes to be applied to debt retirement. They acknowledged, however, that the case for the levy weakened as the shock of the war receded into the past. Viability of the levy hinged upon it being 'accepted with general good will', and the prospects for this grew increasingly dim as the extraordinary wartime shock grew increasingly remote.[40] The majority put the point more strongly. 'Unless a levy were accepted with more good will than it would be possible to anticipate under present conditions, it would be highly injurious to the social and industrial life of the community.'[41] 'Immediately after the War the argument for a levy was much stronger than it is now. . . . In particular, the end of the War was a unique occasion which the more wealthy classes of the nation might well have been asked to mark by a special and personal contribution. In present circumstances the advocates of a levy have a far weaker case.'[42]

The majority paid considerable attention to fears that the levy, once employed, might be resorted to again, with disastrous implications for savings. In addition to the impracticability of constitutional guarantees, they pointed to the unwillingness of the proponents to agree to segregate levy receipts from other government revenues. While some proponents urged devoting the receipts exclusively to retire debt, thereby maximizing the association of the levy with the war debt and, by reducing the debt burden, eliminating much of the rationale for another levy, others recommended instead reducing income taxation or increasing spending on social services.[43]

In 1927 the Labour Party Conference endorsed the surtax proposed by the Minority Report of the Colwyn Committee, acknowledging that the prerequisites for a successful one-time levy were no longer present.[44] By the time Labour reclaimed office in 1929, however, the onset of the Depression and the decline of the stock market rendered new capital taxes beside the point. Eliminating the scourge of unemployment, rather than fine tuning the income distribution, became the central goal of Labour and its opponents alike.

5   The Japanese levy after World War II

An exception to the rule that 20th century capital levies have been unsuccessful is the Japanese levy following World War II.[45] The Japanese capital levy of 1946–47 was one component of a sweeping political and economic overhaul which included tax reform, land reform and constitutional reform. The levy's first objective was to reduce the internal debt burden inherited from wartime. The national debt had risen from 31 billion yen in March 1941 to more than 202 billion yen in March of 1946 (or from roughly 84 to 130 per cent of national income).[46] Reducing this burden was seen as essential for economic recovery.

The levy's second objective was to provide finance for the recovery program. Not only was there an exceptional need for public expenditure to finance physical reconstruction and housing for occupation forces, but economic devastation caused normal tax revenues to lag: with 40 per cent of all urban areas in ruins, taxes as a share of national income had fallen from 13 per cent in 1944 to barely 7 per cent in 1946.

The third objective of the levy was to reduce income inequality. Significantly, this was not an attempt to effect a comprehensive redistribution of wealth. Rather, it was an effort to reduce the wealthholdings of a small minority of exceptionally rich individuals. The perception, particularly among the American occupiers, was that the fulminations of this small minority – the *Zaibatsu* or owners of great holding companies – had been responsible for promoting pro-war sentiment. According to a memo from Allied headquarters to the Japanese government, these individuals had profited handsomely from the war. A levy on their assets would demonstrate that war was unprofitable and contribute to the growth of peaceful and democratic forces.[47] Of the three rationales for the levy, this sociopolitical argument was the most important.

The levy was imposed on households whose property was worth at least 100,000 yen on March 3, 1946. Rates rose from 10 per cent on those properties to 90 per cent on estates worth more than 15 million yen. Initial projections put the yield of the levy at 120 per cent of normal 1946–47 tax revenues and nine per cent of privately-owned national wealth. To minimize underassessment, the law featured a provision entitling the government to purchase property outright at its assessed value. While this provision seems to have been rarely utilized, its existence may have discouraged abuse of the valuation process.[48]

Administrative difficulties led to some delay in implementation. Collection, scheduled to take place in the summer of 1946, did not get under way until the end of the year. Although the nominal yield was quite close to projections, the levy's real value was eroded by inflation. The retail price level in Tokyo more than doubled between March 1946, when property values were assessed, and March 1947, when most payment took place. Nonetheless, this was a remarkable record in comparison with the Central European levies discussed in the previous section.

What accounts for the singular success of the 19467–47 Japanese capital levy? One factor is that the exceptional circumstances of the immediate postwar period limited the scope for evasion. Another is that a levy whose incidence was limited largely to the two or three percent of richest families minimized the scope for effective political resistance. (For a parallel, see the discussion of Czechoslovakia above.) The vast majority of asset holders considered themselves to be exempt. But surely the most important factor was the Allied occupation. If European experience after World War I documents the obstacles to a capital levy in a democratic society, Japanese experience after World War II provides proof by counterexample. With important elements of democracy in suspension, the levy could be quickly and effectively implemented. One might go further and argue that only when political sovereignty is suspended can the measure be pushed through with such alacrity. Under normal circumstances, the argument would run, the wealthy individuals subject to the levy inevitably exercise a disproportionate influence over policy formulation; only when those normal circumstances are in abeyance can the measure be pushed through with a minimum of dispute and delay.

In 1946–47, Japan's sovereignty was radically abridged. While the Japanese government continued to exist, occupation forces possessed absolute authority. Directives and orders were issued by Supreme Commander for the Allied Powers (SCAP) to the Japanese Cabinet, which was responsible for carrying them out. Even when the Japanese government resisted Occupation initiatives, such as the economic provisions of the Initial Postsurrender Policy, it ultimately had no option but to accede. And even when no formal directives were issued, SCAP's influence was pervasive.[49] This is evident in the adoption of the new constitution, which coincided with the capital levy law.[50] When in February 1946 MacArthur rejected the plan for constitutional reform offered by the Japanese government, his staff simply drafted a replacement. Historians continue to debate whether compulsion was involved in the government's decision to accept MacArthur's draft and present it to the Diet, and in the latter's decision to pass it quickly. Even if no direct compulsion occurred, MacArthur clearly had the power to use it if his proposals met with resistance. Next to far-reaching constitutional reform, the demand that the government adopt a capital levy was of relatively little consequence.

6 Conclusions

In this paper I have recast the debate over the capital levy in a contingent capital taxation framework. This shows how in theory the imposition of a levy can be welfare improving when adopted to redress debt problems created by special circumstances, even if its nonrecurrence cannot be guaranteed. If the contingencies in response to which the levy is imposed are fully anticipated, independently verifiable and not under government control, then saving and investment should not fall following the imposition of the levy, nor should the government find it more difficult to raise revenues.

In practice, as opposed to theory, serious problems stand in the way of implementation. A capital levy has profound distributional consequences. Property owners are certain to resist its adoption. In a democratic society, their objections are all but guaranteed to cause delay. This provides opportunity for capital flight, reducing the prospective yield, and allows the special circumstances providing the justification for the levy to recede into the past. The only successful levies occur in cases like post-World War II Japan, where important elements of the democratic process are suppressed and where the fact that the levy was imposed by an outside power minimized the negative impact on the reputation of subsequent sovereign governments. These findings are not encouraging for those who might advocate a capital levy to redress debt problems in present-day Europe.

In addition to these substantive conclusions, the paper has two methodological implications. First, the recent literature concerned with political constraints on economic policymaking and political determinants of the business cycle (Alesina, 1988b) has even broader applicability than sometimes supposed. Second, it can be seriously misleading to draw conclusions about the feasibility of a policy purely on the basis of theory. As Comstock (1928, p. 18) put the point, 'The attempt to judge the practicability or the effects of an untried fiscal device, such as the capital levy . . ., is fantastic if it is based on abstract reasoning alone. The experience of other countries, unlike as they are and must remain, is a better guide.'

NOTES

I am grateful to Alberto Alesina, David Begg, John Black, Steve Broadberry, Alessandra Casella, Allan Drazen, Vittorio Grilli, Herschel Grossman, and Lars Svensson for helpful comments.

1 Following Chou (1945), I refer to a nonrecurrent tax on all wealth as a capital levy, and to an involuntary reduction of interest or principal on government debt as a forced conversion. In this paper, I do not consider taxes on individual assets, including levies on money balances that accompanied inflation stabilization.

2 See for example Prescott (1977), Alesina (1988a), Chari (1988), Chari and Kehoe (1988), Eichengreen (1988a) and Grossman (1988).

3 The effects of the LDC debt overhang have been analyzed theoretically and empirically by Sachs (1989), while the implications for future creditworthiness are the subject of Eichengreen (1988b), Jorgenson and Sachs (1989) and Lindert (1989). The seminal article on time-consistency is of course Kydland and Prescott (1977).

4 Different ways in which this might be accomplished, in addition to outright repudiation, include a forced conversion and inflating away the real value of obligations bearing fixed nominal interest rates.

5 In general, savings and investment will be lower than in a regime in which there is no possibility of the imposition of a levy, however. See Section 2 below.

6 I am far from the first to stress the political dimension of the capital levy. See for example Keynes (1923) and, more recently, Dornbusch (1986).

7 The statement that this is the only 20th century example of a successful capital levy is meant to provoke and is surely overstrong. Belgium, followed by Czechoslovakia, Austria, and Germany, blocked bank accounts and converted them into new currency notes at disadvantageous rates following World War II. But these measures were generally limited to bank accounts and were designed to remove excess liquidity which threatened to ignite inflation rather than to fund government expenditures or eliminate a debt overhang. See Maier (1984). Another candidate is the Italian rearmament levy of 1937–38. Since its success can be attributed to the capacity of an authoritarian government to discuss the policy in secret and impose it unilaterally, this example also supports the point of the exceptional difficulty of utilizing the levy in a democratic society. Moreover, since the levy was imposed in a period when Italy was concluding a war in Ethiopia and preparing for the coming European conflict, it is difficult to regard it as a peacetime measure.

8 More generally, the capital stock would increase at the rate of interest, assuming no consumption out of principal or interest.

9 A more general formulation would specify r as a declining function of the domestic capital stock.

10 Abreu (1988) shows that it is a perfect equilibrium in a variety of non-cooperative games.

11 This device introduces the possibility that the inequality in (6) need not hold. Other assumptions that deliver the same result are discounting of future expenditures by the government (a further advantage of which is that it ensures $U(j)$ is bounded), or the assumption that the government has a non-negligible probability of losing office in each period and attaches no utility to expenditure by its successors. These are more elegant and more rigorously defensible, but they add complexity and change none of the substantive implications.

12 Hobson (1920), p. 210.

13 Hobson (1920), p. 214.

14 Committee on National Debt and Taxation (1927a), p. 259.

15 It is worth noting another reputational argument that figured in the debate.

Edgeworth (1919) and Scott (1918) argued that a debt burden is a form of discipline on the government. It limits the government's ability to indulge in deficit finance. If it is levied away or repudiated, governments will not lower taxes; rather they will fritter away revenues on other forms of spending and increase their deficit finance.

16 There are a number of other interesting theoretical issues in the debate over the capital levy that cannot be pursued here. These include (i) the precise yield of the levy, especially when the reduction in future estate taxes and death duties are netted out from levy revenues (see for example Stamp, 1924), (ii) the appropriate tax base for the levy, and specifically whether there should be an attempt to tax human as well as financial capital (Pigou, 1918), (iii) the effect of a levy on security prices in particular and financial markets in general (Pethick-Lawrence, 1918), and (iv) difficulties of implementation and administration (Arnold, 1918).

17 It is on grounds such as these that we can understand Keynes's volte face from advocacy of a levy immediately following World War I to deep skepticism by the time of the 1923 General Election. Keynes's views in 1927 are recounted in his Colwyn Committee evidence (1927b, p. 534). See also Keynes (1923) and footnote 39 below.

18 A survey of the relevant history is provided by Soward and Willan (1919), chapter 11.

19 See Asso and Barucci (1988) for a detailed analysis of Ricardo's views and Gottlieb (1953) on the surrounding debate.

20 Einaudi (1921), p. 108; *Economist* (May 15, 1920, pp. 1004–05).

21 Hicks, Hicks and Rostas (1941), p. 235; Einaudi (1921), p. 111.

22 Rostas (1940), p. 24.

23 Hicks, Hicks and Rostas (1941), p. 199.

24 Rostas (1940), p. 25; *Economist* (January 31, 1920, pp. 196–97).

25 Van Sickle (1931), p. 138.

26 Hicks, Hicks and Rostas (1941), p. 221.

27 Van Sickle (1931), p. 160.

28 Rostas (1940), p. 28.

29 See Diehl (1918).

30 Silverman (1982), pp. 71–73.

31 Under the provisions of this scheme, all income tax payers who failed to subscribe to the forced loan bearing three per cent interest in amounts equal to one tenth of their total wealth would be levied an exceptional tax equal to the shortfall. Peel (1926), p. 243.

32 Rogers (1929), pp. 252–53.

33 Haig (1929), pp. 124–25.

34 Sauvy (1984), vol. III, p. 82.

35 Comstock (1928), p. 10.

36 Comstock (1928), p. 12.

37 Labour's vision for postwar society is described by Cole (1948).

38 Gottlieb (1952), p. 373.

39 Keynes's speeches on the issue made in connection with the General Election are recounted by Harrod (1951), pp. 338. On Stamp's views, see Stamp (1924), p. 228.

40 They continued, 'We have no hesitation in saying that a capital levy at that time (1919–1920) could have been carried out comparatively easily, and that it

is a matter of great regret that no levy was then imposed.' Committee on National Debt and Taxation (1927a), pp. 410–11.
41 Committee on National Debt and Taxation (1927a), p. 296.
42 Committee on National Debt and Taxation (1927a), p. 248.
43 See Section 3 above.
44 Hicks, Hicks and Rostas (1941), p. 262.
45 The account that follows relies on Shavell (1948).
46 These figures understate the debt income ratio because they divide end-of-fiscal year debt figures by national income for the fiscal year as a whole. Data are from Shavell (1948). Tables 1 and 2.
47 Cited in Shavell (1948), p. 131.
48 While the levy to reduce the great estates of the families that controlled the combines was adopted, early Occupation initiatives intended to break up the combines themselves were not pressed once the Cold War increased the importance the US attached to speedy Japanese economic recovery. Instead, the decision was made to permit Japanese reconstruction to proceed along traditional lines.
49 Borton (1970), pp. 461–62.
50 The first draft of the constitution was written in English in February 1946, translated into Japanese in March, passed by both Houses of the Diet in October, promulgated by the Emperor in November, and made effective in May 1947, coinciding almost exactly with the period from adoption to implementation of the capital levy.

REFERENCES

Abreu, Dilip (1988). 'On the Theory of Infinitely Repeated Games with Discounting', *Econometrica* **56**, 383–96.
Alesina, Alberto (1988a). 'The End of Large Public Debts', in Francesco Giavazzi and Luigi Spaventa (eds.), *High Public Debt: The Italian Experience*, New York: Cambridge University Press, pp. 34–79.
    (1988b). 'Macroeconomics and Politics', *NBER Macroeconomics Annual* (ed. Stanley Fischer), Cambridge: MIT Press.
Arnold, Sydney (1918). 'A Capital Levy: The Problems of Realisation and Valuation', *Economic Journal* **28**, 157–66.
Asso, P.F. and E. Barucci (1988). 'Ricardo on the National Debt and its Redemption: Some Notes on an Unpublished Riciardian Manuscript', *Economic Notes* **2**, 1–36.
Alexrod, Robert (1984). *The Evolution of Cooperation*, New York: Basic Books.
Borton, Hugh (1970). *Japan's Modern Century*, New York: Ronald Press.
Chari, V.V. (1988). 'Time Consistency and Optimal Policy Design', *Federal Reserve Bank of Minneapolis Quarterly Review* **12**, 17–31.
Chari, V.V. and Patrick J. Kehoe (1988). 'Sustainable Plans and Debt', Research Department Working Paper 399, Federal Reserve Bank of Minneapolis.
Chou, Shun-Hsin (1945). *The Capital Levy*, New York: King's Crown Press.
Cole, G.D.H. (1948). *A History of the Labour Party from 1914*, London: Routledge and Kegan Paul.
Committee on National Debt and Taxation [Colwyn Committee] (1927a). *Report*, Cmd 2800, London: HMSO.

(1927b). *Minutes of Evidence*, 2 volumes, London: HMSO.

Comstock, A. (1928). 'From Capital Levy to Surtax', *American Economic Review* **18**, 9–18.

Dalton, Hugh (1923). *The Capital Levy Explained*, New York: Knoff.

Diehl, Karl (1918). 'The Readjustment of German Finance by a Capital Levy', *Economic Journal* **29**, 91–105.

Dornbusch, Rudiger (1986). *Dollars, Debts, and Deficits*, Cambridge: MIT Press.

Edgeworth, F.Y. (1919). *A Levy on Capital for the Discharge of Debt*, Oxford: Clarendon Press.

Eichengreen, Barry (1988a). 'The End of Large Public Debts: Discussion', in Francesco Giavazzi and Luigi Spaventa (eds.), *High Public Debt: The Italian Experience*, Cambridge: Cambridge University Press, pp. 80–84.

(1988b). 'The U.S. Capital Market and Foreign Lending, 1920–1955', in Jeffrey Sachs (ed.), *Developing Country Debt and Economic Performance: The International Financial System*, Chicago: University of Chicago Press, vol. 1, pp. 107–55.

Einaudi, Luigi (1921). 'Taxes on Property and Property Increments in Italy', *Quarterly Journal of Economics* **35**, 108–38.

Fabian Research Society (1916). *How To Pay For the War*, London: Fabian Research Society.

Fischer, Stanley (1980). 'Dynamic Inconsistency, Cooperation, and the Benevolent Dissembling Government', *Journal of Economic Dynamics and Control* **2**, 93–108.

Giavazzi, Francesco and Luigi Spaventa (eds.) (1988). *High Public Debt: The Italian Experience*, New York: Cambridge University Press.

Gottlieb, Manuel (1952). 'The Capital Levy After World War I', *Public Finance* **7**, 356–84.

(1953). 'The Capital Levy and Deadweight Debt in England, 1815–40', *Journal of Finance* **8**, 34–46.

Grossman, Herschel I. (1988). 'The Political Economy of War Debts and Inflation', National Bureau of Economic Research Working Paper No. 2743 (October).

Grossman, Herschel I. and J.B. Van Huyck (1988). 'Sovereign Debt as a Contingent Claim: Excusable Default, Repudiation, and Reputation', *American Economic Review* **78**, 1088–97.

Haig, R.M. (1929). *The Public Finances of Postwar France*, New York: Columbia University Press.

Harrod, Roy (1951). *The Life of John Maynard Keynes*, New York: Macmillan.

Hicks, J.R., U.K. Hicks and L. Rostas (1941). *The Taxation of War Wealth*, Oxford: Clarendon Press.

Hobson, J.A. (1920). *Taxation in the New State*, New York: Harcourt, Brace and Howe.

Jorgenson, Erika and Jeffrey Sachs (1989). 'The Costs of Default: The Settlement of Interwar Defaults in Latin America', in Barry Eichengreen and Peter Lindert (eds.), *The International Debt Crisis in Historical Perspective*, Cambridge, MA: MIT Press, 48–85.

Keynes, John Maynard (1923). *A Tract on Monetary Reform*, New York: Harcourt Brace.

Kydland, Finn and Edward Prescott (1977). 'Rules Rather than Discretion: The Inconsistency of Optimal Plans', *Journal of Political Economy* **85**, 473–91.

220   **Barry Eichengreen**

Lindert, Peter (1989). 'The Debt Crisis: What is Different About the 1980s?' in Barry Eichengreen and Peter Lindert (eds.), *The International Debt Crisis in Historical Perspective*, Cambridge, MA: MIT Press, 227–76.

Maier, Charles S. (1984). 'Inflation and Stabilization in the Wake of the Two World Wars: Comparative Strategies and Sacrifices', in Gerald D. Feldman *et al.* (eds.), *The Experience of Inflation: International and Comparative Studies*, Berlin: Walter de Gruyter, 106–32.

Peel, George (1926). *The Financial Crisis of France*, London: Macmillan.

Pethick-Lawrence, F.W. (1918). *A Levy on Capital*, London: George Allen & Unwin.

Pigou, A.C. (1918). 'A Special Levy to Discharge War Debt', *Economic Journal* **28**, pp. 135–56.

Prescott, Edward C. (1977). 'Should Control Theory Be Used for Economic Stabilization?' *Carnegie Rochester Conference Series on Public Policy* **7**, 13–38.

Rogers, James Harvey (1929). *The Process of Inflation in France, 1914–1927*, New York: Columbia University Press.

Rostas, L. (1940). 'Capital Levies in Central Europe, 1919–1924', *Review of Economic Studies* **8**, pp. 20–33.

Sachs, Jeffrey (1989). 'The Debt Overhang of Developing Countries', in Ronald Findlay *et al.* (eds.), *Debt, Development and Stabilization: Essays in Honor of Carlos Diaz-Alejandro*, Oxford: Blackwell, 80–102.

Sargent, Thomas (1982). 'The End of Four Big Inflations', in Robert Hall (ed.), *Inflation*, Chicago: University of Chicago Press.

Sauvy, Alfred (1984). *Histoire economique de la France entre les deux guerres* Paris: Economica (second edition).

Scott, W.R. (1918). 'Some Aspects of the Proposed Capital Levy', *Economic Journal* **28**, pp. 247–67.

Shavell, Henry (1948). 'Postwar Taxation in Japan', *Journal of Political Economy* **56**, 124–37.

Silverman, Dan P. (1982). *Reconstructing Europe After the Great War*, Cambridge: Harvard University Press.

Snowden, Philip (1920). *Labour and National Finance*, London: Leonard Parsons.

Soward, Alfred W. and W.E. Willan (1919). *The Taxation of Capital*, London: Waterlow and Sons.

Stamp, Sir Josiah (1924). *Current Problems in Finance and Government*. London: P.S. King.

Van Sickle, John V. (1931). *Direct Taxation in Austria*, Cambridge, MA: Harvard University Press.

Discussion

DAVID BEGG

As always, Barry Eichengreen has given us a well argued paper which uses modern ideas to illuminate historical debates and brings interesting, and unfamiliar, evidence from the past to bear on current theoretical analysis.

His subject is the capital levy, a 'once off' tax on capital. Should such a tax be viewed as lump-sum, it will have attractive incentive properties relative to alternative, distortionary, means of raising the same revenue. However this conclusion may be overoptimistic, and modern economics formalises some possible objections.

The literature on time-inconsistency alerts us to the problem that in the future there will again be a temptation to invoke such a tax; foreseeing this, the private sector will impute marginal tax rates on what it regards as a recurrent tax. In such circumstances, as Eichengreen notes, it is possible that a capital levy actually raises the cost of debt service by increasing the *ex ante* interest rate demanded by lenders. This conclusion may be reinforced by applying the idea of repeated games in which the private sector punishes the government for its default on previous implicit commitments, where punishment takes the form of penalty interest rates following a default or an unanticipated capital levy.

Against this background, Eichengreen explores a more sophisticated idea, viewing debt as a contingent claim. Within the state-contingent approach, the rate of capital taxation and hence the post-tax rate of return depends on the state of nature which arises. Traditional smoothing arguments imply that the government will wish to pay a lower effective return on its debt when its revenue-raising opportunities are low, but pay a higher effective return when revenue-raising opportunities are high. *Ex ante*, lenders understand the structure of returns and expect on average to earn the going rate of return. *Ex post*, the government is able to vary capital taxation (in a manner previously agreed) without loss of reputation or the triggering of punishment strategies.

To develop this approach, the paper adopts three lines of attack: a theoretical model, a reinterpretation of historical debates about the possible introduction of a capital levy, and an event history of capital levies in practice. I deal with each in turn.

The theoretical model considers three types of equilibria. If the government was able to precommit itself to follow a state-contingent policy, this would be optimal and the desire to smooth government expenditure leads to high taxation of bondholders in states where revenue is low. If no commitment is possible, bondholders will foresee the temptation to levy high taxes in all states and incorporate this in *ex ante* interest rates. Finally there is the possibility of a reputational equilibrium where the threat of subsequent punishment by the private sector – here taking the form of expecting subsequent cheating and demanding suitably high interest rates *ex ante* to cover this eventuality – is sufficient to discipline the government to pursue the state-contingent policy correctly anticipated by the private sector.

These results are intuitive and Eichengreen's simple model has several attractive features. First, it brings credibility and reputation to the forefront where they belong in such a discussion. Second, by dealing in a multiplicity of states of nature, it gets away from the 'all or nothing' dichotomy which is not sufficiently rich to characterize debates over the capital levy in practice. Third, it introduces naturally the issue of monitoring or verifying which state has occurred, and hence the potential moral hazard problem when the state is defined with respect to criteria which the government can manipulate over time.

This analysis suggests that capital levies will be easiest to implement where monitoring is easiest and where the moral hazard problem can be mitigated, for example by commitments to use the proceeds of a capital levy for direct retirement rather than increasing general government expenditure. To some extent, these conclusions are borne out in the subsequent empirical discussion. However, it should be stressed that it is a central assumption of the theory that the private sector cannot take action *after the state of nature is known* to shelter its assets from taxation. If capital flight is trivially easy, *ex post* attempts to vary taxation according to the state of nature are doomed to failure. This turns out to be an important part of Eichengreen's final empirical judgement of why some levies were more successful than others; to that extent, it appears at first sight that we obtain relatively little mileage out of the elegant state-contingent theoretical treatment.

However this is not entirely fair, as later sections of the paper make clear. The possibility of capital flight depends partly on the size of transactions costs – the presence or absence of foreign exchange controls on the one hand, the extent of disruption of markets and communications in immediate postwar periods on the other hand. But the delay in implementing proposals for a capital levy is also critical: longer delay allows lenders more time to shelter their assets.

Eichengreen's examination of the debate over capital levies highlights the link between implementation delay and ambiguities in monitoring the state of nature. For example, in the UK, where advocates of the capital levy stressed that it could be successful, in the sense of being capable of implementation without fear of repetition, the force of this argument gradually evaporated in the mid 1920s: as the war legacy receded so did any prospect of identifying a capital levy with 'special' postwar circumstances. More generally, Eichengreen draws attention to the difficulty in a peacetime democracy of ever quickly agreeing that the appropriate contingency has in fact occurred.

Let me turn now to the case by case analysis of capital levies in practice. We are told that most of them failed. I should have liked a much more explicit discussion of the criteria by which success or failure should be judged. Implicitly, Eichengreen takes as his yardstick the narrow question of whether or not the levy raised significant amounts of revenue. I agree that failure to raise much revenue is a sufficient condition for the failure of a capital levy, but raising significant revenue is not a sufficient condition for its success. As recognised in the introduction, the further question is whether a levy, even when it raises immediate revenue, so diminishes the reputation of the government that it raises the cost of subsequent debt service to an extent which more than offsets any initial advantage.

To say that successful capital levies are not feasible because delay allows capital flight is a legitimate conclusion, and one the evidence supports to a large extent; but for that we do not need the apparatus of debt as a contingent claim. The latter framework is designed precisely to shed light on when a levy can be introduced without prejudice to reputation or the triggering of punishment. Such a question can be examined only by studying returns on the relevant assets. I appreciate that the paper is persistently silent on this issue not because the author is unaware of its importance but because the relevant data is not available. Nevertheless, it is a pity that the novel theoretical aspect of the paper cannot directly be examined empirically.

Rather, the case studies of the paper catalogue the discussions about capital levies in many European countries after World War I, and in Japan after World War II. This discussion is illuminating and serves to highlight the many difficulties in implementing such a levy. I am wholly in sympathy with the author's conclusion that peacetime levies are extremely difficult in practice.

Discussion

VITTORIO GRILLI

As does most of Barry Eichengreen's research, this interesting work cleverly combines economic history with macroeconomic theory insight. The issue analyzed in this paper is the use of capital levies to finance government expenditure. The particular historical episodes which are investigated are the debt overhangs typical of post-war economies. Most of the evidence provided is from the 1920s, even if one important case (Japan) refers to the post-World War II period.

Time-consistency and capital levies

One well known theoretical issue associated with capital levies is the time-inconsistency of optimal tax policies. Eichengreen solves the problem by using a reputational model in which the government can credibly sustain a capital levy policy. In particular, the government and the public agree, in equilibrium, on an implicit social contract according to which taxes on capital are introduced or increased only in specific contingencies, specifically in the case of exceptionally high revenue requirements. This type of model has appealing results, especially because it produces an endogenous rigidity in the tax rates, a property that conforms to simple empirical observation. The model, in fact, predicts that the variation in the tax rate occurs only 'rarely', that is, only when the 'exceptional' contingency is realized.

However, when Eichengreen explores the empirical implications of the model, he finds that, in reality, the occurrences of the introduction of capital levies are very rare, more so than even this type of model would predict. Reasoning within this framework, Eichengreen argues that a possible justification for the absence of capital levies is the lack, in the real world, of an independent agency which would objectively verify the occurrence of the contingency. In the case under investigation, however, this type of explanation is weak. In fact, one would think that a 'World War' is an excusable enough contingency and that verification is not a problem this circumstance.

Politics and taxes

The poor empirical support of the theory needs to be explained in some other way. A logical alternative interpretation of the evidence is that this type of implicit social contract, at least in the simple form predicted by the theory, does not exist in reality. Eichengreen recognizes this possibility and convincingly suggests that, in several circumstances, it is easy to identify political factors which could be responsible for the absence, or failure, of this type of social arrangement. Often, competing social factions (political parties), use their power and undertake actions, beyond pure economic interactions, to oppose measures whose implementation could hurt them, like a capital levy. However, once we introduce these types of political factors into the analysis, we should recognize that there is no reason to limit our attention to capital levies, since this kind of consideration finds more general applications than simply capital taxation. In fact, even if we restrict our analysis to the problem of government revenues, this type of argument applies to almost all the forms of taxation and, especially, to taxes that imply substantial amount of income redistribution. In other words, while the time-consistency problem might be peculiar to taxes on capital, and thus would justify a separate analysis of this form of taxation, political factors are not. It would seem appropriate, therefore, given the global nature of budget financing and the trade-offs that exist among alternative sources of government revenue, to reformulate the problem in more general terms, by explicitly considering a whole array of possible tax instruments.

As a starting point, one way of posing the question is to view it as a problem of optimal taxation where the government has to decide the best way, according to some well-specified objective function, to finance its expenditure. The logical underlying framework could be similar to the usual optimal taxation models, as in Mankiw (1987) and Grilli (1989), enriched by the introduction of political factors. The inclusion of political factors can be achieved in two distinct, but not mutually exclusive, ways. The first is by introducing a political element directly into the government's objective function. This could be done, for example, by assuming a partisan government, i.e. a government that maximizes a welfare function biased in favour of a part of the population and that, consequently, prefers certain forms of taxation over others. The second is by introducing a political element into the budget constraint by assuming, for example, different degrees of flexibility of revenue instruments, that reflect the different amounts of political opposition received by various form of taxes. Both strategies would deliver, as outcome, an asymmetric time pattern of taxes, which could be reversed over time if we allow for changes in governments and/or changes in the relative degree of the inflexibility of tax rates. This could produce negative correlations between various tax instruments, in contrast to the standard optimal taxation models that predict such correlations to be positive.

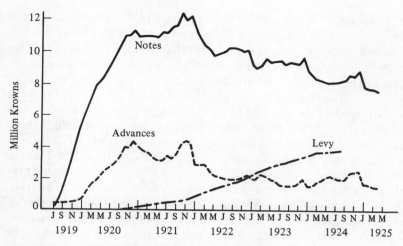

Figure 7A.1 Stabilization in Czechoslovakia, 1919–25.
Source: Young (1925).

Two historical episodes

As an example, it is convenient to review the historical episode of stabilization in Czechoslovakia and the Netherlands during the inter-war period. In both cases it is evident that a shift between different forms of taxation occurred in those years. The case of Czechoslovakia has already been well documented in the paper by Eichengreen, nonetheless it is interesting to see the facts described in the text summarized in a picture. Figure 7A.1 shows the total amount of notes in circulation, the revenues of the capital levy, and the total amount of loans and discounts by the Banking office of Czechoslovakia. This agency was not an independent central bank but an office of the Ministry of Finance, so that this last category is composed mainly of discounts to the government. What is interesting to notice is that before the spring of 1920 (i.e. when the capital levy was introduced) monetization was the main component of government revenues. Immediately after the introduction of the levy, the money supply was stabilized and inflationary finance came to a stop.

A similar story can be told for the Netherlands. The Netherlands was not one of the belligerent countries and, therefore, its revenue requirements were not of the same magnitude as most of the other European countries. Nonetheless, during World War I, the increase in the government deficit was substantial, jumping from 11.3 million guilders in 1913 to a peak of 490 million guilders in 1918. As described in Figure 7A.2, during the war, deficits were in part financed by monetization. However, as early as 1916,

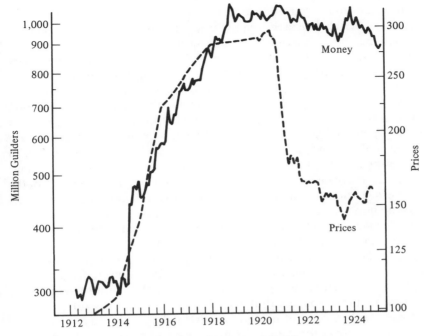

Figure 7A.2   Stabilization in The Netherlands, 1912–25.
Source: Young (1925).

new taxes (war profit and defence taxes) were introduced but only later, in 1919, were income and capital taxes raised to a sufficient amount to bring monetization to a halt.

While I only discuss these two cases, the basic elements are common to the experience of several other countries, including the ones analyzed by Eichengreen. Here I want to point out two factors. First, it is typical that following a major increase in expenditure, taxes are not raised immediately, and debt is allowed to grow beyond what optimal intertemporal tax smoothing would suggest. Taxes are increased only with a considerable delay. Second, until the increase in other taxes was realized, most of the countries used inflation as a source of revenues in the inter-war period. Why are stabilizations delayed? Why is inflation tax used in the interim period?

War of attrition, delayed stabilization and inflation

Simple variations of the optimal taxation model, however, cannot answer these questions in a meaningful way. While they can explain the decrease in inflation and the introduction of levies or other taxes as the consequences of a change in the relative costs of using such taxes, they cannot explain the underlying causes of these variations.

Recent work, which builds on the model of a war of attrition developed by Nalebuff (1982), provides a way of introducing political factors in the resolution of debt crisis and the implementation of stabilization programs. Alesina and Drazen (1989), explain the delays in stabilization programs as the result of a struggle between opposite social parts, each trying to impose the cost of the debt reduction on the other. Stabilization occurs only when one of the parties concedes. This process of social instability could last for several periods depending, among other things, on the degree of heterogeneity of the population and the asymmetry of the tax burden after the stabilization. In this paper inflation is present in the pre-stabilization period by assumption, and thus cannot respond to the question of why inflation characterizes these periods. Related work by Drazen and Grilli (1989) addresses the issue directly. There it is argued that, in the presence of delays in the implementation of a stabilization program due to social conflicts, the monetary authorities may find it optimal to monetize the deficit. Inflation, in fact, will not only provide revenues during the interim period but, more importantly, since it imposes explicit costs of living in an unstabilized economy, it may also provide incentives for the parties to come to an agreement. In this case, stabilization would occur sooner, for the benefit of all.

In conclusion, Barry Eichengreen's paper raises an important issue, given the current need for fiscal stabilizations in several European countries. He points out the inadequacies of the representative agent model which only addresses on the time consistency problem typical of taxation on capital. He is also correct, in my opinion, in directing attention to 'political factors', as a source of additional insight on the problem. This is where future research should be concentrated.

REFERENCES

Alesina, A. and A. Drazen (1989). 'Why are Stabilizations Delayed?', mimeo.
Drazen, A. and V. Grilli (1989). 'The Welfare Benefits of Distortionary Taxes: Can Inflation Be Good for You?', mimeo.
Grilli, V. (1989). 'Seigniorage in Europe', in M. De Cecco and A. Giovannini (eds.), *A European Central Bank*, Cambridge University Press, 53–79.
Mankiw, N.G. (1987). 'The Optimal Collection of Seigniorage: Theory and Evidence', *Journal of Monetary Economics* **20**, 327–41.
Nalebuff, B. (1982). 'Prizes and Incentives', D. Phil. Thesis, Nuffield College.
Young, J.P. (1925). *European Currency and Finance*, Commission of Gold and Silver Enquiry, United States Senate. Washington D.C., Government Printing Office.

8 Episodes in the public debt history of the United States

E. CARY BROWN

1   Introduction

The United States has undergone four major periods of debt reduction over its history: the Revolutionary War and War of 1812 debt repayment extended over the first third of the 19th century; the Civil War debt was reduced in the last third of that century; and the debt repayment of World Wars I and II covered the third decade and third quarter of the 20th century, respectively.

Until the time of the Great Depression of the 1930s, the major reason for borrowing by the United States government was the preparation for or waging of war. Until then a relatively narrow stance had been maintained with respect to the kinds of programs considered appropriate to undertake. State governments, on the other hand, had assumed a broader role in the 19th century in financing transportation and other developmental projects. Local governments grew explosively after the Civil War to provide needed urban utilities and infrastructures.

Up to World War II, the expected and well-accepted policy of the federal government was to repay outstanding debt in a more or less systematic way, even when accompanied, as it often was, by substantial subsidies to creditors through price deflation. It could be characterized as a creditor-dominated policy. In contrast, after World War II debt repayment was minimal; but inflation and economic expansions, even when slow, sharply lowered the debt-GNP ratio in a debtor-dominated policy.

In reviewing these episodes the debt-GNP ratio will be used, when feasible, as a simple measure of debt burden, although other factors are, of course, present. Changes in this ratio come about (1) because the real debt increases or decreases through borrowing or repaying, and through fluctuations in prices; and (2) because the real GNP expands or contracts. For the 18th and 19th centuries, consistent annual estimates of GNP are unavailable, and measurement of annual price changes requires the use of the wholesale price index of Warren and Pearson (1933) which probably exaggerates movements in the general price level. Only in the 20th century are annual estimates of real and nominal GNP available. Tables 8.7 and 8.8 contain the annual data used, and Table 8.4 sums up changes in debt for particular periods when it expanded and contracted.

2   Revolutionary and War of 1812 debt: 1775–1835[1]

The Revolutionary government, virtually unable to borrow until the victory at Saratoga in 1777, depended almost entirely on the issuance of paper currency as the only way it could secure resources. By the end of hostilities, however, it was on a specie basis and emerged with a debt of $36 million. When the constitutional government was organized in 1789, the debt had grown half as much again, as the government struggled with essentially insoluble fiscal problems and met only one-fourth of its debt service. The first major legislative action of the new government was to provide a revenue structure that relied almost exclusively on customs duties, a choice that was to plague the young nation in a variety of ways for at least a century, supplemented by modest amounts from the sale of public lands from the huge public domain. A highly controversial legislative enactment further increased the debt in 1790 to $76 million when the states' war debts were assumed. The total debt at that time was perhaps 20–30 percent of GNP.[2]

Activist in strengthening the national government, the twelve-year Federalist administration, 1789–1800, enlarged the tax structure. Consequently, the debt grew only 10 percent in nominal terms (after the assumption of state debts) and decreased almost one-fourth in real terms. Despite real net borrowing of 9 percent, price inflation had reduced the debt by 32 percent (Table 8.4).

When Jefferson's administration replaced the Federalist in 1801, it initiated a decade of fiscal restraint: expenditures were reduced, especially military, from the high levels of Adams's administration; internal taxes were eliminated; a booming foreign trade doubled customs duties; and large budget surpluses were applied to debt reduction (Table 8.5). Up to the eve of the War of 1812, both the nominal and real debt were reduced by 45 percent entirely attributable to explicit debt retirement (Table 8.4). The debt had fallen to 6–8 percent of GNP through a fiscal policy that cut both taxes and expenditures.[3]

The War of 1812 tripled expenditures, increased internal revenues by much less and with a lag through reenactment of the direct property tax and the Federalist excises, while customs revenues dropped substantially although rates were doubled. The nominal debt had increased to a new peak of $127 million; the real debt had more than doubled by the end of 1815 – increased by net borrowing (140 percent), decreased by inflation (30 percent) (Table 8.4).

Deficits were quickly turned into surpluses as the United States was flooded by imports, especially from Britain. In the years 1816–19 more customs duties were collected than ever before, partly because of the doubling of rates, but also because of large pent-up demand for British goods. Serious unemployment overtook the domestic industries that had gained a foothold during the wartime interruption of trade, and the crisis of 1818 developed into the depression of 1820–21.

This depression and the repeal of wartime taxes eliminated these surpluses briefly. Recovery brought many years of budget surpluses that were heightened in the mid-1830s by heavy speculation in public lands. Revenues averaged 40 percent more than expenditures in the 20 years after the War of 1812 (Table 8.5) and the public debt was completely liquidated in 1834 from its high point in 1815. Since prices were falling in much of this period, the real value of debt repayments exceeded the initial real debt by 60 percent (Table 8.4). This redistribution from taxpayers to bondholders recurred even more dramatically after the Civil War.

The elimination of a public debt by a central government is a rare happening in fiscal history. The maintenance of such large budget surpluses and their application to debt repayment demanded a disciplined approach on both the expenditure and the revenue side. The rigid control of expenditures exercised by the several administrations was extraordinary, especially after 1820 when internal improvements and the provision of enterprise capital became a growing need and a major policy issue for a developing nation. Various presidents, with the ineffective exception of John Quincy Adams, opposed the federal government's undertaking such programs, usually expressing the belief that the constitution prevented it.[4]

States on the other hand had no such constraints. Essentially debt-free after the assumption of the states' war debts by the federal government in 1790, state debt was only $13 million by 1825 (Table 8.6). States were performing only a few elementary functions; their budgets were quite small; interest constituted 50 to 90 percent of their total expenditure, and raising taxes for interest payments was unpopular.[5] Faced by expanding capital demands and the spectacular success of the New York state-financed Erie Canal,[6] state borrowing took off after 1830 most importantly to develop canals, railroads, and, after Jackson's 1832 veto of the bill rechartering the Second Bank of the United States, banks. By 1838 state debt of $174 million exceeded federal debt.[7]

With such a clearly defined and implemented expenditure policy and

232   E. Cary Brown

without any debt, one could imagine the federal government eliminating its primary budget surplus and achieving fiscal bliss forever after: that is, cut the revenues to fit the expenditure program. However, once customs duties were made almost the sole revenue source, their protective usage became irresistible. From the initial debate over the modest rates proposed by Madison in 1789, protectionism moved swiftly forward: rates were doubled in the War of 1812; manufacturers were protected from postwar competition beginning with the act of 1816, especially of products that had sprung up during the war such as cotton and woollen goods, iron, and glass; the tolerable political threshhold of the nonmanufacturing sections was even exceeded by unsustainably high rates in the 1828 Tariff of Abominations, which led some states to threaten nullification of the legislation that was then temporarily moderated in the early 1830s.

A strong defensive argument for high customs duties had been their fruitful revenue yield that could retire the debt. But in the years 1834 and 1835 with no further debt to retire, protectionist supporters had to regroup and develop a new rationale. Political genius found a way. Tariff rates would not have to be reduced (or raised, as was attempted near the end of the century); more federal spending, clearly anathema to President Andrew Jackson, could be avoided; excess revenues would be given back to the states, and they could expand crucial programs foresworn by the federal government.[8] Thus it was voted in 1836 to turn back to the states an estimated $36 million in surplus revenues, more than half the revenues collected in that year. Because of its novelty and perhaps for constitutional reasons, the expenditure was labelled a loan, callable if needed, though it never was.

Before the final quarterly installment was paid, the panic of 1837 terminated this fiscal experiment. This panic also caught most states in the midst of internal-improvement programs with uncompleted canals and railroads. As the severe deflation continued until 1843,[9] it brought losses in market values and default on half of the outstanding state debt, 10 percent of which was repudiated.[10] Unsuccessful efforts were made to persuade the federal government to assume or support these debts, and many foreign lenders failed clearly to delineate the two levels of government. Thus, default and repudiation of state debt may have affected the otherwise impeccable credit standing of the federal government.[11] The financial difficulties and mismanagement that were exposed led to the enactment of various types of constitutional debt limits in most states.

By the time of the Civil War, the federal debt had grown to $65 million after fluctuations resulting from the business cycle and the Mexican War, less than 2 percent of GNP (Table 8.6). State government debt, after shrinking in the 1840s, had a miniboom in the 1850s as developmental programs were reactivated. In the latter decade local government debt rose five-fold to $200 million and, though still smaller than state debt, surpassed the federal (Table 8.6). This expansion was mostly in city debt as the rapid increases in population and income extended city programs and services, and cities competed for railroad connections through offers of loans and subsidies. This substantial borrowing became a heavy burden in the 1857 depression and, again, defaults resulted.[12]

3   The Civil War debt: 1860–93

3.1   The war period: 1860–65

The Civil War resulted in an explosion in size of the public debt, an expansion of expenditures to 12 percent of GNP (compared with 4 percent in the War of 1812),[13] innovations in taxation, both qualitative and quantitative, that substantially broadened tax sources and brought in large amounts of revenue; innovative marketing of the public debt; conscription of military personnel; and major changes in the banking system.

Congress took the lead in designing wartime fiscal policies, enacting the first federal income tax which reached a top rate of 10 percent, and an inheritance tax. The bulk of the revenue was provided by a massive array of excise taxes, both *ad valorem* and specific, that covered a large portion of market transactions, multiple taxes on manufactured products much like a turnover tax, stamp duties on a variety of transactions, and gross receipts taxes on such industries as railroads and utilities. These taxes required the creation of a whole new administrative apparatus – the Office of Internal Revenue in the Treasury – and were slow to reach their potential. Yet, revenues at their peak in fiscal year 1866 raised over half a billion dollars – almost 13-fold more than in 1861 – compared with peak expenditures of $1.3 billion in fiscal year 1865. The nominal public debt rose from $65 million at the beginning of the war to $2.7 billion at its end. By far the largest debt yet incurred, it resulted in the highest debt-GNP ratio, 41 to 49 percent, for the country up to that time.[14]

The Confederacy, on the other hand, could not develop an effective tax program given the structure of its economy and the need for creation of a central government from scratch. During the war only about 10 percent of the government's expenditures were covered by taxes; $2 billion was borrowed, almost as much as the North but mostly in the form of paper money, and repudiated after surrender.

3.2   The period of debt repayment: 1866–93

In the immediate postwar years the federal government reviewed the tariff-tax structure to adjust it to long-term peacetime needs. The economic and political prostration of the South in the reconstruction and postreconstruction periods weakened the effective opposition to protectionism. Budget surpluses were crafted around protective customs duties that were increased substantially above their prewar level. In the decade of the 1850s they averaged $50 million; by the 1866–75 period they jumped to an average of more than $200 million.[15] The ratio of duties to free and dutiable imports rose from a prewar low of 14 percent in 1861 to 41–46 percent up to 1871, then moved down to around 30 percent in the 1870s and 1880s.[16]

The wartime tax structure was dismantled. Income and inheritance taxes, its progressive elements, were eliminated by 1872. Almost all the many excise, stamp, licensing, and other internal duties were swept away by 1874 with the major exception of liquor and tobacco taxes that provided more revenue at lower rates than they had during the war – 30 percent of total 1874 revenues. Expenditures, though well above prewar, were cut back from their wartime levels. Thus, average nominal surpluses were expanded dramatically – from an average of $3.6 million in the prewar decade to an average of $66 million in the decade 1875–84 following repeal of wartime taxes.[17]

In the period following the Civil War to the depression years after 1893, the nation witnessed a remarkable series of economic developments: (1) real GNP growth averaged 5 percent per annum;[18] (2) prices fell at an average rate of 2 or 3 percent per annum;[19] (3) nominal yields on US bonds slowly fell from over 6 percent in the late 1860s to 2–2.5 percent in the late 1880s and early 1890s;[20] and (4) budgets were in surplus almost continuously.

The ratio of real debt to real GNP fell sharply in the postwar period: from 39 percent in 1871 to 8 percent in 1891 (Table 8.1). The factors accounting for this change were: (1) the resumption of specie payments in 1879 eliminated the gold premium; (2) real debt repayment only reduced the real debt by 10 percent after adjusting the data in Tables 8.4 and 8.7 for the difference between Kuznets' implicit GNP price indices and the wholesale price indices of Warren and Pearson; (3) price decreases offset 60 percent of the net debt repayment, again after adjusting for the difference between the two price indices as in (2) above, and (4) real growth of 2.87-fold clearly dominated all other factors.[21]

Real debt repayment exceeded the initial real value of the debt at the end of the Civil War, but the real debt only fell 15 percent (Table 8.4).

Debt–GNP ratio, 1871		39
Resumption of specie payment	− 4	
Real growth to 1891 (2.87-fold)	− 23	
Net real debt repayment	− 10*	
Net price changes	+ 6*	− 31
Debt–GNP ratio, 1891		8

Table 8.1. Factors reducing the US debt–GNP ratio, 1871–91
(per cent)
*Adjusted for difference between price indices (see text).

Nominal interest rates could, of course, have adjusted – in this case to have decreased 2 or 3 percent – and thus maintained debtors and creditors in the same real positions as before the deflation. However, it took nominal interest rates several decades to fall that much. Real interest yields for the 10-year period 1869–78 were a high 10.3 percent compared with the prewar decade of 2.6 percent.[22]

In such a world, one must indeed repay debt rapidly just to hold it constant, similar to Alice's frustrating excursions with the Red Queen. With real interest rates averaging more than the growth rate for much of this period, it was the hard way to grow out of debt. Nevertheless, economic growth at such a rapid rate came to dominate even the falling price level.

Redistribution via the fiscal structure is always a concern when taxes are used to repay debt. The post Civil-War structure must be described as regressive – very few benefits on the expenditure side for the lower income groups and a tax-tariff structure loaded heavily on consumers. The form of this structure was such that price deflation exacerbated it. While *ad valorem* taxes would not have been subject to this defect, specific commodity taxes, such as tobacco and liquor and many of the customs duties, increased in real terms when prices fell.

Nevertheless, despite a regressive internal-external excise-tax program that responded to falling prices with rising real tax rates, it should not be assumed that these taxes imposed a heavier burden on individual taxpayers. While prices were falling, real wages and income were increasing in the latter part of the 19th century.[23] The distributional question would have to be explored in detail to make a reasonably precise assessment of the impact of falling prices on taxes and incomes. This was a period of vibrant business expansion, of heavy immigration, of high protectionism, of growth of large enterprise, of increasing business concentration, and of government corruption.

The distributional strategy of a tight fiscal policy financed by consumption taxes came under increasing political attack as the century waned. Opposition increased to what was seen as a deflationary redistribution of income from debtors to creditors, and a regressive fiscal structure harnessed to repay debt. As the political situation became increasingly unstable, protectionists tried to reduce the surplus by eliminating the excises on tobacco and liquor. They were unsuccessful because the public regarded them as good taxes. With more success, certain expenditure programs were expanded, particularly veterans' pensions and public works,[24] perhaps in a search for some offsets to the regressivity of the revenue side.

The Harrison administration in a last major attack on the surplus furthered the McKinley tariff of 1890 that raised tariff rates (in order to reduce tariff revenues by increased duties) and increased veterans' pensions. These tariff policies were reversed soon after the depression of 1893, and an income tax added after heavy pressures from the Populists and the West. The Supreme Court, however, declared it unconstitutional in a controversial decision before it could become operative. Budget surpluses finally came to an end following the panic of 1893 with the debt down to $1 billion – 8 percent of GNP. By 1900 the depression of the mid-1890s followed by the Spanish–American War increased the debt to $1.3 billion.

The Victorian prose of Henry C. Adams richly sums up this episode.

> The claim that is here urged in support of deficit financeering is especially pertinent when the machinery of taxation is used for other than revenue purposes, for, under such conditions, those interested in the maintenance of existing fiscal laws will show themselves very ingenious in finding occasions for public expenditure. It is not too much to say that the Arrearage Pension Acts, by means of which the treasury was relieved of its plethora of funds, find their true explanation in the desire of Congress to maintain inviolate the system of protective duties. This could not be done in the face of an ever-increasing surplus, and protectionist politicians did not dare to advocate the abolition of the whiskey tax; it only remained for them to spend the money.

He concluded:

> It is the policy of protection that has paid our debts. This was true in the period from 1816 to 1836, and it is true at the present time [1887]. The wisdom of our statesmen consists in this, that they have not used unwisely the surplus revenue forced upon them by a radically pernicious system of taxation.[25]

3.3   The states

The Civil War was to make a tangle of the debts of the Southern states. At the beginning of the war the bulk of Southern state debt was owned by the North, and, not surprisingly, interest was not paid on these bonds during the war. Almost no taxes were imposed by the Southern states at first, but they were turned to more and more as the war went along. After the war President Johnson emphatically directed the states to repudiate them after they had initially taken no action. The repudiation of these debts for all time was a bitter pill for them to swallow, particularly because the Southern banks were major holders of these debts and would be liquidated with the disappearance of such assets.

Reconstruction in the South presented a sorry picture of vindictiveness and venality in the supervision and rebuilding of an impoverished economy. Upon admission of the 11 states by 1870, the control of their governments was in the hands of Congress. Shoddy financial practices permitted state debts to increase from $146 million at the beginning of reconstruction in 1870 to $248 million by the end of 1874, about half of which was repudiated or scaled down in the depression of the 1870s.

The Northern states, on the other hand, steadily reduced their debt from 1870–90 largely through taxation and debt retirement. The total government debt to GNP ratio by 1900 was down to 15 percent – much lower than the 49 percent of 1870, but higher than the 1860 ratio of 12 percent. The substantial increase of local debt – from $0.2 to $1.6 billion – is notable (Table 8.6).

4   World War I debt

4.1   Federal government accumulation: 1917–19

From the depression of the mid-1890s through the era of reform of the first Roosevelt and Woodrow Wilson up to 1916, the eve of entry of the United States into the war, the nominal debt had remained virtually unchanged at $1 billion while the real debt diminished steadily as prices rose from their depression levels. The debt was a low 3 percent of GNP in that year.

War mobilization accelerated government expenditures in the three following years to a peak in 1919 of more than 20 percent of GNP. As in the Civil War, the wartime tax structure was innovative. A constitutional amendment explicitly permitting an income tax had received state ratification by 1913; its availability was quickly exploited and, from a modest beginning of 1 percent, the top bracket by 1919 reached nearly 80 percent.

An excess-profits tax was enacted for the first time, and applied both to unincorporated firms as well as corporations in contrast with later practice. Perhaps the most intriguing fiscal novelty was the passage of a tax act in 1919 after the war had ended with major retroactive tax increases on 1918 incomes and profits.[26]

Corporate and personal income taxes and the excess profits tax provided the bulk of wartime revenues – a dramatically different distributional structure from that of the 19th century. The revenue effort developed more slowly than the expenditure side so that only 30 percent of spending was covered and the nominal debt grew to $25 billion by 1919, 30 percent of GNP.

4.2   Repayment: 1920–30

In the postwar period a return to what was to be called 'normalcy' by President-elect Harding was broadly favoured by the public. Expenditures were quickly reduced to their average for the coming decade, while revenues involved much more controversy and were lowered less rapidly. Moreover, the large 1919 deficit of $15 billion, 18 percent of GNP, was replaced by a modest surplus in 1920 – a large swing in fiscal policy. Output dropped sharply in 1920 and 1921; and in the latter year the inflation turned into a sharp deflation, increasing the real value of the debt, and raising the debt–GNP ratio to 34 percent.

Postwar tax reductions were applied first to the special wartime levies, like the excess-profits tax, and then to the high wartime rates on personal and corporate income. The permanent tax structure developed by the mid-1920s generally followed the views of Secretary of the Treasury Mellon that taxes on higher incomes should be cut sharply to provide incentives for saving and risk-taking. By 1926 the top income-tax bracket had been lowered to 25 percent.

The lag in tax cuts behind expenditure reductions produced surpluses in every year. Applied to debt repayment, they proved as important as the decade's income growth in reducing the debt/GNP ratio. The nominal debt was reduced by a third, or $9 billion, and by 1929 it stood at its postwar low of 16 percent of GNP. This reduction was almost equally accounted for by debt repayment and output growth. Price deflation was a modest though present factor (Table 8.2).

4.3   State and local debt

State and local debt was being added to throughout this decade in about the same amounts as federal debt was being retired. An expanding GNP

Debt–GNP ratio, 1919		30
Real growth to 1929 (1.34-fold)	− 8	
Net real debt repayment	− 8	
Net price changes	+ 2	− 14
Debt–GNP ratio, 1929		16

Table 8.2. Factors reducing the US debt–GNP ratio, 1919–29 (per cent)

brought the total debt–GNP ratio down from 44 percent in 1922 to 35 percent in 1927. By 1932, however, the lowered income and increased depression borrowing pushed this ratio up to 66 percent (Table 8.6).

5   World War II debt experience

The World War II experience had many novel features: the magnitude of mobilization – at its peak half of GNP; falling yields on government securities as the war progressed; debt exceeding GNP by the end of the war; and the postwar reduction of a substantial fraction of the debt by inflation.

With such a huge build-up of expenditures, debt grew rapidly despite much innovation on the tax side: conversion of the personal income tax to a mass tax (a 10-fold increase in taxpayers), the initiation of withholding which made the tax a more effective stabilizing instrument, and an administration proposal for a progressive consumer-expenditure tax that Congress rejected. A major feature of the stabilization program was the distributional compromise that held together disparate groups in a kind of implicit social contract of fair shares: price controls, wage controls, excess-profits taxation, rationing and direct allocation of scarce materials, and low interest rates.

In the postwar period, President Truman followed tight fiscal policies that reduced the nominal debt. Prices rose sharply in 1946 and 1947 after premature elimination (by the standards of the administration) of price and other controls. From then on inflation became virtually the only factor reducing real debt: it took a major or equal postwar position with growth in reducing the debt GNP ratio.[27]

It surely was not the intention of the government to follow a policy of debt reduction through inflation, though it should not be forgotten that the administration's support of early elimination of the excess-profits tax

Debt–GNP ratio, 1945			110
Terminal year	1955	1965	1974
Real growth to	−10	−39	−55
Net real debt repayment to	−3	+3	+10
Net price changes to	−42	−38	−41
Total change	−55	−74	−86
Debt–GNP ratio, terminal years	56	37	23

Table 8.3. Factors reducing the US debt–GNP ratio, 1945–74 (per cent)

in 1945 was probably decisive in breaking the deadlock between the House and the Senate on this issue. Elimination of this tax shattered the wartime stabilization compromise and doomed continuation of wartime price and wage controls.[28] Nevertheless, President Truman was to take many courageous positions in support of a tight fiscal stance: opposition to premature Congressional tax reductions in 1946 and 1947; support of prompt and high taxation in the Korean War that eliminated heavy pressures on direct controls. The Eisenhower administration surely would not have advocated inflationary policies to reduce debt, but by then the wartime debt–GNP ratio had been cut almost in half.

The relative weight of output growth, net real debt repayment, and inflationary changes in real debt are shown in Table 8.3 for three postwar periods beginning with 1945 and ending about a decade apart, the last of which ends with the lowest debt–GNP ratio of the postwar period, 1974. In the first decade, inflation overpowered growth and debt repayment in reducing the debt–GNP ratio; growth and inflation were almost equal in the two-decade postwar period; and in the three-decade period ending with the oil shock in 1974, growth forged ahead, but by then net borrowing had also begun to be a factor. Some inflation has ruled in every postwar year except 1949.

The federal share of total government debt has fallen in the postwar period as state and local governments returned to their normal activities suspended during the war. In 1950 the federal proportion was 76 percent; by 1980 it had reached 26 percent, but has subsequently risen. State and local debt in 1960–85 has kept pact with GNP in the 12 to 15 percent range (Table 8.6).

6   Observations and conclusions

(1) Fiscal policy of the United States in the 19th century could not be described as one driven by an autonomous expenditure structure to which taxes were adjusted: on the contrary.[29] The government began with custom duties as its major revenue source; it became gripped by protectionism and used tariffs to achieve that end. Revenue yields were generated well beyond the expenditure programs, barring wars, desired by the public. Protectionism thus dominated the generally tight fiscal policies of that century and budget surpluses, with a consequent rapid debt retirement, created political 'problems'.

(2) While a government may become a captive of policies that generate more revenue than is normally needed for financial reasons, budget surpluses will result only if expenditures are contained. The expenditure restraint shown in the first half of the 19th century was remarkable. The dominant theme of limited government was anchored at one end by Jefferson and at the other, even in the face of growing needs for transportation development, by Jackson. State governments necessarily became involved in these programs with consequent reductions in efficiency.

Opposition grew to the distributional effects of these tight monetary and fiscal policies, both to the debtor–creditor redistribution and to the regressiveness of the revenue system. As political support weakened, the backers of high customs gave way on the expenditure side, offering pensions and public works; and they surely were surprised on the revenue side when they made an income-tax concession in 1909 that became a constitutional amendment. The income tax changed substantially the impact of the fiscal program in the 20th century, and permitted the debt repayment of the 1920s.

(3) In the 19th century the government usually borrowed when prices were high and repaid when they were low. Even after World War I, the sharp decline in prices in 1921 increased the real value of the debt, although the rest of the decade was one of price stability. Not until the first decade after World War II was real debt repayment accompanied by price changes that reduced, rather than increased, the real debt (Table 8.4).

(4) The Civil War debt was doubled in real terms by falling prices; this price increment was slightly more than offset by substantial debt repayment; but the growth rate was so substantial that it dominated both factors in reducing the debt–GNP ratio. World War I debt reduction came through almost equal parts of repayment and growth. In contrast, World War II's came through inflation and growth, in about equal

Year	Initial debt		Change in real debt		
	Nominal	Real	Total	From net borrowing	From price change
	($ million)				
1790–1800	75.5	116.6	−27.2	10.1	−37.3
1801–1811	83.0	89.4	−39.6	−40.2	0.6
1812–1815	45.2	49.9	54.2	69.8	−15.6
1816–1835	127.3	104.1	−104.1	−166.9	62.8
1836–1859	0.0	0.0	85.6	101.5	−15.9
	($ billion)				
1860–1865	0.06	0.09	1.9	2.40	−0.47
1866–1893	2.68	2.01	−0.30	−2.35	2.04
1917–1919	1	12	148	165	−18
1920–1930	25	159	−45	−61	17
1940–1945	41	326	1,170	1,275	−102
1946–1955	235	1,498	−665	−40	−625
1946–1965	235	1,498	−724	69	−793
1946–1974	235	1,498	−857	262	−1,119

Table 8.4. Periods of US government borrowing and repayment, 1790–1914

Source: Through 1930, from Table 8.7; from 1940, Table 8.8.

proportions over 20 postwar years – inflation dominated in the first decade, growth caught up in the second.

(5) There are some similarities between the present fiscal problems of the United States and the 19th century experience. Like the 19th century revenue structure, the present one has been fixed by nonrevenue considerations: the desire to force down the size of government, rather than promoting protection. Unlike the 19th century structure, it fails to support the expenditure programs desired by the public. As a consequence we are confronted by chronic deficits instead of chronic surpluses. This unstable situation has raised the debt–GNP ratio to nearly double its level in 1974, the lowest point in the postwar period.

	1790–1800	1801–1811	1812–1815	1816–1835	1836–1843	1844–1849	1850–1860	1861–1865
			($ million)					
Net receipts	6.4	13.7	12.9	26.4	25.3	31.5	56.1	178.9†
Customs	5.8	12.8	9.5	22.7	18.5	29.0	52.1	100.6
Land sales	*	0.6	1.1	2.9	6.8	2.5	4.0	0.5
Internal taxes	0.6	0.3	2.3	0.8	0.0	0.0	0.0	72.4
Expenditures	6.2	9.3	28.6	19.1	33.4	36.2	52.5	671.6
Purchases	3.4	5.0	24.9	12.5	24.2	30.6	45.7	610.4
Transfers and interest	2.8	4.3	3.7	6.6	9.1	5.6	6.8	61.2
Surplus	0.2	4.4	−15.7	7.3	−8.1	−4.7	3.6	−492.7

Table 8.5. Federal government: average receipts and expenditures, 1790–1865

†Customs receipts and interest payments valued at the gold premium.
*Less than 0.5 million.
Source: 1790–1860: Trescott (1960) Tables 10, 11.
1861–65: Trescott (1966) Tables 2, 3.

Year	Federal[1] ($ million)	State[2]	Local[2]	Total	GNP nominal[3] ($ billion)	Debt GNP (%)
1825	81	13	—	94	1.0	10
1835	0	46	5	51	1.4	4
1840	5	176	20	201	1.8	11
1843	33	232	28	293	2.0	15
1850	63	190	40	293	2.5	12
1860	65	257	200	522	4.5	12
			($ billion)			
1860	0.1	0.3	0.2	0.5	4.5	12
1870	2.4	0.4	0.5	3.3	6.7	49
1880	2.1	0.3	0.8	3.2	9.2	35
1890	1.1	0.2	0.9	2.2	13.1	17
1902	1.2	0.2	1.6	3.0	20.3	15
1913	1.2	0.4	4.0	5.6	39.9	14
1922	23.0	1.1	9.0	33.1	74.8	44
1927	18.5	2.0	12.9	33.4	95.8	35
1932	19.5	2.8	16.4	38.7	58.4	66
1940	42.8	3.6	16.7	63.1	100.4	63
1950	219.0	5.3	18.8	243.1	288.3	84
1960	237.2	18.5	51.4	307.1	515.3	60
1970	284.9	42.0	101.6	428.5	1,015.5	42
1980	715.1	122.0	213.6	1,050.7	2,732.0	38
1985	1,509.9	211.9	346.6	2,078.4	3,998.1	52

Table 8.6. Public debt in the United States, 1825–1985

[1]Table 8.7.
[2]To 1902, Hempel (1971) Table 6; 1902–70, *Historical Statistics of U.S.* (1970) Series Y747 and Y794; 1980–85, *Statistical Abstract of U.S.*
[3]To 1860, Trescott (1960) Table 14 with this writer's linear interpolations for the years 1825, 1835, and 1843; 1870–1909. *Historical Statistics of the U.S.*, Series F1; 1909 to present, Table 8.8.

Table 8.7

					Change in real debt		
Year	Price index	Price change (%)	Nominal gross debt	Real debt (1929)	Total	From net borrowing	From price change
(1)	(2)	(3)	(4)	(5)	(6)	(7)	(8)
			(Money figures in $ million)				
1790	65		75.5	116.6			
1791	61	−6	77.2	126.2	9.6	2.8	6.9
1792	n.a.	n.a.	80.4	n.a.	n.a.	n.a.	n.a.
1793	73	20	78.4	106.8	−19.4	1.6	−21.0
1794	78	6	80.7	103.9	−3.0	3.0	−5.9
1795	94	21	83.8	88.9	−14.9	3.3	−18.2
1796	105	11	82.1	78.2	−10.8	−1.6	−9.1
1797	94	−10	79.2	84.0	5.9	−3.1	9.0
1798	88	−7	78.4	89.3	5.3	−0.9	6.2
1799	91	3	83.0	91.6	2.2	5.1	−2.8
1800	93	2	83.0	89.4	−2.1	0.0	−2.1
1801	102	10	80.7	79.0	−10.4	−2.3	−8.2
1802	84	−18	77.1	91.6	12.6	−4.3	16.9
1803	85	1	86.4	101.8	10.2	11.0	−0.8
1804	91	7	82.3	90.8	−11.0	−4.5	−6.5
1805	101	12	75.7	74.6	−16.2	−6.5	−9.7
1806	96	−5	69.2	71.8	−2.8	−6.7	3.9
1807	94	−3	65.2	69.7	−2.1	−4.3	2.2
1808	83	−12	57.0	68.9	−0.8	−9.9	9.1
1809	94	13	53.2	56.9	−12.0	−4.1	−7.9
1810	94	1	48.0	50.9	−6.0	−5.5	−0.4
1811	91	−4	45.2	49.9	−1.1	−3.1	2.0
1812	94	4	56.0	59.4	9.6	11.5	−1.9
1813	117	24	81.5	69.9	10.5	21.9	−11.4
1814	131	12	99.8	76.2	6.3	14.0	−7.7
1815	122	−7	127.3	104.1	27.9	22.5	5.4
1816	109	−11	123.5	113.7	9.6	−3.5	13.1
1817	109	0	103.5	95.3	18.4	−18.4	0.0
1818	106	−3	95.5	90.3	−5.0	−7.6	2.6
1819	90	−15	91.0	101.2	10.9	−5.0	15.9
1820	76	−15	90.0	118.0	16.8	−1.3	18.1
1821	73	−4	93.5	127.4	9.4	4.8	4.6
1822	76	4	90.9	119.2	−8.2	−3.4	−4.8
1823	74	−3	90.3	121.9	2.7	−0.8	3.5
1824	71	−5	83.8	118.9	−3.0	−9.2	6.2
1825	74	5	81.1	109.4	−9.4	−3.6	−5.8

Table 8.7 (*cont.*)

Year	Price index	Price change (%)	Nominal gross debt	Real debt (1929)	Change in real debt		
					Total	From net borrowing	From price change
(1)	(2)	(3)	(4)	(5)	(6)	(7)	(8)
			(Money figures in $ million)				
1826	71	−4	74.0	103.9	−5.5	−10.0	4.4
1827	71	−1	67.5	95.7	−8.2	−9.2	1.1
1828	70	−1	58.4	83.7	−12.1	−13.0	1.0
1829	69	−1	48.6	70.4	−13.3	−14.2	0.9
1830	65	−5	39.1	59.7	−10.6	−14.5	3.9
1831	68	3	24.3	35.9	−23.8	−21.9	−1.9
1832	68	1	7.0	10.2	−25.7	−25.3	−0.4
1833	68	0	4.8	7.0	−3.2	−3.2	0.0
1834	65	−5	0.0	0.0	−7.0	−7.4	0.4
1835	72	11	0.0	0.0	0.0	0.0	0.0
1836	82	14	0.3	0.4	0.4	0.4	0.0
1837	83	1	3.3	4.0	3.6	3.6	0.0
1838	79	−4	10.4	13.1	9.2	9.0	0.2
1839	81	2	3.6	4.5	−8.7	−8.4	−0.2
1840	68	−15	5.3	7.8	3.3	2.5	0.8
1841	66	−3	13.6	20.5	12.8	12.5	0.3
1842	59	−11	20.2	34.2	13.7	11.2	2.5
1843	54	−9	32.7	60.6	26.4	23.2	3.2
1844	55	3	23.5	42.4	−18.2	−16.6	−1.6
1845	60	8	15.9	26.6	−15.8	−12.7	−3.1
1846	60	0	15.6	26.1	−0.5	−0.5	0.0
1847	65	8	38.8	59.9	33.8	35.8	−2.0
1848	59	−9	47.0	79.7	19.7	13.9	5.8
1849	59	0	63.1	107.0	27.3	27.3	0.0
1850	60	2	63.5	105.1	−1.9	0.7	−2.5
1851	60	−1	68.3	114.4	9.3	8.0	1.3
1852	63	6	66.2	104.6	−9.8	−3.3	−6.5
1853	70	10	59.8	85.7	−18.9	−9.2	−9.7
1854	78	11	42.2	54.3	−31.4	−22.7	−8.7
1855	79	2	35.6	45.0	−9.3	−8.3	−1.0
1856	76	−5	32.0	42.4	−2.6	−4.8	2.1
1857	80	6	28.7	35.9	−6.4	−4.1	−2.3
1858	67	−16	44.9	67.1	31.2	24.2	7.0
1859	68	2	58.5	85.6	18.5	19.9	−1.4
			(Money figures in $ billion)				
1860	67	−2	0.06	0.09	0.00	0.00	0.00

Table 8.7 (*cont.*)

Year	Price index	Price change (%)	Nominal gross debt	Real debt (1929)	Change in real debt Total	Change in real debt From net borrowing	Change in real debt From price change
(1)	(2)	(3)	(4)	(5)	(6)	(7)	(8)
			(Money figures in $ billion)				
1861	64	−4	0.09	0.14	0.05	0.05	0.00
1862	75	17	0.52	0.70	0.55	0.57	−0.02
1863	96	28	1.12	1.17	0.48	0.63	−0.15
1864	139	45	1.82	1.31	0.14	0.50	−0.36
1865	133	−4	2.68	2.01	0.70	0.65	0.06
1866	125	−6	2.76	2.20	0.19	0.06	0.13
1867	117	−7	2.65	2.27	0.07	−0.09	0.16
1868	114	−2	2.58	2.27	0.00	−0.06	0.06
1869	109	−4	2.55	2.35	0.08	−0.03	0.11
1870	97	−11	2.44	2.51	0.16	−0.11	0.28
1871	94	−4	2.32	2.48	−0.03	−0.13	0.10
1872	98	5	2.21	2.26	−0.22	−0.11	−0.11
1873	96	−2	2.15	2.25	−0.01	−0.06	0.05
1874	91	−5	2.16	2.38	0.14	0.01	0.12
1875	85	−6	2.16	2.54	0.16	0.00	0.16
1876	79	−7	2.13	2.69	0.15	−0.04	0.19
1877	76	−4	2.11	2.77	0.08	−0.03	0.10
1878	65	−14	2.16	3.30	0.53	0.08	0.46
1879	65	−1	2.30	3.55	0.25	0.22	0.04
1880	72	11	2.09	2.91	−0.65	−0.29	−0.36
1881	74	3	2.02	2.73	−0.18	−0.09	−0.08
1882	78	5	1.86	2.39	−0.33	−0.21	−0.13
1883	73	−6	1.72	2.37	−0.03	−0.19	0.17
1884	67	−8	1.63	2.44	0.07	−0.13	0.20
1885	61	−9	1.58	2.58	0.15	−0.08	0.23
1886	59	−4	1.56	2.64	0.06	−0.03	0.09
1887	61	4	1.47	2.40	−0.24	−0.15	−0.09
1888	51	1	1.38	2.23	−0.17	−0.15	−0.03
1889	58	−6	1.25	2.15	−0.09	−0.22	0.14
1890	59	1	1.12	1.90	−0.25	−0.22	−0.03
1891	59	0	1.01	1.71	−0.19	−0.19	0.00
1892	55	−7	0.97	1.77	0.06	−0.07	0.14
1893	56	3	0.96	1.71	−0.06	−0.02	−0.05
1894	50	−10	1.02	2.03	0.31	0.12	0.20
1895	51	1	1.10	2.15	0.13	0.16	−0.03
1896	49	−4	1.22	2.49	0.34	0.25	0.10

Table 8.7 (*cont.*)

					Change in real debt		
Year	Price index	Price change (%)	Nominal gross debt	Real debt (1929)	Total	From net borrowing	From price change
(1)	(2)	(3)	(4)	(5)	(6)	(7)	(8)
			(Money figures in $ billion)				
1897	49	0	1.23	2.51	0.02	0.02	0.00
1898	51	4	1.23	2.41	−0.11	0.00	−0.11
1899	55	8	1.44	2.60	0.19	0.38	−0.19
1900	59	6	1.26	2.14	−0.46	−0.31	−0.16
1901	58	−1	1.22	2.09	−0.04	−0.07	0.03
1902	62	6	1.18	1.91	−0.19	−0.06	−0.12
1903	63	1	1.16	1.85	−0.05	−0.03	−0.02
1904	63	0	1.14	1.82	−0.03	−0.03	0.00
1905	63	1	1.13	1.78	−0.04	−0.02	−0.02
1906	65	2	1.14	1.76	−0.02	0.02	−0.04
1907	68	6	1.15	1.68	−0.08	0.01	−0.09
1908	66	−3	1.18	1.78	0.10	0.05	0.05
1909	71	8	1.15	1.61	−0.17	−0.04	−0.13

Table 8.7. Nominal and real US government debt, 1790–1909

Sources:

(2) Wholesale price index for calendar years, Warren and Pearson (1933) Table 1, pp. 10–14, adjusted to percent of 1929. The year 1792 is missing, hence the subsequent computations combine 1792–93.

(3) Percentage change in price from previous years. For year $t = (P_t - P_{t-1})/P_{t-1}$.

(4) *Historical Statistics of the U.S. to 1957*, Series 257. End of calendar year through 1842; end of fiscal year, June 30, from 1843. In Series 368 the same source reports the same data but from 1791 through 1984 the previous year is shown.

(5) Column (4)/Column (2).

(6) First difference of Column (5).

(7) [First difference of Column (4)]/Column (2).

(8) Column (6) − Column (7) = $D_{t-1}(P_{t-1} - P_t)/P_{t-1}P_t$.

Table 8.8

						Change in real debt		
Year	Price index (1982)	Gross debt	GNP	Debt–GNP ratio	Real debt (1982)	Total	From net borrowing	From price change
(1)	(2)	(3)	(4)	(5)	(6)	(7)	(8)	(9)
				(Money figures in $ billion)				
1909	8.2	1	34	0.03	14			
1910	8.4	1	36	0.03	14	0	0	0
1911	8.3	1	36	0.03	14	0	0	0
1912	8.7	1	40	0.03	14	0	0	−1
1913	8.6	1	40	0.03	14	0	0	0
1914	8.8	1	39	0.03	14	0	0	0
1915	9.2	1	40	0.03	13	−1	0	−1
1916	10.3	1	49	0.03	12	−1	0	−1
1917	12.6	3	61	0.05	24	12	14	−2
1918	13.5	12	77	0.16	92	69	70	−2
1919	16.0	25	85	0.30	159	67	81	−14
1920	18.9	24	92	0.26	129	−31	−6	−24
1921	15.5	24	70	0.11	155	26	−2	28
1922	14.4	23	75	0.31	159	5	−7	12
1923	14.9	22	86	0.26	150	−9	−4	−5
1924	14.7	21	86	0.25	145	−5	−7	2
1925	15.0	21	94	0.22	137	−8	−5	−3
1926	14.8	20	98	0.20	133	−4	−6	2
1927	14.5	19	96	0.19	128	−5	−8	3
1928	14.6	18	98	0.18	121	−7	−6	−1
1929	14.6	17	104	0.16	116	−5	−5	0
1930	14.2	16	91	0.18	114	−2	−5	3
1931	13.0	17	76	0.22	129	15	5	11
1932	11.5	20	59	0.33	170	40	23	17
1933	11.2	23	56	0.40	201	31	27	5
1934	12.2	27	66	0.41	222	21	38	−16
1935	12.5	29	73	0.39	230	7	13	−5
1936	12.5	34	83	0.41	270	41	41	0
1937	13.1	36	91	0.40	278	7	20	−12
1938	12.9	37	85	0.44	288	11	6	4
1939	12.7	41	91	0.45	326	38	33	5
1940	13.0	43	100	0.43	329	3	11	−8
1941	13.8	48	126	0.39	351	21	41	−19
1942	14.7	68	159	0.43	461	110	132	−21
1943	15.1	128	193	0.66	846	385	397	−12
1944	15.3	185	211	0.87	1,208	361	373	−11
1945	15.7	235	213	1.10	1,498	290	321	−31

Table 8.8 (*cont.*)

Year	Price index (1982)	Gross debt	GNP	Debt–GNP ratio	Real debt (1982)	Change in real debt Total	From net borrowing	From price change
(1)	(2)	(3)	(4)	(5)	(6)	(7)	(8)	(9)
			(Money figures in $ billion)					
1946	19.4	242	212	1.14	1,247	−251	35	−286
1947	22.1	224	235	0.95	1,015	−232	−80	−152
1948	23.6	216	262	0.83	917	−98	−34	−65
1949	23.5	214	260	0.82	912	−5	−9	4
1950	23.9	219	288	0.76	916	4	20	−15
1951	25.1	214	333	0.64	854	−63	−19	−44
1952	25.5	215	352	0.61	842	−11	2	−13
1953	25.9	218	372	0.59	843	1	14	−13
1954	26.3	225	373	0.60	854	10	23	−13
1955	27.2	227	406	0.56	833	−21	8	−28
1956	28.1	222	428	0.52	791	−42	−16	−27
1957	29.1	219	451	0.49	754	−37	−10	−27
1958	29.7	226	457	0.50	762	8	24	−15
1959	30.4	235	496	0.47	773	11	28	−18
1960	30.9	237	515	0.46	768	−5	7	−13
1961	31.2	239	534	0.45	765	−3	4	−7
1962	31.9	248	575	0.43	779	14	31	−17
1963	32.4	255	607	0.42	785	7	19	−12
1964	32.9	258	650	0.40	783	−3	9	−12
1965	33.8	262	705	0.37	774	−9	12	−21
1966	35.0	265	772	0.34	756	−18	9	−27
1967	35.9	268	816	0.33	745	−11	8	−19
1968	37.7	291	893	0.33	771	26	61	−36
1969	39.8	280	964	0.29	702	−69	−28	−41
1970	42.0	285	1,016	0.28	678	−24	13	−37
1971	44.4	304	1,103	0.28	685	7	44	−37
1972	46.5	324	1,213	0.27	696	11	42	−31
1973	49.5	343	1,359	0.25	693	−3	39	−42
1974	54.0	346	1,473	0.23	641	−52	6	−58
1975	59.3	397	1,598	0.25	669	28	86	−57
1976	63.1	480	1,783	0.27	761	92	132	−40
1977	67.3	552	1,991	0.28	820	59	106	−48
1978	72.2	611	2,250	0.27	846	26	82	−56
1979	78.6	645	2,508	0.26	820	−26	43	−69
1980	85.7	715	2,732	0.26	834	14	82	−68
1981	94.0	794	3,053	0.26	845	11	84	−74

Table 8.8 (*cont.*)

Year	Price index (1982)	Gross debt	GNP	Debt– GNP ratio	Real debt (1982)	Total	From net borrowing	From price change
							Change in real debt	
(1)	(2)	(3)	(4)	(5)	(6)	(7)	(8)	(9)
				(Money figures in $ billion)				
1982	100.0	929	3,166	0.29	929	84	135	− 51
1983	103.9	1,142	3,406	0.34	1,099	170	204	− 35
1984	107.7	1,313	3,772	0.35	1,219	120	159	− 39
1985	111.2	1,510	4,010	0.38	1,358	139	177	− 38
1986	114.1	1,746	4,235	0.41	1,530	173	207	− 35

Table 8.8. US government debt and GNP, 1909–86

Sources:
(2) Implicit GNP price index as percent of 1982 base, US Department of Commerce (1986–1987).
(3) Through 1939, *Historical Statistics of the U.S. to 1957*, Series 257; 1940 to present, debt in hands of public. *Economic Report of the President*, 1987, end of fiscal year: June 30, through 1976; September 309, 1977 to present.
(4) US Commerce (1986, 1987).
(5) Column (3)/Column (4).
(6) Column (3)/Column (2).
(7) First difference of Column (6).
(8) [First difference of Column (3)]/Column (2).
(9) Column (7) − Column (8) = $D_{t-1}(P_{t-1} - P_t)/P_{t-1}P_t$.

NOTES

1 Dewey (1934) has been an important and reliable source for this and later periods.
2 Trescott (1960) p. 342 is the low figure; Barro (1984) p. 368, using unpublished data of Robert Gallman, is the high one.
3 Trescott (1960) p. 360; Barro (1984) p. 368.
4 Madison near the end of his administration announced his support of internal improvements of *national* interest. John Quincey Adams had a full-scale program involving internal improvements, but Congress successfully thwarted it.
5 Ratchford (1941) p. 46. This work is an indispensable source for state finances and has been relied on extensively in this paper.
6 The Erie Canal debt was repaid from the canal's revenues in 10 years. The cost of freight dropped dramatically – Buffalo to New York City from $100 to $15 per ton – ultimately diverting substantial amounts of traffic from the Ohio and Mississippi valleys to New York City.

7 Classifed by purpose of borrowing, banking accounted for $54 million, canals $60 million, railroads $43 million, turnpikes $7 million and $9 million was of a miscellaneous character. Transportation accounted for almost two-thirds. Ratchford (1941) p. 87.
8 Trescott (1955) p. 140 estimates that most of this distribution promoted capital formation either directly or indirectly, although many of the investments were of doubtful merit.
9 Temin (1969) pp. 155–65.
10 Hempel (1971) pp. 16–18, 32. Of $245 million outstanding in the period 1837–434, $125 million was in default, and $14 million was repudiated.
11 European lenders were ready purchasers of many of the states' debts, but were understandably put off by the defaults and, later, repudiations. Secretary of the Treasury Bibb in his Annual Report for 1844 stated: 'If aliens, not understanding the texture of the National Government, do not distinguish accurately between engagements entered into by the Government of the United States, and those entered into by the several States, . . . have distrusted the credit of the National Government, . . . such distrust is to be regretted'. Quoted in Childs (1947) p. 29.
12 Studenski and Krooss (1952) pp. 133–36.
13 Trescott (1957) p. 62.
14 The government had suspended specie payment in 1862, except for customs duties and 'virtually all interest and principal payments on its debt', not to be resumed until January 1, 1879. Friedman and Schwartz (1963) p. 27. The debt service, therefore, required premium payments in currency, and the debt should logically be valued at the currency price of gold in this period. Trescott (1966) made such adjustments to budget data for 1862–75, and they are incorporated in Table 8.5. This premium as highest in 1864 and would have doubled the size of the debt in currency prices. The $2.7 billion debt at the end of the war shown in Table 8.7 would be increased to $3.8 billion in currency prices. For the gold value of currency, see Warren and Pearson (1933) p. 351.
    The implicit nominal GNP of $9.2 billion, in Barro (1984) p. 368, when applied to the debt figure adjusted for the gold premium, yields a ratio of 41 percent. The higher figure is that obtained from Kuznets' estimate of average nominal GNP for 1869–73 of $6.7 billion increased by 15 percent – the proportion implicit in Barro's data. This $7.7 billion GNP yields the 49-percent ratio in the text. For Kuznets' estimates, see *Historical Statistics* (1957) Series F3.
15 Table 8.5 for the 1850s; Trescott (1966) for the later decade.
16 *Historical Statistics* (1957) Series U19.
17 Studenski and Krooss (1952) p. 163.
18 Kuznets' real GNP measured from the mid-points of his 5-year averages, 1871–91. *Historical Statistics* (1957) Series F3.
19 The Warren and Pearson (1933) wholesale price index fell 2.9 percent per year from 1866–93; 2.2 percent per year from 1871–91. From the mid-points of Kuznets' 5-year GNP averages the implicit GNP deflator fell 1.9 percent per year during 1871–91. *Historical Statistics* (1957) Series F5.
20 Sylla (1975) p. 287 has computed US bond yields for the period from 1869 to 1892 that shows a steady decline from 6.87 percent to a low of 2.11 percent in 1889 ending with 2.69 percent.

21 Before the adjustments, the total in Table 8.4 for 1871 compare with those shown for 1866–93 as follows:

Change in real debt ($ billion)	1866–93	1871–91
Total	−0.30	−0.80
Attributed to debt repayment	−2.35	−2.03
Attributed to price changes	+2.04	+1.22

22 Five-year averages of nominal yields on US government securities (date from Sylla, 1975, p. 287) show a virtually steady decline from the 1869–73 figure of 5.7 percent to 2.4 percent in 1888–92. When these nominal yields are converted to real yields for 10-year periods to smooth the skittish Warren and Pearson (1933) wholesale price index, a 10.2 percent average real yield for 1869–78 drops to a low of 3.2 percent for 1879–88, primarily because of the inflation preceding the 1883 crisis, and finishes in 1883–92, the last 10 years, with 5.8 percent.

   Homer (1963, p. 287) has computed an average nominal yield for the pre-Civil War decade of 4.3 percent that converts to a real yield of 2.6 percent.

23 Warren and Pearson (1933) p. 197.

24 Despite the fact that the price level was falling, the nominal value of pensions increased from a prewar figure of $1 million to $28 million in 1869, $66 million in 1883, and $107 million in 1890. *Historical Statistics* (1957) Series Y p. 356. Public works increases were much smaller. Studenski and Krooss (1952) p. 165.

25 Adams (1887) p. 81.

26 Adams (1887) p. 274.

27 Paul (1954) has been heavily relied on for the World War I and II periods.

28 This view contrasts with Alesina (1988).

29 This difficult decision was undoubtedly intended to soften the New Deal image of business hostility. Labour experts had warned repeatedly that wage controls would never survive beyond the excess-profits tax.

30 Contrast Barro (1989).

REFERENCES

Adams, Henry C. (1887). *Public Debts*. New York: D. Appleton and Company.

Alesina, Alberto (1988). 'The end of large public debts?' in Francesco Giavazzi and Luigi Spaventa, eds., *High Public Debt: The Italian Experience*. Cambridge: Cambridge University Press, 34–79.

Barro, Robert J. (1984). *Macroeconomics*. New York: John Wiley & Sons, Inc.

   (1989). 'The Ricardian Approach to Budget Deficits', *The Journal of Economics* 3, 37–54.

Childs, C.F. (1947). *Concerning U.S. Government Securities*. Chicago: C.F. Childs and Company.

Dewey, Davis R. (1934). *Financial History of the United States*, 12th ed. New York: Longman's Green and Co.

Friedman, Milton and Anna Jacobson Schwartz (1963). *A Monetary History of the United States, 1867–1960*. Princeton: Princeton University Press.

Hempel, George H. (1971). *Postwar Quality of State and the Local Debt*. New York: National Bureau of Economic Research.

254 **Discussion by Barry P. Bosworth**

Homer,Sidney (1963). *A History of Interest Rates.* New Brunswick, N.J.: Rutgers University Press.

Paul, Randolph E. (1954). *Taxation in the United States.* Boston: Little, Brown & Co.

Ratchford, B.U. (1941). *American State Debts.* Durham, North Carolina: Duke University Press.

Studenski, Paul and Herman E. Krooss (1952). *Financial History of the United States.* New York: McGraw-Hill Book Company, Inc.

Sylla, Richard (1975). *The American Capital Market, 1846–1914.* New York: Arno Press.

Temin, Peter (1969). *The Jacksonian Economy.* New York: W.W. Norton & Company, Inc.

Trescott, Paul B. (1955). 'Federal-State Financial Relations, 1790–1860', *The Journal of Economic History* **15**, 227–45.

(1957). 'Some Historical Aspects of Federal Fiscal Policy, 1790–1956', in U.S. Joint Economic Committee, *Federal Expenditure Policy for Economic Growth and Development* (Washington: Government Printing Office, 60–83.

(1960). 'The United States Government and National Income, 1790–1860' in *Trends in the American Economy in the Nineteenth Century.* Princeton: Princeton University Press, 337–61.

(1966). 'Federal Government Receipts and Expenditures, 1861–1875', *The Journal of Economic History* **26**, 206–22.

U.S. Department of Commerce (1960). *Historical Statistics of the United States, Colonial Times to 1957,* Washington, D.C.: Government Printing Office.

(1976). *Historical Statistics of the United States, Colonial Times to 1970,* Washington, D.C.: Government Printing Office.

(1986). *The National Income and Product Accounts of the United States, 1929–82,* Washington, D.C.: Government Printing Office.

(1987). 'National Income and Product Accounts', *Survey of Current Business* **67**.

Warren, George F. and Frank A. Pearson (1933). *Prices.* New York: John Wiley & Sons, Inc.

Discussion

BARRY P. BOSWORTH

Professor Brown has provided a very complete history of US debt stretching over a full two centuries – perhaps a short time by European standards, but for the United States that is all there is. I will focus my remarks on the most recent portion of that history because it seems most relevant

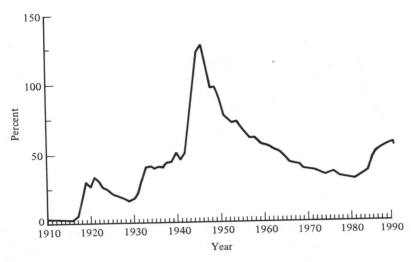

Figure 8A.1   US: ratio of gross federal debt to GNP, 1910–90

to the current situation in other countries. However, I was struck, following Brown's discussion of the episodes of debt repayment in 1815–35 and 1865–93, by how times change. In those days, government taxes were a good and expenditures were a bad, and there was a marked tendency for the government to run a budget surplus during peacetime. I agree with the argument in his paper that this result can be explained by noting that taxes were a synonym for tariffs, and Americans were protectionists who feared the power that flows from central government expenditures. Somewhat facetiously we might be led to conclude that the United States could solve some of the current political and economic problems surrounding the budget and trade deficits by adopting large tariffs. While not optimal, tariffs may be preferable, in a world of flexible exchange rates, to the growing system of quotas and so-called voluntary export restrictions.

Professor Brown's paper does not fit well in a conference where others focus on confidence and funding crises, panics, and debt default. We can find little of that in the history of US debt; but that fact is itself striking, when, as pointed out by Brown, the US debt–GNP ratio has been as high or higher than that of nations that have had serious funding crises.

One reason for this disparity of experience is that the debt–GNP ratio is a very poor proxy for the political–economic consequences of debt financing. The political problems of debt finance are associated with its interest cost, not the level of the debt; it is involuntary, distortionary taxes on citizens, not offset by any evident expenditure program benefits, that

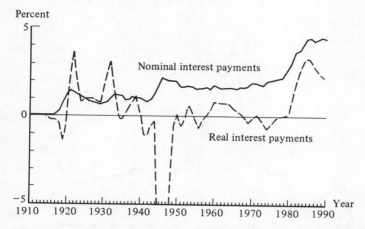

Figure 8A.2   US: ratio of government interest payments to GNP, 1910–90.
Real interest payments excludes the inflation component of nominal interest
payments.

create the difficulty of dealing with budgetary decisions in a rational
fashion. From this perspective I have provided two graphs: Figure 8A.1
shows the debt–GNP ratio with its huge peak in World War II, and
Figure 8A.2 shows the ratio of interest payments to GNP. In Figure 8A.2
the World War II peak largely disappears because it was accompanied by
very low interest rates.

According to Figure 8A.2, the United States has had three episodes of
rising debt burden in this century: World War I, World War II, and the
Reagan era; and the costs of Reagan far exceed those of the two world
wars. Today, interest payments are the fastest growing expenditure
program, as other programs are, in the aggregate, a falling share of GNP.
An alternative perspective is provided by noting that, if it could exclude
the interest cost of debt added since 1980, the United States would have a
balanced federal budget today.

Because of the focus on political models of debt creation in this conference, it is interesting to speculate on the reasons for the outbreak of
peacetime reliance on debt financing – or what is sometimes referred to as
a consumption binge in the United States in the 1980s. One simple answer
may be: what should we expect from a 75-year-old president who never
liked his children very much to begin with?

It appears to reflect, however, a more lasting shift in the political
process. I do not believe that economics has played a relevant role in the
current debate over the budget deficit. The deficit is a result of stalemate
in an ideological debate over the appropriate size of government, not an

argument over fiscal policy. It is an old issue in the United States where there has been considerable resistance to a major role for government in society; but the battle was normally fought over expenditure programs. Liberals emphasized the benefits of these programs; and conservatives, opposed to the expansion of government, were forced into the niggardly position of arguing that the nation could not afford it. It should not be surprising that the liberals often won these public debates.

In the late 1970s, conservatives abandoned this institutionalized role of opposing specific expenditures; and they argued, instead, for the benefits of tax reduction. Liberals were forced into the uncomfortable position of arguing that the nation could not afford it. The two groups found their roles reversed, and the budget deficit became a major tool for blocking the liberals' new expenditure programs. At present, conservatives argue that the deficit is bad, but worse than the deficit would be a tax increase. So too with liberals, but worse than the deficit would be cut in expenditures. The public, not yet affected directly by the deficit, agrees with both. Most recently, both extreme conservatives and extreme liberals, recognizing the threat to their preferred option, have begun to argue that the deficit itself is not a problem.

Finally, Professor Brown is obviously correct that inflation was a major factor behind the decline in the debt–GNP ratio, but we should be careful in the interpretation that this took the form of an involuntary tax on debt holders. He measures the inflation component as a residual, subtracting the budget surplus, measured in constant dollars, from the real value of the outstanding debt. However, if the inflation was anticipated and incorporated in nominal interest rates, interest expenditures, and thus the budget balance, includes an element that represents repayment of principal to bondholders. The change in the residual real value of the outstanding debt would not be a measure of the inflation effect.

However, if we thought that inflation was anticipated and incorporated in nominal interest rates, we are left with a puzzle: why were interest rates so low in the 1940s and 1950s; or, more dramatic, why were real interest rates consistently negative? It was the negative level of real rates that made it so easy for the United States to dramatically lower the debt–GNP ratio in the years immediately after World War II. In fact, as Brown's data shows, inflation wiped out a third of the real debt in the two years of 1946–57.

It is often emphasized that the Federal Reserve pegged interest rates at an artificially low level during the War and continued to do so up to the time of the accord with the Treasury in 1951. However, I am struck by how easy that appears to have been: the lack of major debt purchase by the Federal Reserve and the lack of any pattern of sustained acceleration of inflation.

In addition, there was no substantial surge in interest rates in the years immediately after the accord.

Faced with artificially low yields on financial assets we would expect investors to flee the markets. In part, the low rates could be traced to controls on foreign capital movements during the 1940s and 1950s, although US foreign assets did rise at a substantial rate. Furthermore, the stability of real estate prices, a dividend–price yield nearly twice that of nominal interest rates, and the constancy of the real return on corporate tangible capital seem surprising. I would have expected the return on real assets to reflect some of the decline in returns in financial markets. Finally, the negative real rates could be explained by an argument that opportunities to substitute between real and financial assets were very limited, but few argued that in the 1970s when nominal interest rates did begin to reflect the inflation. What were the institutional changes that allowed investors to avoid the effects of inflation in later decades?

Investors appear to have accepted very large losses from inflation in a very passive fashion. Even in the very short end of the market, there was little or no evidence of serious upward pressure on nominal rates until well after the end of the accord. Perhaps, as some have argued, expectations were dominated by a historical tendency for the price level to fall after wars. It did not take a genius, however, to believe that the 3-month inflation rate was high in 1946; but investors continued to purchase Treasury bills with interest rates below 0.5 percent.

In any case, few of us would believe that governments could currently adopt the post-WWII policies of the United States to reduce their debt burdens. It is no longer so easy to fool investors. Thus, I would conclude that there is little in the debt history of the United States that is relevant to current conditions. And, if we focused on interest costs rather than debt, we would realize that today's problems are actually substantially greater than in the past.

Discussion

GIAMPAOLO GALLI

Professor Brown's paper makes a clear point about an important aspect of the political process. His account of the history of US public finance shows that decisions about spending and revenues were taken separately with little concern about their net outcome, whether deficit or surplus: even less importance appears ever to have been attributed to their cumulative effect on the outstanding debt, except perhaps in exceptional circumstances. Sometimes this point is made in connection with large deficits and large debts; it is easy to conceive of governments taking decisions about expenditure without worrying about who is to pay. Cary Brown presents an altogether different picture. Before the introduction of the income tax in 1913, much of the revenue came from customs duties, but their function was related to international trade, not public finance. The real issue was protectionism. Similarly, the main purpose of the excises on tobacco and liquor was not to raise revenue; public health or morality were deemed to be at stake. One the spending side, there were limits imposed by ideology and by the Constitution; both prevented the federal government from doing the things that 19th-century America needed, namely building roads, railroads and canals. The outcome was large surpluses, with which the US government repaid the debts accumulated during the Revolution, the Napoleonic Wars and the Civil War. What was the political role of the public debt? According to Cary Brown, it provided an economic justification or, better, a pretext for not reducing custom duties: sound finance and debt repayment were more acceptable words than protectionism and special interests. Hence the political dilemma of the 1830s, when the debt was completely repaid.

The story that Cary Brown tells is convincing. It would be interesting to have papers like this on other countries, to assess whether there are common determinants of the propensity to accumulate or deculumate debts. A causal comparison with the case of Italy shows no similarity with the US. After national unification in 1861 the ratio of the debt to GDP soared, from 45 to almost 100 percent in 9 years (see Figure 8B.1). The main causes were two wars, in 1866 and in 1870, and the taking up of regional debts by the central government. After the 1870 war the conservative minister of finance, Quintino Sella, managed to reduce the ratio to 70 percent in three years through higher taxes, privatization of railroads and, more importantly, monetization; prices, which had been stable for a decade, rose by 23 percent from 1871 to 1873. Except for this episode, the debt expanded steadily until the end of the century, because of falling prices, slow real growth and a number of programs enacted by the 'left' government which came into power in 1876. Among these was public support of the railroad system and its gradual renationalization. From the turn of the century until the First World War the debt was reduced by the resumption of growth, a major fiscal correction and the conversion of 1906 (see M. de Cecco in this volume), but never fell below 80 percent of GDP.

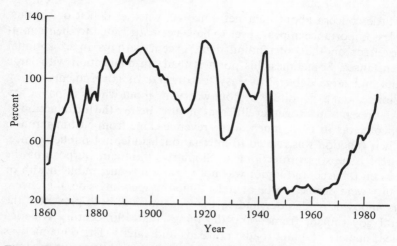

Figure 8B.1   Italy: ratio of public debt to GDP, 1860–1985

From the Great War onwards, the Italian and American stories tend to converge somewhat. The two major wars and the Depression raised the debt to unprecedented levels while in the 1920s and 1940s inflation was a major factor for fiscal soundness. In Italy the inflationary erosion of the debt after the Second World War was much more dramatic than in the US. From 1945 to 1947 the debt plummeted from 91 to 24 percent of DGP, thanks mainly to the doubling of prices.

An implicit assumption here, shared by Cary Brown, is that inflation was largely unanticipated and not incorporated in nominal interest rates. Otherwise it would make little sense to split the growth of the debt into the portion generated by the total deficit, including interest payments, and the portion due to the change in prices. My impression is that this assumption, although perhaps extreme, is largely warranted except in the very recent past.

Figures 8B.2 and 8B.3 display inflation and the yield on long-term government securities in the US and Italy. What is striking is that until the 1960s nominal interest rates are virtually a flat line, rarely diverging from their normal values by more than 1 or 2 points. The fluctuations in inflation meanwhile are very large, often 10 or 20 points away from the mean and in some cases the divergence is sustained for years at a time.

In the US the two major outbreaks of inflation, the first of which lasted five years (1916–20), were accompanied by little or no change in interest rates. In the case of Italy, interest rates held virtually constant from 1880 to 1960, oscillating around 5 percent, rarely moving below 3.5 or above 6

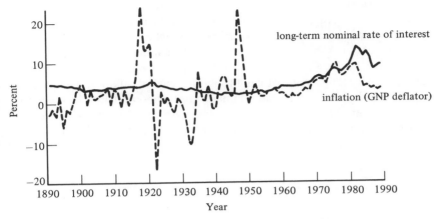

Figure 8B.2   United States: interest rates and inflation, 1980–89

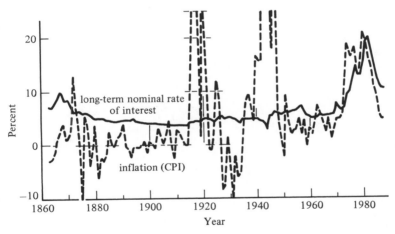

Figure 8B.3   Italy: interest rates and inflation, 1863–1988

percent. Interestingly, the high interest rates of the 1860s were not associated with high inflation. The lira was not depreciating in terms of goods and services, but against foreign currencies and, after the declaration of inconvertibility in 1866, against gold.

The mid-1960s appear to mark a watershed in investor perceptions and behaviour. The market is no longer content to have nominal interest rates hover around 5 percent, plus or minus a point. Inflationary expectations have come to play a major role. We have no convincing explanation why this has happened, nor is it very satisfactory to describe the change, as is often done, simply as the increased 'sophistication' of the average investor. For the average holder of financial wealth is perhaps less sophisticated today than at the turn of the century, when a large portion of the Italian debt was held by a single, highly sophisticated family. More persuasive is the thesis that the recent inflationary episode has been exceptionally long, in historical terms. The level of inflation has not been terribly high, but exponential cumulation of even moderate losses for 10 or more years has probably not left investors indifferent. Whatever the reason, it is clear that this change in attitude is at the heart of debt problems today.

9   The Italian national debt conversion of 1906

MARCELLO de CECCO

1   Introduction

Reducing the weight of interest charges on the public debt is an urgent and declared target of many governments in developing countries, but also in developed ones like Italy. The growth of public debt is now almost exclusively due to the inertial requirements of debt service. The structure of public debt today is very different, and its life expectancy much shorter, than used to be the case before the First World War or even in the interwar period. Nevertheless, it might perhaps be instructive to recall to memory a traditional instrument of debt service reduction, conversion. For this purpose this paper analyses the Italian debt conversion operation of 1906, an important episode in pre-1914 Italian financial history. An attempt is made to place it within the context of the international monetary and financial history of the period, and to study the significance of the operation for both the national and international financial markets. As in the case of other large debt conversions of the period, the Italian conversion can be said to have concluded an age, the age of low interest rates, and it came just before the international financial crisis of 1907 really brought the prewar international financial era to a close.

After a paragraph devoted to reminding modern readers of the main features of a conversion, the paper goes on to describe the Italian conversion operation in some detail. Explanations are offered of its timing and its essential technical features, and a few comparisons are made with similar operations conducted in other countries in the same and earlier periods. The conversion of 1906 is then compared to that effected by Fascist Italy after the First World War.

2   Conversion operations before 1914

In the nineteenth century and up to the First World War national debt consisted, in the main countries, mostly of Consolidated Bonds, which had an indefinite life span but were nonetheless issued by borrowing governments at fixed interest rates.[1] It was precisely the indefinite duration of the loan and its fixed interest coupon which gave juridical justification to this particular right offered to governments. Governments, like other debtors, had the right to repay their debts whenever they wanted to, before their maturity, provided no loss of capital or interest be suffered by creditors. The essential feature of a conversion, accordingly, was the freedom offered by the debtor government to its creditors to get their capital back and to lend the principal again to the same government on the new terms the latter had seen fit to offer. In modern parlance, a conversion can be described as a call option open at all times to the borrower. A conversion operation was launched by a government, of course, only if it had a clear expectation that most of its creditors were likely to convert their old bonds into the new ones the government was issuing. And it was started only if a considerable decrease of interest changes could be obtained. However, given the fact that the bonds involved were Consols of indefinite duration, even a small annual saving of interest could add up, over many decades, to quite remarkable amounts.

To our post-inflationary mentality all this looks irrelevant. Modern governments ever since the great inflations of the 1920s have often resorted to cancelling the real value of their debt by price rises engineered through appropriate monetary policies. This was not, however, the attitude taken by governments and public opinion in the great bourgeois age, the nineteenth century. Governments were supposed, in civilized countries at least, to honour their debts and refrain from inflation. A reduction in interest charges obtained through a conversion operation was, together with the largely illusory and cumbersome device of the Sinking Fund, the only way of reducing the burden of debt in a non-confiscatory fashion.

Conversions were a favoured device of the British Treasury ever since it had developed and brought to perfection the instrument of National Debt. Between 1717 and 1914 there were no fewer than 11 major debt conversions. The French Treasury also used the device repeatedly, although not nearly so often as its British counterpart. The practice also spread from the centre to the periphery. In the closing decades of the pre-World War One period several modernising countries undertook debt conversions.

The prerequisites for a successful conversion were an established falling trend in world interest rates, a stabilized situation in the national accounts, and exchange rate stability for the country concerned. It was also considered to be important that the bonds to be converted were above par, and looked like staying that way for a reasonable time.

Contemporary financial economists gave long descriptions of the details of conversion operations, from which it is possible to discern that remarkable technical ingenuity was displayed in the various instances. A conversion had to appear as much as possible an affair among equals. The government had to induce its creditors to reinvest in its bonds by making the conversion convenient for them. In an age of great freedom of capital movement, as the pre-1914 decades certainly were, investors could choose among literally dozens of different state bonds, and a botched conversion could mean that a good part of the creditors might not easily come back to a government that had once let them down. A successful conversion, therefore, depended vitally on the existence of a semi-captive market for national debt among the non-cosmopolitan bourgeoisie of the country in question. The more the debt was held by nationals and scattered among many final investors, the more easily a conversion would be successful from the purely financial point of view. Of course, citizens who thought that their government had done them down by a too clever conversion would be likely to take their revenge at the next election. But if the national debt was to a large extent in the hands of foreign financial intermediaries, one would be sure that the government would not be allowed much saving of interest charges, if it attempted a conversion. And it was certainly considered prudent by contemporary observers that governments conduct a conversion operation with the approval and open backing of major international financial intermediaries.

It would take too long to list all the different features exhibited by various conversions. It will be enough to say that, according to the judgements of the governments involved about the circumstances of the conversion, creditors were given a greater or smaller share of the capital gain showing on their bonds on the stock exchanges, under the form of a greater or smaller differential between the interest rate corresponding to the present quotation of the bond to be converted and the interest rate offered on the new bond. No government would dare to offer an interest rate exactly equal to that corresponding to the present quotation of the bond. It had to be higher, not to incur the wrath of creditors. The differential could be reduced by other devices, like a capital 'prize' or a two-stage interest reduction, the second stage to occur several years after the first (from 3 to $2\frac{3}{4}$% from 1888 to 1903 and to $2\frac{1}{2}$% from 1903 to 1923, in the case of the Goschen conversion in Britain). And the government could undertake not to subject the same consols to further conversions in the future.

When a conversion was announced, the bonds to be converted were usually above par on the market. The conversion meant that holders could either get their money back *at par* from the state, or convert into the new bonds offered. Some holders tried to cash in their accrued capital gain by immediately selling ahead of conversion. This attempt depressed the price of the bonds to be converted, by increasing their supply on the market. In this way the conversion was not wholly an affair among equals. The state could, by announcing the conversion, deprive bond holders of their accrued capital gains. As was just said, the game was to find the interest rate which, added to other *una tantum* benefits, would maximize the yield to the state from the conversion and minimize the risk of an investors' strike.

3   The Italian debt

Heavy fiscal pressure and a huge national debt were the two birthmarks of the new Kingdom of Italy.[2] The new country was united by a hegemon, Piedmont, which had relied on all means available to it to finance its modernization process and a military policy which allowed it to conquer the rest of the Italian peninsula. The main problem of the Italian modernization process was its financing. It was not that the country was lacking in financial resources. What it really lacked were institutions strong and reliable enough to perform the role of intermediaries between Italian financial resources, which were mostly in the hands of the relics of what had in previous centuries been the most powerful and cosmopolitan European commercial bourgeoisie, and the end-users, infrastructure builders and industrialists, who were not particularly credible in the eyes of Italian capitalists. The latter had for centuries been used to placing their resources completely freely in the whole world and to using the best European bankers as their bankers. It was clear that the role of intermediary had to be played by the state, which would have been required to enter directly into debt, and then to use the resources obtained to build industries and infrastructures or to lend resources to banks which would then lend them on to private industrialists.

Prior to unification, Northern Italy had *de facto* been integrated with France, while the Bourbon Kingdom was within the British financial and economic orbit. Piedmontese hegemony in the new Kingdom meant that French economic and financial links would prevail, and in fact Italy in 1865 became a founding member of the Latin Monetary Union, to which it faithfully adhered until it was dissolved after the First World War. French economic and financial predominance was seen by the Italian ruling elite with ambivalent feelings, as it had immediate and often unwelcome repercussions on foreign policy. The Italian leadership therefore tried until the First World War and even after it, to perform a delicate balancing act between the natural regional hegemon, France, the rising

European great power, Germany, and the world hegemon, Britain. This balancing act had to face obvious difficulties, which emerged from the hard facts of the financial world, which saw France as the almost exclusive source of finance for sovereign borrowers in Europe. If we examine the financial investments of Britain in the whole pre-war period, we see that it specialized in private finance and in non-European sovereign loans, while Germany relied much more on direct investment than it did on portfolio placements. It was only the French who were prepared to purchase political hegemony over Europe with their savings.[3] And the other hard fact was that the French branch of the House of Rothschild, which was by far the predominant power in sovereign finance, had tacitly agreed with their English branch that the latter would look after the rest of the world, while the former took care of Europe. The French Rothschilds had been bankers to the Bourbon Kings and to Cavour. The latter had tried to diversify his sources of finance, by having close relations with Carl Joachim Hambro. But the *basso continuo* of Italian state finance was to remain the French branch of the House of Rothschild, especially after the death of Cavour had put an end to the special relationship with Hambro. It was Rothschilds who made the market in Italian *rentes* in Paris, and who hosted in their house in the Rue Laffitte a permanent delegation from the Italian Treasury, which looked after the servicing of the Italian national debt held abroad.[4]

The services of the House of Rothschild were to be retained by the new Kingdom, when it appeared clear, soon after the lightning unification process, that the subjects of the new state had little intention of footing the bill for the rapid modernization the Italian leadership had planned. The previous states had all been fiscally lenient towards their subjects and the revolutionary governments which had preceded unification had purchased popularity with even greater fiscal leniency. Piedmont was the only exception and the Piedmontese leadership, which was to run the new country, decided to continue with its fiscal methods. Taxes, however, being difficult to exact from the people, modernization had to be financed through debt. The state budget, in the early 1860s, saw only fifty percent of expenditure covered by fiscal revenues.

It was thus decided to float huge state loans for the whole decade of the 1860s, taking advantage of the fact that the international financial market was undergoing one of its periodic booms. After a first attempt at financial 'independence', (which only meant that a different group of French financiers led by the Pereire brothers, the Rothschilds' *bête noire*, underwrote the first Italian state loan, in 1861), the indifferent results of the experiment brought the Italians back into the Rothschilds' lap, where they remained while the loan accumulation of the 1860s lasted. Italy had, at the beginning of the 1860s, decided to have a convertible currency, which seemed a reasonable course for a country which intended to rely heavily on the international financial market.[5] However, the reasons of history had prevailed and dictated that the country adopt the bimetallic system which Piedmont had adopted in Napoleonic times and kept ever since. The pressure of state expenditure and the chronic scantiness of revenues had soon made it impossible to continue with convertibility, especially because the war of 1866 had coincided with the outbreak of the Overend and Gurney crisis in London and the end of the boom in foreign loans on European financial markets. In the six years that the boom had lasted, however, Italy had managed to pile up what could be considered as a very considerable foreign debt, starting from a position of low indebtedness inherited from the pre-unity states. A large part of the debt had been placed in foreign hands, mostly in France. This large foreign debt was to become the bane of the Italian political and economic authorities, and the conversion operation of 1906 was intended also as a celebration of the fact that less than ten percent of Italian debt was left in foreign hands, after a decade of continuous repurchases.[6]

The fact that so much Italian debt was in foreign hands, though continually deprecated by the Italian national leadership, did not prevent the same from moving further into debt, when the international financial market started another of its periodic booms, in the 1880s. The Italians, early in the decade, decided to return to the convertibility they had had to abandon in 1866. This experiment was a rather complicated one, because the international financial atmosphere was right but the political one was not. While entertaining serious pourparlers with the French Rothschilds on the terms of the proposed loan, the Italian government, under the leadership of Agostino Depretis, decided to join the Triple Alliance, thus slapping its traditional ally, France, in the face. It was not very difficult to imagine that, after that, the Rothschilds would want out, as they did. Their place was taken by British finance. The Houses of Hambro and Baring underwrote the operation, which was not officially quoted in Paris, but in which some French financial houses participated. Soon after the flotation it was found that the loan could be sold only with difficulty, as the only serious market for Italian state bonds was in Paris. The help of German banks had to be sought and obtained, and henceforward it had very often to be resorted to, to support the value of the Italian debt on the international market, after the French had declared what in the end amounted to more than ten years of economic warfare against Italy.[7]

4   Overseas debt

The knowledge that we have today of capital flight from developing countries is very helpful in understanding Italian financial history in the first fifty years of Italian unity. Having considerable financial resources in the hands of its citizens but not enough monetary and exchange stability and no credible financial intermediaries, Italy discovered to its cost the meaning of the words 'international arbitrage'. When the price of Italian state bonds fell on the Paris market, it became convenient to export bonds back to Italy, where the quotation was higher, to sell them there. This was done by Italians, and in doing so they exported capital and lowered the exchange rate of the lira. The same happened if the exchange rate was high. When the lira was inconvertible, on the other hand, Italian citizens would demand that their bonds be paid in Paris, in gold Francs, by exporting the bonds. Against this movement, which depleted Italian reserves, the government had repeatedly to resort to the *Affadavit*, a form of exchange control which was reasonably effective in stemming the outflow of Italian bonds.[8]

The Italian experiments in convertibility were traumatic and short-lived. They were undone especially by the overhang of Italian public debt in foreign hands, or in the hands of Italian citizens pretending to be foreigners in order to enjoy the privilege of being paid interest in gold currency.

5   The Italian balance of payments

By the early 1890s, when the era of low world interest rates came to a close, the Italian national debt had reached a very considerable level. Italy's national income was still very far from that of other developed European countries, and income per head was even further below theirs. Debt per head, on the other hand, was almost as high in Italy as it as in France and Britain, and higher than in Germany or Austria-Hungary. Debt servicing, moreover, involved annually a very high share of total Italian public expenditure. After military expenditure was considered, a very small amount indeed was left to provide for the other tasks of the state, such as health, education, promotion of industry, etc. (see Tables 9.1, 9.2 and 9.3).

The international crisis of 1893, which reverberated in Italy with extremely grave repercussions, marked a watershed for Italian finances, bringing to a close a decade of overvaluation, increasing foreign indebtedness and banking scandals and also terminating the second Italian experience of convertibility. As on previous occasions, the Italian financial crisis

	1891 (million It. Lire)	1904	Difference
Germany	12,699	17,642	+4,943
Great Britain	16,942	19,959	+3,017
Austria–Hungary	12,188	14,921	+2,733
France (Consols only)	25,985	26,066	+81
Italy	12,765	12,731	−34
Russia	12,745	17,678	+4,933

Table 9.1. Public debt in various countries in 1891 and 1904

Source: Flora (1905) p. 8, note 2.

	Revenues (million It. Lire)	Interest charges	%
France	3,528	1,180	33.45
Russia	4,673	736	15.77
Great Britain	3,543	585	16.51
Germany	6,418	705	10.98
Austria–Hungary	3,149	643	20.41
Italy	1,702	575	33.77

Table 9.2. Public revenues and debt service in various countries in 1902

Source: Flora (1905) p. 9, note 1.

	1893	1899	1903
Germany	n.a.	26.92	25.01
Italy	48.40	52.98	58.08
France	65.13	89.85	61.05
Russia	58.41	43.07	32.40
Great Britain	62.91	69.91	64.19
United States	23.91	40.09	34.74
Japan	49.98	58.42	48.06

Table 9.3. Military expenditure as a percentage of total public expenditure in various countries, 1893–1903

Source: Zahn (1906).

1875	32	1883	51	1891	73	1899	28
1876	35	1884	28	1892	73	1900	25
1877	35	1885	45	1893	83	1901	23
1878	37	1886	49	1894	85	1902	22
1879	38	1887	53	1895	34	1903	18
1880	38	1888	67	1896	32		
1881	37	1889	69	1897	29		
1882	32	1890	68	1898	29		

Table 9.4. Percentage of interest on the Italian public debt paid abroad, 1875–1903

Source: de Johannis (1904).

was brought to a head by an international crisis. But the decade which began in 1895 saw a very remarkable case of radical financial reconstruction, which was facilitated by international cyclical movements, but did not follow what was happening at the same time to the public finances of other major European countries.

The *deus ex machina* of Italian financial reconstruction was emigrants' remittances and income from tourism (see Table 9.5). The former were rendered possible by the insatiable demand for emigrants generated by the Transatlantic economies. Millions of Italian peasants emigrated to North and South America in that decade, and began to send back a veritable torrent of convertible currencies. As to the latter, Italy enjoyed with France a first-comer position in world tourism and benefited from this fast-growing activity of the middle classes of prosperous countries. Taken together these two items (see Table 9.5) came in the two decades before the First World War to cover more than fifty percent of Italian imports, thus allowing the country to participate in the world economic boom without experiencing the balance of payments crises which had been so frequent in previous decades. Imports of essential raw materials, food and investment goods were allowed to grow unfettered, as the bill was footed by invisible exports. And the permanent undervaluation of Italian state bonds in Paris which took place in the same period induced Italians to practice once again their old game of repurchasing the debt (see Table 9.4). This time, however, the results were virtuous, as the foreign debt overhang radically decreased, and the exchange rate was prevented from rising to uncomfortable heights, as it would otherwise have done because of large invisible exports and emigrants' remittances. It did, however, occasionally rise above par, amidst the surprised

Five-year averages, million current lire

	Visible trade		Service income	Emigrants' remittances			
	Imports	Exports					
	(1)	(2)	(3)	(4)	(3 + 4)	(4/1) %	(3 + 4/2) %
1861–65	565	864	99	21	120	4	14
1866–70	738	858	140	52	192	7	22
1871–75	1,078	1,137	184	73	257	7	23
1876–80	1,075	1,151	208	114	322	11	28
1881–85	1,105	1,260	252	144	396	13	31
1886–90	956	1,324	307	187	494	20	37
1891–95	977	1,101	329	254	583	26	53
1896–1900	1,230	1,310	364	347	711	28	54
1901–05	1,524	1,744	450	691	1,141	45	65
1906–10	1,908	2,808	650	846	1,496	44	53
1911–15	2,299	3,145	782	858	1,640	37	52

Table 9.5. The Italian balance of payments, 1861–1915
Source: ISTAT (1957).

admiration of Italians and foreigners alike, who well remembered the evils of a very recent past (see Table 9.2).

6   The Italian debt, 1893–1905

I have said that Italy, in this period, did not imitate the policies of other European countries. This is particularly true for what concerns the fiscal stance of the government. With a policy of very strict austerity coupled to a radical reform of the banking system, it was able to redress the internal balance completely and achieve that great Victorian dream, a balanced budget, for several years. There was, as a result, no more need to increase the national debt. Between 1983 and 1905, the Italian national debt remained virtually stable, while other European countries increased their public debt very considerably. This was particularly true of Britain and France, as appears clearly from Table 9.1.

Throughout the 19th century, Italian public debt had always been considered a rather unsafe, very speculative, high yield financial invest-ment.[9] The fact that it was very speculative is shown by its oscillations, which are depicted in Figure 9.1. The highs remain very distant from the lows for a long time, but begin to converge in the final years of the century and in the first ten years of the new century.

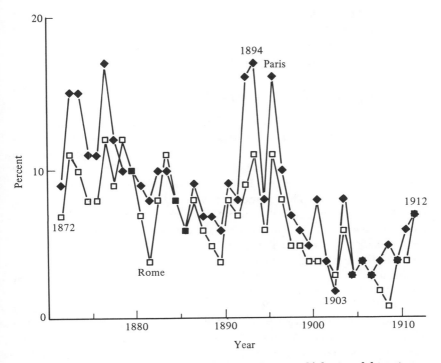

Figure 9.1 Italian 5% consols: % differences between highest and lowest quotations, 1872–1912.

Source: Author's calculations based on data provided in *Annuario Statistico Italiano*, various issues.

When the age of low interest rates came to a close, in the early 1890s, a new and interesting phenomenon began to be noticed. The national debt of the richest and most solid countries, like Britain, France and Germany, started on a steady and considerable decline in capital values, thus reversing the opposite movement which had taken place throughout the 'great depression' decades. The decrease in interest rates which had occurred in those years had prompted several major countries to go in for large conversion operations. The largest had been that brought about by Lord Goschen on the British debt in 1888, which was supposed, rather curiously, to take effect beginning in 1903.

After 1895, however, while the capital values of prime state bonds began to decline, the opposite started to occur to more speculative, lower-grade state bonds. The flight to quality of the previous twenty years, prompted by the decline in prices, industrial profits and dividends, and private and state bankruptcies, became a flight to yield, as prices, profits and dividends rose, and investors' bad memories receded into the background. The Italian *rentes* were among the state securities which benefited from this movement. They rose solidly after 1897, and reached values well above par.

7   Italian conversions before 1906

Ever since the beginning of Italy's financial reconstruction, the Italian economic authorities had begun to contemplate the possibility of converting the national debt. They were following the example of major European countries. In 1888, in fact, Lord Goschen, then Chancellor of the Exchequer, had converted the British consolidated debt, with a two-stage reduction of interest. The second stage was to take place in 1903, bringing the interest rate down to 2.5%. In 1902 the French national debt as converted by Rouvier, then Minister of Finance, with an operation which had not been considered particularly brilliant, as the price of French consols was not even above par and French state accounts were still in the red. Both the British and French conversions had been prompted by the fall in interest rates (the French were late, as rates had already started climbing when they launched their conversion). Both could not on any account be considered great successes. The price of French consols fell considerably after the operation, and the second stage of the British operation came soon after the end of the Boer War, which had forced the Exchequer to go to the market for new funds, thus causing British Consols to fall even as low as 87. Some contemporary observers thought that it had been the declared intention of the financial authorities in major countries to reduce interest charges on their debt that had made the latter's values fall on the stock exchanges and those of lesser countries, which had a higher coupon, to rise. As to Italy, the government had been authorized by Parliament as early as 1895 to convert the Italian debt on terms which had not been considered realistic by the financial authorities. In an article written in the *Corriere della Sera* in December 1897, Luigi Einaudi had advised against an early conversion, reminding the authorities of the fact that their debt was not to be compared to the British of French debt. It was still not properly *classé* – he noted – and therefore still too much entrusted to the hands and whim of national and international speculators. Italian state securities were thus subject to deep oscillations on both national and foreign exchanges. Italy could not yet behave as a developed country. It had to wait until cicumstances were more favourable.

The Italian authorities officially kept their peace for several years. (A sort of conversion of the debt, 'by stealth', or 'forced' according to contemporary writers, had already occurred anyway, when the Italian government had been repeatedly compelled by the imperative of fiscal necessity to impose a tax on national debt coupons which, in 1894, had been lifted to 20%).

Secret diplomacy, however, started moving in the direction of conversion once good relations with France were reestablished, in the last years of the century. Italian statesmen realized that financial reconstruction would not be possible without the previous assurance of French financial neutrality or assistance. This was sought and obtained especially by Luigi Luzzatti, who was notoriously a francophile. He wanted to be considered the 'father' of the conversion operation, whose happy conclusion was in the end to be snatched from him by one of the classic Italian government crises. In his memoirs he therefore went to great pains to document that he had himself done most of the preparatory work, which had culminated in the passing of the Law of 12 June 1902, No. 166, which created a new 3.5% consolidated bond with the aim of converting redeemable securities, mainly state railway bonds which had been floated in the course of the early decades of Italian unity. This was intended to be little more than a 'ballon d'essai conversion' because most of the securities involved were in the hands of Italian para-governmental institutions. There remained only 262 million, out of a total of 1,356 million lire, which were really open to conversion. The fall of the government brought to the Treasury ministry an obscure Northern MP, Di Broglio, who by his incompetence managed to botch an operation which had been considered almost risk-free. In order to appear as someone who tried to save public money, Di Broglio cancelled an already concluded deal with a powerful syndicate, led by the Bank of Italy and the French Rothschilds, and including the major Italian banks, which had offered to underwrite 75 million of the new consols at 94, and gave the loan, but only for 30 million, to a doubtful group of small speculators and minor banks, who had offered a price of 96. They were unable to support the issue when it was launched, and its poor performance on the stock exchange led questions to be asked in Pariament, which were answered by Di Broglio by slandering the name of Bonaldo Stringher, Director General of the Bank of Italy. The latter in the end was persuaded to rescue the issue by purchasing the remaining 45 million at 96.

This rather unsavoury episode was not the best prelude to the following operation, which Luigi Luzzatti, back in the government, managed to launch in December, 1903. This involved a capital of 1,356 million lire, equivalent to a coupon of 61 million, at 4.5%, to be converted into 3.5% bonds. Again, it was little more than an anticipation of the real conversion, because more than $\frac{4}{5}$ of the bonds involved were owned by para-governmental institutions which were compelled to convert them. But the remaining bonds were freely converted and the operation was declared a success. Italian state bonds did not follow other state securities in the fall induced by the Boer crisis.

8   The 1906 conversion

Time was thus ripe for the real conversion, which involved the Italian 5% consols. There were more than 8 billion lire of these, making the operation the largest since the Goschen conversion of 1888–1903, and overtaking the Rouvier conversion of 1902. The new Giolitti cabinet accordingly set out to launch the operation in December 1903, but the outbreak of the Russian–Japanese War, and the international financial crisis it unleashed, convinced the government that it should be postponed. Financial disturbances had involved particularly the French market, as France had notoriously financed the Russian state budget for over a decade, and only the utmost effort on the part of the *Haute Banque* stopped the fall on the bourse from becoming a rout. The French market was also the place where the deepest repercussions would have been felt of any operation on Italian state debt, as the French were supposed to hold about 400 million lire of it, having purchased it heavily from the Germans after the Franco–Italian political rapprochement. The Far Eastern War was followed by revolution in Russia, and by the Conference of Algeciras, where Germany was politically isolated. All these events were certainly unfavourable to the launching of a giant operation like the Italian one, which would have required the unanimous agreement of European political and financial circles. German and British financial houses in fact had enough Italian bonds in their hands to disrupt any operation launched without their consent. A mass conversion from abroad would again have depressed the lira exchange rate, which had behaved favourably in the previous five years.[10]

There was a certain amount of debate on how the giant conversion ought to be conducted. It was pointed out, first of all, that only half the debt subject to conversion consisted of bearer bonds, the other half being made up of bonds in individual names. Half of the latter was, moreover, 'tied up' in wills and trusts; the Bank of Italy held 129 million, and the *Cassa Depositi e Prestiti* held 290 million; about 700 million was held abroad. Of the 3,347 million in bearer bonds, 543 million was in the hands of Italian financial institutions. Only 2,804 million was in the hands of the public. It must also be said that, in the previous ten years, ownership of government securities had spread to the lower classes, as emigrants' savings had been invested in Consols. And from these nonspeculative holders no massive requests for reimbursement were to be expected, unless the conversion terms were openly confiscatory. These details made the conversion operation appear less difficult than it would have seemed at first sight. Still, when the Russian–Japanese War had broken out, in February 1904, the Italian 5% had slumped from 102 to 92. It would have been a delicate affair.

It is therefore understandable that, with 10% of the Consols still in foreign hands, the Italian authorities exercised utmost care in securing the international financial community's support for the operation, and did the same with respect to the Italian financial community, as about 20% of bearer bonds were in its hands. Their approach was to encourage the formation of two syndicates, one of domestic, the other of foreign, bankers, to underwrite the operation. There was some talk about staggering the operation in two halves, one involving the bearer bonds, the other the 'nominative' bonds.[11] In the end that solution was discarded and the operation was launched in a single instalment. Some thought was also given to another type of staggering, more usual in conversion operations conducted in other countries. This involved reducing the interest rate in two instalments, encompassing the second one to occur five years after the first. This solution was in the end adopted, the net interest rate going from 4 to 3.75% immediately and to 3.5% after five years. Also adopted was the device of guaranteeing that the Consols converted would not be converted again for fifteen years. This was a bet on future interest rates, which could have been lost, but was in fact won by the government. They were severely reproached from the left, as having in fact, by their conversion, put a solid floor under both the capital values and the yield of Italian state debt, rescuing the rentier from his expected euthanasia. When the conversion operation was accomplished, in June 1906, interest rates were depressed, and Italian state bonds yielded some two points more than savings deposits or prime state bonds. The Italian authorities, however, expected a firmer market for the future and they were proved right.

A few details of the operation might be of interest. First of all, its lightning rapidity. It took the government only a few hours between the introduction and the approval of the Conversion Law in Parliament. This was an all time record, compared to the several days similar operations had required in France and Britain. It was done to prevent speculation, of course, which would have exploited any delays. Rather unfavourable comments were written about the very short conversion period the public was allowed: only six days. It was again a world record. The international syndicate which was formed to guarantee the foreign part of the conversion was in fact, after long and complex negotiations with Rothschilds, reduced in its status. On March 28, 1906 Bonaldo Stringher met with Edmond de Rothschild in Mentone to negotiate the terms of the foreign syndication of the operation. The French financier told him that his House was well disposed towards the proposed deal, but that any Italian operation would have had to wait until the Paris market was clear of a massive Russian debt operation which was awaiting only the conclusion of the Algeciras Conference to be launched, and French elections were out of the way. This procrastination on the part of Rothschilds also proved useful to the Italian side, as the Sonnino Cabinet, which had been conducting negotiations, fell after only three months of life. The new Giolitti Cabinet continued negotiations in Paris as of June 14th, sending Stringher as its plenipotentiary representative. The two sides had different views as to the length of time the converted debt was to yield 3.75%. The international financial syndicate wanted it to be at least eight years. They also offered rather stringent terms to stand by the operation. First of all they only offered their guarantee for the conversion period, and refused to support the debt price after it ended. Second, they offered to compute both the bonds reimbursed and those repurchased during the conversion period at par, thus guaranteeing the Italian Treasury only against the possibility that the bonds fell below par. Third, they demanded a hefty banking commission, of about 2.5%, as the price of their guarantee. These conditions were judged too onerous by Stringher and the Italian government, who decided that the Treasury might take the chance of going it alone, as they could rely on sufficient reserves to support Italian bond prices abroad and on a large post-conversion institutional demand for bonds at home. They thus agreed with the international banking consortium, on June 26th, that the latter would act simply as an agent of the Italian Treasury, buying up whatever bonds were presented for redemption on its behalf. The Consortium undertook to make available a total of 400 million lire to be able to face up to all possible redemption requests abroad and to support Italian bond prices on European stock exchanges during the conversion period. The Italian Treasury has one year to repay the Consortium any sums it might have invested for reimbursements and open market purchases, and would pay a 4% interest rate on the sums advanced until January 1st, 1907, and 3.75% afterwards. A fee of 1% on the 400 million was granted to the Consortium. This assured the Italian Treasury that the Consortium would try to spend as little as possible of the sum made available on market purchases and redemptions, to make the most of the 4 million lire it was to get anyway, thus making it the price of its 'moral support' for the operation.

The Consortium also acquired the right to exercise its option on all the bonds it had withdrawn from the market or which had been redeemed during the period of conversion within one month from the end of the conversion period, at the price they had actually paid for them, minus one per cent as banking commission. In this way the Treasury hoped to induce the Consortium to keep bond prices high, as the Consortium had also agreed to exercise its option first on the bonds it had purchased above par and only afterwards on those it had repurchased at par.

If the Consortium renounced its option, the bonds they had repurchased would be sold by the Treasury on terms such as not to perturb markets, and the Consortium would receive a banking commission of only one-eighth of one percent on the sums effectively disbursed.

The Italian Consortium was headed by the Bank of Italy and included most Italian credit institutions. They agreed to convert the whole of the 5% bonds they owned. The Italian banks received commissions fixed at approximately fifty percent of the those agreed with the international Consortium.

Having established these two powerful safety nets, the Italian government benefitting from a good deal of luck, which made the conversion period and those immediately preceding and following it devoid of grave international crises, managed to finish the operation with complete success. Only three million lire worth of bonds were redeemed abroad, most of them in London, and only 700,000 lire in Italy. In addition, only 48 million were repurchased during the conversion period, of which 32 million were in Italy and only 16.5 million abroad. The total cost of the operation was a little more than 9 million lire, of which one million was given to Rothschilds to pay for notices in the international, and especially the French press. It was considered a reasonable price, at a time when the Russian Treasury had given the French press very bad habits.

9   The benefits from conversion

What did the Italian Treasury gain from the conversion? Apart from the obvious prestige accruing from the successful completion of the giant deal, concluded, as we have seen, without a full international guarantee, the actual savings from the conversion amounted to about 20 million lire a year in reduced interest loan the debt, which would become 40 million after January 1st, 1912. The staggered conversion ran the risk of a fall in the new bonds below par, if interest rates had risen in 1912 when the Consols' interest would be reduced from 3.75 to 3.5%. This had in fact happened to the second round of the Goschen conversion which had coincided with the Boer War financial requirements. On the other hand, the Rouvier conversion, done in one go, had caused an immediate fall of the new bond price below par, as the rentiers had pocketed the premium which went with the conversion and sold their bonds on the market immediately afterwards. The Italian conversion did not give any actual premium to the rentiers. It gave them a loyalty price of 0.25% a year for five years, at a cost to the Treasury of 100 million lire in missed interest savings relative to a one-step reduction to 3.5%. As we said above, it was a bet on the future. Rentiers also received a bonus, in the form of a guaranteed period of nonconvertibility for the new Consols, which extended to 1921. It was a floor placed under interest rates, as Filippo Turati, the socialist parliamentarian, was quick to remark. In 1912, moreover, the second instalment of the operation, with the decline of the Consols' interest rate to 3.5%, contributed to a decline of their price below par. Times had changed since 1906. A great European war looked more probable every day. The Italian government had itself gone in for colonial warfare. The exchange rate of the lira again showed a discount against gold. Up to 1911, however, the price of Italian Consols remained above par. It withstood very well the international financial crisis of 1907, jumping back to 105 in Paris in 1908, even above the Italian quotation (average price for the whole year). It also withstood quite well the return of the Italian budget to deficit, which had more or less coincided with the operation. Turati's fear, that the Italian rentier would be saved from his inevitable enthanasia, proved to be unfounded, because world interest rates kept edging up after 1906.

10   Comparisons with other countries

The relative merits of the 1906 conversion can be judged by comparing it to similar operations conducted in other countries in approximately the same period. This we have done, rather sketchily, in the previous pages, using examples from British and French financial history. The Italian conversion comes out rather well from these comparisons with the blue blood of world finance. It would compare even better with equivalent operations conducted by lesser countries, like Russia, the Austro-Hungarian Empire, Portugal and Spain. The Italian authorities' ambition to convey, by the conversion, the message that the financial reconstruction of Italy had been successfully concluded, was, however, thwarted by the immediately following financial history of the country. As noted already, internal balance was again lost, the Italian debt went below par at home and in Paris, and the exchange rate of the lira also dipped below par. Unlike other developed countries, Italy never fully recovered, before 1914, from the 1907 crisis. The Italian debt recovered until 1911, but the main economic indicators did not. The 1906 conversion, therefore, concluded a brief era of financial reconstruction but did not lay durable foundations of public financial strength. Taken as just a way of saving the state a considerable amount of interest payments, however, it was a greater success than several similar experiments conducted elsewhere. And it was concluded without the least perturbation of national and international financial markets, as witnessed by the fact that the 1907 crisis was brilliantly overcome by the Italian debt, if not by the Italian economy. Because of its very success, however, the conversion did not induce any funds to be shifted from the state bonds to private debt and ordinary industrial shares. The Italian public remained firmly anchored to a portfolio almost exclusively composed of gilts.

11   Comparisons with the 1920s conversions

The 1906 conversion also compares very well with the perhaps better known conversions brought about after the First World War. This comparison is, however, slightly unfair. The 1906 conversion was conducted in the most favourable period of contemporary Italian economic history before the 1906s, after 40 years of European peace. It was designed and executed in the nearest thing Italy has ever had to equilibrium conditions in all the main economic variables. The international financial market, compared to what it was to become in the 1920s, was also a much more orderly place, even if it was suffering from the impact of the Russian–Japanese war and of the Russian revolution of 1905. At the end of the First World War, the only index which compared favourably with the pre-war period was the Italian debt–GNP ratio, which had remained approximately unchanged, while it had grown enormously in countries like Britain and France. This favourable comparison revealed its cosmetic nature soon after peace was concluded, when the foreign loans which had kept the Italian economy afloat stopped. The government had to issue an avalanche of floating debt, which it considered, with some reason, to be a better solution than the printing press, but which possessed almost no stability.[12] It was thus decided by Francesco Severio Nitti, professor of public finance and prime minister, to convert the floating debt. He declared his conversion – called the Sixth National Loan – a success, but it was at best a holding operation, because the national accounts were still very unbalanced and the floating debt had to be increased again soon after the conversion operation had concluded, in 1920. As a famous confidential Treasury Report written in 1940 on the Italian inter-war debt experience was to remark, the 1920 conversion had to be supported by massive market intervention, even while it was going on, and the conversion period had to be extended.

Not much greater luck was reserved to another two conversion operations launched by the Fascist government, in 1924 and 1926. They were to crown the radical improvement in Italian public finances obtained by the Fascists in the early phase of their regime, and the stabilization policy of 1926. The problem – as the quoted Treasury Report appropriately noted, was that both conversions, the voluntary one conducted by De Stefani in 1924 and the forced 'Prestito del Littorio' launched by Volpi di Misurata in 1926, were conducted in times of dear money, while a conversion, by definition, had to coincide with a relatively cheap money period. Another anomalous feature of the interwar conversions was that they were meant to consolidate the floating debt, while pre-war ones had been exchanges of Consols for Consols, or consolidations of redeemable debt mostly owned by para-governmental institutions which were compelled to convert. And, in any case, they were not floating bills, but long-dated securities. The two Fascist conversions amounted to a confiscation. Launched in times of high and rising interest rates, they induced a radical depression of the prices of gilt-edged securities, as their owners, who were largely entrepreneurs who had owned short-term state securities as temporary liquid placements, had to sell the Consols they had been forced into, to regain the liquidity they needed because of the credit squeeze.

It is perhaps useful just to reproduce the conclusions the Treasury Report of 1940 reached on these experiments:

4 to 5 billion lire were lost by the owners of the converted bills, plus about a billion lost by those who had panic-sold their long-dated gilts when their prices had slumped;

Enormous losses were experienced by the credit institutions, especially savings and loan associations, which held large amounts of gilts and whose balance sheets had to be brought back to a false normality by allowing their holdings of gilts to be valued at cost;

The state suffered a radical loss of credibility and could not issue Treasury Bills for almost ten years;

The whole stabilization programme failed, because the state was compelled, in the following period, to borrow heavily from the central bank, i.e. to monetize its deficit. The Treasury's account with the Bank of Italy went from a credit of 2.6 billion lire in March, 1926, to a debit of 688 million lire in December, 1926.

Moreover, having foreclosed himself from the Treasury Bill market by his botched conversion, Vittorio Volpi was compelled, in the following months, to expropriate various para-governmental institutions, like the Cassa Depositi e Prestiti, the municipalities of Rome and Milan, of their liquid assets, raising, even in those dictatorial times, heavy criticism in the not yet dissolved Parliament.

Pre-war Italian governments, when confronted with dear money, had preferred taxing heavily the coupon on gilt edged securities to converting them. The Nitti cabinet tried to do both (as its capital tax was soon reduced to no more than a tax on capital income), and failed. The Fascist Treasury ministers had to resort to even rougher methods. We have already mentioned Volpi's quasi-confiscation of the liquidity of public institutions. Alberto de' Stefani had tried in vain to channel private investors' funds away from industrial shares and into state securities by adopting punitive measures against share ownership, which deflated the stock exchange boom but did not induce people to buy gilts. They preferred to export capital and to buy real estate.

NOTES

This paper is a by-product of my collaboration with the Historial Research Department of the Bank of Italy. I am grateful to Valeria Sannucci and Massimo Roccas of the Bank of Italy, and to Francesco Asso, of the European University Institute, who were of great help to me. I would also like to thank Ignazio Visco, who made an important bibliographical item available to me. Usual disclaimers apply, however.

 1 Most of what I have learned about conversions, and about the Italian conversion in particular, comes from two very good contemporary essays on the subject. They are Polizio (1904) and Flora (1905). Both were written on the eve of the Italian conversion of 1906. A detailed account of the Italian conversion is given in a confidential Report written soon after the event by Bonaldo Stringher, Director General of the Bank of Italy, who had masterminded the operation, for the Italian Treasury Minister, A. Majorana. This Report, Stringher (1906) is in the Bank of Italy archives, and will be published, with other documents relating to Italian financial history, in a forthcoming volume edited by M. de Cecco, with the collaboration of M. Roccas, V. Sannucci and P.F. Asso.
 2 Usual references on these matters are Luzzatto (1963) and Confalonieri (1974), See also Sannucci (1989).
 3 Herbert Feis's interpretation (Feis, 1930) still stands. Recent literature has reiterated these main differences between major lending countries. See Eichengreen and Lindert (1989).
 4 On the role of the House of Rothschild in European and Italian finances, see Gille (1967).
 5 See Sannucci (1989).
 6 Almost no one among contemporary Italian writers took a non-nationalistic, free market view of foreign holdings of Italian state bonds.
 7 A very good contemporary account of the convertibility loan of 1882 is given by C. Rozenraad (1883), who was involved in the operation, in an article he wrote for the *Journal of the Institute of Bankers*.
 8 The *Affadavit* was a sworn declaration, to be made by the owners of Italian state bonds presented to Treasury agents abroad for coupon payment, that the bonds did not belong to Italian subjects. It was imposed and repealed several times between 1878 and 1904.
 9 James Rothschild, to a friend who asked his advice on Italian bonds, replied: 'If you want to eat badly and sleep well buy British Consols; if you want to eat well and sleep badly buy Italian bonds'. Quoted in Flora (1906).

10 Domenico Polzio, however, by an ingenious comparison of interest rate differentials and exchange rate movements in Berlin, Paris and London *vis-à-vis* Rome, showed that the arbitrage margin which opened up between Paris and Rome was immediately closed by transactions in Italian bonds, while it was not closed between Berlin and Rome or London and Rome. (See Polizio, 1904). It must be remembered, however, that the only large market for Italian bonds was in Paris.

11 The following account of the conversion borrows much from the Stringher Report to the Treasury Minister (1906).

12 An excellent account of the interwar history of the Italian public debt is contained in Confalonieri (1987), which also reproduces the 1940 Treasury Report.

REFERENCES

Confalonieri, A. (1974). *Banca e Industria in Italia.* Milano: Comit.

(1987). *Il Debito Pubblico in Italia.* Milano: CARIPLO.

de Johannis, A. (1904). *La Conversione della Rendita.* Firenze: Barbera.

Eichengreen, B. and P. Lindert (eds.) (1989). *The International Debt Problem in Historical Perspective.* Cambridge, MA: MIT Press.

Feis, Herbert (1930). *Europe, the World's Banker.* New York: Yale University Press.

Flora, F. (1905). *La Conversione della Rendita.* Milano: Società Editrice Libraria.

(1906). 'La Conversione del Consolidato Italiano', *Giornale degli Economisti* **40**, 71–89.

Gille, B. (1967). *Histoire de la Maison Rothschild.* Geneva: Libraire Droz.

ISTAT (1957). 'Indagine Statistica sullo Sviluppo del Reddito Nazionale dell'Italia dal 1861 al 1956', *Annali di Statistica, 1957.*

Luzzatto, G. (1963). *L'Economia Italiana dal 1861 al 1914.* Milano: Comit.

Polizio, D. (1904). *Sul Miglior Sistema di Conversione.* Napoli: Pierro.

Rozenraad, C. (1883). 'The Italian Convertibility Loan of 1882', *Journal of the Institute of Bankers.*

Sannucci, V. (1989). 'The Establishment of a Central Bank: Italy in the Nineteenth Century', in M. de Cecco and A. Giovannini (eds), *A European Central Bank?* Cambridge: Cambridge University Press.

Stringher, B. (1906). 'Rapporto al Ministro del Tesoro sulla Conversione della Rendita'. Roma: unpublished typescript.

Zahn, F. (1906). 'Les Finances des Grandes Puissances', *Revue Economique Internationale* **3**, 509–34.

Discussion

RICHARD PORTES

Marcello De Cecco tells a good story very well. There is no model, nor any underlying thesis, so a discussant cannot do much more than either add to the story or indicate that he profited from it, as I did. It might be seen as a religious tale of vice and virtue – it is basically Christian, culminating in a conversion, but the Rothschilds did get a share of the action, though they did not of course ever convert. They got shut out of the 1902 operation by the hapless Di Broglio, and they then procrastinated in 1906 and ultimately played only a minor role. Their main fee appears to have gone to paying to advertise the operation.

The new Kingdom of Italy started with heavy fiscal pressure and a 'huge' debt – 95% of GDP, rising to 115% fifteen years later, and peaking at 120% in 1895. These figures exceed even those which are causing so much concern today and may indeed make us wonder whether that concern is exaggerated. According to De Cecco, foreign debt was 'the bane of Italian political and economic authorities'. He should perhaps tell us why they found it such a burden; after all, they did not hesitate to borrow more abroad in the 1880s.

The paper tells an interesting story about capital flight, the repatriation of bonds, and the effect on the exchange rate. The 'repurchases' here are not buybacks by the state, but rather repatriation by private residents. From 1895 onwards, the circumstances were ideal. A flood of emigrants' remittances permitted financial reconstruction, and debt repatriation kept the exchange rate from appreciating. With fiscal austerity there were balanced budgets – with such virtue, who needs to convert? Perhaps it was because they had sinned with the tax on national debt coupons that was raised in 1894 – the motive is not obvious, because the budget was balanced from 1893 onwards.

It is also hard to understand why the 1906 conversion should deserve so much emphasis. It was an easy and successful operation with apparently little payoff. On the other hand, though it tried to signal the conclusion of the successful financial reconstruction of Italy, in fact the budget went into deficit immediately thereafter and the exchange rate fell. The interest saving appears to have been negligible, at 1–2% of total public revenues.

The postwar postscript is amusing. Francesco Saverio Nitti declared his conversion a success although it did not really eliminate the floating debt. Perhaps he should have tried total immersion.

Discussion

IGNAZIO VISCO

> . . . of all nations, Italy is the one that most needs to reduce the expense
> of servicing its National Debt. [. . .] When this expense – which amounts
> to approximately 575 million lire for the whole debt – was compared
> with the saving of 20 million lire in the first five years, the conversion
> [. . .] seemed, in the end, to be but a modest thing, and many, who only
> saw this, obstinately believed that, as in Shakespeare's comedy, there
> had been *Much Ado about Nothing*.
>
> Flora (1906), p. 89.

Professor De Cecco has produced yet another lively and instructive
reconstruction of an important and much quoted episode in Italian
financial history, albeit one only superficially investigated by economic
historians. There is still something to be learned, he claims, from recalling
what used to be, in the nineteenth century and in the first decades of the
twentieth, the major instrument available to governments for reducing the
weight of interest charges on National Debts, which were mostly in the
form of consolidated bonds (consols) with fixed coupons. Only by chance,
however, did the latter coincide with market interest rates, since the bonds
were seldom quoted at par. Governments, then, had the right to convert a
particular issue of consols with a given coupon into a new issue with a
lower coupon; the exchange between the two issues was generally at par
with creditors being given the right to choose between conversion or the
reimbursement of capital.

It must be observed that this instrument was only used when market
interest rates were steadily below the fixed interest paid on the consol, and
that governments usually coupled the conversion operation with some
incentive to discourage reimbursements of capital. These incentives were
in the form of a 'premium' on the price of the bonds, a stepwise interest
reduction, a promise of a long period of inconvertibility or some other
comparable technical device. The Italian National Debt conversion of
1906 was carried out without giving any premium to bond holders but
involved a two-step reduction in the net interest paid on the consols: from
4% to 3.75% in 1907 and to 3.5% five years later. Furthermore, a 15-year
period of inconvertibility was also granted. As De Cecco rightly observes,
the conversion was not only remarkable for the size of the operation, but
also highly successful when one considers its limited cost and the negligible amount of reimbursements.

There is no need to go further into the political and technical details of the operation. They are brilliantly described in Section 8 of De Cecco's paper and there is simply nothing to add to the picture, except perhaps to emphasize that in 1906 the Italian Public Debt was equal in size to 100% of national income, exactly as it is today, even if 20% below the 1897 peak. Most of it, as in all other nations, was in the form of consols. The 8 billion lire that were converted amounted to 60% of the total debt.

My comments will then be very brief and will only concern two issues of De Cecco's paper: one he raises explicitly, while he is more silent on the other. Unfortunately so, since his insights on the matter would have been most welcome. The first is the title of Section 9 of the paper and the subject of the quotation at the start of my comment: 'What did the Italian Treasury gain from the Conversion?' The latter concerns the reasons for which 'it might perhaps be instructive to bring back to memory' the Italian National Debt conversion of 1906: that is, what can we learn from it?

1   The gains from the 1906 Conversion

As observed, even though it was falling, the Italian Public Debt was extremely large at the time. Not only was its 'size' a matter of concern (the debt was approximately $\frac{1}{2}$ that of France, $\frac{3}{4}$ that of Great Britain and almost equal to those of Germany, Austria-Hungary and Russia) but its service was extremely high as a percentage of total public expenditure. Out of a total of slightly less than 2 billion lire of public expenditure, only 400 million were not on military items or interest payments. The former were on a headlong upward trend and never considered to be reducible. There was thus considerable pressure to reduce the latter by taking advantage of the 'age' of low interest rates mentioned by Professor De Cecco. As a matter of fact, in relative terms Italian interest payments on the Public Debt were the highest in Europe (as a percentage of total revenues they were over $\frac{1}{3}$ as opposed, for instance, to about $\frac{1}{10}$ in Germany, where Railroad revenues more than matched interest payments.)[1]

Accordingly, it was widely agreed that advantage should be taken of Italy's good economic and political conditions to reduce the service of the debt. The only way to do so was to convert the 5% consols (4% net of taxes) into 3.5% ones,[2] with a 'real' reduction of interest charges equal to half a percentage point, i.e. approximately 40 million lire. It was also generally agreed that the funds made available from the conversion should be used to reduce taxes, rather than to increase public expenditures. Differences of opinion existed, however, on which taxes to cut.[3]

A reduction of market interest rates was also commonly expected to be one of the consequences of the conversion (if it were successful) with obvious benefits for agricultural and industrial firms.[4] On the political side, everybody agreed that the success of the operation would have given proper recognition to the improvement of the credit of the nation, after years of good budgetary conditions and substantial growth. Indeed, as De Cecco observes, it proved to be a great political and diplomatic success. But what about the economic consequences?

The conversion implied a once-and-for-all saving for the Treasury of 0.15% of GDP, in 1907 and rising to 0.30% in 1912. It is not difficult to see, then, that it could not have a significant 'macroeconomic' impact.[5] This explains why, according to some, it all amounted to 'much ado about nothing'. Furthermore, as Griziotti (1908) pointed out, in opposition to the general opinion, there was no reason for the conversion to have had either good or bad macroeconomic effects, with one *single* exception. It could not induce a reduction in the cost of capital (contrary to the above-mentioned belief of Luzzatti and many others),[6] nor could it stimulate economic activity or push up wages. Nor could it provoke an economic crisis as a result of 'excessive speculation'. These were all partial effects that would just disappear once a general equilibrium analysis had been conducted.[7] Griziotti recognized that if the conversion had not been a complete success, reimbursements might have caused interest rates first to rise (as the State would need to borrow to satisfy its creditors) and then to fall (as those who were reimbursed brought their funds back to the market.) But this effect would only have been of a temporary nature. In particular, had the new consol fallen below par, it would have been wrong to consider this a consequence or a sign of failure of the conversion operation.

The single exception concerned the possibiity of a large number of reimbursements to foreign holders of the debt. This would have caused a loss of reserves and a variation of the exchange rate with possible serious consequences for the economy. As De Cecco appropriately observes, this explains why so much care was given to the international aspects of the operation.

The success of the 1906 Conversion should thus be seen more in terms of the political achievement than of the (aggregate) economic benefit. It was concluded without significant costs for the Treasury, and even more importantly, without any change in international money flows or consequences for the exchange rate. In fact, as was appropriately observed, it was extremely important since it reinforced 'the credit of the State, guarantee of its independence'.[8] It also helped to enhance the reputation of the Italian monetary authorities.

2   What can we learn?

As De Cecco observes, 'the structure of Public Debt is today very different, and its life expectancy much shorter, than what it used to be . . .'. Consols with indefinite life spans and issued at fixed interest rates are no longer a popular instrument for the financing of public deficits. Certainly, in Italy's case they are only an echo of the past. It would be wrong, then, to look at the 1906 National Debt conversion in the hope of finding specific suggestions for today's problems. Thus, the question is obvious: why should we be interested at all in that remote episode? Or, more properly, what can we learn from it? It seems to me that there are at least two things.

First, on the management of the Public Debt. Even a widely accepted and apparently risk-free operation such as the 1906 Conversion called for a long period of careful preparation and for the monetary authorities to establish their credibility firmly. The size of the operation was obviously a major factor, and especially important was the fact that 10 percent of the sum to be converted was held by foreigners. But it only became possible to reduce the interest burden on the debt when the market started to acknowledge the significant results achieved by fiscal policy, with the budget basically in balance by the turn of the century. In fact, at the time of the conversion Italy was the only European country to have seen a slight reduction in its Public Debt over the previous decade. It was generally accepted that this was the main force behind the 'solid' rise of the Italian *rentes* that started at the end of the 1890s. The shift, at the international level, from 'the flight to quality' to 'a flight to yield' – to use De Cecco's words – benefitted Italian government securities, but the sound budgetary conditions eventually achieved by the State were a significant factor in reaping this benefit. The market acknowledged the achievement: by 1901 the Italian *rentes* were steadily quoted above 100, and by 1902 the market interest rate fell below 4%.[9]

The second thing to be learned concerns the role and performance of capital markets. Nobody would deny that they were (are?) at times somewhat gullible and volatile. However, in the occasion of the 1906 Conversion they were working properly and this was of significant help in timing the conversion correctly and fixing the most suitable conditions for the operation.

After the event, some criticism was levelled at the stepwise nature of the conversion. It was observed that an immediate passage from 4% to 3.5% consols (avoiding the first step to 3.75% for 5 years) would have produced a further benefit of 100 million lire (i.e. a saving of a quarter of a percent

290   Discussion by Ignazio Visco

applied to a total sum of 8 billions for 5 years.) It was also suggested, however, that the care with which the operation was conducted might have been excessive, since the market price of the bonds to be converted (4% net) was equivalent to the market quotation of the bonds into which the conversion was to be made (3.5%) 'with the addition of a conversion premium anticipated by the market to be approximately equal to one lira and a quarter'.[10]

How was this figure derived? And what did it imply? As recalled by De Cecco, it was a common procedure at the time to back a conversion operation with the concession of a premium on the price of the bonds to be converted. This was the case, for example, of the 1902 French conversion by Rouvier, which was not particularly successful precisely because of the premium: holders' attempts to realize the capital gain led to a considerable fall of the market price of French consols after the conversion. The Italian government's intention to convert was announced well in advance, even if the technical details, the necessary negotations and the timing of the operation obviously were all kept rigorously secret. As a matter of fact, it is likely that the conversion would have taken place a couple of years earlier, had it not been for the outbreak of the Russian–Japanese war. And a premium of 1.20% on the capital was judged to be appropriate by several authoritative observers, both in 1904 and on the eve of the conversion.[11]

It is easy to show that the market had already discounted such a premium when the conversion took place. In 1905 and in the first semester of 1906, in fact, the 5% (4% net) consols were quoted at around 105, with a rate of return about 3.80%. The price of the 3.5% consols previously issued by the Government (even if in limited quantity) was above 103, with a rate of return about 3.38%.[12] The difference between the two rates, then, is indicative of the fact that the market was discounting the probability of a conversion taking place in the near future. More precisely, defining with V_A and V_B the ex-coupon prices of the 5% (4% net) and 3.5% consols, respectively, and with C_A and C_B their coupons, we can write:[13]

$$V_A = V_B + \sum_{i=1}^{\infty} [(C_A - C_B)p_i + \pi(1 - p_i)]/(1 + r)^i \qquad (1)$$

where p_i is the probability perceived by market participants that the conversion would not take place in period i and π is the expected conversion premium. r is the interest rate at which the expected income from holding the consols to be converted is discounted; it is assumed to be constant and equal to that of the consols into which the conversion was to be made, that is 3.5% (approximately equal to C_B/V_B).

For $p_i = 1$ for all i, we thus have:

$$V_A^* = V_B + (C_A - C_B)/r = C_A/r \tag{2}$$

that is equal, for $C_A = 4$, to 114.29, as already noticed by Flora.[14] When $p_1 = 0$, we have instead:

$$V_A^{**} = V_B + \pi/(1 + r) \tag{3}$$

In the three and half years that preceded the conversion it was always the case that $V_B < V_A < V_A^*$. As a matter of fact, $V_A - V_B$ touched a maximum of 3.93 in May of 1903 (a figure that should be compared with the theoretical maximum, for the same month, of $V_A^* - V_B = 114.29 - 98.16 = 16.13$.) The difference between V_A and V_B then decreased to 1.38 in the second semester of 1903 and was equal to 1.26 in February 1904, when the outbreak of the Russian–Japanese war made the conversion impracticable. In the next month the difference peaked at 2.78 and it was only in the second half of 1905, with the end of the war, that it became quite small again (1.23 on average). It continued to be small in the first half of 1906 and in the month of June, on the eve of the conversion, it was equal to 1.21. The probability of a conversion taking place being extremely high at the time (with $V_A \simeq V_A^{**}$), it is fair to conclude that the premium π anticipated by the market was just about one lira and a quarter for every 100 lire of the 'old' consols.

It is easy to see that applying this premium to the 8 billions to be converted gives a total of 100 million lire. This is exactly what was given to the holders of the Italian 5% consols with the reduction of the 4% (net of taxes) coupon to 3.75% for five years, rather than to 3.5% from the very first day. The cost of the stepwise operation was thus exactly equal – as it had to be – to the premium that the market had already discounted.[15]

NOTES

1 Flora (1905), pp. 8–9.
2 The 'normal' market interest rate was in fact considered to be approximately 3.5 percent.
3 It was quickly noticed by some commentators that the total sum freed by the conversion was clearly not sufficient to meet all the objectives indicated by politicians. In particular, rather than dissipating it in many directions, it was suggested that the sum should be used to abolish one single duty, namely 'the heaviest, most immoral and noxious of all: the tax on salt, the highest that is known, since it amounts to 660 per cent of the cost of this product' (Flora, 1906, p. 84).
4 See, among many others, Luzzatti (1906), p. VII.
5 After all, the reduction of a quarter of a point in the fixed interest paid on the consols (to become one half of a point by 1912) was smaller than the reduction imposed on debt holders by the 1894 tax rise from 13.2 to 20 percent.

292   Discussion by Ignazio Visco

6 'Anyway, there is only one effect for the rentier: a capital but not an income loss' (Griziotti, 1980, p. 376).
7 It should be noticed that Griziotti studied under Pareto.
8 Flora (1906), p. 83.
9 Bianchi (1979).
10 Flora (1906), p. 76. Against the further criticism that the Treasury might have dispensed with the backing of 1 billion lire by the two banking consortia established for the operation, and especially the international one led by the House of Rothschild, the counter-objection was raised that 'without such an arrangement it is certain that the Germans – who hold more than 100 millions of our consols – would have gone for reimbursement' (*ibid.*, p. 77, n. 1).
11 See De Johannis (1904), Einaudi (1904) and De Johannis (1906).
12 These figures are taken from Necco (1915). By allowing for the semi-annual payment of the coupons, Bianchi (1979) obtains, for the same period, an average rate of return of 3.88% for the 5% (4% net) consols. A similar calculation for the 3.5% (net) consols gives an average yield of 3.44%. In the 1903–04 period, when the Conversion was already considered to be a likely event, the rates of return were, respectively, 3.96% and 3.54%, with very small variations around the average values. At the time of the conversion the '3.5% net' consols issued by the Italian government amounted to 942 million lire, as opposed to the 8.1 billion lire of the '5% gross' (4% net) consols that were to be converted.
13 I wish to thank Emerico Zautzik for a useful discussion on this point.
14 See Flora (1906), p. 74, n. 1.
15 Actually it was slightly less if one considers that it was distributed over a 5-year period: indeed, discounting the yearly cost of 20 million lire at the 3.5% rate gives a present value of about 90 million lire.

REFERENCES

Bianchi, B. (1979). 'Appendice statistica; il rendimento del consolidato dal 1862 al 1946', in F. Vicarelli (ed.), *Capitale industriale e capitale finanziario: il caso italiano*, Bologna, Il Mulino.
De Johannis, A.J. (1904). *La conversione della rendita*, Firenze, Barbera.
   (1906). 'La spesa per la conversione della rendita', *L'economista*, 10 June.
Einaudi, L. (1904). 'I problemi della conversione in Italia', *Corriere della Sera*, 25 August.
Flora, F. (1905). *La conversione della rendita*, Milano, Soc. Ed. Libraria.
   (1906). 'La conversione del consolidato italiano', *Giornale degli economisti*, July, pp. 71–89.
Griziotti, B. (1908). 'Sugli effetti della conversione della rendita', *Giornale degli economisti*, May, pp. 353–84.
Luzzatti, L. (1906). 'La conversione della rendita italiana', *Nuova Antologia*, 16 September, pp. I–VIII.
Necco, A. (1915). *Il corso dei titoli di Stato in Italia dal 1861 al 1912*, Soc. Ed. Dante Alighieri, Milano.

10 Fear of deficit financing – is it rational?

MARCUS MILLER, ROBERT SKIDELSKY
and PAUL WELLER

1 Introduction

A *sine qua non* for successful international cooperation to combat the
spread of infectious diseases proved to be emergence of a scientific
consensus on the way they are transmitted; and, by analogy, Richard
Cooper has argued that broad agreement on the likely effects of fiscal and
monetary actions is an essential prerequisite for the effective coordination
of macroeconomic policy. The omens, however, are none too promising.

On the one hand, Bryant, Helliwell and Hooper conclude their survey of
the consequences of changes in US fiscal policy (as revealed by simulation
of several global macroeconomic models) with observations that seem
consistent with a conventional Keynesian approach; at least for the short
run. In their words: 'An unanticipated cut in U.S. federal purchases could
have a substantial negative impact on the level of U.S. real output for
several years, . . . and to a lesser but still significant extent on output
outside the United States'; though they go on to observe that: 'the
declines in U.S. prices, interest rates and the dollar would eventually
stimulate domestic demand and net exports enough to reverse most of the
decline in output within five or six years' (Bryant *et al.*, 1989, p. 101).

On the other hand, some economists argue that changes in federal
spending have contrary effects on GNP. Fels and Froehlich, for example,
not that an 'anti-Keynesian' policy of fiscal consolidation in the Federal
Republic of Germany coincided with a rapid recovery of the economy
from the 1981–82 recession, and attribute this 'coincidence' in large part
to the benign effect of fiscal consolidation on expectations in the private
sector. 'The measures were welcomed as a return to fiscal stability and
predictability. The process of psychological crowding out was quickly
reversed. Just as adverse expectations may prevent a fiscal expansion from
raising overall demand, a gradual reduction of the fiscal impulse may be
expected to stimulate private demand if indeed such a policy is in line with

preferences in the private sector' (Fels and Froehlich, 1987, p. 184). The concept of 'psychological crowding out' mentioned here had actually been elaborated earlier by the German Council of Economic Experts (SVR) in 1981 to refer to the negative feedback which fiscal expansion might induce in the private sector owing to its deleterious impact on the public finances: these were judged so powerful as to make the overall public budget multiplier *negative* in the Federal Republic of Germany (Fels and Froehlich, p. 181).

In short, there is evidence of sharp disagreement amongst policy analysts in the US and the Federal Republic of Germany as to the very sign of the effects of federal spending on GNP. It is a disagreement, moreover, which is based on psychological elements not usually captured in macro-economic models (elements which may, presumably, vary from country to country).

However, the idea that such factors might play a key role in determining the efficacy of policy is not new. The famous debate between Keynes and the Treasury in the 1930s hinged largely on the role of psychological considerations, as Roger Middleton (1985) emphasizes in his discussion of the debate. Both saw psychology and confidence as central – and recognized that it might be irrational: but while the Treasury (like the German SVR) treated the fear of 'unsound finance' as an insurmountable obstacle to running fiscal deficits, Keynes took the view that it was irrational and needed to be changed. We begin our discussion below with an account of Keynes's views on the nature of expectations, indicating the key role he (as well as the Treasury) assigned to psychological factors.

In the light of 'the rational expectations revolution' it seems natural to ask whether and to what extent psychological fears are 'model-consistent.' Thus, in commenting on Fels and Froehlich, Blanchard (1987, p. 197) asks 'Can we construct models with *rational* firms and individuals in which such psychological effects can arise?' (italics added). His affirmative answer includes two elements, first that a reduction of spending may be taken as a signal of lower distortionary taxes in the future, and second that it may change the likelihood of 'bad news' in circumstances where, 'when public debt reaches some critical level, something very bad happens, repudiation, monetization, or civil war, in which capital suffers large losses.'

In the second part of the paper, we pursue further this line of thought, and use some results in stochastic process-switching to see to what extent such psychological elements may be treated as 'rational' estimates of possible levies on financial claims. These results are discussed in the last section of the paper.

2   Keynes and expectations

Although Keynes attached importance to expectations, he did not consider the possibility that these could be 'rational' in the modern technical sense, i.e., mathematical predictions generated by a model of the economy.

In his view, expectations were based on (1) the belief that present conditions will continue indefinitely into the future; as he wrote: 'the facts of the existing situation enter, in a sense disproportionately, into the formation of our long term expectations; our usual practice being to take the existing state of affairs and project it into the future' (Keynes, VII, p. 148); (2) the assumption that 'the *existing* state of opinion as expressed in prices and the character of existing output in based on a *correct* summing up of future prospects . . .' (Keynes, XIV, p. 114); (3) conventional judgement – 'we endeavor to fall back on the judgement of the rest of the world . . .' (Keynes, XIV, p. 114).

Keynes's expectations are thus essentially static. To the extent that they reflect the state of public opinion, or the state of confidence, they are liable to be swept away by any change in the 'news', however ephemeral and irrelevant. 'The practice of calmness and immobility, of certainty and security, suddenly breaks down. New fears and hopes will, without warning, take charge of human conduct. The forces of disillusion may suddenly impose a new conventional basis of valuation' (Keynes, XIV, pp. 114–15).

One consequence of the importance of the state of confidence is that 'economic prosperity is excessively dependent on a political and social atmosphere which is congenial to the average business man. If the fear of a Labour Government or a New Deal depresses enterprise, this need not be the result either of a reasonable calculations or of a plot with political intent; – it is the mere consequence of upsetting the delicate balance of spontaneous optimism. In estimating the prospects of investment, we must have regard, therefore, to the nerves and hysteria and even the digestions and reactions to the weather of those upon whose spontaneous activity it largely depends' (Keynes, VII, p. 162).

One criticism of Keynes's account of expectations formation is that it appears to exclude learning by experience, or the efficient utilization of information – including judgments of relevance. In his world, anything may go wrong, and it usually does. However, it is more helpful to see his account as a product of an age so prone to shocks and disasters, so bereft of stable parameters, that it would have been irrational to form expectations 'rationally'. It was a world sliding from the settled expectations of the Victorians into the chaos of the interwar years. It as a world too full of 'noise' to give clear signals. The conventions which had served the

Victorians well enough could no longer be relied on. As he wrote: 'It is unsound to base the policy of the future on the decaying conventions of the present' (Keynes, XIX, p. 315).

Keynes's theoretical work in the 1930s was designed to justify systematic government policy to recreate and maintain a set of expectations consistent with full employment: a combination of raising the marginal efficiency of capital and lowering the long-run rate of interest. In the 1920s he had defined the government's duty as to guarantee that 'the index of prices will never move far from a fixed point' (Keynes, XIX, p. 161). In the 1930s its duty was to bring about full employment level of demand.[1] But Keynes's comments on the American New Deal in the 1930s showed that he fully understood the dangers of 'psychological crowding out' associated with an expansionary fiscal and monetary policy. 'The average City man,' he wrote in an Open Letter to Roosevelt, 'believes you are engaged on a hair-brained expedition in face of competent advice . . .' A policy perceived to be 'crack-brained and queer' will 'upset the confidence of the business world and *weaken its existing motives to action* before you have had time to put other motives in their place' (our italics) (Keynes, XXI, p. 290).

Indeed, in a recent analysis of the famous 'Treasury View' of the 1930s, Middleton (1985) has suggested that an expansionary fiscal policy, carried out in the expectational environment in the 1930s, would have proved abortive. An increase in public spending would not have had the expansionary effect predicted by Keynes because businessmen's lack of confidence in the programme would have led them to revise downwards their estimates of expected profitability of investment. Given such expectations, . . . 'the application of a fiscal stimulus fails to effect a commensurate increase in income because it sets in chain a sequence of deflationary forces which act to offset, or even completely neutralize, the initial increment to demand.' 'Crowding out' can reduce the multiplier to zero even when unemployment is high (Middleton, 1985, p. 163).

In this account of the Treasury view, expectations largely determine outcomes. The question is: was it reasonable for businessmen to hold such expectations in the 1930s? In his book, Middleton suggests not. But his analysis does not deal explicitly with public concern as to the 'sustainability' of fiscal deficits. Since this is an important element of the 'psychological crowding out' described by Fels and Froehlich, we decided to examine this issue further.

3   Psychological crowding out, debt and disasters

Our aim in this section is to explore the extent to which one might tell a convincing story to explain 'psychological crowding out' within an orthodox rational expectations context. The idea is simply stated. Suppose that agents are concerned about the sustainability of high levels of government debt. In particular, suppose that they anticipate that when the cost of servicing the debt reaches some critical level, the government will introduce some policy measure which is 'bad news' for bond holders. At one extreme this might be a permanent default on coupon payments, which in the case of consols would render them worthless. Perhaps more plausibly, the government could levy a tax upon coupon payments. It is also more reasonable, given the nature of the problem, to imagine that such a tax would not be introduced permanently, but rather would be contingent upon the level of (gross of tax) coupon payments. This latter is the scenario we analyze. We do so in a rational expectations model in which the 'disaster', namely the imposition of a coupon tax is correctly anticipated by all.

Our treatment of this question in a macroeconomic model can be more easily understood by first considering the impact of various taxes on the price of perpetual bonds in order to illustrate the techniques involved. In Section 3.1 we therefore analyze the impact of coupon and capital gains taxation in a deterministic model of rational bond valuation, and in Section 3.2 we consider the effects of various state-contingent shifts of tax regime in a stochastic environment. Then, in Section 3.3 we specify a macroeconomic model (with a similar mathematical structure) to see what the 'rational expectations' effects of possible future disasters might be for bond prices in the present.

3.1 The taxation of coupons and capital gains in a deterministic environment

For simplicity, it is assumed that the short interest rate follows a first-order autoregressive process which, in the absence of stochastic shocks, is written

$$\dot{r} = - \gamma(r - \bar{r}) \tag{1}$$

The price of bonds, q, is determined as the present discounted value of the fixed coupon, c, after allowing for the incidence of both a proportional coupon tax (represented by a constant θ) and a proportional tax on capital gains (represented by τ). The arbitrage condition that this implies is

$$(1 - \tau)\frac{\dot{q}}{q} + \frac{c}{q}(1 - \theta) = r$$

or, equivalently,

$$(1 - \tau)\dot{q} = rq - c(1 - \theta) \tag{2}$$

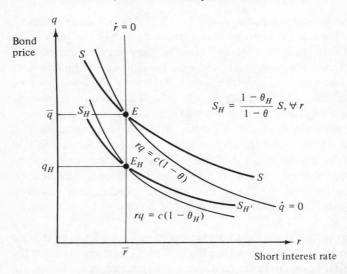

Figure 10.1   Saddlepoint equilibrium at E; and the effect of increasing θ

Note that the 'tax rates' appearing in equation (2) are effectively 'normalized' on that applying to interest receipts, r. Thus, if $\theta = \tau = 0$, this will represent the case where all tax rates are uniform: while if $\theta > 0 > \tau$, then coupons are taxed more heavily than interest receipts, which in turn are taxed more than capital gains.

The phase diagram corresponding to these equations has the saddlepoint structure shown in Figure 10.1. The lines of stationarity are the vertical line through $\bar{r}$ and the rectangular hyperbola which is drawn passing through E. The stable manifold SS is shown leading towards equilibrium, $\bar{r}, \bar{q}$, where

$$\bar{q} = \frac{c(1 - \theta)}{\bar{r}}$$

Clearly an increase in the rate of coupon tax will lower the equilibrium price and shift the stable trajectory from SS to $S_H S_H$ in the figure. A change in the rate of capital gains tax, however, leaves equilibrium unchanged but affects the trajectory SS.

The effect of capital gains taxation may be obtained straightforwardly by taking a linear approximation of equations (1) and (2) around $\bar{r}, \bar{q}$, as follows

$$\dot{r}_0 = -\gamma(r - \bar{r}) = -\gamma r_0 \tag{3}$$

$$(1 - \tau)\dot{q}_0 = \bar{r}(q - \bar{q}) + \bar{q}(r - \bar{r}) + \bar{r}\bar{q} - c(1 - \theta) = r_0 \bar{q} + q_0 \bar{r} \tag{4}$$

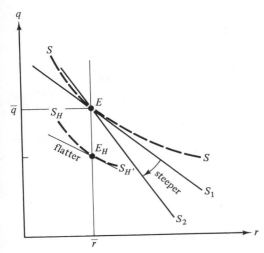

Figure 10.2   Linearized solutions (with the flattening due to higher θ and steepening due to higher τ)

using r_0, q_0 to denote the deviations from equilibrium. In matrix form this becomes

$$
\begin{bmatrix} \dot{r}_0 \\ \dot{q}_0 \end{bmatrix} = \begin{bmatrix} -\gamma & 0 \\ \dfrac{\bar{q}}{1-\tau} & \dfrac{\bar{r}}{1-\tau} \end{bmatrix} \begin{bmatrix} r_0 \\ q_0 \end{bmatrix}
\tag{5}
$$

with roots $-\gamma$ and $\bar{r}/(1-\tau)$. The slope of the stable eigenvector, S_1, which is tangent to the nonlinear stable manifold SS at E, follows immediately from the requirement that $A \begin{bmatrix} 1 \\ \omega \end{bmatrix} = -\gamma \begin{bmatrix} 1 \\ \omega \end{bmatrix}$ and so

$$
\frac{\bar{q}}{1-\tau} + \frac{\bar{r}}{1-\tau}\,\omega = -\gamma\omega
$$

where A denotes the matrix in equation (5) and $\begin{bmatrix} 1 \\ \omega \end{bmatrix}$ denotes the stable eigenvector. Consequently,

$$
\omega = \frac{-\bar{q}}{\bar{r} + (1-\tau)\gamma}
\tag{6}
$$

So the (negative) slope of the stable manifold becomes steeper as the result of an increase in the rate of capital gains taxation.

The corresponding 'swivelling' of the manifold through E is shown in Figure 10.2. It occurs because for points to the right of E, prices are expected to rise to $\bar{q}$ over time, so a higher gains tax means loss of value;

while for points to the left of E the converse applies – assuming that capital losses can be used to reduce net tax payments. We also note from equation (6) that the effect of a higher rate of capital gains tax (higher τ) has the same effect as an equivalent reduction in the coefficient γ measuring the speed with which short rates return to equilibrium.

The effect of changing the tax on the fixed bond coupon is also shown in the figure. It lowers the equilibrium from E to E_H and also flattens the slope of the linearized stable manifold. (This 'flattening' is evident from the expression for ω, which measures the slope of S_1 and can be written as

$$\omega = \frac{-c(1-\theta)}{(\bar{r}+(1-\tau)\gamma)\bar{r}}$$

by substitution for $\bar{q}$ in equation (6) above).

3.2　Stochastic shocks and probabilistic shifts to the tax regime

In what follows we will, for reasons of analytical tractability, work with the linear approximations derived. We allow first for the process determining the short interest rate to be disturbed by a white noise error, so

$$dr = -\gamma r dt + \sigma dz \tag{3'}$$

where r is now used to denote the deviation from equilibrium and z is a Brownian motion process. Reformulating the bond arbitrage equation as

$$Edq = \frac{\bar{q}}{1-\tau} r dt + \frac{\bar{r}}{1-\tau} q dt \tag{4'}$$

where E is the instantaneous expectations operator, one may show that such a system will generate a diffusion along the (linear) stable manifold (with an asymptotic distribution centered at the deterministic equilibrium).

Now consider the effects of a 'state-contingent' shift of tax regime. Specifically let us assume that $\theta = \tau = 0$ at equilibrium, but that θ is stepped up for all $r \geq r^* > \bar{r}$. To see what effect this will have on bond prices we refer to Figure 10.3 where the locus FF shows how the bond price depends on the short rate in these circumstances.

To see how the function FF is derived we note first that there are two manifolds appearing in the figure, that through E_1 for the 'uniform tax' regime (where $\theta = \tau = 0$) and that through E_2, for the regime with the higher coupon tax ($\theta > \tau = 0$). But the tax regime only switches at $r = r^*$, so the question is how to splice the two regimes together.

One can see that a switch from one manifold to the other at $r = r^*$ would involve a discrete movement in bond prices which is inconsistent with

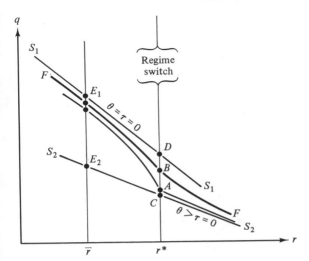

Figure 10.3 **Bond prices when coupon taxes rise for** $r \gtreqless r^*$

arbitrage. At points on S_2 to the right of C for example, the general expectation is of a fall of interest rates towards $\bar{r}$, (and so of a switch of regime) and this will tend to raise bond prices even before the interest rate falls to r^*. Conversely bond prices will tend to be depressed below S_1 to the left of r^*, by the risk that higher coupon taxes may be imposed.

What we find is that for any point above $\bar{r}$ between C and D we can find a function which satisfies the stochastic differential equations for each tax regime (i.e., $\theta = 0$ to the left, and $\theta > 0$ to the right) and converges asymptotically to the relevant manifold. Take point A for example; the path shown through it is continuous by construction; but its first derivative is not. And this violates the smooth transition which must hold when there is reversible stochastic switching at r^*. We conclude that the behaviour of the bond price will be characterized by a path such as FF, which has the property of satisfying the differential equations of whichever regime is in operation and also of meeting the necessary boundary condition implied by smooth transition. (For an analysis of the technical issues involved, see Whittle, 1982).

We note that the impression given by Figure 10.3 that the two manifolds S_1 and S_2 will ultimately *intersect* is false, an artifact of the local linearization. It is straightforward to see that the correct nonlinear manifolds would not intersect since if they did there would be a contradiction – two bonds facing the same discount factors, priced at the same price despite having post-tax coupons which are systematically different.

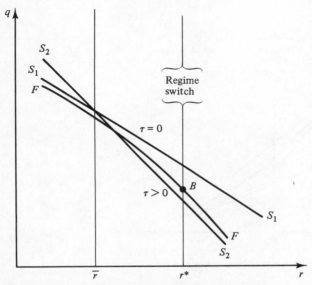

Figure 10.4   Bond prices when gains taxation increases for $r \gtreqless r^*$

When a capital gains tax is imposed, however, this does cause the manifolds to intersect as the stable manifold rotates around equilibrium. Thus, in Figure 10.4, the effect of a higher rate of capital gains tax is to steepen the manifold from S_1 to S_2. If the higher rate of capital gains tax is only applied when the short rate lies above r^*, however, then one must solve for the appropriate stochastic solution using the principles discussed above. The result is shown by the path FF, with a point of inflexion at B.

It is the macroeconomic model to be analyzed in the next section which prompts the last example of tax switching illustrated in Figure 10.5. In the macroeconomic illustration there is an increased tax on bond coupons which is applied when the short rates of interest are high. (The actual trigger for the tax increase turns out to be the stock of bonds, but this is closely correlated with short rates via portfolio effects in the demand for money equation.) The effect of this tax on the rate of convergence of the system is to speed it up – that is indeed what it is designed to do. But such an increase in analogous to a change in the rate of capital gains tax, as we have already seen above. As an increase in gains tax was like a reduction in the (absolute magnitude of the) stable root, consequently it will be a *reduction* in the rate of tax which will mimic faster convergence.

The switch of tax regime shown in Figure 10.5 therefore is of a *raising* of coupon tax and a lowering of the gains tax for short rates to the right of r^*. As before, there are two manifolds: S_1 where taxes are uniform

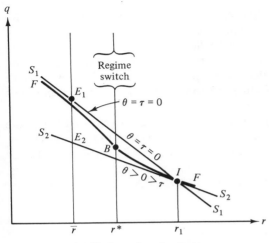

(a) 'Bad news' predominates

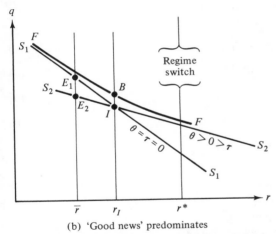

(b) 'Good news' predominates

Figure 10.5 Bond prices when both taxes switch (θ rises and τ falls for $r \gtreqless r^*$)

($\theta = 0 = \tau$) and S_2 where θ is increased and τ is lowered ($\theta > 0 > \tau$). Since the second manifold is made flatter by the reduction of the capital gains tax, the intersection shown in the picture reflects a genuine economic possibility and does not arise from the linearization. (At point I, for example, two bonds would have the same price given the same rates of discount because the lower tax on the substantial capital appreciation to be expected as short rates fall from r_I to $\bar{r}$ will precisely offset the lower post-tax coupon available.)

In the upper panel of the figure, we illustrate the path for bond prices which is relevant where the switch of regime takes place well to the left of any such intersection. The locus FF lies below S_1 to the left of r^* and above S_2 to the right, approaching each manifold asymptotically, and going through a point of inflection at the switch point r^*. It is this pattern of bond pricing behaviour which we will observe in the macroeconomic example of the next section.

For completeness, we also illustrate in Figure 10.5(b) the case where the switch point lies to the right of I. In this case the locus lies above S_1 since, by construction, a higher coupon tax is only imposed when interest rates are high enough for the relaxation of gains tax to offset it. In other words, the 'good news' of tax relief on gains will more than offset the 'bad news' of higher coupon tax.

3.3   The macroeconomic model

We consider first a deterministic model of bond price dynamics, and incorporate a simple link between short-run interest rates and the stock of bonds. The equations of the model are as follows:

$$y = \alpha(y - \phi b - \theta b) + \beta q + g \tag{7}$$

$$m = \omega b - \lambda r \tag{8}$$

$$q\dot{b} = (g + b(1 - \phi - \theta) + \bar{s}r) \tag{9}$$

$$\dot{q} = rq - (1 - \theta) \tag{10}$$

The variables are defined as follows:

y = level of GNP
b = stock of consols
q = price of a consol
g = government spending
m = real money supply
$\bar{s}$ = (exogenous) stock of short-term government debt
r = short-term interest rate
ϕ = factor tax parameter
θ = coupon tax rate.

Equation (7) is an IS equation, where α is the marginal propensity to consume, and ϕb is a component of tax revenue which is, as a matter of policy, directly related to the level of the bond stock. The purpose of this device is to avoid the well-known instability associated with such models without explicit recourse to wealth effects in consumption. The term βq is

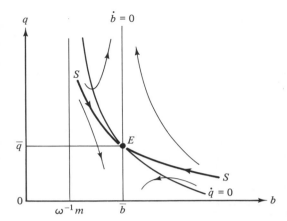

Figure 10.6 The stable path of adjustment for the bond stock

a stylized investment function. The yield on a consol with a coupon of unity is $1/q$ and it is this long interest rate which is assumed to influence investment decisions.[2] Next we have a simplified LM equation, where the domestic price level is omitted because we shall assume throughout that it is constant. We include a simple wealth effect, neglecting the influence of the consol price. Equation (9) captures the government budget constraint, and states that the value of new bond issues, $q\dot{b}$, must be equal to the shortfall between revenue, $(\phi + \theta)b$, and expenditure, $g + b + \bar{s}r$, where b and $\bar{s}r$ are respectively the coupon and interest payments on long and short-term debt.

We now turn to consider the dynamics of the system we have just described. The system has a nonlinear saddlepoint structure (if ϕ is sufficiently large to ensure stability of the autonomous equation determining the bond stock), as depicted in Figure 10.6. The locus $\dot{q} = 0$ is a curve with equation $q(b - \omega^{-1}m) = \lambda\omega^{-1}(1 - \theta)$. Given the presence of a fully flexible asset price, expectations adjust so as to position the system on the unique stable path of adjustment to long-run equilibrium at $(\bar{b}, \bar{q})$.

To proceed further with the analysis, we work with the linearized system below:

$$\begin{bmatrix} \dot{b}_0 \\ \dot{q}_0 \end{bmatrix} = \begin{bmatrix} \dfrac{1 - \phi - \theta + \omega\lambda^{-1}\bar{s}}{\bar{q}} & 0 \\ \omega\lambda^{-1}\bar{q} & \bar{r} \end{bmatrix} \begin{bmatrix} b_0 \\ q_0 \end{bmatrix} \qquad (11)$$

The variables b_0, q_0 rerpresent deviations from equilibrium. Thus $b_0 = b - \bar{b}$, $q_0 = q - \bar{q}$. We solve for the various equilibrium values, which are

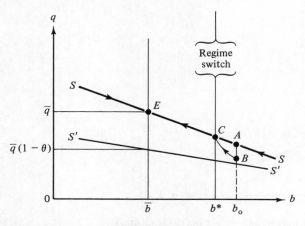

Figure 10.7   A coupon tax announced at b_0

$$\bar{b} = \frac{g - m\lambda^{-1}\bar{s}}{\phi + \theta - 1 - \omega\lambda^{-1}\bar{s}}; \quad \bar{r} = \omega\lambda^{-1}\bar{b} - m\lambda^{-1}; \quad \bar{q} = \frac{1 - \theta}{\bar{r}}$$

In order to isolate the effect of differential tax discrimination against bond holders, we consider the case of a coupon tax θ introduced with an offsetting increase in g designed to hold the equilibrium bond stock constant at the level when $\theta = 0$.[3] As one would expect, the coupon tax reduces the long-run equilibrium price of a bond. For saddlepoint dynamics, we need to assume that $(1 - \phi - \theta + \omega\lambda^{-1}\bar{s} < 0$ whereupon this term becomes the stable root of the system. The slope of the stable manifold is

$$\theta = \frac{-\omega\lambda^{-1}(1 - \theta)^2}{\bar{r}^2(\phi - \omega\lambda^{-1}\bar{s})} \tag{12}$$

which is negative, and increases in value with θ. Thus we can compare the stable manifold of the two systems, with and without a coupon tax levied at rate θ. This is illustrated in Figure 10.7,[4] by the lines SS ($\theta = 0$) and $S'S'$ ($\theta > 0$).

We consider first the effect of announcing that a coupon tax at rate θ will be applied if $b + \bar{s}r \geq k$, or $b \geq (k + \bar{s}m\lambda^{-1})(1 + \omega\lambda^{-1}\bar{s})^{-1} \equiv b^*$. In a deterministic environment this will obviously have no effect if $b < b^*$. If $b = b_0 > b^*$ then the announcement will lead to an abrupt drop in bond prices, followed by a subsequent recovery. The effects are illustrated in Figure 10.7. The bond price q drops from A to B, and subsequently rises to C, whereupon the tax is removed and the system proceeds along SS to equilibrium E.

A clearly unsatisfactory feature of the deterministic analysis is that such announcements have no effect at all upon the behaviour of the system if the bond stock lies below the critical level at b^*. This runs very much counter to the intuitive arguments we have presented earlier for regarding such contingent tax regimes as having an impact on the equilibrium of the system when no tax is in place through the expectational mechanism. This points to the need for a stochastic analysis, to which we now turn.

We suppose that the LM equation is perturbed by a white noise process. This implies, from equation (8) that we may write

$$r = \omega\lambda^{-1}b - m\lambda^{-1} + \sigma dz \qquad (13)$$

This means that we may rewrite (11) as

$$\begin{bmatrix} db_0 \\ Edq_0 \end{bmatrix} = \begin{bmatrix} \dfrac{1 - \phi - \theta + \omega\lambda^{-1}\bar{s}}{\bar{q}} & 0 \\ \omega\lambda^{-1}\bar{q} & \bar{r} \end{bmatrix} \begin{bmatrix} b_0 dt \\ q_0 dt \end{bmatrix} + \begin{bmatrix} (\bar{s}/\bar{q})\sigma dz \\ 0 \end{bmatrix} \qquad (14)$$

The term Edq_0 denotes the instantaneous expected rate of change in the bond price, and our formulation of the bond price arbitrage equation assumes risk neutrality.

In order to analyse (14) we will make substantial use of earlier work on qualitative analysis of stochastic saddlepoint models (Miller and Weller, 1988). There we showed that the dynamic behaviour of a system such as (14) could be obtained by postulating a determination functional relationship between asset price q and the 'sluggish' fundamental, here the bond stock. One obtains, by applying standard techniques of stochastic calculus, a nonlinear second order differential equation, which will in general have no closed form solution.[5]

The way in which we proceed to analyze the impact of imposing a contingent coupon tax regime is as follows. We apply the boundary condition (described in the previous section) which can be shown to apply generally in the case of reversible regime switches in which fundamentals are driven by a Wiener process. The condition states that the transition between regimes must be smooth (see Whittle, 1982, so the trajectories in the two regimes must be tangent at the point of transition. If this condition did not hold, profitable arbitrage would be possible. We then look for solution trajectories in the two regimes which are asymptotic to their respective stable manifolds, and also satisfy smooth transition. It is possible to show that such asymptotic trajectories always exist.

The picture that emerges, illustrated in Figure 10.8, is one where the 'kinks' that are a feature of the deterministic solution are stochastically 'ironed out', and where, *even if* the system is in the region of $\bar{b}$ and no coupon tax is currently imposed, the possibility of adverse shocks driving

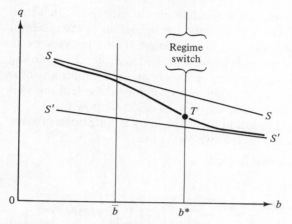

Figure 10.8   A coupon tax anticipated at b^*

the economy beyond b^* leads to an immediate effect upon bond prices. If the economy has only a relatively low capacity to absorb debt, i.e., b^* is 'close' to $\bar{b}$, then the anticipation of possible *future* coupon taxes will have a significant *current* impact, providing a close parallel to the 'psychological crowding out' story. But if, on the other hand, the economy has large absorptive capacity, then the effect of such anticipated taxes will be negligible.[6]

4   Conclusions

In seeking to draw practical policy conclusions from models in which agents are assumed to form rational expectations, it is easy to lose sight of the fact that the assumption is more convincing as a *long-run* theory of expectations formation; so there must be sufficient stability in the environment for the theory to be convincing. Keynes clearly recognized the importance of this, given the emphasis he placed upon the 'normal' state of affairs in his discussions of expectations. He viewed the first decades of the twentieth century, and particularly the interwar period, as a time of 'turbulence' following on from the settled stability in the Victorian era. It was his experience of such times which led him to place such importance upon psychological factors in his theory of expectations. But he saw the desirability of a return to stability and a world in which individuals could accurately anticipate future events. Of central importance for this was the requirement that individuals agree upon the general principles governing the functioning of the economy system. A central objective in the writing of the *General Theory* was to being about this state of affairs.

It seems to us, in short, that there is more common ground between much of Keynes's thinking on expectations and the modern theory of rational or model consistent expectations, than might appear from the great difference of emphasis – which can no doubt be partly explained in historical terms. Nevertheless, it is abundantly clear that there are certain kinds of events which by their very nature are not easily incorporated into a theory of rational expectations. These are infrequently occurring events to which it may not even be very sensible to attach any objective probability. One such event is the 'crisis' people perceive as likely to occur consequent upon an excessive accumulation of debt.

So far as we have boldly assumed that the public correctly assesses both the nature of the 'crisis' and the contingency which will precipitate it; and we have seen how, in these circumstances, forward-looking asset prices will adjust to incorporate the appropriate discount or premium. (Specifically bond prices adjust appropriately to reflect the possible introduction of a 'coupon tax' designed to alleviate the tax burden imposed on those who are *not* bond holders.) This provides a rational expectations account of 'psychological crowding out'.

But – as noted above – it may be very difficult for the public to form decent estimates of the nature of crises and when they will occur, so it is easy to see how psychological factors could take over. It is our impression, indeed, that the 'psychological crowding out' referred to by Fels and Froehlich is to a large extent based on *exaggerated* fears. This possibility immediately suggests an important role for policy – namely that of trying to inform the market of events that are, in principle, better known to policy makers (how and when they plan to act). One can see a role here for policy commitments designed to bring about rational expectations.

There are a number of questions this paper has not specifically addressed, which might repay further investigation. One is the quantitative significance of the effects we describe. Another is the effect of formulating the nature of the 'crisis' in different ways, and of allowing for some degree of uncertainty about the level of debt at which 'crisis' will occur.

For macroeconomic modelers to ignore the possibility of such crises is as unsatisfactory as it is for their critics to exaggerate the risks. But the methods described in this paper provide a way for modelers to include a rational estimate of what such a crisis might mean for current asset values (and for economic decisions which depend upon them). Applying them could help to reduce the yawning gap between the econometric and psychological assessment of policy effects we described at the outset.

310   Marcus Miller, Robert Skidelsky and Paul Weller

NOTES

We would like to thank Alan Sutherland for able research assistance.
1 It would be wrong to assume that the second goal supersedes the first. Keynes never thought in terms of a 'menu of choices' open to policymakers with different degrees of employment and price stability. His goal was a state of demand sufficient to maintain full employment but insufficient to lead to any expectations of a persistent rise in prices (Keynes, XXIX, p. 235). In the 19th century, an expected zero rate of inflation was associated with a 5% unemployment 'norm'. This was what Keynes wanted to get back to; in his view, it could no longer be achieved by a combination of *laissez-faire* and 'decaying conventions'.
2 This implies that we should really think of the 'coupon tax' as a more general capital tax.
3 This implies that we should really think of the 'coupon tax' as a more general capital tax.
4 The possibility that SS and SS' will intersect appears to be an artifact of the linearization of the system, which is confirmed by numerical computation of the nonlinear solutions for a range of parameter values.
5 In the special case considered here, in which there is no feedback from the asset price to the fundamental, the solution can be characterized in terms of Kummer's function. This is useful when it comes to obtaining numerical solutions.
6 Indeed, it seem quite possible that for b^* sufficiently far to the right of $\bar{b}$, the anticipated tax could even be 'good news' for bond holders.

REFERENCES

Blanchard, Olivier (1987). 'Germany and the World Economy: A US View', *Economic Policy* 1, issue 4, 195–200.
Bryant, Ralph C., John F. Helliwell and Peter Hooper (1989). 'Domestic and Cross-border Consequences of U.S. Macroeconomic Policies' in Bryant *et al.* (eds.), *Macroeconomic Policies in an Interdependent World*, Washington: International Monetary Fund.
Fels, Gerhard and Hans-Peter Froehlich (1987). 'Germany and the World Economy: A German View', *Economic Policy* 1, issue 4, 178–95.
Keynes, John Maynard, *The Collected Writings of*, Sir A. Robinson and D.E. Moggridge, eds. London: St. Martin's Press for the Royal Economic Society, volumes referred to are specifically:
Vol. VII *The General Theory* (1936)
Vol. XIV *The General Theory and After: Defence and Development*
Vol. XIX *Activities: The Return to Gold and Industrial Policy, 1924–9*
Vol. XXI *Activities: World Crises and Policies in Britain and America 1931–1939*
Vol. XXIX *Supplement: The General Theory and After.*
Middleton, Roger (1985). *Towards the Managed Economy: Keynes, the Treasury and the Fiscal Policy Debate of the 1930s*, London: Methuen.
Miller, Marcus and Paul Weller (1988). 'Solving Stochastic Saddlepoint Systems: a qualitative treatment with economic applications', Warwick Economic Research Paper No. 309, also CEPR Discussion Paper No. 308.
Whittle, Peter (1982). *Optimization Over Time: Dynamic Programming and Stochastic Control*, Vol. 2, New York: J. Wiley.

Discussion

GIUSEPPE BERTOLA

This interesting paper touches upon a wide range of issues. The authors remind us of the importance of psychological factors in Keynes' view of how an economy works; propose an application of state-of-the-art stochastic techniques to issues of government deficits and debt repudiation; and argue that nonlinear policy reactions can, even in a rational expectations framework, produce results that are somewhat reminiscent of Keynesian phenomena.

The three short sections below deal with the first point; with the general features of the technique proposed; and with their applicability to fiscal policy and debt management.

1   Psychology vs. rationality

Forward-looking behaviour has an essential role in correctly specified macroeconomic models. Investment depends on expected future profitability, asset prices on expected future dividends and capital gains, consumption on expected future incomes, and so on.

In Keynes's view, the future can be so unmeasurably uncertain as to make it impossible to specify objective probabilities for the relevant realizations of future variables. Expectational variables are then essentially subjective, and can shift in arbitrary ways as agents change their mind. In this framework, any phenomenon could be interpreted (but not really *explained*) in terms of exogenous, unpredictable expectational shocks – an unpleasant state of affairs from an economist's point of view. The rational expectations school set out to pin down expectational variables: taking the probability distribution of future exogenous variables and the structure of the economy as given, it becomes possible for agents to compute objective probability distributions and expectations, and for economists to undertake prediction and normative analysis.

Simplifying a little, the paper argues that Keynesian and rational expectations can be reconciled, to some extent, by making the former concept more precise and considering new twists in the latter. On the first count, the authors' careful reading of Keynes reveals that he thought rational expectation assumptions realistic, provided that the structure of the economy would not itself be viewed as uncertain by agents.[1] This brings up a normative prescription of sorts: governments should aim to provide agents with a consistent model of the economy, and the very availability of clear rules of the game should instill stabilizing confidence in the economy.

The authors do not pursue this point further. Rather, they note that expectations, even psychological ones, may shift *because* news about exogenous variables becomes known, and that such 'psychological crowding out' may cause conventional causal relationships to disappear or to be reversed. Still, prediction and normative analysis would be feasible if the phenomenon could be modelled and rationalized. The bulk of the paper explores this possibility, using recent stochastic extensions of well-known saddlepath phase diagram techniques.

2   Saddlepath and stochastic regime switches

In the absence of uncertainty, saddlepaths (or stable manifolds) offer a characterization of endogenous dynamic convergence to the steady state from a given starting point. They can also be used to study the impact and dynamic effects of exogenous changes in parameters and exogenous variables: in nonstochastic models, however, such changes must be either completely unexpected, or expected to occur with certainty at some given time.[2]

Recent work by Miller and Weller makes an explicit, realistic treatment of uncertainty possible.[3] The idea is to model the stochastic behaviour of a state variable, or parameter, in terms of a sequence of 'small' shocks, with known probability distribution: 'large' changes of parameters and or exogenous variables are then assumed to be triggered endogenously when a state variable reaches a prespecified point in the state space.

In this framework, probability assessments about the timing of large shocks (or regime switches) depend on the current state of the system. The farther we are from the trigger point, the less likely it is that small shocks will bring about a regime switch in the near future and, because of discounting, possible regime switches have negligible effects. Conversely, as we get closer to the trigger point from either direction the probability of switches in the immediate future approaches one, and the behaviour of the system in the two regimes becomes more similar – eventually meeting smoothly, to first order, at the trigger point.

3   Fear of deficit financing

To work with these techniques on an economic problem, one has to specify dynamic relationships between the variables of interest; 'small' and 'large' shocks; and a trigger point. The paper proposes applications to bond markets and to standard Keynesian models. The dynamics are determined by standard arbitrage relationships between bond prices and short-term interest rates; 'small' shocks are applied to short-term interest rates (or to the money market); and the 'large' shock is a partial, temporary repudiation of government-issued consols, triggered by high values of short-term rates or of debt stocks.

The applications are interesting but do not directly address issues of 'psychological crowding out' or expectational shifts. In the introduction, the authors discuss informally the possibility of perverse effects of fiscal policy on output: intuitively, this may be the case if changes in current policies were to increase disproportionately the likelihood of drastic policy reversals in the near future.

The stochastic saddlepath framework can address these issues. For example, the exchange rate determination model of Flood and Garber (1989) has a stochastic money supply process, with continuous, small changes and large changes (unsterilized intervention) when the exchange rate reaches the limits of a predetermined fluctuation band. Flood and Garber show that positive money supply blips can lead to exchange rate appreciation when the exchange rate is close to the level that triggers for large, negative money supply shocks. It appears possible to adapt these arguments to fiscal policy issues: to do so, however, it would be necessary to specify *policy* itself as stochastic. For example, the small shocks could be applied to government spending, g, rather than to the LM equation (8).

In the setting of this paper, fiscal policy issues could alternatively be addressed by analyzing output responses to unexpected, once-and-for-all changes in g, starting from different debt stock levels. This is a somewhat backward step (in the direction of nonstochastic saddlepath models), and would probably require numerical solutions, but still appears to be a worthwhile exercise.

The notion of 'excessive' government debt should also be made more precise in future work. Debt accumulation is stable in the macroeconomic model considered, not only because government expenditure g has no dynamics but also because taxation is directly linked to the stock of government debt equation (9). Under these assumptions, the government is always solvent and there is no compelling economic reason for debt repudiation: it would be interesting (but difficult!) to explore models in which a sequence of expansionary fiscal policy shocks would produce insolvency in the absence of a regime switch.

In conclusion, this paper deals with very interesting issues and takes important steps in what I think is the right direction. Technical problems, however, prevent it from reaching definitive conclusions: much difficult work remains to be done in future research.

NOTES

1 Some formal work has been done along these lines, assuming that agents make rational attempts to learn by experience: see, for example, the work in Frydman and Phelps (1983). In fact, the rational expectations approach does not survive such extensions very well: expectations are quite unlikely to converge, vindicating Keynes's point of view.
2 See e.g. Dornbusch (1976) for an early application, Obstfeld and Stockman (1985) for complex models.
3 Others have contributed to this branch of literature; see e.g. Froot and Obstfeld (1989).

REFERENCES

Dornbusch, Rudiger (1976). 'Expectations and Exchange Rate Dynamics', *Journal of Political Economy* **84**, 1161–76.
Frydman, Roman and Edmund S. Phelps (eds.) (1983). *Individual forecasting and aggregate outcomes: 'rational expectations' examined*, Cambridge University Press.
Flood, Robert P. and Peter M. Garber (1989). 'The Linkage Between Speculative Attack and Target Zone Models of Exchange Rates', mimeo.
Froot, Kenneth A. and Maurice Obstfeld (1989). 'Stochastic Process Switching: Some Simple Solutions', NBER working paper.
Obstfeld, Maurice and Alan C. Stockman (1985). 'Exchange Rate Dynamics', in P.B. Kenen and Ronald W. Jones (eds.) *Handbook of International Economics*, Vol. 2, North Holland.

11 Government domestic debt and the risk of default: a political–economic model of the strategic role of debt

PHILIPPE AGHION and PATRICK BOLTON

1   Introduction

Until recently, most research and controversy on macro fiscal policies was about when and whether debt-financed government deficits have real effects on aggregate output and employment. This problem has typically been studied in a model of a representative agent (or overlapping generations of representative agents) interacting with a benevolent government maximizing a Social Welfare Function. Naturally, only a limited set of issues (such as the role of fiscal policy in favouring optimal capital accumulation or in minimizing the deadweight loss of distortionary taxation) can be addressed within this framework (see Blanchard and Fischer, 1989, for an extensive discussion of this approach). Thus, a particularly important aspect of fiscal policy suppressed in this model is the (intragenerational) redistributive effect of fiscal policy and the consequent political conflicts arising from these distributional concerns. Behind the representative agent lurks a lot of heterogeneity, whether in terms of income and asset-holdings or of preferences. This paper focusses on the question of how differences in income and asset-holdings give rise to differences in preferences concerning fiscal policy and investigates how democratic political institutions solve the social choice problem of what fiscal policy to implement, when agents have conflicting preferences.

Our model is much inspired by the experience of public debt management and the political conflicts surrounding it in several European countries during the interwar period. This was a time when one of the major problems confronting the various governments was how to deal with the huge debt-overhang problem inherited from World War I. Very broadly, in several countries there was a clear conflict over fiscal policy between right-wing parties representing the interests of the rentiers (among others) and thus favouring conservative fiscal policies aimed at preserving the real value of government debt and other forms of nominal domestic savings, and left-wing parties representing the interests of the workers and unemployed and who favoured reflationary fiscal policies as well as increased expenditures on public goods. In several instance when left-wing parties were elected (as for instance the 'Cartel des Gauches' in 1924 and the 'Front Populaire' in 1936 in France) there shortly followed a period of more or less high inflation (fed by sharp increases in government spending) which amounted to a *de facto* default on public debt. Conservative governments on the contrary practiced severe fiscal restraint and endeavoured to curb inflation (see Alesina, 1988, for an illuminating survey of interwar debt policies in Europe).

We construct a model where these conflicts over fiscal policy clearly emerge as a result of differences in incomes between agents. We then analyse how fiscal policy is determined when the government is assumed to be in the hands of a political party elected through majority voting. The political party in power is assumed to pursue the interests of it own constituency rather than a general Social Welfare Function. In this paper, we restrict attention to a two-party system: the left-wing party identifies with the interests of agents having incomes below the average while the right-wing party represents those agents with incomes above the average. These party objectives give rise to fiscal policies where the left-wing party favours large government expenditure on public goods with concomitant high levels of taxation and/or high levels of indebtedness, and the right-wing party favours low levels of expenditure, low taxes and low levels of outstanding debt. The fiscal policy that is implemented is that of the party which wins the elections.

Within this model we address two sets of questions: first, what role if any does public debt play in the dynamic political game between the two parties in constraining the actions of future administrations? Second, to what extent does current fiscal policy have an impact on the outcome of future elections? Concerning the first question, large levels of outstanding debt constrain future governments both in terms of limiting future expenditure on public goods and in forcing higher levels of taxation to repay the debt. We show that a left-wing government anticipating the victory of its conservative rival in the next elections finds it worthwhile to accumulate large levels of government debt in order both to 'substitute intertemporally' the provision of public goods and to increase redistribution in the future by imposing higher levels of taxation.[1] Surprisingly, however, this is the only instance where a government wishes to exploit the commitment effect of debt. Conservative governments do not wish to constrain future left-wing governments by excessively accumulating debt. Our results are thus in contrast with the earlier work of Alesina and Tabellini, (1987a, 1988), and Persson and Svensson (1989). Section 4 deals extensively with the *commitment effect of debt*. It discusses the precise connections between these papers and ours. It also points out that the commitment value of debt disappears when future governments are allowed to default on inherited outstanding debt. We show that current fiscal policies have an impact on the outcome of future elections only if future administrations contemplate the possibility of default (either through inflation or explicit default). Our model is one of complete information with forward-looking agents, where current fiscal policy only matters if it changes agents' preferences about future fiscal policies. It turns out that preference reversals can only occur if there is a risk of default. The basic point is as follows: a current conservative government accumulating large levels of debt can swing the outcome of future elections in its favour because its left-wing rival is rationally expected to default on the debt while the conservative party is rationally expected to repay it. The larger the outstanding debt the more voters become concerned with maintaining the real value of debt and thus the more favourably inclined they are towards a conservative administration. Large levels of debt change the outcome of elections to the extent that they shift the conflict about fiscal policy away from issues of more or less expenditure on public goods towards issues of more or less monetization of the debt. Interestingly, left-wing parties may be able to use debt in the same way as the conservative government above. The circumstances in which this happens are described in Section 5.

2   The model

We consider a closed economy with no foreign debt or lending. This economy is composed of a continuum of agents who all live for two periods. At the beginning of each period, elections are held to appoint a new government. Agents have identical preferences but different incomes. Each agent is identified by a parameter α which measures his income in each period (agents earn the same income in both periods). The source of agents' earnings is not modelled. The economy's income distribution in the absence of intertemporal transfers is given by $f(\alpha)$ with support $[0, 1]$. The individual voters' preferences are assumed to be represented by the utility function:

$$U(c_t; g_t) = \log(c_1 + g_1) + \beta \log(c_2 + g_2) \tag{1}$$

where c_t is consumption of the private good in period t and g_t is consumption of the public good; β is the discount factor. Of course, this is a rather special utility function. We adopt it mainly to make calculations tractable. Our results hold for a much wider class of utility functions.[2]

The public good, g_t, is provided by the government.[3] In fact, in our model the government's role is limited to determining the level of current expenditure on the public good and the method of financing it. In period 1 the government can choose between various combinations of tax and debt financing. In period 2 only taxes are available to finance both debt repayments and expenditure on the public good.

Throughout most of the paper we assume that income-tax rates are uniform and, to begin with, we shall make the additional assumptions that:

(i) taxes are not distortionary.

(ii) the rate of transformation between the private and the public good is equal to one. Later in the paper we relax the latter assumption.[4] We denote by τ_1 and τ_2 the tax rates in periods 1 and 2 respectively. The government can choose any tax rate between zero and one.[5] Finally, given the tax rate τ_1 in period one and given the government's expenditure on public goods g_1, and amount of public debt accumulated in period 1 is given by the government's budget constraint:

$$D = g_1 - \int_0^1 \tau_1 \, \alpha f(\alpha) \, d\alpha \tag{2}$$

The interest rate at which the government can borrow, r, will be determined endogenously in the model.

Now, an agent with income α, anticipating government expenditures on the public good, g_1 and g_2, financed with tax rates τ_1 and τ_2 solve the following intertemporal consumption problem:[6]

$$\left. \begin{aligned} \max_{c_1; c_2; s} \ & \log(c_1 + g_1) + \beta \log(c_2 + g_2) \\ \text{s.t.} \quad & c_1 + s \le \alpha(1 - \tau_1) \\ & c_2 \le \alpha(1 - \tau_2) + s \cdot \rho \end{aligned} \right\} \tag{3}$$

where $\rho \equiv 1 + r$.

We model the political process as follows:

At each period there are two political parties competing to be elected: a left-wing party and a right-wing party.[7] Once a party is in power it has total control over τ_t and g_t. Prior to the election, a party cannot commit itself to pursuing a particular fiscal policy if it is elected.[8] To fix ideas, we represent the sequences of moves and events in the time-line (Figure 11.1): Whichever party get more votes is elected. How do we distinguish between a left-wing and a right-wing party? We assume that the left-wing party represents primarily the interests of those individuals whose income is below the *average income* in the economy. The right-wing party represents primarily the interests of those whose income is above the

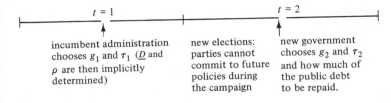

Figure 11.1 The time line

average. More specifically, we suppose that the left-wing party maximizes the interests of some income group $\alpha_L < E\alpha$; and that the right-wing party maximizes the interests of some income group $\alpha_R > E\alpha$. Both α_R and α_L are exogenously given, and we do not consider the question of how a party may wish to choose α in order to maximize the probability of being elected.

We shall be interested in the subgame-perfect equilibria of this game. As usual, one solves for these equilibria backwards. This is particularly straightforward in this model since there is perfect information and no uncertainty.[9] The only potential difficulty arises from the endogeneity of the interest rate. The individual agents' savings decisions depend on their (rational) expectations about future policy as well as on the equilibrium interest rate; and the latter simultaneously influences and depends on future policy. Before solving for the perfect equilibria of the game described above, we shall consider various scenarios which will serve as helpful benchmarks. We begin by solving for the optimal government policies when the government is respectively a social planner, a right-wing dictator and a left-wing dictator, assuming that the government does not default on outstanding public debt in period 2. Then we solve for the political equilibrium, first assuming no default and secondly, allowing the period-2 governments to default on outstanding public debt.

3 Optimal policy decisions of a social planner and of right-wing and left-wing dictators

Throughout this paper we only consider optimal time-consistent policies. These are the relevant benchmarks to compare with the dynamic political equilibrium. We call a dictator a government pursuing the interests of his own clientele and who remains in power in periods 1 and 2.[10] A social planner, on the other hand, maximizes the utility of a representative average consumer. We are particularly interested in finding out how much debt each type of government wants to accumulate in period 1.

To begin with, consider the optimal savings behaviour of an agent with income α. Solving the maximization problem (3) yields the following savings function:

$$s(\alpha;\, \rho,\, \tau_t,\, g_t) = \frac{\beta\rho(g_1 + \alpha(1 - \tau_1)) - (g_2 + \alpha(1 - \tau_2))}{(1 + \beta)\rho} \tag{4}$$

The equilibrium interest rate r is then given by the following equation:

$$\int_0^1 s(\alpha;\, \rho,\, \tau_t,\, g_t) f(\alpha)\, d\alpha = D \tag{5}$$

where $\rho = 1 + r$.

The LHS represents the net supply of savings and the RHS the demand for savings. Using equation (4) and the two government budget constraints, $g_1 = \tau_1 E\alpha + D$ and $g_2 = \tau_2 E\alpha - D\rho$ (where $E\alpha$ denotes the average income in the economy), one easily solves for the equilibrium interest rate:

Lemma 1: In equilibrium we have $\rho = 1/\beta$ for all levels of debt $D \in [0;\, E\alpha \cdot \beta]$.

Proof. Obvious.

The level of outstanding debt cannot exceed $E\alpha \cdot \beta$, for otherwise the government is unable to pay back all the public debt in period 2.[11]

Consider first the optimal policy chosen by a social planner in periods 1 and 2. We suppose that the social planner maximizes the utility of a representative average consumer. The main reason for selecting this social welfare function is that it allows us to characterize a point on the Pareto-frontier abstracting from distributional issues between high- and low-income agents. This is not the case, for instance, with the utilitarian welfare function which corresponds to maximizing the sum of the utilities. The latter welfare function leads to perfect equality as the social optimum in our model.[12]

Thus, in period 2 the social planner chooses τ_2 and g_2 to maximize the utility of the consumer with income $E\alpha$:

$$\log\left[g_2 + E\alpha(1 - \tau_2) + \frac{s(E\alpha;\, \rho,\, \tau_t,\, g_t)}{\beta}\right] \tag{6}$$

where $g_2 = \tau_2 E\alpha - \dfrac{D}{\beta}$. (Recall $\rho = 1/\beta$ from lemma 1).

Substituting for g_2 in (6) it is clear that the social planner is indifferent between any second-period tax rate $\tau_2 \in \left[\dfrac{D}{\beta E\alpha};\, 1\right]$.[13] Since taxes are non-discretionary, and since the rate of transformation between the private and the public good is equal to one, *the social planner is indifferent between any feasible level of expenditure on public goods.*

A similar result holds in period 1. In the first period, the social planner chooses τ_1, D and g_1 to solve:

$$\max_{\tau_1; D} \log(c_1 + g_1) + \beta \log(c_2 + g_2)$$

$$\text{subject to: } c_1 = E\alpha(1 - \tau_1) - s(E\alpha; \rho, \tau_t, g_t)$$

$$g_1 = \tau_1 E\alpha + D \qquad (7)$$

$$c_2 = E\alpha(1 - \tau_2) - s(E\alpha; \rho, \tau_t, g_t) \cdot \frac{1}{\beta}$$

$$g_2 = \tau_2 E\alpha + D\rho$$

Now, notice that $\dfrac{d(c_i + g_i)}{d\tau_i} = 0$; $(i = 1, 2)$. Consequently, the social planner is indifferent between any level of taxation $\tau_i \in [0, 1]$. It is also straightforward to see that $\dfrac{d(c_i + g_i)}{dD} = 0$; $(i = 1, 2)$, so that *the social planner is indifferent between any feasible level of debt and therefore between feasible level of period 1 expenditure on public goods.* This result is reminiscent of the *Ricardian equivalence theorem,* to the extent that the government's financial structure is indeterminate as a result of individuals' intertemporal arbitrage behaviour. That is to say, when the government deficit increases today, agents save more to pay future increases in taxes (note that $\dfrac{ds(\alpha; \rho, \tau_t, g_t)}{dD} = 1$ so that one extra dollar of deficit today is exactly offset by an extra dollar of savings). However our result is more general than the Ricardian equivalence theorem, since government expenditure decisions here are endogenous. The indeterminacy is not only in the financial structure, but also in the optimal level of government expenditure. One might refer to this result as 'Ricardian super indeterminacy'. To complete our characterization of the social optimum note that if the social planner were allowed to default on public outstanding debt in period 2, it is easy to show that he would be indifferent between default and no default. This is altogether not surprising given that taxes are assumed to be nondistortionary.

As will become clear below, the social planner's optimal policy differs from that of a left-wing or right-wing dictator. Consider first the optimal fiscal policy of a dictator of type α in period 2 (in other words, the optimal policy of a government which represents the interests of the income-group α): the government then chooses τ_2 and g_2 to solve:

$$\max_{\tau_1; g_2} \log(c_2 + g_2)$$

$$\text{subject to: } c_2 = \alpha(1 - \tau_2) + \rho \cdot s(\alpha; \rho, \tau_t, g_t)$$

$$\text{and} \qquad g_2 = \tau_2 \cdot E\alpha - D\rho \qquad (8)$$

where s, ρ, D are taken as given).

Solving (8) one easily obtains the result that if $\alpha > E\alpha$, the government chooses $g_2 = 0$ and $\tau_2 = \dfrac{D\pi}{E\alpha}$. In other words, the government chooses to minimize expenditure on the public good. Vice-versa, if $\alpha \leq E\alpha$, the government chooses $\tau_2 = 1$ and $g_2 = E\alpha - D\rho$; that is, the government maximizes expenditure on the public good.

In period 1, a dictator of type α chooses τ_1 and D to solve:

$$
\left.
\begin{aligned}
&\max_{\tau_1;\,D} \ \log(c_1 + g_1) + \beta\log(c_2 + g_2^*) \\[4pt]
&\text{subject to: } \ c_1 = \alpha(1 - \tau_1) - s(\alpha;\, \rho,\, \tau_t,\, g_t) \\[4pt]
&\qquad\qquad\quad c_2 = \alpha(1 - \tau_2^*) + s(\alpha;\, \rho,\, \tau_t,\, g_t)\rho \\[4pt]
&\text{and} \qquad\quad g_1 = \tau_1 E\alpha + D \\[4pt]
&\qquad\qquad\quad g_2^* = \tau_2^* E\alpha - D\rho
\end{aligned}
\right\} \qquad (9)
$$

where g_2^* and τ_2^* are the solutions to problem (8) and where

$$
\begin{aligned}
&s(\alpha;\, \rho,\, \tau_t,\, g_t) \\[4pt]
&= \frac{\tau_1 E\alpha + D + \alpha(1 - \tau_1) - (\tau_2^* E\alpha - D/\beta + \alpha(1 - \tau_2^*))}{\dfrac{(1 + \beta)}{\beta}}
\end{aligned}
$$

One can easily verify that if $\alpha \leq E\alpha$, then both $c_1 + g_1$ and $c_2 + g_2$ (as defined in (9)) are increasing in τ_1. It follows that the optimal solution is to set $\tau_1 = 1$. Vice-versa, if $\alpha > E\alpha$, then $c_1 + g_1$ and $c_2 + g_2$ are decreasing in τ_1 so that the solution then is to set $\tau_1 = 0$. Thus if a dictator wants to maximize tax revenues (and expenditure on public goods) he wants to do so in both periods. The same is true if he wants to minimize taxes. Given our assumptions on α_L and α_R, this means that *a left-wing dictator wants to maximize expenditure on public goods*, and a *right-wing dictator wants to minimize expenditure*.

It remains to determine how much debt each type of dictator is willing to incur in period 1. *A left-wing dictator, who sets $\tau_1 = \tau_2 = 1$, will be indifferent between any level of debt below $E\alpha \cdot \beta$.* This follows from the fact that both $c_1 + g_1$ and $c_2 + g_2$ (as defined in (9)) remain constant as the level of debt is changed. The left-wing dictator is indifferent between debt and taxes, since any increase in debt today implies a corresponding reduction in expenditure on the public good tomorrow so that the increase in utility from more expenditure on public goods today is exactly offset by a reduction in utility tomorrow.

To determine how much debt a right-wing dictator is willing to accumulate in period 1, it suffices again to see how $(c_1 + g_1)$ and $(c_2 + g_2)$ vary with D. The right-wing dictator minimizes public expenditures and thus sets $\tau_1 = 0$; $\tau_2 = \dfrac{D\rho}{E\alpha}$. Total consumption in periods 1 and 2, respectively, for an individual of type α_R then becomes:

$$c_1 + g_1 = D + \alpha_R - \frac{D + \dfrac{\alpha_R D}{E\alpha} \cdot \dfrac{1}{\beta}}{\dfrac{1 + \beta}{\beta}} \tag{10}$$

$$c_2 + g_2 = \alpha_R \left(1 - \frac{D}{E\alpha} \cdot \frac{1}{\beta}\right) + \frac{D + \dfrac{\alpha_R D}{E\alpha} \cdot \dfrac{1}{\beta}}{(1 + \beta)} \tag{11}$$

Differentiating (10) and (11) with respect to D, one obtains:

$$\frac{\partial(c_1 + g_1)}{\partial D} = \frac{1}{1 + \beta}\left(1 - \frac{\alpha_R}{E\alpha}\right); \quad \frac{\partial(c_2 + g_2)}{\partial D} = \frac{1}{1 + \beta}\left(1 - \frac{\alpha_R}{E\alpha}\right) \tag{12}$$

Since $\alpha_R > E\alpha$ by assumption we obtain the conclusion that a *right-wing dictator strictly prefers not to issue any public debt in period 1*. This result is all the more striking in that taxes are not distortionary in our model. The intuition behind this result is straightforward. The consumers with incomes above the average bear most of the taxation cost of servicing the debt in period 2. In fact, it is easy to verify that those consumers with incomes below the average pay less than one dollar in taxes for any one dollar of debt repayment they receive. Therefore, debt accumulation indirectly serves the role of a redistributive tax. This explains why right-wing administrations strictly prefer noↄ to accumulate debt. It does not, however, explain why left-wing administrations are indifferent between debt accumulation and no debt accumulation. The latter result is obtained because taxes and expenditure on public goods are a (weakly) superior instrument of income redistribution; so that the role of debt in redistributing income becomes irrelevant.

4   Dynamic political equilibrium with no default

If elected, a right-wing administration will choose to minimize expenditure on the public good by setting the period-2 tax rate $\tau_2 = \max\left\{0; \dfrac{D\rho}{E\alpha}\right\}$. A left-wing administration will do the opposite and set $\tau_2 = 1$. This was established in the previous section. Note that the policy objective in period 2 of each type of administration is the same *regardless of what fiscal policy was implemented in period 1*. What affects the policy objective in period 2 is only the location of the political party in power ($\alpha_L < E\alpha < \alpha_R$).

Voters know the policy objectives of each party and rationally foresee what fiscal policy each party will implement. We assume that voters always vote and that they vote for the party implementing the fiscal policy which is in their individual best interest.[14] Our model has a useful feature which considerably simplifies the derivation of the political equilibrium in period 2: we can define an income-group, denoted by $\hat{\alpha}$, such that all voters with this income are indifferent between the policies of a right-wing government and those of a left-wing government. This income group is uniquely determined, and all voters with incomes α less than $\hat{\alpha}$ vote for the left-wing candidate and all voters with incomes above $\hat{\alpha}$ vote for the right-wing candidate. In other words, our model has the feature that income is a perfect predictor of voting behaviour. In Section 3, it was shown that a government representing the income group $E\alpha$ is indifferent between minimizing or maximizing expenditure on the public good for any given first-period fiscal policy. It follows that in our model $\hat{\alpha} = E\alpha$, and that there is a left-wing majority if the median income $\alpha_m \leq E\alpha$ and a right-wing majority when $\alpha_m > E\alpha$. Our discussion so far not only characterizes the second-period political equilibrium, but also establishes our first important result:

Proposition 1: *When governments cannot default on outstanding domestic debt, then past and current budget deficits have no strategic effect. In other words, public debt cannot be used to influence the outcome of future elections.*

Proposition 1 follows from the fact that each candidates' period 2 fiscal policy and the median voter's preferences remain the same for any $D \in [0, E\alpha \cdot \beta]$. Thus, with no default, public debt can only be used to *constrain* the policies of future administrations as in Alesina and Tabellini (1987a) and Persson and Svensson (1989). The remaining part of this section will be devoted to the analysis of optimal first-period fiscal policy when the incumbent party knows that it will be replaced in period 2. We determine to what extent the party in place in period 1 wants to constrain the policies of its opponent in period 2.

We begin with the case where a left-wing administration in period 1 knows that it will be followed by a right-wing administration in period 2. Such a situation might arise, for instance, if after the period-1 elections there was a shift in income distribution (or a change in tastes) such that in the new elections in period 2 there is a right-wing majority (that is, $f(\alpha)$ is such that $\alpha_m > E\alpha$). Then, the left-wing administration will choose its fiscal policy, $\oint \equiv (\tau_1, D, g_1)$ to maximize the utility of its clientele, anticipating the policy followed by the right-wing administration in period 2:

$$\begin{cases} \max_{\tau_1, D, g_1} \log(c_1 + g_1) + \beta \log(c_2 + g_2) \\[2mm] \text{subject to:} \quad c_1 + g_1 = \tau_1 E\alpha + D + \alpha_L(1 - \tau_1) - s(\alpha_L; \rho) \quad (13) \\[2mm] \qquad\qquad c_2 + g_2 = \alpha_L \left(1 - \dfrac{D\rho}{E\alpha}\right) + s(\alpha_L; \rho) \cdot \rho \end{cases}$$

where $s(\alpha_L; \rho) = s(\alpha_L; 1/\beta) = \dfrac{\tau_1 E\alpha + D + \alpha_L(1 - \tau_1) - \alpha_L \left(1 - \dfrac{D\rho}{E\alpha}\right)}{(1 + \beta)/\beta}$.

Again, it is easy to verify that $\dfrac{\partial(c_1 + g_1)}{\partial \tau_1} > 0$ and $\dfrac{\partial(c_2 + g_2)}{\partial \tau_1} > 0$, so that the left-wing government sets $\tau_1 = 1$. More interesting is the debt policy; we have:

$$\frac{\partial(c_1 + g_1)}{\partial D} = 1 - \frac{1 + \dfrac{\alpha_L}{E\alpha} \cdot \dfrac{1}{\beta}}{(1 + \beta)/\beta} = \frac{1}{1 + \beta}\left[1 - \frac{\alpha_L}{E\alpha}\right] \quad (14)$$

and

$$\frac{\partial(c_2 + g_2)}{\partial D} = \frac{1}{1 + \beta}\left[1 - \frac{\alpha_L}{E\alpha}\right] \quad (15)$$

since $\alpha_L < E\alpha$ (by assumption), we have that both period 1 and period 2 utility is increasing in D. We thus obtain our second noteworthy result:

Proposition 2: *A left-wing government followed by a right-wing government will run budget deficits in order to 'constrain' the right-wing government.*

In fact the left-wing government will choose to accumulate the maximum sustainable public debt: $D = E\alpha \cdot \beta$. The intuition behind Proposition 2 is simple. By accumulating public debt, the left-wing government can increase expenditure on public goods in period 1. This increases the period-1 utility of all consumers with incomes below the average. It is perhaps more surprising that it also increases their utility in period 2. This follows from the fact that most of the tax burden of servicing the debt falls on wealthy consumers with incomes above the average. For any one dollar of debt repayment by the right-wing government in period 2, a consumer with income less than the average is taxed less than one dollar. Thus debt accumulation with no default amounts to an indirect income transfer from the wealthy to the poor. The only income group that is neither hurt nor favoured by debt accumulation is the average-income group. It follows that, from the perspective of a left-wing party, being replaced by a right-wing party accumulation is favourable in both periods.[15]

We close this section with the case where a right-wing administration is followed by a left-wing administration. We know that the left-wing administration will choose $\tau_2 = 1$ and $g_2 = E\alpha - D\rho$, so that the right-wing administration chooses $\oint = (\tau_1, D, g_1)$ to solve:

$$
\begin{cases}
\max_{\tau_1, D, g_1} \log(c_1 + g_1) + \beta \log(c_2 + g_2) \\[2mm]
\text{s.t.} \quad c_1 + g_1 = \tau_1 \cdot E\alpha + D + \alpha_R(1 - \tau_1) \\[2mm]
\qquad\qquad - \dfrac{\tau_1 E\alpha + D + \alpha_R(1 - \tau_1) - (E\alpha - D/\beta)}{(1 + \beta)/\beta} \\[4mm]
\qquad c_2 + g_2 = E\alpha - D/\beta \\[2mm]
\qquad\qquad + \dfrac{1}{\beta}\left[\dfrac{\tau_1 E\alpha + D + \alpha_R(1 - \tau_1) - (E\alpha - D/\beta)}{(1 + \beta)/\beta}\right]
\end{cases}
\tag{16}
$$

Again it is straightforward to check that a right-wing administration will minimize taxes in period 1 ($\tau_1 = 0$). If we differentiate $(c_1 + g_1)$ and $(c_2 + g_2)$ with respect to D, we obtain:

$$
\frac{\partial(c_1 + g_1)}{\partial D} = 1 - \frac{1 + 1/\beta}{(1 + \beta)/\beta} = 0
\tag{17}
$$

$$
\frac{\partial(c_2 + g_2)}{\partial D} = -\frac{1}{\beta} + \frac{1}{\beta}\left[\frac{1 + 1/\beta}{(1 + \beta)/\beta}\right] = 0
\tag{18}
$$

This implies that a right-wing administration followed by a left-wing administration is indifferent between any level of debt $D \in \left[0, \dfrac{E\alpha}{\beta}\right]$:

Proposition 3: *A right-wing administration followed by a left-wing administration does not gain by constraining the future administration's policy choices through the accumulation of debt.*

This result is in sharp contrast to the conclusions obtained by, say Persson and Svensson (1989); and also to those obtained in the present model when a right-wing administration is followed by another right-wing administration. The reason why the right-wing incumbent is indifferent is because debt plays no indirect redistributive role when all income is taxed away in period 2. As a result, any increase in debt today resulting in an increase in period-1 utility is exactly offset by a decrease in utility in period 2, since the equilibrium interest rates is $\rho = \dfrac{1}{\beta}$.

7 Dynamic political equilibrium with costless default

We have already pointed out in Section 3 that with no distortionary taxes, a social planner is indifferent between default and no default in period 2. Our first important result of this section is that both a left-wing government and a right-wing government strictly prefer default in period 2, even though taxes are non-distortionary. We go on to show, however, that this conclusion crucially depends on the assumption that the rate of transformation between the private and the public good is (less than or) equal to one. As soon as the rate of transformation exceeds one, it is no longer generally true that both types of government strictly prefer default.

Consider first the default decision of a left-wing administration ($\alpha_L < E\alpha$) inheriting a total debt of D. We know that such an administration maximizes expenditure on public goods by setting $\tau_2 = 1$. If it defaults, total expenditure on public goods is given by $E\alpha$, and every consumer in the economy gets utility $\log E\alpha$.[16] If it does not default, then total expenditure on the public good is $E\alpha - D/\beta$ and a consumer with income α gets period-2 utility of $\log[E\alpha - D/\beta + s(\alpha, 1/\beta) \cdot 1/\beta]$. Thus a left-wing administration prefers to default if and only if: $E\alpha > E\alpha - D/\beta + s(\alpha_L; 1/\beta) \cdot 1/\beta$

$$D > s(\alpha_L; 1/\beta) \tag{19}$$

We know from the credit-market equilibrium that

$$D = \int_0^1 s(\alpha; 1/\beta) f(\alpha) \, d\alpha = Es(\alpha; 1/\beta) = s(E\alpha; 1/\beta) \tag{20}$$

The last equality in (20) follows from the linearity of the savings function $s(\alpha; 1/\beta)$ in α. Since $\alpha_L < E\alpha$, it follows that (19) is verified for all $D \in (0, E\alpha \cdot \beta)$. Thus we obtain:

Proposition 4: *A left-wing administration (such that $\alpha_L < E\alpha$) strictly prefers to default on any positive level of outstanding public debt.*

By refusing to repay the outstanding debt, a left-wing administration can increase even further its expenditure on public goods. Since savings are an increasing function of income, default becomes another form of redistributive taxation. A left-wing government represents the interests of those agents who benefit from this redistribution and therefore favours default. This is altogether not very surprising. We were, however, astonished at first to get the next result about the incentives to default of a right-wing administration. We know that the latter wants to minimize expenditure on the public good and therefore sets $\tau_2 = \max \left\{ 0, \dfrac{D}{\beta E\alpha} \right\}$ if it does not default. In that case, an individual with income α gets a period-2 utility of

$\log \left[\alpha \left(1 - \dfrac{D}{\beta E\alpha} \right) + s(\alpha; 1/\beta) \right]$. If the right-wing government defaults, period-2 utility becomes simply $\log \alpha$. Thus a right-wing government defaults if and only if:

$$\alpha_R > \alpha_R \left[1 - \frac{D}{\beta E\alpha} \right] + s(\alpha_R; 1/\beta) \cdot 1/\beta \tag{21}$$

where $\alpha_R > E\alpha$).

In words, if the cost of increased taxation required to finance debt repayments outweigh the benefits to those individuals with incomes above the average, then the right-wing government prefers to default. It turns out that the costs are always greater than the benefits for any positive level of inherited debt:

Proposition 5: *A right-wing administration such that $\alpha_R > E\alpha$ defaults on any positive level of outstanding debt.*

Proof. Condition (21) is equivalent to

$$\alpha_R \frac{D}{E\alpha} > s(\alpha_R; 1/\beta)$$

where:

$$s(\alpha_R; 1/\beta) = \frac{D + \alpha_R(1 - \tau_1) + E\alpha \cdot \tau_1 - \alpha_R \left[1 - \dfrac{D}{\beta E\alpha} \right]}{(1 + \beta)/\beta}$$

$$\leqslant \frac{D \left[1 + \dfrac{\alpha_R}{E\alpha} \cdot \dfrac{1}{\beta} \right]}{(1 + \beta)/\beta}$$

but

$$\alpha_R \frac{D}{E\alpha} > \frac{D \left[\beta + \dfrac{\alpha_R}{E\alpha} \right]}{(1 + \beta)} \geqslant s(\alpha_R; 1/\beta)$$

since

$$\alpha_R(1 + \beta) > \beta E\alpha + \alpha_R \Leftrightarrow \alpha_R > E\alpha \qquad \Box$$

We pointed out earlier that if there is no default, then the agents with incomes above the average pay more in taxes to finance debt repayment than the value of their bond holdings. It is then obvious that they should prefer the government to default. The implications of Propositions 4 and 5 are far-reaching. *If default is costless, there does not exist a rational-expectations political equilibrium where government expenditures are financed through debt* (except in the degenerate case where

$\alpha_L = \alpha_m = E\alpha = \alpha_R$). This is all the more striking as taxes are not distortionary. The reason why there cannot be positive public debt in equilibrium is that no one will agree to lending to the government in period 1 if they anticipate default in period 2. Another obvious consequence of these propositions is that public debt plays neither a strategic nor a constraining role when default is costless *ex-post*.[17]

To leave it at that, however, would be misleading. It turns out that Propositions 4 and 5 are not robust to small changes in the parameters of the model. Specifically, if the rate of transformation between the private good and the public good is $1 + \lambda$ ($\lambda > 0$) instead of 1, then Propositions 4 and 5 are no longer generally valid.[18]

The main modification introduced into the model the rate of transformation is given by $1 + \lambda$ is that the subset of income groups preferring expenditure maximization (respectively, expenditure minimization) on public goods no longer coincides with the subset of income groups who prefer default on public debt when period-2 tax rates are maximized (respectively, minimized). As a result, there exists a range of middle-income groups who strictly prefer no default. We demonstrate this last point rigorously below and investigate the implications of this result for the dynamic political equilibrium.

When the rate of transformation between the private and the public good is less than one, supplying the public good becomes less attractive, other things being equal. As a result, one should expect fewer income groups to prefer expenditure maximization on public goods than before. This is indeed the result we obtain here: if a government representing income group α is elected in period 2, it will set the tax rate τ_2 to solve:

$$
\left.
\begin{aligned}
&\max_{\tau_2} \ \log(c_2 + g_2) \\
&\text{subject to:} \quad c_2 = \alpha(1 - \tau_2) + s(\alpha; \rho)\cdot\rho \\
&\qquad\qquad g_2 = \frac{\tau_2 E\alpha - D\rho}{1 + \lambda}
\end{aligned}
\right\}
\tag{22}
$$

(assuming that there is no default on public debt). Notice that any dollar raised through taxes and spent on the public good yields $\dfrac{1}{1 + \lambda}$ more units of the public good. From the first-order conditions we obtain that

$$
\left.
\begin{aligned}
&\tau_2^* = 1 &&\text{if } \alpha \leq \frac{E\alpha}{1 + \lambda} \\
&\tau_2^* = \max\left\{0; \frac{D\rho}{E\alpha}\right\} &&\text{if } \alpha > \frac{E\alpha}{1 + \lambda}
\end{aligned}
\right\}
\tag{23}
$$

While in the previous sections all income groups below the average income strictly preferred maximum expenditure on public goods, now only those income groups below $\dfrac{E\alpha}{1+\lambda}$ prefer expenditure maximization.

If the public good is more expensive to produce one should also expect that fewer income groups prefer default in order to increase expenditure on the public good, and consequently that fewer possible administrations would choose to default in period 2.

The next result shows that this intuition is indeed correct! Assuming that the first-period tax rate has been set equal to zero,[19] consider how an elected government located at α assesses a default decision:

Suppose first that $\tau_2 = 1$. In that case default is attractive if and only if:

$$\frac{E\alpha}{1+\alpha} > \frac{E\alpha - D\hat{\rho}}{1+\lambda} + s(\alpha;\hat{\rho})\cdot\hat{\rho}$$

or $\qquad \dfrac{D}{1+\lambda} > s(\alpha;\hat{\rho})$ $\qquad\qquad\qquad\qquad$ (24)

where:

$$s(\alpha;\rho) = \frac{\beta\rho\left(\dfrac{D}{1+\lambda}+\alpha\right) - \dfrac{E\alpha - D\rho}{1+\lambda}}{(1+\beta)\rho} \qquad\qquad (25)$$

and $\hat{\rho}$ is the (correctly anticipated) equilibrium interest rate in period 2 when $\tau_2 = 1$ and the elected government does not default:

We can then establish the following lemma:

Lemma 1: $\exists \underline{\alpha} \in (0, E\alpha)$ such that if τ_2 is to be chosen equal to 1, then all income groups $\alpha \in (0, \underline{\alpha})$ prefer *default* whereas all income groups $\alpha \in (\underline{\alpha}, 1)$ prefer *no default*. Furthermore $\underline{\alpha}$ is increasing in D, and $\underline{\alpha}(0) = E\alpha$.

Proof. First, the equilibrium interest rate $\hat{\rho}$, when the period-2 government is expected both to set $\tau_2 = 1$ and to avoid default, is defined by:

$$Es(\alpha;\hat{\rho}) = s(E\alpha;\hat{\rho}) = D,$$

where $s(\alpha;\rho)$ is defined in (25).

We then have, for all α:

$$s(\alpha;\hat{\rho}) = D + (s(\alpha;\hat{\rho}) - s(E\alpha;\hat{\rho}))$$

$$= D + \frac{(\alpha - E\alpha)\beta}{1+\beta} \qquad\qquad\qquad (26)$$

Hence (24) can be rewritten as:

$$\frac{D}{1+\lambda} > D + \frac{(\alpha - E\alpha)\beta}{1+\beta}$$

Which in turn is equivalent to:

$$\alpha < \underline{\alpha}(D) = E\alpha - \frac{(1+\beta)\lambda D}{(1+\lambda)\beta} \tag{27}$$

We immediately verify that: $\underline{\alpha}(0) = E\alpha$ and that $\underline{\alpha}$ is decreasing in D. $\square$

In words: when the rate of transformation between public and private goods is greater than one and if $\tau_2 = 1$, the range of middle incomes which strictly prefer no default increases with the amount of outstanding debt, D.[20] Furthermore, our analysis so far implies that a (left-wing) government located between $\alpha = 0$ and $\alpha = \underline{\alpha}$ chooses $\tau_2 = 1$ and defaults on its outstanding debt; whereas a government located between $\underline{\alpha}$ and $\dfrac{E\alpha}{1+\lambda}$ chooses $\tau_2 = 1$ and no default.

Consider next how agents assess the default decision when the government in place in period 2 minimizes expenditure on the public good (i.e., when $\tau_2 = 0$ or $\tau_2 = \dfrac{D\rho}{E\alpha}$ depending on whether the government honours its debts). Then an agent earning income α strictly prefers the government to default if and only if:

$$\alpha > \alpha\left(1 - \frac{D\rho}{E\alpha}\right) + \rho \cdot s(\alpha; \rho)$$

or: $$\frac{\alpha D}{E\alpha} > s(\alpha; \rho) = \frac{\beta\rho\left(\dfrac{D}{1+\lambda} + \alpha\right) - \alpha\left(1 - \dfrac{D\rho}{E\alpha}\right)}{(1+\beta)\rho} \tag{28}$$

($s(\alpha; \rho)$ is derived assuming that the government will not default).

We can then prove the following lemma which is similar to Lemma 1.

Lemma 2: If τ_2 is to be minimized by the period-2 government, then all income groups $\alpha < E\alpha$ prefer *no default*, and all income groups above $E\alpha$ prefer *default*.

Proof. We begin by deriving the equilibrium interest rate, ρ^*, when the period-2 government is expected to set $g_2 = 0$: the equilibrium interest rate is given by the equation:

$$Es(\alpha; \rho^*) = s(E\alpha; \rho^*) = D \tag{29}$$

where $s(\alpha; \rho)$ is defined in (28).

Now, let $g(\alpha) = \dfrac{\alpha D}{E\alpha} - s(\alpha; \rho^*)$

From (29), we have: $g(E\alpha) = 0$.

Furthermore g is linear in α and therefore monotonic in α. Next, we can show that the function g is increasing in α. Indeed, we have $g(1) > 0$ and

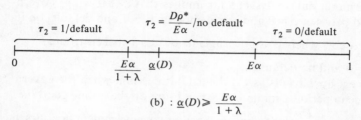

(a) : $\underline{\alpha}(\underline{D}) < \dfrac{E\alpha}{1 + \lambda}$

(b) : $\underline{\alpha}(D) \geqslant \dfrac{E\alpha}{1 + \lambda}$

Figure 11.2   The optimal default decision

$g\left(\dfrac{E\alpha}{1 + \lambda}\right) < 0$. This follows from the fact that when $\alpha = 1$, inequality (28) becomes equivalent to:

$$(1 + \lambda)D > D\lambda + D \cdot E\alpha,$$

which is automatically true since $E\alpha < 1$; this establishes: $g(1) > 0$; when $\alpha = \dfrac{E\alpha}{1 + \lambda}$, inequality (28) becomes equivalent to:

$$\beta\rho^*(1 + \beta)D > \beta\rho^*(1 + \beta)D + \beta \cdot (\rho^*\beta - 1),$$

which is violated since

$$\beta\rho^* = \dfrac{E\alpha(1 + \lambda)}{E\alpha(1 + \lambda) - D\lambda} > 1$$

hence $g\left(\dfrac{E\alpha}{1 + \lambda}\right) < 0$ and Lemma 2 is proved.   □

Lemma 2 then implies that a moderate-right-wing government located between $\dfrac{E\alpha}{1 + \lambda}$ and $E\alpha$ chooses both no default and minimum taxation in period 2 $\left(\text{i.e. } \tau_2 = \dfrac{D\rho^*}{E\alpha}\right)$; on the other hand a government located between $E\alpha$ and 1 chooses to default and sets $\tau_2 = 0$.

Figure 11.2 representing the support of the income distribution function summarizes our results about optimal tax rates in period 2 and the default decision when $\tau_1 = 0$:

As we shall now see, the presence of the middle-class of incomes $\alpha \in [\underline{\alpha}, E\alpha]$ *can create a situation where it is in the interest of a moderate right-wing party in power to excessively accumulate public debt in order to raise the likelihood of being reelected.* Recall that a left or right-wing party was (somewhat arbitrarily) defined to be a party representing primarily the interests of the income groups respectively *below* the *average* and *above* the average. Casual empiricism suggests that this is not always an unreasonble approximation. In the same spirit we shall define a *moderate-left-wing party* as one that puts more weight on middle-income groups but remains favourable to large public expenditure on public goods and a *moderate-right-wing* party as one that puts more weight on middle-income groups but prefers fiscal restraint. In terms of our model, a *moderate-left party* defends the interests of income groups $\alpha \in \left(\underline{\alpha}, \dfrac{E\alpha}{1 + \lambda} \right)$ and a *moderate-right* party represents the interests of those groups $\alpha \in \left(\dfrac{E\alpha}{1 + \lambda} ; E\alpha \right)$.

The next two propositions establish that under certain conditions a moderate right-wing party in power in period 1 may:

(i) successfully modify the voting behaviour of the median voter by accumulating debt and thus ensure its reelection.

(ii) be better off by following that strategy of debt accumulation.

Consider the situation where $\alpha_m < \dfrac{E\alpha}{1 + \lambda}$. Then with zero outstanding debt in period 2, there is a majority in favour of a left-wing candidate $(\alpha_L < \alpha_m)$ standing against a right-wing incumbent $\alpha_R \in \left(\dfrac{E\alpha}{1 + \lambda}, E\alpha \right)$.

We show in the first proposition that for a large enough outstanding debt, a new majority arises favouring this 'moderate' right-wing incumbent.

Proposition 6: *When α_m is close enough to $\dfrac{E\alpha}{1 + \lambda}$, there exists a level of outstanding debt D such that all $\alpha \in [\alpha_m, 1]$ strictly prefer the right-wing candidate over the left-wing challenger.*

Proof. In what follows, we suppose that $\alpha_m < \dfrac{E\alpha}{1 + \lambda}$ with α_m close to $\dfrac{E\alpha}{1 + \lambda}$.

Let $D > 0$ be a level of debt such that:

(a) $\underline{\alpha}(D) < \dfrac{E\alpha}{1 + \lambda}$.

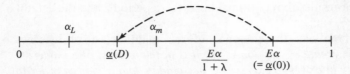

Figure 11.3   Shifting the median voter's preferences to the right

(b) $D \cdot \rho^* \leqslant E\alpha$ (where ρ^* is defined in Lemma 2).
(This condition says that it is feasible to repay the amount of debt D!).
Condition (b) is equivalent to:

$$D \leqslant \frac{\beta \cdot E\alpha}{1 + \beta \cdot \dfrac{\lambda}{1 + \lambda}} \tag{30}$$

Whereas condition (a) is equivalent to:

$$D > \frac{\beta \cdot E\alpha}{1 + \beta} \tag{31}$$

Note that these two inequalities (30) and (31) are consistent; they define a *non-empty set* of debt levels D.

Using the fact that $\underline{\alpha}(D)$ is continuously decreasing in D, we can always choose D sufficiently close to $\dfrac{\beta \cdot E\alpha}{1 + \beta}$ in order to have:

$$\alpha_L < \underline{\alpha}(D) < \frac{E\alpha}{1 + \lambda} \tag{32}$$

(see Figure 11.3).
For such a level of debt the left-wing candidate α_L will default in period 2 if elected; furthermore we know from the foregoing analysis that this left-wing candidate will set:

$$\tau_2 = 1 \quad \text{and} \quad g_2 = \frac{E\alpha}{1 + \lambda}.$$

On the other hand the right-wing candidate α_R will *not* default on this outstanding debt, D, if elected, since we have assumed $\alpha_R < E\alpha$; furthermore we know that such a right-wing candidate will set:

$$\tau_2 = \frac{D\rho^*}{E\alpha}; \quad g_2 = 0.$$

Clearly, if the median voter α_m were located below $\underline{\alpha}(D)$, he would automatically vote for the left-wing candidate α_L since both α_m and α_L would choose $\tau_2 = 1$ *and default* in that case. However, if α_m is sufficiently close to $\dfrac{E\alpha}{1 + \lambda}$, the level of debt D can always be chosen such that:

$$\alpha_L < \underline{\alpha}(D) < \alpha_m$$

(by continuity of $\underline{\alpha}$ w.r.t D).

For such a choice of D by the incumbent government, the median voter's most preferred period-2 policy becomes: $\tau_2 = 1$ and *no default*. However, the left-wing candidate will default on D if elected ($\alpha_L < \underline{\alpha}(D)$); and the right-wing candidate will minimize taxes τ_2

$$\left(\alpha_R > \frac{E\alpha}{1 + \lambda} \right)!$$

So, the median voter must compare the losses involved in electing either of the two candidates: if the left-wing candidate is elected, the median voter gets: $\dfrac{E\alpha}{1 + \lambda}$; if the right-wing candidate is elected he gets:

$$\alpha_m \left(1 - \frac{D\rho^*}{E\alpha} \right) + \rho^* \cdot s(\alpha_m; \rho^*).$$

(It is easy to show that the first period choice of τ_1 by the right-wing incumbent is given by $\tau_1 = 0$. Given this choice of τ_1, a left-wing party will indeed always default). Thus the median income earner (and therefore the median voter) votes for the right-wing incumbent if and only if:

$$\alpha_m \left(1 - \frac{D\rho^*}{E\alpha} \right) + \rho^* \cdot s(\alpha_m; \rho^*) > \frac{E\alpha}{1 + \lambda} \tag{33}$$

Let $\alpha_m = \dfrac{E\alpha}{1 + \lambda}$, then (35) is equivalent to

$$\frac{D\alpha_m}{E\alpha} < s(\alpha_m; \rho^*) \tag{34}$$

But from the proof of Lemma 2 we know that (34) is satisfied when $\alpha_m = \dfrac{E\alpha}{1 + \lambda}$. By continuity, the same inequality will hold for $\alpha_m < \dfrac{E\alpha}{1 + \lambda}$ but sufficiently close to $\dfrac{E\alpha}{1 + \lambda}$. □

By accumulating debt the moderate right-wing incumbent makes the left-wing challenger look bad in the eyes of moderate voters. The latter care about preserving the real value of their savings (i.e., the government not defaulting); they also like large expenditures on public goods. The problem for the left-wing candidate is that he cannot commit himself both to maximizing expenditure on public goods and not defaulting on the public debt. *When it comes to choosing between no default but fiscal restraint on the one hand and increased spending on public goods, but default on outstanding debt on the other, a lower-middle class voter may well prefer the former alternative.* An incumbent moderate-right-wing party can foresee this and thus use public debt to enhance its likelihood of re-election. The question remains, whether it is in the interest of a right-wing party to follow that strategy. The next proposition establishes this.

Proposition 7: *When λ is sufficiently small and α_m is sufficiently close to $\frac{E\alpha}{1 + \lambda}$ it will be in the right-wing incumbent's interest to accumulate a positive amount of debt ($D > 0$) in order to ensure its reelection.*

Proof. If the incumbent sets $D = 0$, the left-wing challenger wins the next election so that the right-wing party's total utility is given by

$$\log(\alpha_R - s(\alpha_R;0,\hat{\rho})) + \beta\log\left(\frac{E\alpha}{1 + \lambda} + s(\alpha_R;0,\hat{\rho}).\hat{\rho}\right) \tag{35}$$

where: $s(\alpha_R;0,\hat{\rho}) = \dfrac{\beta\hat{\rho}.\alpha_R - \dfrac{E\alpha}{1 + \lambda}}{(1 + \beta)\hat{\rho}}$

and $\hat{\rho}$ is given by: $s(E\alpha;0,\hat{\rho}) = 0$

i.e.: $\hat{\rho} = \dfrac{1}{\beta(1 + \lambda)}$

We can then reexpress (35) as:

$$\log\left(\alpha_R - \frac{\beta(\alpha_R - E\alpha)}{1 + \beta}\right) + \beta\log\left(\frac{E\alpha}{1 + \lambda} + \frac{\alpha_R - E\alpha}{(1 + \lambda)(1 + \beta)}\right) \tag{35'}$$

Now, suppose that the incumbent chooses the minimum amount $\underline{D}$ of debt necessary for him to reverse the outcome of the elections; when $\alpha_m = \dfrac{E\alpha}{1 + \lambda}$, this amount is simply defined by the equation:

$$\alpha(\underline{D}) = \frac{E\alpha}{1 + \lambda} \text{ where } \alpha(D) = E\alpha - \frac{(1 + \beta)\lambda D}{(1 + \lambda)\beta} \tag{36}$$

which yields:

$$\underline{D} = \frac{\beta E\alpha}{1 + \beta} \tag{37}$$

The incumbent right-wing's total utility in that case will be given by:

$$\log\left(\alpha_R + \frac{D}{1+\lambda} - s(\alpha_R;\underline{D},\rho(\underline{D}))\right) + \beta\log\left(\alpha_R\left(1 - \frac{D\rho(\underline{D})}{E\alpha}\right) + \right.$$

$$s(\alpha_R;\underline{D},\rho(\underline{D})).\rho(\underline{D})) \tag{38}$$

Now we can show that for λ sufficiently small:

$$\alpha_R - \frac{\beta(\alpha_R - E\alpha)}{1+\beta} < \alpha_R\left(+\frac{D}{1+\lambda} - s(\alpha_R;\underline{D},\rho(\underline{D}))\right) \tag{39}$$

and

$$\frac{E\alpha}{1+\lambda} + \frac{\alpha_R - E\alpha}{(1+\lambda)(1+\beta)} < \alpha_R\left(1 - \frac{D\rho(\underline{D})}{E\alpha}\right) + s(\alpha_R;\underline{D},\rho(\underline{D}))\rho(\underline{D}) \tag{40}$$

First, from the proof of lemma 2 we know that for $\underline{D} > \underline{D}$ the equilibrium rate $\rho(\underline{D})$ is given by:

$$\rho(\underline{D}) = \frac{(1+\lambda)E\alpha}{\beta[(1+\lambda)E\alpha - \underline{D}\lambda]} \tag{41}$$

The corresponding savings for the α_R income group are equal to:

$$s(\alpha_R,\underline{D}),\rho(\underline{D})) = \frac{\beta\rho(\underline{D}).[\dfrac{D}{1+\lambda} - \alpha_R(1 - \dfrac{D\rho(\underline{D})}{E\alpha}}{(1+\beta)\rho(\underline{D})}$$

Inequality (5) is then equivalent to:

$$E\alpha - \alpha_R(-2\beta\lambda - 1 - \lambda - \beta^2\lambda) > 0 \tag{39'}$$

which is automatically satisfied for λ small since $\alpha_R < E\alpha$ by assumption. Inequality (40), on the other hand, can be expressed as:

$$E\alpha\left[\frac{1}{1+\beta+\lambda} - \frac{(1+\beta)(1+\lambda)}{\beta(1+\beta+\lambda)} - \frac{1}{1+\lambda} + \frac{1}{(1+\beta)(1+\lambda)}\right] >$$

$$\alpha_R\left[\frac{1}{(1+\lambda)(1+\beta)} - 1 + \frac{1+\lambda}{1+\beta+\lambda} - \frac{(1+\lambda)(1+\beta)(1+\lambda+\beta\lambda)}{\beta(1+\beta+\lambda)}\right] \tag{40'}$$

which is automatically satisfied when $\lambda > 0$ and $\alpha_R < E\alpha$.

Proposition 7 now follows immediately from a term by term comparison of (35) and (38).

6   Conclusions

To sum up, what have we established in this section? We have shown that, even though agents are forward-looking, debt can play an important strategic role in the political game between a left-wing and a right-wing party. The particular illustration of the strategic role of debt considered here was about a right-wing party[21] accumulating excessively large amounts of debt so as to change the preferences of the median voter in its favour by creating a situation where the left-wing party appears financially irresponsible in the eyes of a majority of voters holding a substantial fraction of their savings in government bonds.

The fact that voters become more concerned about the government monetizing the debt, when they hold a substantial fraction of their savings in government bonds, seems rather plausible. In light of historical experience (at least in the 20th century) it seems equally plausible that left-wing administrations may be more inclined to erode the real value of outstanding public debt than right-wing administrations. The next step in the argument, following logically from these two observations – namely, that a right-wing administration may deliberately increase the government's indebtedness to create a problem of potential monetization of the debt so as to ensure its reelection – somehow seems less plausible. Are governments perhaps not as cynical as we make them appear in this model?

Alternatively, they may have superior instruments available to manipulate the outcome of elections. For instance, it has often been argued that a policy inducing more voters to become home-owners on even shareholders is pursued by right-wing administrations partly because home-owners tend to vote more conservatively. Exactly how this works is not clear but is the mechanism perhaps similar to the one highlighted in this paper? A third reason might be that governments may not know exactly the distribution of bond-holdings in the economy. They may then not be able to predict exactly the preferences of voters concerning default. A fourth reason, (perhaps the most important of all) is that a government accumulating large deficits may itself appear financially irresponsible and thus be voted out of office for incompetent management (recent events, however, do not seem to corroborate this explanation).

In any event, we do not wish to argue that the main interest of the model developed here is summarized in Propositions 6 and 7. Rather the whole reasoning about government action (and specifically about fiscal policy) behind these propositions is as instructive as the conclusions. Other interesting aspects of the model relate to how empirically plausible predictions about fiscal policy of one or the other party emerge from simple assumptions about which income group's interests each party seeks to promote. Moreover a general lesson from this section is that *conflicts of interest may exist between the middle-income groups and the extremes* (very low and very high income groups). In this respect our model has similar properties as the one in Cuikerman and Meltzer (1988). These conflicts of interest are quite general and rise whenever the public good is not a perfect substitute for the private good. We expect that even if there is perfect substitution between public and private goods, such a conflict may exist if the income-tax schedule is sufficiently progressive, for then the higher income groups bear most of the costs of servicing the debt. As a result, a conflict may arise concerning the default decision between middle-income earners and the other income groups. Many aspects relating to this model of course need much further development. A systematic treatment of uncertainty is necessary. More needs to be said about the political system: how do parties choose their location and what determines the equilibrium number of parties? If there are more than two parties what political equilibrium emerges? Finally, this paper along with those of Alesina and Tabellini (1987a and b) and Persson and Svensson (1989) has highlighted some of the costs of a democratic two-party system. An interesting and important project is to investigate and formalize the benefits of such a system.

NOTES

We are particularly grateful to Alberto Alesina for introducing us to the field of Macroeconomics and Politics and for many useful comments. We would also like to thank Olivier Blanchard, Jean-Pierre Danthine, Rudiger Dornbusch, Pietro Reichlin and Philippe Weil for very helpful discussions.

1 In our model even a proportional income tax has redistributive effects.
2 Our results can be obtained for any utility function satisfying the following properties:
   – private and public consumption are substitutes
   – the marginal rate of substitution between the private and the public good is increasing with consumption of the private good:

$$\frac{d}{dc_1}\left\{-\frac{\partial U/\partial c_1}{\partial U/\partial g_1}\right\} < 0$$

A utility function with these properties gives rise to the basic conflict about fiscal policy in our model where agents with income below average prefer large expenditure on public goods. Similarly, the conflict in our model regarding default on public debt would arise with any utility function with the properties above.

   Moreover it one assumes intertemporal separability one also obtains our result about Ricardian super indeterminacy (provided of course that the social planner only cares about Pareto-efficiency). (See Section 3 for a derivation of the result of Ricardian super indeterminacy.)

3 Given the form of the utility function, we only consider such public goods as public education, health care, social security, etc.; these can be viewed quite naturally as substitutes for private consumption.

4 Introducing distortionary taxation would not alter our main results about the political equilibrium and the commitment and strategic roles of debt. Interesting additional effects probably arise if taxes are distortionary. For instance, the political equilibrium may depend on the well known trade off between equity and efficiency. We shall pursue these additional aspects in future research.

5 In our model we have normalized the set of taxable incomes to be $[0, 1]$. Equivalently, we could have taken this set to be $\underline{\alpha}, 1 + \underline{\alpha}]$, with an income tax schedule composed of a tax exemption equal to $\underline{\alpha}$ and a uniform tax rate $\tau \in [0, 1]$, and redefined the consumers' utility function to be:

$$u(c) = \log(c - \underline{\alpha})$$

Note that introducing a lower bound on taxable incomes amounts to imposing an upper bound $\bar{\tau} < 1$ on the tax rate when there is no tax-exemption. By doing so, we avoid an unpleasant feature of our savings functions: namely, that agents may have positive savings even if all their income is taxed away (see footnote 11).

6 Agents can save by holding three different assets: they can hold cash which provides zero interest; they can buy government bonds with interest rate ρ; or they can lend to other agents who wish to borrow. Holding cash is always dominated by either lending to other agents or buying government bonds.

We assume that there is a perfectly competitive capital market and that private agents never default on their debts. Given these assumptions, the interest rate on private loans must always be equal to the interest rate on government bonds (when the government does not default on its debt).

7 An interesting extension of our model would be to analyse the implications for fiscal policy of having more than two parties. We shall investigate this in future research.

8 We thus assume that parties in power break their campaign pledges if this is in their interest and that there is no reputational loss from doing so. Electoral campaigns then are pure 'cheap talk'. Electoral programs have no commitment value and nobody is fooled by them. Judging from recent campaigns, this does not seem to be a very unrealistic assumption.

9 A full-blown analysis of the political game with uncertainty is beyond the scope of this paper. Several interesting issues arise with the introduction of uncertainty. We shall just mention two: to begin with, uncertainty about future income may result in uncertainty about the outcome of future elections. This may bring about default in equilibrium so that government bonds become a risky asset. Agents then face a portfolio-choice problem *ex-ante* instead of a simple savings decision. Secondly, when governments choose their debt policy in the first period they also have to make difficult compromises because of the uncertainty of the electoral outcome. Thirdly, interesting issues arise concerning default when the government is uncertain about the distribution of bond-holdings in the economy.

10 In all other respects, the dictator is identical to a democratically-elected government. In particular, our dictator is not above the law and behaves so as to respect all constitutional rules imposed on him.

11 An extremely useful property of $s(\alpha; \rho, \tau_t, g_t)$ for our purposes is the linearity with respect to α. This allows us for instance to easily solve for the equilibrium interest rate. While the shape of $s(\alpha; \rho, \tau_t, g_t)$ simplifies our analysis considerably, none of our results seem to depend directly on its specific form. This is reassuring since linearity is probably not a robust property.

There are several other noteworthy features about $s(\alpha; \rho, \tau_t, g_t)$. First, when the government runs no deficits so that $D = 0$, one observes that agents with income below average borrow from the capital market and those with incomes above average lend at the equilibrium interest rate $\rho = 1/\beta$, if and only if $\tau_1 \geqslant \tau_2$. Otherwise, the borrowing and lending functions are reversed. That is, if $\tau_1 < \tau_2$ then low-income agents save and high-income agents borrow. These predictions are modified when the government runs deficits only to the extent that the higher the supply of government bonds, the more all income-groups tend to save.

Second, a slightly awkward feature of our savings function is that agents may have positive savings even if $\tau_1 = 1$. They save, even though all their income is taxed away. This is possible since we allow for negative consumption. In foonote 5 we have argued that this unpleasant feature of our model is simply the result of a normalization. A tax rate such as $\tau_1 = 1$ should not be interpreted literally. In practice, governments have upper bounds on how much they can effectively tax income. This upper bound is normalized to equal one if our model.

12 Since individual utility functions are strictly concave and identical, the utilitarian welfare function is maximized when all individuals' consumption is equal to the average income. This outcome can be implemented by setting $\tau_1 = \tau_2 = 1$. For $\tau_1 = \tau_2 = 1$, it can be shown that the utilitarian social planner is indifferent between any level of debt $D \in [0, E\alpha \cdot \beta]$.

13 Since τ_2 is chosen in period 2, savings must be treated as a constant.

14 We assume here to rule out voting behaviour driven by ideological considerations. This is clearly a very strong assumption. However, in our defence, we should point out that it has been widely observed that income is the best predictor of voting behaviour.

15 Recall that a left-wing government followed by another left-wing government does not need to accumulate debt to redistribute income, since income is more efficiently redistributed through high taxes in both periods. Debt is used only because the right-wing government sets low tax rates in period 2.

16 We assume here that the government defaults on its outstanding nominal debt by running an infinitely-high inflation, so that not only the real value of government debt is totally eroded but also the real value of other nominal assets. In practice, implicit default through inflation (monetization of the debt) seems more common than explicit default.

This is why we have focussed on this form of default. In addition, default through inflation is more costly than explicit default to the extent that it also wipes out the real value of other nominal assets. If we establish that a government has incentives to default via inflation even though this hurts its own constituency by eroding their private savings then *a fortiori* these incentives are present if the government defaults explicitly and thus does not afffect the real value of its constituency's savings.

In footnote 17 we briefly analyse the effects of explicit default. In particular we consider whether a government prefers explicit default over monetization if given a choice.

17 The difference between explicit default and monetization is that in the former case only government bonds becomes worthless while in the latter case all other nominal assets as well as government bonds see their value being eroded. Creditors therefore prefer explicit default over monetization and debtors have the reverse preferences. Given a choice between monetization or explicit default a government is all the more tempted to default explicitly on the outstanding public debt (instead of monetizing the debt) if it represents the interest of agents who are borrowers. Thus, to find out how the incentives for explicit default differ from the incentives of monetization in our model we must determine who are the borrowers and who are the lenders in the internal capital market.

The identity of the borrowers and lenders is most easily identified when there is no outstanding government debt ($D = 0$). Then the savings function is given by:

$$s(\alpha; 1/\beta, \tau_1, \tau_2) = \frac{(\tau_1 - \tau_2)(E\alpha - \alpha)}{(1 + \beta)/\beta}$$

One notes immediately that intertemporal transfers then only take place when $\tau_1 \neq \tau_2$. The reason is that an individual agent only wishes to perform intertemporal transfers at the equilibrium interest rate, when $\rho = 1/\beta$ if his or her consumption is different in the two periods. *Consumption smoothing* is the motive for intertemporal transfers! Now, an individual agent's consumption in both periods differs only if the tax-rates in both periods differ. Given that optimal tax rates in both periods are either equal to zero (when a right-wing administration is in place) or one (when the left-wing party is in power), there are only two cases to consider:

(i) $\tau_1 - \tau_2 = 1$
(ii) $\tau_1 - \tau_2 = -1$

(i) In this case, agents with incomes $\alpha < E\alpha$ save and those with incomes $\alpha > E\alpha$ borrow. When $\tau_1 = 1$ and $\tau_2 = 0$, the agents with incomes below average get a higher consumption in period 1, because of the government's policy of maximum redistribution in that period, than in period 2 (where a policy of minimum redistribution is selected). Consumption smoothing then dictates that they save. The opposite is true for agents with income above average, which is why they borrow.
(ii) This case is entirely symmetric to (i); here low-income agents borrow, in anticipation of a more redistributive policy in the future and for the exactly opposite reasons the wealthy save. (Note that these rather intuitive results depend critically on our assumptions of rational expectations on the one hand on our assumptions on the tax-treatment of savings on the other. In our model interest revenue from savings is not taxed. We appeal to the principle of no double taxation to justify this assumption. Of course this principle is never systematically applied in practice, for obvious reasons. An interesting extension of our model, thus might be to allow taxation of interest income).

Next, consider how an individual agent's savings change when the government increases the level of outstanding government debt. We have:

$$s(\alpha; 1/\beta, \tau_1, \tau_2, D) = \frac{(\tau_1 - \tau_2)(E\alpha - \alpha) + D(1 + 1/\beta)}{(1 + \beta)/\beta}$$

Thus, $\dfrac{ds(\cdot)}{dD} = 1$.

As the government increases D, everyone saves more so as to exactly compensate for expected future increases in taxes. Thus the identify of the borrowers and lenders of private funds is independent of the level of government debt. (Only the volume of borrowing and lending varies with D to the extent that now $\tau_2 \in \left\{1, \dfrac{D}{E\alpha \cdot \beta}\right\}$. In fact, the higher is D the lower is the volume of funds exchanged in the internal capital markets). Since the identity of the borrowers and lenders does not change with D it is now straightforward to determine the difference in incentives to default explicitly rather than through monetization. Basically, a left-wing government following a right-wing government ($\tau_2 = 1$; $\tau_1 = 0$) prefers monetization since its constituency is mainly composed of borrowers. In the opposite case where a right-wing government follows a left-wing government $\left(\tau_1 = 1; \tau_2 = \dfrac{D}{E\alpha \cdot \beta}\right)$, the right-wing government prefers monetization again, since its constituency is then composed mainly of borrowers (case (i)). In the case where a left-wing government is followed by another left-wing administration ($\tau_1 = \tau_2 = 1$) the issue does not arise. Finally when the right follows the right $\left(\tau_1 = 1; \tau_2 = \dfrac{D}{E\alpha \cdot \beta}\right)$ explicit default is preferred to monetization. Since, in this final case, we establish that monetization is better than no default, it follows that *a fortiori* explicit default is better than no default.

18 λ can be interpreted in several different ways. It may be a pure technological cost: to produce one unit of public good one requires $1 + \lambda$ units of private good. Alternatively, it may represent *a cost of public funds* (λ then measures the efficiency-loss of allocating funds to the public sector). Whatever interpretation one takes it is a strong assumption to suppose that the rate of transformation is constant and independent of the level of production of public goods. We maintain this assumption mainly to remain in the spirit of the model where everything is linear.

Finally, note that propositions 4 and 5 are false, only if $\lambda > 0$. When $\lambda \le 0$, *all types of government $\alpha \in [0, 1]$ prefer to default in period 2.* (See footnote 20 for details).

19 It is easy to show that $\tau_1 = 0$ is optimal for a right-wing incumbent government. We restrict attention to the case where $\tau_1 = 0$ for expositional reasons. In fact a more general result can be established that holds for all $\tau_1 \in [0, 1]$. (See footnote 20).

20 If $\lambda < 0$, this set of income-groups is empty. All governments, no matter which income-group's interests they seek to promote, favour default *ex-post*. This can be seen as follows:

Consider first the case where $\tau_1 = 1$. Then, condition (24) becomes:

$$\frac{d}{1 + \lambda} > s(\alpha; \rho) = s(E\alpha; \rho) = D, \text{ since } \tau_2 = \tau_2 = 1.$$

In other words, default is attractive, if and only if $\lambda \le 0$. Note that $\tau_2 = 1$ for all $\alpha \le \dfrac{E\alpha}{1 + \lambda}$. Next, when $\alpha > \dfrac{E\alpha}{1 + \lambda}$ and $\tau_2 \in \left\{0, \dfrac{D\rho}{E\alpha}\right\}$, we can apply the following lemma and conclude that all types $\alpha > E\alpha$ wish to default:

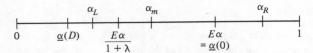

Figure 11.4   Shifting the median voter's preferences to the left

Lemma: $\dfrac{\alpha d}{E\alpha} > s(\alpha; \rho) \Leftrightarrow \alpha \in [E\alpha, 1]$.

Proof. We begin by deriving the equilibrium interest rate, ρ^*, when the period-2 government is expected to set $g_2 = 0$: the equilibrium interest rate is given by the equation

$$\int_0^1 s(\alpha; \rho) f(\alpha)\, d\alpha = Es(\alpha; \rho) = s(E\alpha; \rho) = D$$

or

$$\beta\rho \left[\frac{D + \tau_1 E\alpha}{1 + \lambda} + E\alpha(1 - \tau_1) \right] - \left[E\alpha \left(1 - \frac{D\rho}{E\alpha} \right) \right] = D(1 + \beta)\rho$$

Rearranging terms one obtains:

$$\rho^* = \frac{(1 + \lambda) E\alpha}{\beta[E\alpha(1 + \lambda(1 - \tau_1)) - D\lambda]} \tag{28}$$

Let $\hat{\alpha}$ be the income group indifferent between default and no default, then

$$\frac{\hat{\alpha}D}{E\alpha} = s(\hat{\alpha}; \rho^*)$$

or using (29)

$$(1 + \beta)\rho^* \frac{\hat{\alpha}D}{E\alpha} = \beta\rho \left(\frac{D + \tau_1 E\alpha}{1 + \lambda} + \hat{\alpha}(1 - \tau_1) \right) - \left(\hat{\alpha} - \frac{\hat{\alpha}D\rho^*}{E\alpha} \right)$$

The lemma now follows from the monotonicity and linearity of the savings function w.r.t. α.   □

Notice that the proof works for any value $\tau_1 \in [0, 1]$ and for any λ. The condition $\dfrac{\alpha D}{E\alpha} > s(\alpha; \rho)$ simply says that any income group α satisfying this property prefers default when $g_2 = 0$. To summarize, when $\tau_1 = 1$ and $\lambda \leq 0$ all types of government prefer default. Moreover, when $\tau_1 = 0$ and $\tau_2 \in \left\{ 0, \dfrac{D\rho}{E\alpha} \right\}$ all types $\alpha > E\alpha$ prefer default. It remains to verify the incentives to default when $\tau_1 = 0$ and $\tau_2 = 1$. Here, it suffices to apply Lemma 1 which states that all $\alpha < \underline{\alpha}(D) \equiv E\alpha - \dfrac{(1 + \beta)\lambda D}{(1 + \lambda)\beta}$ prefer default (this lemma applies for all values of λ).

Note that for $\lambda \leq 0$ we have $\underline{\alpha}(D) \geq E\alpha$. Thus, when $\lambda \leq 0$, all governments who wish to set $\tau_2 = 1$ prefer default and all governments into wish to set $\tau_2 = 0$ prefer default as well.

21 The strategic use of debt-accumulation is not the exclusive attribute of right-
    wing administrations. Our model allows for the symmetric possibility that a

moderate left-wing party accumulate excessively large amounts of debt so as to ensure its reelection against a right-wing opponent. Such an (implausible) situation corresponds to the political configuration shown in Figure 11.4:

(1) $\alpha_R > E\alpha$, so that the right-wing candidate defaults on the outstanding debt if reelected.

(2) $\alpha_m \in \left(\dfrac{E\alpha}{1 + \lambda}, E\alpha \right)$, so that without debt-accumulation the right-wing candidate is elected, and with debt-accumulation the median voter prefers *no default* on the oustanding debt.

(3) $\alpha_L < \dfrac{E\alpha}{1 + \lambda}$ but close to $\dfrac{E\alpha}{1 + \lambda}$, so that by accumulating a sufficient amount of debt D, the left-wing party ends up being located *above* the cut-off point $\underline{\alpha}(D)$: this in turn provides the guarantee that the left-wing party will not default on D if reelected.

REFERENCES

Alesina, Alberto (1988). 'The End of Large Public Debts', in L. Spaventa (ed.), *High Public Debt: the Experience in Italy*, New York: Cambridge University Press.

Alesina, Alberto and Guido Tabellini (1987a). 'A Political Theory of Fiscal Deficits and Government Debt in a Democracy', NBER Working Paper No. 2308, July.

(1987b). 'External Debt, Capital Flights and Political Risk', Mimeo, Harvard University.

(1988). 'Voting on the Budget Deficit', MIT CEPR Discussion Paper No. 269.

Blanchard, O.J. and S. Fischer (1989). *Lectures on Macroeconomics*. Cambridge, MA: MIT Press.

Cuikerman, Alex and Allan Meltzer (1988). 'A Political Theory of Government Debt and Deficits in a Neo-Ricardian Framework', Mimeo, Carnegie–Mellon University.

Persson, Torsten and Lars Svensson (1989). 'Why a Stubborn Conservative Would Run a Deficit: Policy with Time-Inconsistent Preferences', *Quarterly Journal of Economics* **65**, 325–46.

Discussion

JEAN-PIERRE DANTHINE

Can public debt be used in a strategic sense by political parties? More specifically, can one envision governments altering significantly the level of their countries' public debt with a view to improving their chance of being reelected? Aghion and Bolton show that the answer to the first question may be positive. However, they (realistically) refrain from following up with a positive answer to the second, admitting in their conclusions that one does not seem to observe the political behaviour predicted by their model: 'Are governments perhaps not as cynical as we make them appear in this model?'

Despite this discrepancy between the model and reality, this paper is both enjoyable and interesting and I agree with the authors that its contribution goes beyond one provocative but special result. At a general level it can be viewed as extending to the public debt issue, and to a world where the government's action is purely redistributive, the fundamental idea of the political business cycle literature: electoral considerations may be useful, perhaps necessary, to explain certain elements of economic policy, originally taken to mean macroeconomic policy.

In the first part of the paper, that is, as long as the rate of transformation between the private good and the public good is one, Aghion and Bolton's world is perfectly polarized: all citizens below the mean income level want full taxation and production of the public good at the maximal rate; all citizens above the mean income level want just the opposite: no public good and minimal taxation. This is due to the fact that the most efficient way to redistribute income in this economy is to tax income (proportionately) and redistribute the proceeds equally in the form of public goods (which are perfect substitutes for private goods). Thus if the economy is run by a dictator, i.e. a government that is guaranteed to stay in power in the second period, public debt plays no role whatsoever.

There is, however, another way of redistributing income in the Aghion–Bolton world. It consists in defaulting on the public debt. This favours the rich if the saving thus realized is used by the government to decrease taxes. On the contrary, default is welcome for the poor if the saving is used to produce public goods. This feature of the model explains one of the more striking results obtained: with no cost to default, both the right-wing and the left-wing party, if they were in power in the second period, would want to default. And, as a result, there cannot exist a rational expectations equilibrium where government expenditures are financed by debt.

If default is excluded, debt takes on significance in one instance: a left-wing government that know for sure that it will be displaced by its right-wing opponent will accumulate the maximum amount of public debt in period 1, so as to constrain the behaviour of the future government, and use the proceeds to increase public good production.[1] The contrary is not true if the right is followed by the left: since the latter will tax everything anyway, the allocation of goods in the second period cannot be altered.

In order to introduce a strategic role for public debt one has to do away with this polarization of preferences (or political opinions). This is done by assuming that the rate of transformation between the private and the public goods is less than one. With this less efficient technology, there exists an income group, just below the average income level, who do not want public expenditures to be maximized and also do not want default on the public debt, even if its representatives (the 'moderate right-wing party') are in power. The trick is to show that by accumulating debt this party indeed enlarges the number of people favouring its policy of zero public expenditures, minimal taxation and no default. For sufficiently high levels of debt (relative to the values of other parameters), the median voter is included in this group and all voters with higher incomes favour the moderate-right incumbent over the left-wing challenger. Furthermore, this policy of debt accumulation is preferred by the government's natural constituency.

This description shows that giving public debt a strategic role requires a richer set-up than the original left–right polarized situation. With that requirement, Aghion and Bolton's modelling becomes somewhat less clean. Thus this more complicated world does not quite fit the two-party political scene they assume: there are more than two groups and the extremes are not politically represented. Moreover, one has to ask how the moderate right-wing party has come to power: presumably, there was no public debt outstanding at the beginning of the game and if so it is not clear that it could have gotten a majority of the votes. In addition, both the notion of default and the notion of elections are difficult to give sense to in the absence of genuine uncertainty. And indeed, some form of randomness is relied upon informally by the authors to justify changes in political preferences between the two periods (Section 4). However one expects the nature of the game to be significantly altered if this is the case. In particular, in the presence of uncertainty, the possibility of default on the public debt dramatically changes the nature of the relationship between private and public assets. Finally, one would think that reputational considerations are of first importance when dealing with the potential strategic use of public debt by political parties. In that respect, the current modelling horizon of two periods is a serious limitation and it should be extended in future attempts.

NOTE

1 Borrowing by the government is possible because the model allows for negative consumption. See Aghion and Bolton's Note 11 for a discussion of this point.

Discussion

PIETRO REICHLIN

This paper basically provides an example showing that the provision of a public good by the government may imply some income redistribution when tax rates are equal for all agents and private and public goods are represented as perfect substitutes in every consumer's utility function. Assuming that political parties are sufficiently polarized and represent the interest of different income groups, this model allows us to consider the way in which opposing economic policies will be implemented.

The approach is very interesting and has great potential for stimulating a new way of analysing basic problems of economic policy in terms of their effects on the distribution of total resources. However, I have some doubt that the model used in the paper is really suitable for analysing the questions raised by the authors.

My basic objection is that the model is too simple, so that all interesting propositions about the strategic role of debt management only arise in the second part of the paper, in connection with the assumption that the rate of transformation between private and public goods is greater than one. I find this assumption somewhat disturbing in the context of the paper, since it implies that the left-wing party has a Pareto-inefficient policy. In my opinion, this conclusion stimulates a number of questions. Why does nobody come up with a new policy of government transfers and taxes which is Pareto-improving with respect to the program of the left-wing party? Why should anyone vote for the left-wing party if there may exist a Pareto-superior program? I think that, to be more convincing, the authors should provide some argument to show why alternative redistributional policies are not feasible so that the government has to engage in the provision of an excessively expensive public good just to reallocate resources.

A second question concerns Proposition 5, i.e., the statement according to which even a right-wing government inheriting a positive level of outstanding debt, prefers to default. At first sight this proposition seems to be quite surprising. In fact, since the right-wing administration is only interested in setting $g_2 = 0$ and since it can achieve this goal with or without default, one may wonder why default should matter at all. My impression is that Proposition 5 really depends on a special characteristic of the model, mainly, the fact that default implies a zero interest factor on agents' financial assets. In particular, when default is allowed, the government is able to affect individuals' capital income in period 2, not only by choosing the level of g_2, but also by setting the interest factor on agents' assets equal to zero. Since a particular feature of the model is that rich people are always better off with zero tax rates and interest earnings than with positive values of τ and D, one can understand why Proposition 5 holds.

However, assume now that there exists a storage technology such that, if an agent stores one unit of the consumption good in period 1, then R units of the same good become available in period 2. Then, agents have real and nominal assets to choose from, and in the absence of any arbitrage opportunities, an equilibrium where agents store some of the good must be such that $R\beta > 1$ and $R \geq \rho$. In this case the government's default decision should be completely irrelevant, once the level of g_2 has been set equal to zero.

The paper takes a very simple and appealing approach: groups of agents are identified with income groups (where incomes are really gifts from nature) and the interest of all groups is to maximize their own utility.

In terms of the model presented by the authors, the above approach seems to be quite reasonable and allows them to derive some clearcut propositions. In particular, most of the arguments are based on the consideration that, with public goods, agents who have resources below the average pay less than one dollar in taxes for any one dollar of debt-repayment they receive.

But, what happens in a model where we are able to distinguish groups of agents having different levels of labour income, financial wealth and real capital? In my view the model does not capture a potential conflict of interest between agents having different source of earnings. For instance, suppose we have a group of 'wage earners' (i.e., deriving most of their income from wages) and a group of 'owners' of capital (i.e., deriving most of their income from interest). Then, we could expect that a bigger proportion of the outstanding government debt is in the hands of the owners. When government debt increases, revenue from income taxes increases as well to cover interest payments. This may easily imply a redistribution of income from wage earners to capital owners when taxes on labour income are more easily raised than taxes on capital income.

One may also argue that the redistributive effects of government financial policies are very much affected by the different individual income profiles across periods. In fact, since raising public debt is equivalent to substituting future taxes for current taxes, one should really be interested in checking which individuals are interested in paying more taxes tomorrow rather than today. Actually, it can be reasonably argued that a policy of deferring taxation always favours those groups of agents who are relatively richer today than tomorrow.

These considerations may cast some doubt on the general validity of the proposition according to which right-wing parties should be against the growth of public debt.

Index